Confounding the Color Line

Confounding the Color Line

The Indian-Black Experience in North America

EDITED BY JAMES F. BROOKS

University of Nebraska Press, Lincoln and London

The following essays were pre-
viously published in *American
Indian Quarterly* 22:1–2 (win-
ter/spring 1998): "Intimacy
and Empire: Indian-African In-
teraction in Spanish Colonial
New Mexico, 1500–1800," by
Dedra S. McDonald; "'The En-
glish Has Now a Mind to Make
Slaves of Them All': Creeks,
Seminoles, and the Problem of
Slavery," by Claudio Saunt; and
"Strategy as Lived: Mixed
Communities in the Age of
New Nations," by Daniel H.
Calhoun.
Library of Congress Catalog-
ing-in-Publication Data
Confounding the color line :
the Indian-Black experience in
North America / edited by
James F. Brooks.   p. cm.
Includes bibliographical refer-
ences and index.
ISBN 0-8032-1329-8 (cloth : alk.
paper)   ISBN 0-8032-6194-2
(pbk. : alk. paper)
1. African Americans — Rela-
tions with Indians. 2. Indians of
North America — Mixed de-
scent. 3. Indians of North
America — Ethnic identity.
4. Indians of North America —
Cultural assimilation. 5. Ex-
slaves of Indian tribes — United
States — History. 6. Indians in
popular culture — United States.
7. United States — Race relations. I. Brooks, James, 1955–
E98.R28 C66 2002
303.48'2 — dc21
2001052233

For Tamara Lynne Brooks-Lipford, 1965–1996
sister, mother, woman of colors

Contents

PART THREE. Complicating Identities

Illustrations

Confounding the Color Line

Introduction

Older Negro woman seen on Ignacio street . . .
Omer Stewart field notes, 18 June 1953

This volume has at least as many origins as it does authors, but for me it began at the end of a dirt road. The rutted track to Euterpe Cloud Taylor's house cut through freshly mowed alfalfa fields along the bottomlands of the Pine River on the Southern Ute reservation of Colorado. In transit from graduate school in California to conduct research in New Mexico, I had paused to visit family and friends in Bayfield and Ignacio, seat of the Southern Ute tribe. This day found my partner, Rebecca, and me jouncing along behind Frances Leon Quintana and her husband, Miguel, as we engaged in the reservation pastime of "visiting" – informal drop-ins among neighbors to swap stories, share food, and keep abreast of the latest *chisme* (gossip). Fran had lived and worked among the "tri-ethnic" peoples of the reservation for more than thirty years, beginning in the 1960s as a Ph.D. candidate at the University of Colorado and since her 1977 marriage to Miguel as an affinal member of that complicated, contentious, yet enduring Indian-Hispano-Anglo regional community. As the most knowledgeable living resource on the cultures and histories of the area, Fran had long played mentor to my work on Spanish-Indian relations across the eighteenth and nineteenth centuries. But today she had something different in mind.

Euterpe Cloud Taylor's small frame house rested beneath the shade of cottonwood trees grown heavy and brittle with time. Her dog stirred listlessly as we crossed the dusty yard and entered her curtain-darkened front room. An antique buffet featured a parade of framed family photographs, from stiff sepia poses in Indian regalia to recent high school graduation portfolios. Rebecca and I seated ourselves on the cool floor while

"Grandma Chiefie," ninety-four years old, her burnt-caramel skin some-how youthful despite deep lines of age, welcomed Fran and Miguel as old friends.

Of course, they were more than that. Like most of the long-term residents of the reservation area, along several filaments of their shared social constellation they were linked by kinship as well. After some minutes of revisiting marriages and births, divorces and deaths among nieces, nephews, grandchildren, and *ahijados* (godchildren), Fran introduced me as her *novio* (boyfriend) from California and Rebecca as my *novia segunda* (second girlfriend) *como los indios* (in the Indian style). Mrs. Taylor responded "*y como los manitos, que no?*" (and like the Hispanos, no?) with a knowing chuckle. I thanked her for letting us visit and told her a little about my own family's background in ranching north of the reservation. These situating rituals enacted, we moved on to the topic that had drawn us together – the "Black Ute clan" of the Southern Ute tribe.

I had long been intrigued by ascription of this label to the extended Taylor family, and not only by its ethnological inaccuracy, since the Southern Utes had never maintained a clan-based organization. Its use in the area by Whites, Hispanos, and Indians alike evoked a cautious respect, tinged with more unsettling undertones of racial resentment. The very presence of Black Utes tinctured the tidy three-way ethnic balance that had characterized the community since the nineteenth century and that had drawn anthropologists' attention to the reservation in the 1960s.[1]

Local folklore embodied the basics of the story: in the late nineteenth century John Taylor, a Black Civil War veteran and interpreter for the U.S. Cavalry, had arrived on the reservation and married fourteen-year-old Kitty Cloud, daughter of a prominent Ute family. Only four of Taylor and Cloud's eighteen children survived to adulthood, but among those was their eldest, Euterpe Cloud Taylor. And these four adult children had produced a subsequent four generations of "biracial" descendants who now numbered more than a hundred tribal members and constituted, at least to outsiders, the Black Ute clan. And "Terpe," as friends and neighbors knew her, served as their "matriarch."

She laughed at this term but recounted with pride her ongoing role as "keeper of the Ute language," which she continued to teach youngsters in Ignacio schools. "Those Utes," she explained, "they can only learn well in Ute, that's why I go over there all the time. My little granddaughter, she can already count to one hundred in Ute." Indeed, like her father, purportedly fluent in seven Indian languages, Mrs. Taylor was a gifted linguist – she spoke English, Spanish, Ute, and Navajo with ease. "I *had* to learn," she joked, "my mother didn't know any English when she met my father, and he was just coming up from Navajo country. There was languages all over our house."

Of her father, who "came from Africa," Mrs. Taylor spoke with unreserved esteem. "He was born a slave in North Carolina. He joined the army and fought for his people, then came out here with the cavalry. He didn't come here right away, you know, he was down in Arizona. That's when he married first, a Navajo girl." She smiled again, wryly. "At least I think she was first; there were some other wives, I believe. Then he came up here and married my mother – well, he married her, in the Indian way. They got married in the [Catholic] Church later, after I was born.[2] He was a good farmer, and he taught me how to work in my garden, and to milk my cow. My parents had eighteen children, you know, but only four of us lived very long. Now [my brother] Henry [b. 1917] is the only one left. But my father was a good man – my mother got his pension after he died in 1935. You know, she only died a few years ago [1989]; she was 105! Maybe I'll live that long!"

It is likely that John Taylor's pension derived from his service as a Black Civil War veteran, since his file may be found in the pension records of the Military Branch. Unlike local tradition, his service was with the infantry.[3] But his federal service extended beyond the military. He also played a central role in Ute affairs between 1896 and 1935 as the agency interpreter. This might explain the material roots of some local resentments, for in that role he was able to guide his family through the allotment programs that swept the reservation in the wake of the 1887 Dawes Act.[4] While much of the best ("surplus") farming land on the reservation drifted into White ownership during this period, Taylor and Kitty Cloud maintained eighty acres of irrigated hay-and-pasture land along the Pine River, upon which Terpe continued to live. From their position of influence inside the Bureau of Indian Affairs agency, the family also managed to insert itself solidly into Ute tribal politics. Terpe's uncle Julius Cloud served as tribal chairman twice (1939–48, 1950–52), while she herself sat three times on the Tribal Council and continued to attend Committee of Elders meetings. The tradition of politically active women continues with her granddaughter Lillian Seibel serving on the council and with her granddaughter Arlene Millich acting as director of the Peaceful Spirit Lodge, the tribal program for the treatment of alcohol abuse.

Like many reservation families, Mrs. Taylor's had suffered the ravages of alcoholism. But this issue cast in some relief a pattern that was emerging from our conversation – the "primordial" depth and essence of her "African" blood identity over the situational, negotiated nature of her Ute cultural identity. Although Mrs. Taylor had lost sons and daughters to auto wrecks and other alcohol-related tragedies, she insisted that her biracial family maintained greater immunity to alcoholism than other (presumably "pure") Indian residents of the reservation. "I believe our African heritage protects us more than those Utes . . . we aren't so weak for the bottle. That's why my granddaughter Arlene is so good with the Peaceful Spirit Lodge, she has the African to draw on."

As I reflected upon introducing the essays collected for this book, it became clear to me that Mrs. Taylor treated the African and Indian elements of her family's background in particular and mutually distinguishing ways. More often than not, she spoke in terms that connected the African elements to a timeless "heritage," whereas the Southern Ute cultural elements appeared malleable and subject to cultural-historical change.[5] Her father, although "born a slave in North Carolina," also "came from Africa," a remarkable foreshortening of the African diaspora and enslavement in the Americas. Although his military service freed him from any stigma attached to these early identity narratives, it was the positive quality in his blood that seemed his most noteworthy bequest. Her Ute identity, however, was more flexibly asserted. On the one hand, she was "keeper of the language" and an active member in tribal education, politics, and culture, and she recounted proudly that she had recently "gone gambling at Towaoc" (seat of the Ute Mountain Ute tribe), where she had won one hundred dollars through her skill at singing their "gambling songs." Yet she also distanced herself from "those Utes" who had difficulty learning in English, were landless, or suffered from alcohol and drug abuse. Throughout our conversation, Mrs. Taylor alternated in her self and family identification between claiming African blood and Indian culture as central family attributes. She never put forth a synthetic identity in which these two elements were expressed as a "mixed" or "ethnogenetic" biological or cultural expression.

Equally intriguing was the almost complete elision of other significant biological strains and cultural influences. The family's history of intermarriage with the local Hispano population (including Terpe's own union with Joseph Mercedes Valdez, which produced daughters Francis and Ruby) was extensive, and they claimed as well strong connections to Navajos through her brother John Frances Taylor's marriage to Victoria Waratza in 1949. One additional African American did marry into the family (Roy Payton to Ruby Taylor in 1939), but that relationship produced no children. In the 1990s, therefore, after some five generations of intermarriage, the "Black Ute clan" was only ¹⁄₃₂ African American, while containing equivalent or larger percentages of Ute, Navajo, and Hispano "blood." Terpe certainly recognized and explored these latter relationships in her conversation with Fran and Miguel, but these connections seemed to lie within an ahistorical universe of kinship that imposed but little on the African "heritage" and Ute "cultural" identities at the forefront of her consciousness.[6] How could I account for the asymmetrical emphases on African "heritage" vis-à-vis Ute "culture" and the virtual erasure of other Hispano and Indian lines, even though the former was most manifest in day-to-day interactions with her Spanish-speaking neighbors?

One portion of the answer lay in my own guiding questions and those of earlier researchers. Potential and tangible relationships between Africans and Native Americans triggered fear and fascination from the time the two groups met under the force of European colonization. Despite abundant local traditions of mixed descent ("We Sorts" in Maryland, "Cros" in North Carolina, "Mustees" in South Carolina, "Redbones" in Louisiana), the colonial incentive to keep the two peoples apart found continuity in separate historiographical traditions well into the twentieth century. The Native American experience, if treated at all, came to be known as the history of "Indian-White Relations," while the African American past developed primarily under the rubric of historical "Race Relations" in which Indians remained virtually invisible. Even as interest in (and funding for) pluralistic historical studies emerged after World War II, the Indian Claims Commission and civil rights initiatives encouraged "tribal" histories on the one hand and "Negro" histories on the other.[7]

But the socially progressive impulses of the postwar era also gave birth to a generation of scholars whose personal politics inspired them to a wider vision. The shared Indian-African experience of sexual violence, capture, enslavement, and racial marginalization suggested a unified field of analysis, if not overt political action. The presence of Africans and their descendants residing among Native American peoples was sufficiently evident, albeit rare, to drive these historians and ethnographers toward archives and field sites in the hope of recovering moments of alliance between these victims of Euro-American expansion. In that search they also wrote deeper studies of the less-heartening moments in the relationship, especially the widespread (if culturally variable) institutions of Black slavery among Indian tribes of the Southeast and later Indian Territory. The founding members of this community of scholars – Gonzalo Aguirre Beltrán, Karen Blu, Jack D. Forbes, William Loren Katz, Daniel Littlefield, William G. McLoughlin, Magnus Mörner, Theda Perdue, Kenneth W. Porter, Peter H. Wood – delivered a substantial body of work to the current generation, extensively referenced in the essays that follow. In general, the charter generation focused on questions of how Indians and Blacks experienced their lives within the larger constructs of conquest, slavery, and White supremacy and how these forces facilitated or prevented the realization of shared interests or ethnogenetic identities. I had presumed that my conversation with Mrs. Taylor would lead in similar directions.

Instead, I spent the afternoon with a woman little bothered by these issues. Her concerns were those of her neighbors, kinspeople, and other tribal members: family, health, and the particular stories by which she made sense of her life. It seemed that in completing his life, her father, John Taylor, had laid to rest the Middle Passage, slavery, and emancipation. In fulfilling her even longer life, her mother, Kitty Cloud, had dealt with conquest, dispossession, and assimilation. It remained to Euterpe Taylor and her descendants to lay out a new narrative mosaic by which contemporary issues of reservation inequalities, early childhood health and education, alcohol and drug abuse, and socioeconomic regeneration could be addressed. If there existed "multiplicity" in these stories, arbitrary and shifting distinctions between blood and culture, heritage and history, insiders and outsiders, Indian and African, such multiplicity allowed her to occupy several identity stances at once as she searched for answers. Likewise, the erasure or bracketing of other ethnocultural elements made sense in context – she had implicitly acknowledged those in a different register by exploring the constellation of kinship she shared with Fran and Miguel. The notion of "situational multiethnicity" would probably have seemed laughable academic jargon to her, but she might have conceded that it did encompass her own world and the shifting challenge that awaits a new generation of scholars. Our own intellectual frameworks remain slow to admit complexity beyond the discovery and analyses of "biracial" or "tri-ethnic" communities, to engage carefully with the crosscutting tensions and ambiguities of dynamic cultural hybridity and to do so as much as possible from the standpoint of these mixed-and-multiple-descended peoples themselves – to confound the color line (or color lines) in ways as yet beyond imagination.[8]

The essays collected here take real strides toward that end. The contributors to this volume number historians, ethnographers, ethnomusicologists, literary critics, religious studies specialists, and legal scholars, many of whose own lines of descent mirror the intellectual pluralism herein. Perhaps this collection's greatest strength is its holistic, multidisciplinary investigation of the deeper, often contradictory diversity within Indian-Black relations. Their efforts yield some noteworthy results. Not the least of these is the realization that, while we know well that racial boundary-setting in formative states loomed large in imposing artificial divisions over the reality of ethnic and racial intermixture, we must also come to terms with the role of hybrid peoples themselves in the assertion and continuing construction of ethnic and racial difference. Mixed-descent peoples in the following studies show recurrent unease with their own hybrid histories, a discomfort resolved in some cases by bifurcations and erasures like I witnessed in the language of Euterpe Cloud Taylor. This phenomenon requires, of course, that we historicize particularities of cases in which "race" dims and burns in intensity within the larger context of colonialism, state building, and changing political economies. But it also demands a willingness to look within local societies for the micropolitics that give racial difference (or mixture) an autonomy within that field of power relations, whether at the level of family, tribe, or village. We are left to reside in the question of where and how there is "a groupness to mixedness."[9]

Three major themes organize the collection, broadly chronological in form but whose overlap is inescapable. Forging Relations, the Legacy of Slavery, and Complicating Identities move us forward in time, with each theme finding reflection in the others.

Dedra S. McDonald begins this effort with her "Intimacy and Empire: Indian-African Interaction in Spanish Colonial New Mexico, 1500–1800." McDonald finds substantial evidence for an African presence in New Spain's northernmost colony, beginning with the inauspicious death of the "Black Moor," Esteban de Dorantes de Amazor, at the hands of the Zunis of Hawikuh in 1539. But with the founding of permanent settlement (interrupted by the Pueblo Revolt hiatus of 1680–93), she argues that the "Spanish system of racial stratification and coerced labor placed Africans and Indians in a context of deep cultural contact." The ramifications of this contact were various. They ranged from sexual liaisons and intermarriage to the formation of small marginal communities of mulattos and *zambohijos*, from criminal alliances to occasional anti-Spanish collaboration, especially before 1750. As the colony matured as a protocapitalist, caste-conscious society, however, African descent so tinged *limpieza de sangre* (purity of bloodlines) that Indians and Europeans alike suppressed memories and evidence of Black forebears. By 1821, don Pedro Baptista

Pino could proudly declare that "at no time has any *casta* of people of African origin been known" in the province. More poignantly, McDonald concludes that her intensive "surveys of Pueblo art, tribal histories, and folktales" revealed "no references to historical interaction with Africans and their descendants." There is one ironic exception, however: the contemporary presence in Zuni ritual practice of the black kachina Chakwaina, or monster kachina, wherein Esteban's role as "horrible ogre" of the Spanish conquest lives on in their cosmological history. In this case, Indian or European "heritage" trumps a tangible African "history" in the pasts of both communities, the memory of which lingers only in the spiritual realm. Whether the absence of African ancestors in the collective memory of New Mexicans may be attributed to the hegemonic success of Spanish "divide and conquer" tactics, as McDonald suggests, deserves further scholarly inquiry.

Africans played a more active and enduring role among the Creek and Seminole peoples of the colonial Southeast, according to Claudio Saunt in his essay, " 'The English Has Now a Mind to Make Slaves of Them All': Creeks, Seminoles, and the Problem of Slavery." Undertaking a careful reading of heretofore neglected Spanish sources, Saunt argues that Creeks watched closely the emergence of African slavery in South Carolina and "rapidly became divided over how to respond." In those divisions lay an overlooked root cause for the Redstick/Whitestick civil war of 1813–14. While some prominent Anglo-Creek mixed-descent families enslaved Africans in emulation of their fathers' planter aspirations, Creeks and Seminoles in peripheral towns on the lower Chattahoochie River and in north-central Florida formed different relations with the fugitive (or captive) Africans among them. Neither the lands upon which they lived nor the decentralized and dispersed communities within which they resided lent themselves to the institution of slavery. Africans never found complete assimilation or equality within lower Creek or Seminole society, but they did create affinal ties and mutually supportive economic and military alliances. The outbreak of war in 1813 pitted, in the words of one Indian, the "idle" mixed communities of farmers and hunters along the Florida frontier against the "industrious" Whitestick planters of South Carolina. The subsequent Redstick defeat forced even closer associations between the Africans, Creeks, and Seminoles who sought refuge in Florida. But the "race wars" that followed left both Africans and Indians vulnerable to enslavement or expulsion. Saunt concludes that African slavery is an inescapable part of domestic Indian histories, as is Indian history a crucial element in understanding African American experiences in the Deep South

Interior. Yet however much those histories were intertwined, we still must come to a better grasp of the relative silence regarding any "mixed" or "ethnogenetic" African-Indian communities in these stories, a void that may say much about the existence of racialized thinking among Indians and Africans alike in early America.[10]

If slavery played a key role in forging relations in the Spanish Borderlands, racial marginalization was equally important to the experience of Indian and African peoples in New England. Russel Lawrence Barsh argues in "'Colored' Seamen in the New England Whaling Industry: An Afro-Indian Consortium" that, contrary to popular literary traditions that claimed Indians as the dominant labor force in early New England whaling and recent historiography that asserts Blacks in a similar role, "in reality, African American and Indian communities were so extensively intertwined by kinship and employment that they should be considered together as a single antebellum socioeconomic class." Skillfully interweaving a history of the industry with demographic and community analysis, Barsh finds a "consortium," if not a full-fledged community identity, of Indians and Africans bound together by shared experiences in the dangerous, poorly paid whaling trades and racial subordination on shore. These common experiences helped to "forge a common consciousness," but they also proved vulnerable to economic change. As the whaling industry declined after 1845, so too does evidence for the multiracial consortium: after 1860 interrelated "Afro-Indian" lineages came to sort themselves into various "Black" and "Indian" identities that submerged their mutual pasts.

Mixed African-Indian-European communities lie at the center of Daniel H. Calhoun's "Strategy As Lived: Mixed Communities in the Age of New Nations," an ambitious and original synthesis ranging across the nineteenth century from Mexico into Canada. With the 1820 census of Parras, Coahuila, as a microcosmic metaphor for the North American continent, Calhoun lays out the strategies available to mixed communities residing in core areas into which expanding states were poised to intrude: "the Native/African symbiosis was a shifting, labile connection among some families seeking agricultural subsistence and others pursuing military action." These strategic stances impinged on each other, of course, but Calhoun makes a compelling case that the "soldier/fieldworker nexus" can elucidate dynamics as historiographically disparate as Vicente Guerrero's "peasant" revolts in Mexico's "South" after 1821, the Seminole Wars, Yaqui resistance to incorporation in the new Mexican nation, the Fredonia Rebellion of 1826, and even James Dickson's effort in 1836 to crown himself "Moctezuma II" and lead an "Indian Liberating Army" from the Métis country of Canada to Santa Fe, whence he intended to proclaim "a vast secessionist realm in which only Indians could own land." Where previous scholars have seen only local tactics and cultural myopia, Calhoun sees a system: "the 'essence' of such a system was that it had no essence but was a network of adopted and transmuted identities, protean 'all the way down.'" He even offers a contemporary diagnosis of this system in a congressional floor speech delivered by John Quincy Adams in 1836. Adams warned his colleagues that the young United States stood in danger of fighting a multifront "Mexican, Indian, negro, and English war." The next several decades would prove his vision not sufficiently expansive. Calhoun hints that the continental upheavals of the U.S. Civil War and Mexico's decades-long wars of reform and intervention were the final elaboration of a Creole-driven modernization that would corral the Native-African symbiosis by 1877.

If occasional Indian-Black symbiosis took place on haciendas and in backcountry maroon settlements, its most obvious and contested arena of formation or deformation lay with the enslavement of African Americans by certain members of southeastern nations like the Cherokees, Choctaws, Chickasaws, Creeks, and Seminoles. This variegated process and its equally disputed legacy are treated in the next section.

Tiya Miles begins this set of essays by delving into asymmetries of power and their dissonance in the memory of slavery. In "Uncle Tom Was an Indian: Tracing the Red in Black Slavery," she argues for interpretive continuities in the transformation of Indian peoples from slaves in the colonial era to slave owners in the nineteenth century. Central to her work are dynamics of kinship: "tracing bloodlines across Black and Indian communities" as an "effective means of locating further dimensions of Native Americans' experience with slavery." Whether as slaves or slave owners, Indian peoples exercised relations of blood with Africans in ways that point to the importance of a focus on women and gender systems in historical analysis. Indian customs of matrilineal kinship might enfranchise mixed-blood children born to Indian women, but they provided opportunity to exclude children born of unions between Indian men and African women. Miles's careful reading of Works Progress Administration (WPA) interviews with once-enslaved African and "Black Indian" women sounds a cautionary note to interpretations that posit a milder form of bondage among the Five Nations. "The depravities and ideologies of slavery," she writes, "when adopted by Native people, had the potential to warp kinship ties between Indians and Black Indian relatives." Those same forces, as she shows in her case of "Uncle Tom," could encourage Black Indians to cherish their "Indian Blood" in positive terms while subordinating or dismissing their African heritage.

Celia E. Naylor-Ojurongbe follows by summoning evidence to support shared spiritual and cultural customs among Indian peoples and their African slaves. In "'Born and Raised among These People, I Don't Want to Know Any Other': Slaves' Acculturation in Nineteenth-Century Indian Territory," she draws primarily upon WPA interviews with ex-slaves conducted in the 1930s to explore the ways in which former slaves of the Five Tribes in Indian Territory recalled the cultural adjustments and relationships they and their progenitors developed with their Indian owners. In a form of historical ethnography, Naylor-Ojurongbe looks at the everyday – clothing, language, foodways, and traditional medicines – to gauge the creative and often complementary relationships between "mixed-blood" and African slaves and their masters. However much these relations were mutual and mitigating to the experience of slavery, she cautions, slaves and ex-slaves among the Five Tribes always dwelt in a condition of "dual belonging": they had belonged to Native American owners, "but they were also persons who believed they were part of, and belonged to, Native American communities in Indian Territory." The legacy of this paradoxical and often painful dual belonging would not be easily resolved.

However subdued, associations between Africans and Indians persisted into the twentieth century. In "'African and Cherokee by Choice': Race and Resistance under Legalized Segregation," Laura L. Lovett continues to investigate tensions between racial oppositions, affinal connections, and structural constraints or opportunities. Jim Crow–era African Americans found that claims to Indian ancestry proved a useful foil against racial stereotyping. Making sensitive use of family histories, Lovett shows that Black men and women could inject a tinge of romance and danger into local narratives with the recovery of an Indian progenitor (usually Cherokee) and in so doing counter some of the most damaging psychological poison of regional White racism. Likewise, she argues that Black intellectuals like Carter G. Woodson and Alain Locke researched the historical reality of African-Indian intermixture to offer a rational critique of social and scientific notions of racial hierarchy and fixity. She also shows how modest and sometimes fruitless these efforts became in the face of increasingly strident racist ideologies that inspired eastern Indian groups like Lumbees, Pamunkeys, and Monacans to disassociate themselves from their African American kinspeople and neighbors.

The rejection of affinal and fictive kinship across racial lines figures prominently in Circe Sturm's "Blood Politics, Racial Classification, and Cherokee National Identity: The Trials and Tribulations of the Cherokee Freedmen." Sturm looks at the long and painful history of the Cherokee Nation's relationship with African Americans once held in bondage by Cherokee slaveholders. Drawing on her ethnographic fieldwork in Oklahoma and archival research, she takes seriously and treats carefully the charge by one descendant of a Cherokee freedman: "I think you should write about the racism that permeates these Indian programs [re: tribal benefits]. And point out that many of the so-called Indians running the Oklahoma tribes are exclusive if the hyphenated Indian is black and inclusive if the hyphenated Indian is white." Even though the federal government threw its weight behind the creation of "kinship" by requiring in 1866 that Cherokee freedmen "shall have all the rights of native Cherokees," descendants of those freedmen remained excluded from tribal benefits and politics. Although the Cherokee Nation, unlike most other tribes in the United States, has no "blood quantum" requirements for tribal membership, Sturm finds that this progressive notion has been "stretched to the point of 'whitening the tribe' to a controversial level." In the process, Cherokee freedmen, despite repeated efforts at inclusion, find themselves shunned and are increasingly turning away from their "Cherokee heritage." Instead, many of the younger generation are attempting to reclaim a "historical" identity as African Americans. Blood politics, Sturm concludes, might deny freedmens' descendants Cherokee status today but may also in time be turned against the Cherokee Nation itself within the changing racial politics of the United States.

The Cherokee Nation is not the only site of increasingly complicated identities and identity politics today. The essays in the final section are situated solidly in the present, although they continue to reflect the ways that relations are yet being forged between Indians and African Americans and how the legacy of slavery remains unresolved. Ann McMullen's "Blood and Culture: Negotiating Race in Twentieth-Century Native New England" picks up many of the disputes in the Cherokee story and details their particular valences in Connecticut, Rhode Island, and Massachusetts. Her focus is on the "problematic nature of blood and culture within Native societies" in the region and the fact that the identity-constituting power "of 'blood' or 'culture' is a matter of disagreement both within and between tribes." McMullen's essay moves us into the murky history of racial ascription in New England, whereby in the nineteenth century many Indians and Africans found themselves descriptively and legally merged within the "Colored" population, then reinterpreted by anthropologists in the twentieth century as either "Indian" or "Negro" depending on whether Whites or Blacks represented the dominant source of intermixture. Today, ascribed and assumed identities confront one another in the arenas of federal, state, local, and intertribal recognition as increasing numbers of peoples of mixed Indian-African-White descent attempt to claim or reclaim an indigenous identity. Most lack a "chain of blood" to establish their cases indisputably, and McMullen shows how in this absence ethnic symbols and narratives of genealogy and cultural ancestry are mobilized to establish individual or group legitimacy – or to delegitimate the cause of competing groups. These symbols and stories invariably admit some ethnoracial mixture but presume that White ancestry is less compromising to "Indianness" than is Black descent. McMullen concludes that as long as "race is salient in America . . . it will remain salient in Indian country."

Ron Welburn's "A Most Secret Identity: Native American Assimilation and Identity Resistance in African America" speaks from within some of the same communities of contention that McMullen analyzes, thereby offering insights into the intimate politics of family and racial memory. His autobiographical and literary contemplation of Black Indian (or Indian Black) identities makes clear that painful issues of passing or masquerading have long occupied peoples of mixed descent. He asks why Indianness, whether in the past or present, seems so vulnerable to subsumption within Blackness and finds that "the color line that constructs the phenomenon of Indians in African American differs markedly from its Black-White counterpart." Welburn sets himself squarely within the "turbulent and resentful understandings" of Indian-Black relations in the Northeast and shows through his own life story how the wider currents of racial politics in the United States heightened or dampened his willingness to explore his Indian and multiracial background. In exploring the myths and realities of shared experience, he notes that racial pride within the African American community works to subvert the memory of an Indian past: "privileging Indian heritage creates a breach in Black community stability, cohesion, pride, and unity." The odious "one-drop rule," long the mainstay of White supremacy, is twisted to deny the Indianness of many peoples of mixed Indian-African ancestry (in the same way, it must be noted, that Indians may reject attempts by Blacks to assert an indigenous stance). In the end, he makes clear the ongoing and dynamic nature of Indian-Black identity movements, the continuing and hotly debated processes by which "the child remembers what the parent tried to forget."

Malinda Maynor addresses both the corrosiveness of racialist thinking and the possibilities for multiracial community reconciliation in "Making Christianity Sing: The Origins and Experience of Lumbee Indian and African American Church Music." Her careful reading of historical texts describing southeastern Indian musical performance blends with her first-hand knowledge of North Carolina's Lumbee and Black Christian musical conventions to mark the continuities and divergences by which the contemporary spiritual communities are elaborated. Crucial to her analysis is a critical stance regarding the notion of "tradition." Equating tradition with authenticity, she argues, "solidifies the very color lines that our ancestors, through their persistence and intelligence, struggled to undermine." Orality, seasonality, heterophonal and responsorial techniques, and a mutual emphasis on healing and rebirth are just a few of the elements she finds uniting the past and present. Occupying a precarious racial, economic, and political position in the eighteenth-century South, Lumbees proved aggressive in establishing and maintaining a "religious life apart from both Blacks and Whites." As a "third race" in the biracial world of Jim Crow southern society, Lumbees utilized their church music – a creative blend of tradition and innovation, of Indian, Black, and White cores and borrowings – to foster and protect a people "who value exchange and relationships above maintaining a strict boundary of ethnic identity." Maynor believes that this durability and flexibility are the substance of the Lumbees' ongoing critique of the "dominant paradigm of racial markers" that "limits the possibilities of new revelations."

From social intimacy and uplift in religious music to crass commercialism and racial stereotyping on the football fields of America – perhaps nothing better illustrates the extraordinary range of issues at work in Indian-Black relations than the dissonance between Maynor's essay and C. Richard King's "Estrangements: Native American Mascots and Indian-Black Relations." King's ethnographic look at the "images and practices that have knitted together and torn apart Blacks and Indians" challenges us to think self-reflexively about the cultural products and productions that either "facilitate or discourage mutual recognition between African Americans and Native Americans." The widespread spectacle of Black athletes playing for college and professional sports teams that portray often outrageous stereotypes of Indian peoples has long been noted, but King draws us into the history and psychology of these events with a cold eye. Among the disturbing ironies he places before us is that while official and public outcry over John Rocker's blatantly racist diatribe in *Sports Illustrated* in 1999 was an encouraging show of multiracial unity, few thought to raise the point that Rocker played for the Atlanta Braves baseball club, an organization that trades heavily on stereotypes of Indian warfare and brutality. Even historically Black colleges like Alcorn State University engage in what King terms "racial drag" when students and alumni dress in feathers, do the "tomahawk chop," and identify the campus as "the reservation" while urging on their own Braves. Most claim they do so to mimic, not mock, American Indians. Countering this widespread indifference to the hurtful qualities of Indian stereotyping are those rare occasions of cross-racial alliance, as in 1998 when the National Association for the Advancement of Colored People (NAACP) condemned the ongoing use of "Chief Illiniwek" as the mascot at the University of Illinois, Urbana-Champaign. More often, Indian activists find little support either at the local or national level from African Americans and their civil rights organizations when they seek to bar the deployment and profit-taking from Indian images. King situates this estrangement within a field of alienating variables such as differing structural positions within U.S. society, failure of memory, mass culture, reinterpretation, and irreflexivity, all of which interact to inhibit shared Indian-Black consciousness. King concludes that only through relentless exposure of the "arbitrariness of power" and its legitimating symbols can such barriers to mutual consciousness be dismantled.

Finally, in April 2000 Dartmouth College hosted a conference under the title " 'Eating Out of the Same Pot': Relating Indian and Black (Hi)s-tories," at which several hundred scholars, educators, community representatives, and political activists engaged in three days of intense discussion and debate over the past and future of Indian-Black relations. It was a historic event, whose repercussions and ultimate meaning will only be known when those in attendance produce their own curricular innovations, scholarship, and new political alignments. Valerie Phillips, a professor of business law at the University of Tulsa and of mixed Eastern Cherokee and Black descent, was one of those in attendance. Noting her avid critical engagement with many of the papers and roundtables, I suggested she submit a "reflections" piece to serve as both epilogue to this volume and prologue for what may be yet to come. The epilogue is her personal and professional revisitation of the conference proceedings. As editor, I chose to intervene very little in her text, for it seemed to me to capture precisely one person's experience with the pain and passion Indian-Black histories and futures elicited at the conference. Other attendees, myself included, heard some of the papers and comments very differently than did Phillips. But her responses should provoke us into a larger realm of research, writing, and argumentation, which will, I hope, lead to the "new revelations" so necessary for the generations to come.

Euterpe Cloud Taylor died at her home outside Ignacio on 26 March 1994. Nine grandsons and great-grandsons from the "Black Ute clan" carried her casket down the aisle of the Sky Ute Community Center, accompanied by the Seven Rivers Drum and singers. Hundreds of Whites, Hispanos, and Indians turned out for the ceremony, an impressive and moving combination of Ute and Catholic funeral rites. With her died a treasure of memory and cultural knowledge, and her loss will be felt for a long time in the greater reservation community. With her also perished some of the clues to how African and Indian identities have resided in individuals and communities over time, how heritage and history may be both mutually antagonistic and constitutive. Whatever the contradictions, Euterpe Cloud Taylor carried them with singular grace.

But she is not the end of such experiences. In 1998, twenty-three-year-old Radmilla Cody received the crown of Miss Navajo Nation and was designated the tribe's goodwill ambassador. "I am of the Red Bottom people," said Cody, "born for African American," using the traditional Navajo form of designating her maternal and paternal clan affiliations. Fluent in Navajo and English, she impressed the tribal judges with her fry bread making, sheep butchering, traditional singing, and knowledge of the foundational stories of the Diné people. The judges made no mention or issue of her race during the competition. But her victory was not easy, for it provoked some Navajos to angry denunciations of her mixed-racial background. "Miss Cody's appearance and physical characteristic are clearly black, and are thus representative of another race of people," wrote Orlando Tom of Blue Gap, Arizona. "It is the very essence of the genetic code which is passed down to us from generation to generation that makes us who we are. Miss Cody should focus on her African American heritage and stay out of Navajo affairs."

Tom's letter triggered a storm of letters in support of Cody's role as Navajo spokesperson. Daphne Thomas of Leupp, Arizona, summed up the response: "ethnic blood cleansing has no place in Navajo society, because the Navajo way teaches that beauty is everywhere." Cody herself had entered the contest in order to make a statement that "biracial people should not be judged as 'half' of anything. I went into this competition with a goal, a goal that not only was I going to open eyes, but I was going to open doors."[11] The impressive positive response from many Navajo people suggests that those doors were already open.

1. The conversation recounted here took place on 6 July 1993, as transcribed in author's field notes. For background on the Southern Utes, Hispanos, and Taylor family, see Frances Leon Quintana, *Pobladores: Hispanic Americans of the Ute Frontier* (Aztec NM: Quintana, 1991); rev. ed. of *Los Primeros Pobladores: Hispanic Americans of the Ute Frontier* (Notre Dame IN: University of Notre Dame Press, 1974). The archives of the Tri-Ethnic Project are housed in the Western History Collections of Norlin Library, University of Colorado, Boulder.

2. In 1911, in an effort to "stabilize" the serial monogamous nature of Ute marriages, Agency Superintendent Werner "compelled" his charges to undergo marriage ceremonies in the Catholic Church by barring their children from agency rolls until their marriages were formalized. See Frances Leon Quintana, "Ordeal of Change: The Southern Utes and Their Neighbors," unpublished manuscript in possession of author, 184–85.

3. John (Jack) Taylor was attached to Co. H, 24th U.S. Infantry; Co. H, 38th U.S. Infantry; and the 118th U.S. Colored Infantry (see Pension File #C-2,475,293, Federal Records Center, Pittsfield MA).

4. For the Southern Ute experience during and after the Dawes era, with special attention to women and gender, see Katherine M. B. Osburn, "'Dear Friend and Ex-Husband': Marriage, Divorce, and Women's Property Rights on the Southern Ute Reservation, 1887–1930," in *Negotiators of Change: Historical Perspectives on Native American Women*, ed. Nancy Shoemaker (New York: Routledge, 1994), 157–75; Osburn, *Southern Ute Women* (Albuquerque: University of New Mexico Press, 1998); and Frances Leon Quintana, "Ordeal of Change."

5. I draw upon here E. Valentine Daniel, who develops an illuminating discussion of distinctions between ethnic identities lodged within "heritage" or "history," in his case Sri Lankan Tamils and Sinhalas, respectively. See Daniel, *Charred Lullabies: Chapters in an Anthropography of Violence* (Princeton NJ: Princeton University Press, 1997), esp. 13–42.

6. In a similar case of dissonance between "national" identity narratives and on-the-ground complications, Anastasia N. Karakasidou terms local narratives of relationality "mundane personal and family histories . . . not considered to be 'history'" by the villagers of Assiros, Greek Macedonia. Their potential subversiveness to "national" identities (in this case, either "African" or "Indian") is eliminated by relegation to "family stories." See Karakasidou, *Fields of Wheat, Hills of Blood: Passages to Nationhood in Greek Macedonia* (Chicago: University of Chicago Press, 1997), esp. 228–37.

7. There were, of course, important exceptions. Annie Heloise Abel researched and wrote about slaveholding among the Five Tribes of Indian Territory in the first

decades of the century, while Alain Locke and Carter G. Woodson investigated Black-Indian intermixtures in their intellectual critiques of Jim Crow–era racial dualism. See Lovett, this volume.

8. Paul Spickard and Jeffrey Borroughs offer a wider exploration of mixed-descent and multiple ethnic identities in their edited volume, *We Are a People: Narrative and Multiplicity in Constructing Ethnic Identity* (Philadelphia: Temple University Press, 2000); for close focus on issues of sex, gender, and power in interracial unions, see Martha Hodes, ed., *Sex, Love, Race: Crossing Boundaries in North American History* (New York: NYU Press, 1999).

9. W. Jeffrey Borroughs and Paul Spickard, "Ethnicity, Multiplicity, and Narrative: Problems and Possibilities," in Spickard and Borroughs, *We Are a People*, 247.

10. For an exploration of this issue, see Nancy Shoemaker, "How Indians Got to Be Red," *American Historical Review* (June 1997): 625–44.

11. "Queen of Two Cultures," *Albuquerque Journal* 1 March 1998.

PART ONE   Forging Relations

1. Intimacy and Empire

Indian-African Interaction in Spanish Colonial New Mexico, 1500–1800

DEDRA S. MCDONALD

In 1539, Esteban de Dorantes of Azamor, an enslaved Black Moor, ventured into Pueblo Indian territory in the vanguard of Fray Marcos de Niza's expedition to the unexplored north. Esteban had traveled in the northern reaches of New Spain before – he, along with three Spaniards including the famed Álvar Núñez Cabeza de Vaca, had survived Panfilo de Narváez's disastrous attempt to colonize Florida. Cabeza de Vaca's tales of the group's eight years of wanderings through present-day Texas and northern Mexico piqued Spanish interest in the "Northern Mystery." Although the survivors repeatedly claimed to have seen no signs of exploitable wealth in the north, New Spain's viceroy, Antonio Mendoza, and others hoping to find an "otro México" planned an expedition. Cabeza de Vaca, however, refused to return to the north, and Mexican officials could not allow a slave to lead this expedition. Hence, Viceroy Mendoza purchased Esteban and selected Franciscan Fray Marcos de Niza to head the journey northward, to be accompanied by Esteban.

Ranging several days ahead of Fray Marcos with a group of Christianized Pimas (who had followed Cabeza de Vaca to Mexico) and Mexican Indians (Tlaxcalans), Esteban reached the Zuni settlement of Hawikuh. He was the first non-Native to visit Pueblo lands, an event made more significant by his African, rather than European, heritage. During his travels north to Zuni, Indians had treated Esteban as a "black god," regaling him with gifts of turquoise and women. Although no one knows for sure what transpired when Esteban entered Hawikuh, legend has it that his arrogance led him to expect similar privileges and to make demands for gifts and women. This angered the Zunis, who killed him. Another twist to the legend involves a gourd rattle Esteban carried as part of his "black god" persona. The gourd rattle offended the Zunis, thereby leading to the slave's death. Additionally, some scholars have postulated that Esteban interrupted Zuni ceremonials, thereby angering them to the point of murder.[1]

Zuni oral tradition corroborates the tale of Esteban's demise related in Spanish documents. While living at Zuni during the late nineteenth century, Smithsonian ethnologist Frank Hamilton Cushing heard stories of a murdered Black Mexican. In a lecture given to the American Geographical Society in 1885, Cushing admitted that when he first heard the "Zuni legend of the Black Mexican with the thick lips," he had no knowledge of Fray Marcos de Niza's 1539 northern expedition. Cushing described the story to archaeologist Adolph Bandelier, who matched it to events described in Spanish documents. In Bandelier's account of the events in Hawikuh, "The Zunis definitely informed Mr. Cushing, after he had become . . . adept by initiation into the esoteric fraternity of warriors, that a 'black Mexican' had once come to O'aquima [Hawikuh] and had been hospitably received there. He, however, very soon incurred mortal hatred by his rude behavior toward the women and girls of the pueblo, on account of which the men at last killed him."[2] Hence, both Zuni oral tradition and Spanish written documents recorded the ill-fated encounter between Native Americans and the advance guard of the Spanish conquerors. As Bandelier noted, "A short time after that the first white Mexicans, as the Indians call all white men whose mother-tongue is Spanish, came to the country and overcame the natives in war."[3]

What transpired at Hawikuh between the Zunis and Esteban resulted in a black kachina known as Chakwaina, or monster kachina, throughout the Pueblo world. Esteban served as a harbinger of the Spanish conquest, which permanently altered Pueblo life. Thus, Chakwaina kachina emerged as a tangible symbol of Pueblo interpretations of the Spanish conquest. According to anthropologist Frederick Dockstader, legendary accounts attribute the impetus for Chakwaina to Esteban. Dockstader notes that "the appearance of this kachina and the fact that Chakwaina is known in all the pueblos as a horrible ogre, support this legend. Esteban would be remembered because of the color of his skin, because he was the first non-Indian seen in Cíbola, and because of the circumstances surrounding his fate."[4] Anthropologist E. Charles Adams argued that in modern western Pueblo societies, kachinas in the form of ogres and whippers fill the role of disciplinarians and overseers of communal work groups.[5] As the impetus for the ogre kachina Chakwaina, Esteban lives on, reminding us of changes wrought in the Pueblo world by the aggressive presence of White and Black outsiders. Although they effectively defused the threat posed by Esteban, the Zunis could not so easily evade the Spaniards who followed.

Scarcely a year passed before explorer Francisco Vásquez de Coronado and his entourage of several thousand Spaniards and Mexican Indians appeared in Zuni lands, occupying Hawikuh from July to November of 1540.[6]

This less-than-auspicious beginning for African-Indian relations in to-day's American Southwest, however, did not keep the two groups apart. Sometimes at odds with one another, other times brought together in the most intimate of relations, sexual liaisons sometimes resulting in formal marriage – African descendants and Native Americans in northern New Spain interacted throughout the Spanish colonial era. These interactions formed a web in which one group's actions affected the other group, resulting, for example, in the Pueblo kachina Chakwaina or, in the case of the Black Seminoles, in ethnogenesis, the formation of a new group of people. Children of African and Native American sexual unions, known throughout the early colonial period as mulattoes and later as *zambos*, at particular times and places formed new, third groups, such as the Black Caribs or the Black Seminoles. In New Mexico, however, a third group never emerged. The small African population – at the very least 2.5 per-cent, according to one scholar – was partially responsible for this failure.[7] The close connection between the absence of mixed-blood group forma-tion and exploitation, however, provides a better explanation for the ab-sence of a New Mexico version of Black Indians.

Despite the relatively small African population in colonial New Mex-ico, the Spanish system of racial stratification and coerced labor placed Africans and Indians in a context of deep intercultural contact. As ethno-historian Jack Forbes explained, "The nature of these contacts varies . . . according to the region and the time period."[8] This essay will examine interactions between Indians and persons of African descent in New Mex-ico, the northernmost outpost of New Spain, focusing on the seventeenth and eighteenth centuries. First, the essay will briefly survey the history of Spanish American slavery and initial relations between Africans and Indians.

Next I will discuss specific intercultural contacts, particularly episodes in which Africans and Indians worked together – episodes that emanate from the marginalization and disempowerment the two groups faced. Documentary evidence illustrates frequent collaborations between Afri-cans and Indians against Spanish exploitation, ranging from joint mass uprisings to assaults on individual hacendados and their horses.[9] While Indian and mulatto residents of Parral, a mining town in northern Chi-huahua, frequently filed criminal cases against one another for theft, assault, rape, and even murder, no such cases reached New Mexico court dockets. Indeed, in the latter locale, the two groups appeared together as instigators of crimes against church and state. As Forbes suggested and Esteban's death illustrated, however, Native Americans and Africans did not automatically become allies. Indeed, the Spanish government frequently sought to keep the two groups apart, implementing "divide and conquer" policies in an attempt to prevent episodes like the Pueblo Revolt. Additionally, in places like Peru, Africans at times emulated Spaniards, exploiting Indians through their higher status as artisans and supervisors of native agricultural workers.[10]

Third, this essay will examine sexual liaisons and intermarriages, the ultimate deep intercultural contact, and the cultural discussions surrounding the creation of new bloodlines, such as the mulatto and the *zambo*, as illustrated in a popular eighteenth-century genre of paintings known as *las castas*. Marriage records for northern New Spain depict a landscape of interaction between Indians and African descendants, providing hints of cultural crossovers in which African-Indian children identified with both of their cultural antecedents, at times forming an altogether new group, such as the Black Seminole tribe that arose in Florida in the seventeenth and eighteenth centuries. Then, the essay will discuss pertinent literature in the study of Black-Indian relations.

Finally, this study will draw some conclusions responding to the central question raised by Esteban's reincarnation as the Chakwaina kachina and by Indian and Black collaboration in Spanish colonial New Mexico: What is the nature of interaction between Blacks and Indians in New Mexico, and what do those interactions suggest about the relationship between the absence of mixed-blood group formation and imperial exploitation? The answer to these questions, I will show, changed over time and space. During the early colonial period (1500–1750), the frequent contact between the two groups and the myriad laws governing their relations suggest that Native Americans, Africans, and their offspring formed a community. In the late colonial period (1750–1821), however, racially based class differentiation and concomitant exploitation kept Black Indians in New Mexico from maintaining a separate identity. By the mid- to late eighteenth century, a colonial caste system embodied elite "divide and conquer" strategies, successfully defusing the threatening Indian-African alliances. In protocapitalist New Spain, mixed bloods with European ancestry could aspire to be honorable, a rank unattainable for those without *limpieza de sangre* (clean bloodlines). Non-European mixed bloods, on the other hand, gained increasing notoriety as a violent and dangerous element of society.

AFRICANS AND INDIANS IN THE AMERICAS

Africans accompanied the earliest Spanish explorers in the Americas and thereby made contact with Native Americans from the beginning of the Spanish conquest. As Jack Forbes stated, "In America itself Black Africans and, to a lesser extent, North Africans were thrown into intensive contact with Americans soon after 1500 in the Caribbean and shortly thereafter in Brazil, Mexico, Central America, and Peru." Initial Spanish settlement of Caribbean colonies between 1493 and 1530 included freedmen and freed-women of color. Additionally, introductions of large numbers of African slaves, mostly Christians from Seville, Spain, occurred from 1501 to 1503. By the middle of the sixteenth century, as many as 18,500 Africans and their descendants populated New Spain (Mexico).[11]

Because Indians and Africans both were considered laborers, if not outright slaves, the first extensive relations between the two groups centered around their mutual enslavement. Historian Kenneth W. Porter postulated that interracial unions likely occurred first in the West Indies, particularly due to the highly imbalanced sex ratio among Africans brought to the New World. According to Forbes, a high number of Indian females offset the high number of African males. In a discussion of early African arrivals in Spanish America, Magnus Morner claimed that "logically, their partners were usually Indian women. In fact, it seems as if many Indian women preferred them to their own husbands."[12] Another motivation for African men to intermarry with Indian women centered on the Spanish law of the womb; that is, a child's freedom rested on that of its mother. This motivation became even more salient after 1542, when many Native Americans gained liberation from formal slavery. After that year, Indian women, at least theoretically, could not be enslaved. For their part, Indian women may have found motivation for intermarriage in the sexual imbalance in their villages.

Given the above incentives, the population of free "Red-Black people" rose steadily throughout the sixteenth century. Forbes maintained that "this free population, freed not by individual Spaniards but by its native mothers' status, represented a threat especially whenever [that population] existed near hostile native groups or communities of Red-Black *cimarrónes* (runaways)."[13] Sixteenth-century Spanish authorities issued numerous laws and decrees in often futile attempts to control Indian-African alliances and offspring. A 1527 law required that Blacks only marry other Blacks. In a similar vein, a 1541 decree required slaves to marry legally, in reaction to reports that African slaves frequently kept "great numbers of Indian women, some of them voluntarily, others against their wishes." A decree (*cédula*) issued in 1551 and reissued in 1584 noted "that many negros have Indian females as *mancebas* (concubines) or treat them badly and oppress them." In 1572, authorities issued a law requiring children of African men and Indian women to pay tribute "like the rest of the Indians [although] it is pretended that they are not [Indians]." King Philip II in 1595 ordered that unmarried non-Natives living among Natives be expelled from Indian villages. These shifting laws governing the status of African descendants reveal the Spanish colonial state's ambivalence over the racial/ethnic identity of this group.

Another branch of decrees and laws focused on revolts and communities of runaway slaves. A 1540 decree allowed for *cimarrónes* to be pardoned only once. A decree issued the same year stated that *cimarrónes* should not be castrated as punishment for having run away. Two years later, laws appeared that placed limitations on Black mobility. As of 1542, Blacks were not permitted to wander through the streets at night. Additionally, in 1551, Africans could no longer serve Indians and neither free nor enslaved Blacks or *lobos* (offspring of Indians and mulattoes) could carry weapons. In a further limitation of African freedom, a 1571 law forbade free and enslaved Black and mulatto women from wearing gold, pearls, and silk. An exception could be made, however, for free *mulatas* married to Spaniards, who had the right to wear gold earrings and pearl necklaces. Another reduction on African and Afro-Hispano liberties came in 1577 with a decree that free Blacks and mulattoes should live with known employers, which would facilitate the payment of tribute and keep African descendants under control. In addition, a census would be taken in each district, and free people of color were obligated to advise the local justice when they absented themselves from their employer's household. Finally, a report in 1585 noted that mestizos and mulattoes frequently played leading roles among Chichimeca rebels in the Zacatecas-Coahuila region.[14] Such armed resistance made the earlier restrictions placed on African and Indian movements and public behavior all the more necessary, at least in the eyes of Spanish authorities. Whether these laws had any impact on the two groups remains unknown, but the very existence of such rules suggests that Africans and Indians frequently participated in all the activities forbidden to them.

New Mexico's status as a province of New Spain meant that the above laws applied to Indians and Africans living on the far northern frontier. The Spanish Archives of New Mexico include copies of decrees and declarations of kings and viceroys that clarified or changed earlier rulings. For example, a 1706 order compelled African descendants to attend church. In 1785, New Mexico governor Joseph Antonio Rengel received a letter advising that the custom of branding Africans on the cheek and shoulder had been abolished. A 1790 viceregal order granted freedom to slaves escaping into Spanish territory. In the interests of agriculture, in 1804 King Carlos IV renewed the privilege held by Spaniards and foreigners of importing African slaves into specified Spanish American ports. A related 1804 *cédula* renewed the privilege of free importation of African slaves. Finally, in 1817, King Fernando VII abolished the African slave trade. Hence, extant documents in New Mexico archives trace the gradual abolition of African slavery. These same archives, however, contain no evidence of continued attempts to exert Spanish authority over African-Indian relations.[15]

PARTNERS IN REBELLION AND WAR

Beginning with their initial contact, Native Americans and Africans collaborated in committing armed resistance against Spanish exploiters. Porter noted that "from the earliest appearance of Negro slavery in the Spanish possessions, the Negroes, when not engaged in fomenting revolts among the neighboring Indians or starting insurrections on their own account, seem to have contented themselves with running away to take refuge among the natives."[16] This type of interaction characterized relations between Africans and Indians in New Mexico from the earliest exploration and settlement ventures. On the 1594 Leyva y Bonilla expedition, which wandered as far as Wichita tribal lands in present-day Kansas, soldier Antonio Gutiérrez de Humaña murdered Leyva y Bonilla and then took over the expedition. At Quivira, Wichitas killed the entire entourage, except for one Spanish boy, Alonso Sanchez, and a mulatto woman who was half-burned. A 1601 expedition led by New Mexico colonist Juan de Oñate learned that the boy and the woman still lived and endeavored to locate them. Oñate, in fact, brought to New Mexico in 1598 several African slaves. Given the proximity of the initial Spanish settlement at San

Gabriel to San Juan Pueblo, it is probable that Oñate's slaves frequently intermeshed with the San Juans.[17]

In the decades leading up to the Pueblo Revolt of 1680, intense church and state rivalry for jurisdiction over the Pueblos, among other things, split the less than two hundred *vecinos* (citizens, including Spaniards, mestizos, and African descendants) into two vitriolic factions. In 1643, Governor Pacheco executed eight leading citizens of Santa Fe. Incensed Franciscan friars claimed he could not have done so without the support of strangers, a Portuguese man, mestizos, *zambahigos* (sons of Indian men and African women), and mulattoes. This charge suggests the existence of a "racial cleavage in New Mexico, with the persons of non-Spanish ancestry supporting the secular side of the dispute."[18]

Such venomous disputes between New Mexico's civil and religious authorities showed Puebloans the weaknesses in the Spanish governing structure. Additionally, nearby tribes attempted to throw off the oppressive Spanish yoke. In his book *Apache, Navaho, and Spaniard,* Jack Forbes recounted a rebellion by Concho and Suma Indians in the area that is now El Paso, instigated by a mulatto servant. Forbes argued that priests frequently employed mulattoes to control mission Indians. As mentioned earlier, mulatto servants at times emulated the overbearing attitudes of Spanish overlords. When this happened, Forbes suggested, Indians revolted. In 1667, following the death from natural causes of a mission friar, Sumas and Conchos rebelled, killing a mulatto servant and abandoning the mission altogether.[19] At times, the marginalization suffered by both Indians and Africans pitted them against one another. In this case, Africans who did their Spanish masters' bidding incurred Native American wrath.

On the other hand, marginalization and intolerance by Spanish colonials also threw members of the two groups together in attempts to oust their oppressors. Rumors surrounding the Pueblo Revolt illustrate this type of cooperation. In 1967, Fray Angelico Chavez published an article on the successful 1680 revolt, arguing that it was not led by the Puebloans themselves, but by a mulatto. Employing a racist argument in which he questioned the intelligence and ability of Pueblo Indians to pull off a successful rebellion, Chavez sought to give credit for the organization and leadership of the entire uprising to Naranjo, a big Black man with yellow eyes mentioned in Indian testimonies about the revolt. Comparing Puebloans and Africans in words reflective of racist assumptions of the 1950s and 1960s, Chavez claimed that the revolt was "not the first time that an African spoiled the best-laid plans of the Spaniard in American colonial times, but it was the most dramatic. More active and restless by nature than the more passive and stolid Indian, he was more apt to muddle up some serious Hispanic enterprise."[20] Using records of Indian testimonies, Chavez argued that Naranjo, a mulatto of Mexican Indian roots who called himself the representative of Pueblo god Pose-yemu, directed the course of the Pueblo Revolt from his hiding place in a Taos kiva. Some twenty-three years later, in 1990, historian Stefanie Beninato challenged Chavez's controversial argument, interpreting the same documents but using a wider cultural framework. She agreed that a mulatto worked with the Puebloans as a tactical leader but postulated that a non-Pueblo man could not have been a leader in the revolt. Hence, she suggested that Naranjo's roots were Puebloan rather than Mexican Indian.[21]

Both Chavez and Beninato, however, overlooked the significance of the mulatto Naranjo's involvement in an event that epitomized Indian resistance to Spanish colonial rule. According to Jack Forbes, the Pueblo rebels included "mestizos and mulattoes and people who speak Spanish."[22] Since the early sixteenth century, Spaniards had feared just such an alliance, and with good reason. The Pueblo Revolt had been preceded by numerous similar alliances throughout Spanish America. Forbes argued that slavery and general labor oppression created an atmosphere of resistance among marginalized peoples, making conditions favorable for the establishment of intimate relationships between African descendants and Native Americans.[23]

Reports by New Mexico governor Antonio de Otermín and his military officers demonstrate that African-Indian interaction in the province led to what Spaniards perceived as a frustrating and threatening alliance. In a document dated 9 August 1680, the day Puebloans launched their attack on the Spaniards, Otermín related events reported by captured Indians. "There had come to them from very far away toward the north a letter from an Indian lieutenant of Po he yemu to the effect that all of them in general should rebel, and that any pueblo that would not agree to it they would destroy, killing all the people. It was reported that this Indian lieutenant of Po he yemu was very tall, black and had very large yellow eyes, and that everyone feared him greatly."[24] Encouraged by the successful example set by the Puebloans, neighboring tribes also planned revolts. Worried Spaniards recorded these rumors in reports and letters as they tried to ascertain the extent of the threat. On 29 August 1680, Andrés López de Gracia wrote to don Bartolomé de Estrada concerning a Suma plot. Similar to the 1667 Concho and Suma rebellion discussed above, this revolt resulted from a mulatto servant's abuse of Indians. López de Gracia reported that the Suma actions were "instigated by only a few Indians, who do not number more than eight. . . . According to the information I have, the cause of it all is a mulatto who is on the Río de los Janos, a servant of . . . Father Juan Martínez, because of what he did to an Indian, whose ears he cut off." In hopes of defusing the Suma rebellion, López de Gracia ordered the mulatto servant arrested.[25] Mistreatment from any source incurred Indian retaliation.

Rebel Indians also formed alliances with other mistreated groups, making the Pueblo Revolt even more widespread and threatening to Spaniards. Otermín on several occasions noted his frustration with such alliances. In order to counteract a rear action conducted by mounted Pueblo and Apache Indians and led by Picuris leader Luís Tupatú, the ousted New Mexico governor retreated downriver toward his Isleta stronghold. In his report of this action, Otermín described a much-feared alliance formed by Tupatú's followers and "the confident coyotes, mestizos, and mulattoes, all of whom are skillful horsemen and know how to manage harquebuses and lances, together with the main body and column of the rest of the people of all the nations." Several days later, in a report regarding the pacification of Isleta Pueblo, Otermín castigated the Pueblos and their allies:

Obstinate and rebellious, they have left their pueblo houses, the grain upon which they subsist, and other things, taking their families and fleeing with them to the roughest of the sierras, joining together to resist and willing to lose their lives rather than submit. Many mestizos, mulattoes, and people who speak Spanish have followed them, who are skillful on horseback and who can manage firearms as well as any Spaniard. These persons incited them to disobedience and boldness in excess of their natural iniquity.[26]

The importance of these alliances to Pueblo strategy remains unknown, but Spaniards forced to abandon New Mexico viewed *casta* (mixed blood) cooperation with Indians as a disloyal and threatening act, particularly in that such alliances symbolized the rejection of Spanish civilization. Although scholarship and extant documents surrounding the revolt do not reveal whether the Indian-*casta* alliance continued after 1682, it is likely that allied mestizos and mulattoes intermarried with Puebloans during the revolt years (through 1696). Native Americans and *castas* shared a marginal status in Spanish New Mexican society, in which pretensions to power required at least the illusion of *limpieza de sangre*. Both groups stood to gain from rebellion against Spanish authority. By joining Pueblo rebels, New Mexico *castas* constructed a group identity as "not-Spanish," which meant they would no longer acquiesce, at least for the revolt years, to Spanish domination over Puebloans and *castas* alike.

Witchcraft provided another means for the two groups to work together toward a specific end. In one such case, mulatto Juana Sanches, wife of Captain Juan Gomes, obtained herbs from a Tewa Indian woman living at San Juan Pueblo. Juana Sanches wanted to make her husband stop treating her badly. She claimed that he beat her and that he was engaged in a "bad friendship" with a concubine. The Indian woman gave Sanches two yellow roots and two grains of blue corn with points of white hearts inside. She chewed the corn and anointed her husband's chest with it and repeated the exercise with the herbs. Sanches added to her 1631 testimony to New Mexico's agent of the Inquisition that ten or twelve years prior, Hispanicized (*ladino*) Mexican Indian Beatris de los Angeles, wife of the *alférez* Juan de la Cruz, visited her. Finding Juana Sanches to be sad from her husband's mistreatment, Beatris de los Angeles counseled her to take a few worms that live in excrement and toast them, then put them in her husband's food. With this, he would love her very much and stop beating her. Sanches did this, but to no avail. The potion did not alleviate her situation.

Sanches also implicated her sister, Juana de los Reyes, also a mulatto, in committing similar activities. Sanches declared that five or six years before, her sister claimed to know something about herbs and roots, which she had given to her husband, mulatto Alvaro Garcia, so that he would stop visiting concubines. An Indian woman supplied Reyes with the herbs and roots to anoint her husband's chest. Juana de los Reyes made her own declaration, stating that she had been very sad because her husband was sleeping around and not staying in the house with her. So, she asked her sister, Juana Sanches, for help. Sanches said that she had an herb, given to her by an Indian woman, that was good for such occasions. She gave Reyes three or four grains of corn, and Reyes gave this potion to her husband in his food twice and also made an ointment for his chest. With this potion, her husband loved her very much and forgot his vices. She gave him the potion another time in his food and anointed his chest once more, with the result that he woke up, threw off her hand, and left her. Because the potion now had no effect, she left the situation in God's hands. Juana de los Reyes also described another remedy told to her by the

Indian woman: Suck on your two big fingers and give the saliva from the sucked fingers to your spouse in his food and he will love you well and stop seeing concubines. Reyes declared that she tried this once and did not want to try it again because it made her nauseous and it had no effect on her husband. Finally, at the same time that the above testimonies were made, Beatris de la Pedraza also made a declaration. She claimed to be the Indian woman who gave advice and herbs to Sanches and Reyes.[27]

Unfortunately, the records do not indicate whether the Inquisition pursued the case. In New Mexico during the 1630s, the Inquisition pursued cases of heresy more often than those of witchcraft. Moreover, the New Mexico inquisitor did not have the power to try cases. He could only make arrests and send those under suspicion to Mexico City to be tried.[28] Thus, it is likely that nothing came of Juana Sanches's and Juana de los Reyes's experiments in herbal remedies. A far more interesting question surrounds the two *mulata* women's close working relationship with Indian *curanderas*. How they made connections with Indian women and why they did not implicate medicine women by name in their depositions remain unanswerable questions. Perhaps gender concerns brought Native American and African women together. Additionally, as Jack Forbes has argued, in early Spanish colonial usage, *mulato* frequently referred to a person of Indian and African heritage rather than its later usage as a referent for the offspring of African and European unions.[29] Given this insight, it is possible that Juana Sanches and her sister, Juana de los Reyes, sprang from African and Indian parentage. If so, they may have long held knowledge of Indian and African *curanderas* and the types of situations that could be remedied with herbal potions. Additionally, Sanches and Reyes used their connections with Indian medicine women in desperate attempts to control their husbands' abusive behavior. In order to gain control, the women relied on female knowledge and cross-cultural community.

In a similar case in 1632, a mulatto servant named Diego de Santiago and two mestizo soldiers, Pedro de la Cruz and Gerónimo Pacheco, participated in Pueblo religious ceremonies held at San Juan Pueblo. Another soldier, Diego García, testified that a Tewa Indian interpreter from Santa Clara Pueblo named Luisillo told him that Pedro de la Cruz took part in idolatry with the Indians. He had "a creature dead there in the oven" (a kachina in the kiva) and offered cotton and other things to the devil. Additionally, Diego de Santiago had been overheard commenting on the beauty of Indian ceremonies performed at Alameda Pueblo. In his own testimony, Santiago discussed dances he witnessed at Alameda Pueblo three years prior. He described in great detail, but not in a negative tone, the activities he saw in the kiva:

They danced for a while and when they stopped dancing they went to sleep and they returned in the morning and danced and later they went dancing to the kiva, and went around the whole pueblo and together at a corner they put everyone in a row and everyone gathered straw and earth and with this, one Indian from among them took an arrow in his hands and passed by everyone touching the arrow to the chest, and at the end he threw the arrow to the west and all the Indians tossed the earth and straw that they had kept in their hands up to that point.[30]

This 1632 New Mexico Inquisition investigation illustrates the great interest and awe with which *castas* viewed and discussed Pueblo religious ceremonies. Their enthusiasm for Native religion sometimes resulted in troublesome and potentially dangerous Inquisition investigations. For their part, Puebloans seemed willing to allow mestizos and African descendants access to their sacred rituals, perhaps based on *casta* Indian and African ancestry.

Despite imperial efforts to keep Africans and Indians apart, social and economic disempowerment sometimes led those at the bottom of the Spanish empire's racial hierarchy to join forces against exploitive *ricos* (elites) and middling Hispanos. On 23 June 1762 in Santa Fe, testimony began in the criminal case against mulatto Luis Flores and *genízaro* (detribalized Indian) Miguel Reaño for the robbery of a cow. Santa Fe officials surveyed the houses of all citizens living on the edges of the mountains on the outskirts of town, searching for signs of a recently butchered beef cow. They found what they were looking for at the home of Luis Flores. He had indeed butchered the cow, and Miguel Reaño had brought the animal to Flores's home. New Mexico governor Tomás Velez Cachupín ordered that the beef be distributed among Santa Fe's widows and other poor men and women and that the two suspects be imprisoned.

The testimonies that follow reveal a confused situation in which middling Hispanos seem to have taken advantage of their poorer and hungrier neighbors. Miguel Reaño testified that Antonio Sandobal owned the cow and that his son, Juan Sandobal, had sold the cow to him in exchange for a horse. In his declaration, Flores claimed that he planned to cut the brand from the cow and give it to Antonio Sandobal, the owner of the cow, and that he and Reaño would share the meat. Juan Sandobal, however, declared that he had not sold a cow to Reaño and that he had not left his house at all, much less to barter with Reaño. Two witnesses verified that Sandobal had not left his house except to look for a horse to ride to mass, so he could not have engineered the sale of a cow.

In light of these testimonies, Governor Velez Cachupín declared Flores and Reaño guilty as charged for the robbery of a cow and condemned the "criminals" to pay for the animal. Because Reaño had no personal effects other than his labor, Velez Cachupín ordered him to serve Antonio Sandobal until he had earned one-half the cost of the cow. Luis Flores, for pain of his sin and for setting a bad example for the Indian Miguel Reaño, was sentenced to repair Santa Fe's royal adobe buildings.[31] The bureaucratic language that Spanish interrogators and scribes employed makes it difficult for readers two and a half centuries later to determine guilt. It does seem, however, that Luis Flores and Miguel Reaño, as members of the lowest rung in Spanish society, never stood a chance. In all likelihood, the Sandobals passed off a rejected cow on the unsuspecting duo, gaining a monetary return, a horse, and free labor to boot. The town of Santa Fe benefited as well, gaining food for its poor as well as free refurbishing work on royal buildings. Flores and Reaño stood as the only losers. More important, this case illustrates the ease with which Native Americans and African Americans interacted.

PARTNERS

Spanish colonial censuses and marriage registers contain records of numerous legal unions between Native Americans and African Americans – unions regulated under the same "divide and conquer" strategy that guided colonial officials' thinking in matters of crime and legal slavery. Social laws forbade marriages between elite Spaniards and mixed bloods. Many unions between these groups took place, however, despite efforts to maintain social honor and "pure" bloodlines.

Intermarriages between the two groups involved people in a variety of circumstances: Indian and African slaves; free people of color in the Americas; Africans who fled to Indian nations and were initially enslaved but later became members of the group through marriage and adoption; Africans who escaped slavery to form *quilombos* or *cimarrón* (runaway) communities; and individual African runaways.[32] Thus, especially in New Mexico, frontier areas served as a "cultural merging ground and a marrying ground." In historian Gary Nash's pithy words, "Nobody left the frontier cultural encounters unchanged."[33]

Marriage records in the Archives of the Archdiocese of Santa Fe show the extent to which New Mexico fit the above description. Although pre-1680 ecclesiastical documents disappeared in the Pueblo Revolt, many of the records from the 1690s forward have survived. Marriage investigations (*diligencias matrimoniales*) and entries in Roman Catholic matrimonial books (*libros de casamientos*) record significant numbers of marital unions between persons of African descent and Native Americans throughout New Mexico's colonial period. Moreover, *diligencias* often provide information beyond the names and racial or ethnic identities of betrothed couples. Details about personal histories, such as work or residential mobility, are mentioned in these documents. Pieced together, *diligencias* and other sacramental records depict a landscape of interaction between Indians and African descendants on the intimate level of marriage, as well as in society and the economy.

From 1697 to 1711, several mixed couples residing in New Mexico initiated marital proceedings. In 1697, mulatto widower José Gaitín, native of San Luis Potosí, married Indian widow Geronima de la Cruz, native of San Felipe, Chihuahua. Likewise, in 1711, mulatto Fabián Naranjo married Tewa Indian Micaela de la Cruz. Both spouses were New Mexico Natives.[34] Similar unions took place in El Paso del Norte, which was a part of New Mexico throughout the colonial period. María Persingula, Indian from Ysleta del Sur Pueblo, married free mulatto Cayetano de la Rosa, native of Santa Fe, in 1736. Two other marriages between mulatto men and Indian women took place that same year. The following year, Apache Indian María Ysidora, who had previously been married to a mulatto slave, united in matrimony with another Apache, Salvador María. In 1738, another Apache woman, Antonia Rosa, married free mulatto Juan Pedro Vanegas. Yet another Apache-African union occurred in 1760, between Black slave and Congo native Joseph Antonio and Apache Indian servant Marzela. A similar marriage took place in 1764. Finally, two 1779 unions featured Indian grooms and free mulatto brides.[35]

While frontier fluidity facilitated cross-cultural unions, it also fostered a chaotic atmosphere in which bigamy flourished. In one such case, occurring in 1634, two traveling soldiers discovered that mulatto Juan Anton, a recent arrival in New Mexico from Nueva Vizcaya, had two wives. He had married a Mexican Indian named Ana María in Santa Fe. The soldiers met Juan Anton's first wife, an African slave woman, in Cuencamé, Nueva Vizcaya, while en route to Mexico City. The first wife had four or five children, all fathered by Juan Anton. When he heard that denunciations had been made against him for the crime of bigamy, he disappeared.[36]

Juan Anton's choice of wives – first a Black slave and then a free Mexican Indian – comprises a striking element of this case. He may well have chosen his second wife in order to facilitate the birth of free rather than enslaved offspring, as the status of children followed that of the mother. Additionally, his marriages illustrate the ease with which *castas* and Indians intermarried. Indeed, New Mexico Inquisitor Fray Estevan de Perea declared in 1631 that New Mexico's population consisted of mestizos, mulattoes, and *zambohijos* (offspring of Indians and mulattoes).[37]

Similarly, the 1750 Albuquerque census well illustrates the deep intercultural contacts precipitated by frontier demographics and dynamics. Out of 191 families, 18 households included both Native Americans and African descendants. Some of these households, like that of mulatto couple Juan Samora and Ynes Candelaria, included Indian servants. In this case, nine-year-old María served Samora, Candelaria, and their four children, who ranged in age from two years to nine years. In other households, Indians and mulattoes lived together as husbands and wives. For example, mulatto Chrisanto Torres, age thirty, and his forty-year-old wife, Indian Luisa Candelaria, lived with their four daughters, who ranged in age from two to ten years. Out of the eighteen mixed households, however, fifteen featured Indians in service roles, although in some cases Indians served alongside mulatto or Black servants. Clearly, by 1750, some mulatto families achieved socioeconomic distinction over the Native Americans with whom they had once been equally marginalized.[38]

Other Indian and mulatto families, however, joined forces in land grant ventures. In 1751, Governor Velez Cachupín issued the Las Trampas grant as part of New Mexico's Indian defense policy. The grant location would serve as a barrier to nomadic raiders and would increase the amount of agricultural land available to Santa Fe's poor. Las Trampas petitioners hailed from the Barrio de Analco region of Santa Fe, whose residents were primarily presidio soldiers, Mexican Indian servants, and *genízaros*. Additionally, Las Trampas settlers included African descendant Melchor Rodríguez, his son, and his daughter. Hence, Las Trampas settlers represented mixed *genízaro*, Tlaxcalan, African, and Spanish bloodlines. As in the *genízaro* settlements of Abiquiu and San Miguel del Bado, "the task of holding frontier outposts against Indian attack fell primarily to other Indians and mixed-blood Spaniards."[39]

Additionally, after 1750 only one marriage between Indians and African descendants gained mention in the marriage record books for Albuquerque, the 1763 union of mulatto Gabriel Barrera and Apache Indian María.[40] This lack of marriage records could be attributed to a change in the way priests recorded marriages: As the eighteenth century progressed, priests recorded ethnicity less and less frequently. Or the lack of evidence for marriages between African Americans and Native Americans may signal that class and racial distinctions became far more salient in the late colonial period. Indeed, historian Ramón Gutiérrez argues that increasing numbers of *castas* in New Mexico frightened *ricos*, "who expressed concern over the pollution of their blood lines and the loss of honor." In an attempt to control these racial demographic changes, New Mexico elites turned to a legal skin color–based categories, borrowing heavily from schema adhered to in central New Spain.[41]

A genre of paintings known as *las castas* appeared in New Spain in the mid to late colonial period. While these paintings depicted the complex mixtures of people in Spanish America, they also underscored the colony's strict social hierarchy, based largely on skin pigmentation. Mexican scholar Nicolás Leon's 1924 pamphlet, *Las castas del méxico colonial o nueva españa*, detailed this genre of paintings. According to Leon, the *castas* distinction arose from a societal understanding that the products of intermarriages could not be considered of equal category and importance before society. Therefore, the distinction of castes emerged, "each one with a special name according to the class of the original primitive element that formed it."[42]

Caste paintings simultaneously illustrated awareness of racial distinctions and the widespread nature of racial mingling. They showed husband, wife, and their mixed-blood child, usually with a label describing the process. For example, a *casta* painting by Ignacio Castro, now housed in Paris, proclaims, "*De indio y negra, nace lobo*" (of a male Indian and a female Black a lobo is born). In this portrait, the Black woman is young, gracious, and operates an open-air food stand. Her husband, the Indian, extends his hand to receive a plate of chiles, which the little lobo hands to him with a look of curiosity.[43] In sum, this caste painting embodies a scene of domestic tranquillity. Indeed, Gary Nash argued that the caste paintings of intermarriages "mostly invited tolerance, common compassion, and some understanding of 'the fundamental cohesion of the human race.'"[44]

On the other hand, caste paintings also carried overt messages regarding the vices of the lower classes – vices that interracial unions exacerbated. As Nash explained, "some caste paintings registered domestic discord, and they are especially revealing in associating marital turbulence with the mixing of African and Indian bloodstreams, whereas the dark-skinned African or Indian who married a Spaniard could count on a child with a favorable temperament."[45] Inscriptions on caste paintings ensured that audiences would understand the artist's message about dangerous racial mixtures. Yet, one wonders if *casta* artists captured the mood of Spanish colonial society with such portraits or if they served a more didactic purpose, providing yet another means through which colonial officials attempted to "divide and conquer" the lower classes.

Another interesting element of caste paintings concerns their implicit encouragement of interracial relationships between Spaniards and other groups. Some paintings suggested that domestic tranquillity increased in direct proportion to amounts of Spanish blood, or *limpieza de sangre*. Inscriptions even went so far as to credit success and intelligence to the presence of European blood. For example, one family portrait announces that "the pride and sharp wits of the mulatto are instilled by his white father and black mother." In contrast, the *cambujo* (child of a lobo father and Indian mother) "is usually slow, lazy, and cumbersome."[46]

One type of caste painting featured a chart of racial mixtures, beginning with the highest level of Spanish blood and ending with the lowest level. Even the names given to offspring of the latter intermarriages indicated societal disdain. For instance, the product of a union between a *calpan mulata* and a *sambaygo* carried the name *tente en el aire* (grope in the air). The next lower rung, the child of a *tente en el aire* and a *mulata*, was called *no te entiendo* (I don't understand you). Finally, the offspring of *no te entiendo* and an Indian woman became known as *hay te estas* (stay where you are).[47] Hence, the upper rungs of Spanish colonial society, or at least the artists, did not oppose interracial marriages as such. They did, however, associate danger and violence with unions between the most marginalized and disempowered groups. The marriage records cited above indicate that intimate relations between Native Americans and African Americans continued, albeit at a reduced rate, in late-eighteenth-century New Mexico, despite class-based assumptions about lower-class intermarriages. Indeed, it is likely that racist assumptions embedded in caste paintings had little impact on the very groups depicted. Caste paintings served to buttress upper-class attempts to distinguish themselves from lower classes rather than to discourage interracial marriages.

In addition, caste paintings symbolized elite attempts to revise New Mexico's racial heritage. Father Juan Agustín de Morfi penned an *Account of Disorders* in 1778, in which he delineated the myriad problems facing New Mexico. One area of great concern to Morfi centered on the exploitation of Indian Puebloans by other *castas*. The priest lamented that laws prohibiting Spaniards, mulattoes, mestizos, and Blacks from living in Indian pueblos were not enforced. "And," Morfi added, "it is difficult to judge if the resulting intermingling of races is useful or harmful to the Indians themselves and to the State." For their part, Morfi continued, Spaniards and *castas* find life in Indian pueblos much preferable to farming their own lands, and all too often "they shrewdly take advantage of the natural indifference of those miserable people to heap upon them new obligations." These obligations include domestic service and the elections of mulattoes and coyotes as Indian pueblo governors. According to the priest, "this rascal's treatment of the Indians is guided by hatred and arrogance." Morfi recommended that all outsiders be expelled from Indian pueblos, and non-Indian partners in mixed marriages should not hold public office in the pueblo. Interestingly, Morfi had nothing but scorn for non-Indian *castas*, particularly mulattoes, whom he viewed as exploiters of victimized Puebloans. While he certainly disapproved of *casta* pretensions, Morfi by no means ignored their presence. His *Account* stands as one of the latest documents to include African descendants and to link them in interactions with Indians.[48]

Writing some thirty-four years later, New Mexico *rico* don Pedro Baptista Pino, in his *Exposition on the Province of New Mexico, 1812*, declared that "in New Mexico there are no *castas* of African origin. My province is probably the only one with this prerogative in all of Spanish America. At no time has any *casta* of people of African origin been known there." In making this claim, Pino deliberately revised New Mexico's racial history, denying the existence of a small yet visible group of Africans and their descendants, many of whom held Indian heritage as well. Pino's denial symbolized an overt attempt by elites to obliterate a history of racial mixtures and alliances born of resistance to dominate group exploitation.[49] As Pino's comments suggest, constructions of racial identity in New Mexico increasingly moved toward a fantasy "White" heritage decades before Anglo-Americans arrived on the scene. Such racial reification all but obliterated African descendants and their interactions with Native Americans from the historical record.

A FAILURE OF HISTORICAL MEMORY

Not surprisingly, given Pino's denial of New Mexico's mixed racial heritage, recent discussions of intermarriages between African Americans and Native Americans fail to address the long history of such unions. Indeed, Pueblo women who alluded to the topic in oral histories recorded in the late 1960s did not indicate any awareness of the five centuries of "Red-

Black" interaction and deep cultural contacts. Rosalinda Lucero of Isleta Pueblo placed African Americans at the bottom of the list of desirable marriage partners. As Lucero stated: "I've heard elderly people where they have heard where these younger girls have married colored, why they say how would the clan leader look having a colored sitting in among the clanships there. Because he's dark. That's what I've heard 'em say. But of course, I mean, these are the clan members speaking, you know. But in the path of religion, there's no difference."[50] Similarly, San Juan Pueblo resident Tillie Decker noted that the few African Americans connected with the pueblo, including a school principal and one married to Decker's cousin, "get along" and "had no trouble."[51] Granted, these few interviews cannot speak for all New Mexico Indians. However, surveys of Pueblo art, tribal histories, and folktales reveal no references to historical interaction with Africans and their descendants, with the exception of Zuni legends about Esteban recorded by Frank H. Cushing and Adolph Bandelier over one hundred years ago.[52]

Hence, few people outside the world of academe (and not so many inside that world) remember the historical prevalence of Black-Indian interaction. Rhett Jones bemoaned this historical omission in a 1986 article, "Social-Scientific Perspectives on the Afro-American Arts." In the article, Jones listed specific reasons for this lack of scholarly and popular treatment. First, he argued, "the racially mixed children of these unions have often been uncertain as to their racial identity." Second, many of these racially mixed offspring prefer not to identify themselves as Black. Third, the demographics of history factor into the problem. There were very few societies in which large numbers of Blacks and Indians interacted and still fewer studies of those societies. Moreover, anthropologists rather than historians have engaged in those studies.[53]

In spite of Jack Forbes's prolific attention to the etymology of the terms *mulatto* and *zambo*, the most frequently treated Black Indian subgroup remains the Black Seminoles.[54] Daniel Littlefield and Kevin Mulroy have closely examined the history of this group. Additionally, Theda Perdue and William McLoughlin have discussed African slavery among the Cherokees.[55] Two of the most engaging treatments of the Black Seminoles examine the group in comparison with other Black Indians, particularly the Black Caribs, who now live in Central America and on several Caribbean Islands. In her article "Africans and Indians: A Comparative Study of the Black Carib and Black Seminole," Rebecca Bateman used ethnohistorical methods to discuss how the Black Caribs and the Black Seminoles originated as distinctive "new peoples." She "focuse[d] on the role that the structure of domestic and community relations has played in preserving their distinctiveness and discusse[d] the differences between these groups in regard to their relationships with the Indians whose names they bear."[56] Another comparative article, written by Jan Carew, provided an overview of Indian and African cooperation during the early colonial period. In "United We Stand! Joint Stuggles of Native Americans and African Americans in the Columbian Era," Carew focused on today's southeastern United States. He argued that "from the very beginning of the Columbian era . . . Africans and Native Americans had consciously set about laying the foundations for a new civilization through a joint struggle and a fusion of their cultures."[57]

Two additional articles addressed the cultural fusion to which Carew alludes. In "'Make Like Seem Heep Injin': Pidginization in the Southwest," Elizabeth Brandt and Christopher MacCrate examined the influence of Black, Chinese, Mexican, and Anglo presence on Southwest Indians' development of American Indian pidgin English. They argued that "through the presence of thousands of Blacks in the Southwest . . . we are provided with the opportunity and motive for their participation in an American Indian pidgin English," a language "which met the needs dictated by the contact between different ethnic groups."[58] Similarly, Mary Ellison traced parallels in Native American and African American folktales and myths in her article "Black Perceptions and Red Images: Indian and Black Literary Links." She found that trickster figures, particularly the rabbit, "contain the key to Black and Indian responses in repressive situations." Furthermore, she connected the persistence of trickster figures in late-twentieth-century Black and Native American literature to the continuing economic and political marginalization faced by both groups.[59]

Folktales featuring tricksters comprise a twentieth-century remnant of the early cooperation and affinity shared by Africans and Indians. Thomas Patterson argued that "from early on . . . African slaves and Native Americans recognized the commonality of their interests and experiences; they had a sense of community that was continually forged and reproduced in their everyday lives by virtue of the places they shared in that system of exploitation called the colonial class structure."[60] I would add that the same colonial class structure chipped away at African-Indian community alliances by elevating mixed bloods with European roots at the expense of Africans, Native Americans, and the children of their unions. The "divide and conquer" strategy, under the guise of class differentiation, kept Black Indians in New Mexico from forming an identity as a distinctive third group. In addition, American and European liberalism pushed New Mexico elites like Pino to redefine the province's racial heritage, separating and elevating "White" civilization from darker-skinned noble "savagery." Yet, as this essay has shown, African descendants and Native Americans interacted as partners in rebellion and war, as partners in crime, and as sexually intimate partners. These interactions reveal a web of cooperation but also a web of silence. Such linkages are now the stuff of obscure archival records and little-known oral tradition, such as Zuni stories of a murdered Black Mexican related to Cushing over a century ago. Yet Black-Indian interaction surely left subtle legacies. It seems likely that African and Indian cultural elements meshed together, forming something that centuries later appeared to be exclusively Indian in heritage. For example, Native American healing arts, trickster folklore, and creative arts may have been reconfigured over the course of centuries of interaction with Africans.

Late-eighteenth-century class differentiation whitewashed the cross-cultural alliances and shared experiences that gave birth to African–Native American interaction. Elites like don Pedro Baptista Pino and the artists responsible for the *castas* paintings tried valiantly to make the web of interaction invisible. The fiction of *limpieza de sangre* and desire for legitimacy in a place in which mixed bloods were increasingly salient required the denial of African roots. Moreover, imperial exploitation had the unintended consequence of pushing powerless groups into alliances, such as that of the Pueblo Revolt. Hence, the case of colonial New Mexico shows that exploitation can foster linkages between marginalized groups and simultaneously squelch group formation, resulting in a fictionalized, sanitized historical memory of racial and ethnic identity.

NOTES

1. Frederick Dockstader, *The Kachina and the White Man: The Influences of White Culture of the Hopi Kachina Cult*, 2nd ed. (Albuquerque: University of New Mexico Press, 1985), 61. Dockstader argues that Esteban's murder stemmed from Pueblo distaste for arrogance and a realization that, given his Indian costume, he was not a god. The pueblo held a council and decided to deny him entrance into Hawikuh. "In the ensuing melée he was killed by arrows, and the southern Indians who had accompanied him fled."

2. Jesse Green, ed., *Cushing at Zuni: The Correspondence and Journals of Frank Hamilton Cushing, 1879–1884* (Albuquerque: University of New Mexico Press,

1990), 10, 335; and Adolph F. A. Bandelier, *The Gilded Man (El Dorado)* (New York: D. Appleton and Company, 1893), 159.

3. Bandelier, *Gilded Man*, 159.

4. Dockstader, *The Kachina and the White Man*, 12–13. In *When Jesus Came, the Corn Mothers Went Away: Marriage, Sexuality, and Power in New Mexico, 1500–1846* (Stanford: Stanford University Press, 1991), 40–41, Ramón Gutiérrez describes Esteban as a Black kachina who promised the future arrival of many White kachinas. Gutiérrez speculated that Zuni elders asked each other, "Who was this black katsina [*sic*]? Whence had he come? What did he want? Would more katsina shortly arrive, as Estevanico said?"

5. E. Charles Adams, "The Katsina Cult: A Western Pueblo Perspective," in *Kachinas in the Pueblo World*, ed. Polly Schaafsma (Albuquerque: University of New Mexico Press, 1994), 35–46, especially 44.

6. Gutiérrez, *When Jesus Came*, 45.

7. Adrian Bustamante, "Los Hispanos: Ethnicity and Social Change in New Mexico" (Ph.D. diss., University of New Mexico, 1982), 66. This estimate is based on eighteenth-century censuses, especially the 1750 census. I believe that this is a low estimate. Documents for the seventeenth century were destroyed in the Pueblo Revolt of 1680, but Blacks and mulattoes appear frequently in the few extant records.

8. See Gary B. Nash, "The Hidden History of Mestizo America," *Journal of American History* 82, no. 3 (December 1995): 947; and Jack Forbes, *Black Africans and Native Americans: Color, Race, and Caste in the Evolution of Red-Black Peoples* (New York: Basil Blackwell, 1988), 61.

9. Forbes, *Black Africans*, 61.

10. Forbes, *Black Africans*, 61; and Nash, "Hidden History," 951.

11. Thomas C. Patterson, "Early Colonial Encounters and Identities in the Caribbean: A Review of Some Recent Works and Their Implications," *Dialectical Anthropology* 16 (1991): 7; Forbes, *Black Africans*, 61; and Nicolás Leon, "Las castas del México colonial o Nueva España," *Noticias etnoantropológicas* 1 (1924): 7.

12. Kenneth W. Porter, "Negroes and Indians on the Texas Frontier," reprinted in *The Negro on the American Frontier* (New York: New York Times and Arno Press, 1971), 15; Magnus Morner, *Race Mixture in the History of Latin America* (Boston: Little, Brown and Company, 1967), cited in Forbes, *Black Africans*, 182.

13. Forbes, *Black Africans*, 184.

14. Leon, *Las castas*, 9–11; Forbes, *Black Africans*, 184–86.

15. Spanish Archives of New Mexico, Twitchell numbers 914, 1094, 1684, 1723, 1761, 2437, 2704, microfilm, Center for Southwest Research (CSWR), Zimmerman Library, University of New Mexico, Albuquerque.

16. Porter, "Negroes and Indians," 28.

17. Jack D. Forbes, *Apache, Navaho, and Spaniard* (Norman: University of Oklahoma Press, 1960), 76.

18. Forbes, *Apache*, 135, 138–39.

19. Forbes, *Apache*, 162.

20. Fray Angelico Chavez, "Pohé-Yemo's Representative and the Pueblo Revolt of 1680," *New Mexico Historical Review* 42, no. 2 (April 1967): 85–126, quote from 89.

21. Stefanie Beninato, "Popé, Pose-yemu, and Naranjo: A New Look at Leadership in the Pueblo Revolt of 1680," *New Mexico Historical Review* 65, no. 4 (October 1990): 417–35.

22. Forbes, *Black Africans*, 186.

23. Forbes, *Black Africans*, 161.

24. Antonio de Otermín, "Autos Drawn Up as a Result of the Rebellion of the Christian Indians, Santa Fe, 9 August 1680," in *Revolt of the Pueblo Indians of New Mexico and Otermín's Attempted Reconquest, 1680–1682*, vol. 1, ed. Charles Wilson Hackett, trans. Charmion Clair Shelby (Albuquerque: University of New Mexico Press, 1942), 5.

25. Letter of Andrés López de Gracia to don Bartolomé de Estrada, 29 August 1680, in Hackett and Shelby, *Revolt of the Pueblo Indians*, vol. 1, 46–47.

26. "Auto of Antonio de Otermín," Hacienda of Luís de Carbajal, 24 December 1681, and "Auto for the Conclusion of the Opinions of the Junta," Place opposite La Isleta, 1 January 1682, in Hackett and Shelby, *Revolt of the Pueblo Indians*, vol. 1, 338, 354–55.

27. Archivo General de la Nación (AGN), Inquisición, Legajo 372, photostat copies, CSWR. From transcriptions by France V. Scholes, "The First Decade of the Inquisition in New Mexico," *New Mexico Historical Review* 10, no. 3 (July 1935): 195–241, transcriptions in appendix, 230–32.

28. John L. Kessell, "New Mexico History" (course at University of New Mexico, Albuquerque, 22 February 1996).

29. Forbes, *Black Africans*, 165.

30. AGN-Inquisición, Legajo 304, from Scholes transcriptions, 239–41.

31. Spanish Archives of New Mexico, microfilm reel 9, frames 325–36, CSWR.

32. Forbes, *Black Africans*, 61–63.

33. Both quotes from Nash, "Hidden History," 947.

34. Fray Angelico Chavez, *New Mexico Roots, Ltd.*, CSWR.

35. Diligencias Matrimoniales, Nuestra Señora del Paso del Rio del Norte Record Group, boxes 90–94, Spanish and Mexican Manuscript Collection, Catholic Archives of Texas (CAT), Austin.

36. Scholes, "First Decade," 228.

37. Quoted in Gutiérrez, *When Jesus Came*, 103.

38. Spanish Colonial Census of New Mexico, 1750, in *Spanish and Mexican Censuses of New Mexico, 1750–1830*, compiler Virginia Langham Olmsted (Albuquerque: New Mexico Genealogical Society, 1981), 75–87. Originals from photostat copies, Biblioteca Nacional, Legajo 8, Parte 4, CSWR.

39. Malcolm Ebright, *Land Grants and Lawsuits in Northern New Mexico* (Albuquerque: University of New Mexico Press, 1994), 146–47.

40. Marriages, Archives of the Archdiocese of Santa Fe (AASF), microfilm reel 26, frame 187, CSWR.

41. Gutiérrez, *When Jesus Came*, 196.

42. Leon, *Las castas*, 5.

43. Leon, *Las castas*, 31–32.

44. Nash, "Hidden History," 952–53.

45. Nash, "Hidden History," 952–53.

46. Quoted in Nash, "Hidden History," 953.

47. Leon, *Las castas*, 9.

48. Father Juan Agustín de Morfi, "Account of Disorders, 1778," in *Coronado's Land: Essays on Daily Life in Colonial New Mexico*, ed. Marc Simmons (Albuquerque: University of New Mexico Press, 1991), 127–61, especially 148–51.

49. Don Pedro Baptista Pino, *The Exposition on the Province of New Mexico, 1812*, trans. and ed. Adrian Bustamante and Marc Simmons (Santa Fe and Albuquerque: El Rancho de las Golondrinas and the University of New Mexico Press, 1995), 40.

50. Rosalinda Lucero interview, Isleta Pueblo, Pueblo Transcripts, American Indian Oral History Collection, reel 7, tape no. 604, p. 12, CSWR.

51. Tillie Decker, interviewed by Pat Gregory, 8 July 1969, San Juan Pueblo, Pueblo Transcripts, American Indian Oral History Collection, reel 10, tape no. 230, p. 19, CSWR.

52. Works surveyed include J. J. Brody, *Anasazi and Pueblo Painting* (Albuquerque: University of New Mexico Press for the School of American Research, 1991); *The Zunis: Self-Portrayals*, by the Zuni People, trans. Alvina Quam (Albuquerque: University of New Mexico Press, 1972); Frank Hamilton Cushing, *Zuni Folk Tales* (New York: G. P. Putnam's Sons, 1901); Polly Schaafsma, ed., *Kachinas in the Pueblo World* (Albuquerque: University of New Mexico Press, 1994).

53. Rhett S. Jones, "Social-Scientific Perspectives on the Afro-American Arts," *Black American Literature Forum* 20, no. 4 (winter 1986), 443–47, quote from 444.

54. Forbes's works include several articles that gained inclusion in his 1988 book *Black Africans and Native Americans*. These articles include "Mustees, Half-breeds and Zambos in Anglo North America: Aspects of Black-Indian Relations," *American Indian Quarterly* 7, no 1 (1983), 57–83; "Mulattoes and People of Color

in Anglo-North America: Implications for Black-Indian Relations," *Journal of Ethnic Studies* 12, no. 2 (1984), 17–61; and "The Use of the Terms 'Negro' and 'Black' to Include Persons of Native American Ancestry in 'Anglo' North America," *Explorations in Ethnic Studies* 7, no. 2 (1984), 11–26.

55. Daniel J. Littlefield Jr.'s books include *Africans and Creeks: From the Colonial Period to the Civil War* (Westport CT: Greenwood Press, 1976); *Africans and Seminoles: From Removal to Emancipation* (Westport CT: Greenwood Press, 1977); and *The Cherokee Freedmen: From Emancipation to American Citizenship* (Westport CT: Greenwood Press, 1978). See also Kevin Mulroy, *Freedom on the Border: The Seminole Maroons in Florida, the Indian Territory, Coahuila, and Texas* (Lubbock: Texas Tech University Press, 1993); Theda Perdue, *Slavery and the Evolution of Cherokee Society, 1540–1866* (Knoxville: University of Tennessee Press, 1979); and William G. McLoughlin, *Cherokees and Missionaries, 1789–1839* (New Haven: Yale University Press, 1984).

56. Rebecca B. Bateman, "Africans and Indians: A Comparative Study of the Black Carib and Black Seminole," *Ethnohistory* 37, no. 1 (winter 1990): 1–24, quote from 1.

57. Jan Carew, "United We Stand! Joint Struggles of Native Americans and African Americans in the Columbian Era," *Monthly Review* 44, no. 3 (1992): 103–27, quote from 125.

58. Elizabeth Brandt and Christopher MacCrate, "'Make Like Seem Heep Injin': Pidginization in the Southwest," *Ethnohistory* 29, no. 3 (1982): 201–20, quotes from 209, 217.

59. Mary Ellison, "Black Perceptions and Red Images: Indian and Black Literary Links," *Phylon* 44, no. 1 (1983): 44–55, quote from 48.

60. Patterson, "Early Colonial Encounters," 7.

2. "The English Has Now a Mind to Make Slaves of Them All"

Creeks, Seminoles, and the Problem of Slavery

CLAUDIO SAUNT

In the opening decades of the eighteenth century, residents of the Deep South Interior (defined here roughly as the present-day states of Florida, Georgia, and Alabama) confronted a strange new development on the northeastern edge of the lands they hunted. There, between the Savannah and Santee Rivers, people, known to Native Americans mainly as purchasers of deerskins and war captives, began using slaves to burn the clear large areas of coastal land, to build dikes, to dig water channels, and to plant rice.[1] Though Southeasterners may have employed forced labor centuries earlier to build the ceremonial mounds that still dot the landscape, in the eighteenth century no Native American in the Deep South Interior could recall ever seeing or hearing about such slavery.

Indians soon realized that the emerging slave society, which called itself Carolina, would be a substantial and distinct presence in the region. Between 1710 and 1730, the number of slaves in this British colony more than quadrupled, to over twenty thousand. Farther south, in Spanish Florida in the third decade of the eighteenth century, in contrast, slaves numbered just over one hundred.[2] Unlike their northern counterparts, who spent daylight hours cultivating rice, Spanish slaves worked as household servants and skilled craftsmen in Pensacola and Saint Augustine. These settlements stood on the periphery of the Spanish empire and never attracted the people or capital necessary for the development of a plantation economy. West of the Deep South Interior, along the Mississippi River, lay the French colony of Louisiana, also neglected by its homeland. It had fewer than four thousand slaves in the 1730s and would not begin to emerge as a profitable slave colony for another thirty years.[3] Native Americans took note of these differences. In 1738, Creek Indians who lived along the Chattahoochee River (which divides the present-day states of Georgia and Alabama) agreed that they preferred the masters of the land be the Spanish who "enslave no one as the English do."[4]

Despite the growing scholarship on Indian slavery and on the related subject of Indian-Black relations, we still do not understand the momentous challenge that slave colonies presented to Native Americans in the Southeast.[5] In one sense, the impact of plantation slavery on Indians is clear: large-scale rice and tobacco cultivation diminished the importance of the deerskin trade to the colonial economy and encouraged Whites to appropriate Indian lands. But Native Americans were not simply buffeted about by impersonal historical forces. They made conscious decisions about the justice of the slave labor camps in the Southeast.[6] In the Deep South Interior, a close examination of the evidence, and particularly of long-neglected Spanish documents, suggests that Creeks were deeply troubled by the brutality of slavery and by the skewed hierarchy it created. In fact, the racial component of plantation slavery may have been one of its least disturbing aspects.[7] Frightened by the degree of oppression in South Carolina, Creeks closely monitored developments in the expanding slave colony and rapidly became divided in their responses.[8]

This division played a key role in shaping the direction of Creek history in the eighteenth and early nineteenth centuries. In 1813–14, slavery was one of the issues dividing Creeks in the civil conflict known as the Redstick War. After their defeat, Creek dissidents, or Redsticks, fled from their enemies into Florida, where they took refuge with the Seminoles. This violent war marks a turning point in the history of the Creeks and Seminoles as well as the Deep South Interior. It hastened the removal of the Creeks from what soon became the antebellum states of Alabama and Georgia, but at the same time it steeled Seminoles and Redsticks against leaving Florida. To understand fully the origins of this conflict and to ascertain why Redsticks found allies among the Seminoles, we must go back to the early eighteenth century, when Creeks first observed growing numbers of slaves on the northeastern perimeter of their hunting grounds.

In the eighteenth century, the Creeks, or Muskogees, lived along two river systems that drain into the Gulf of Mexico. In central Alabama, the Tallapoosa and Coosa Rivers join just north of the capital city of Montgomery to form the Alabama River, which winds its way southwest, eventually emptying into Mobile Bay. Nearly two hundred miles east, in the swamps of the Florida panhandle, lies the mouth of the Apalachicola River, formed some seventy miles upstream by the Chattahoochee and the Flint. Though not truly reflective of Creek social organization, European observers used these river systems to divide the Muskogee peoples into two main groups, the Upper Creeks along the Coosa-Tallapoosa-Alabama and the Lower Creeks along the Chattahoochee-Flint-Apalachicola. Europeans attached another name to Creeks who moved into north-central Florida in the mid-eighteenth century. Seminoles, as the English called these Indians, were actually renegade Creeks. They would not firmly establish their independence from the central Muskogee towns until the Redstick War of 1813–14.[9]

Creeks welcomed the first Carolina settlers in 1670 and initially found no objection to their requests for slaves.[10] Even before the settlement of Carolina, they had commonly taken prisoners and disposed of them, either through adoption (thus turning them into full members of Creek society) or through ritual murder.[11] The emerging slave trade with Carolina fit in neatly with Creek practices: Creeks dispatched enemy warriors, as was customary, and sold women and children to the newcomers.[12] In the early years of Carolina, the demands of establishing a new colony created a kind of frontier equality among its inhabitants, slave and free, and consequently Creeks did not observe the violent relationships between master and slave that would trouble them in the future.[13] In addition, the vast majority of the Indian captives sold in Carolina were sent out of the colony, usually to the West Indies, where they would be less able to escape from bondage.[14] For these reasons, Creeks did not at first recognize the full implications of the slave trade.

By 1720, the emergence of rice as a cash crop in South Carolina had changed the nature of this early slavery. Indian servitude declined when White South Carolinians began importing hundreds, then thousands, of Africans annually in order to meet their much-increased labor needs.[15] South Carolina's Black population more than doubled in the second decade of the eighteenth century, and by 1720, it was nearly twice the White population – and exceeded the entire Creek population as well.[16] Ten years later, one Cherokee expressed the difference between Native American and colonial slavery in a vivid image. Objecting to a treaty article that stipulated the return of fugitive slaves, he stated, "This small rope we shew you is all we have to bind our slaves with, and may be broken, but you have Iron Chains for yours."[17] If Creek visitors to Carolina in the past had not been unduly concerned about the limited trade in Indian slaves, they could now see – in the changing populace and in the steady expansion of cultivated coastal lands – that a new social order was emerging.

The development of plantation slavery in South Carolina preoccupied Creeks because it violated their notion of just power. The Creek peoples, according to a creation story recounted by two warriors in early summer 1735, followed the "white path" – that is, kept peace with each other – not because they were compelled to do so. Rather, they remained united by "fair persuasions."[18] Storytelling, not chains and jail cells, kept order in their towns. As Edmond Atkin, the future British superintendent to the Southern Indians, wrote in 1755:

The old Head Men of Note, who being past the fatigue of War and constant Hunting for their Livelyhood, but on Account of their Age held in great Veneration for their Wisdom and Experience, spend the remainder of their days almost intirely in the Town Round Houses, where the Youth and others daily report; relating to them the History of their Nation, discoursing of Occurrences, and delivering precepts and Instructions for their Conduct and Welfare.[19]

Unlike the stories written in history books, spoken stories are performed before responsive audiences. The storyteller can emphasize certain themes and even alter content according to the reactions of listeners. When political circumstances change rapidly, overnight or even during the course of a narration, storytellers can adapt immediately. Storytelling consequently allowed Creeks to maintain order through persuasion and negotiation.[20]

The novelty of the Creeks' political organization led colonists to comment on their "great love of Liberty," as one British official put it in 1766.[21] They "maintain very little Distinction," a Georgia colonist wrote in the 1730s.[22] James Oglethorpe of Georgia explained that "there is no coercive power in any of their nations; their kings can do no more than to persuade."[23] The naturalist William Bartram, who traveled through Creek and Seminole lands just before the American Revolution, concluded that when the power of an Indian leader became "dangerous to the liberty of citizens, . . . he must be a very cunning man if the tomahawk or rifle do not cut him short."[24]

Given the Creeks' commitment to persuasion rather than coercion, it is not surprising that they reacted strongly to the hierarchical societies they saw in colonial settlements. In 1754, for example, a Cherokee headman, probably alluding to the social organization he observed in South Carolina, told a party of Creeks that "he hoped it would never be in the Power of one Head Man to create a War Betwixt their Two Nations."[25] Five years later, when Lower Creeks responded to the insults of the governor of Florida by raiding Spanish settlements, a Creek warrior asked a resident of Saint Augustine: "Why didn't they kill the micco [governor] as many innocent people had to pay for such a bad man, for in their land in having someone who was so, everyone would join together and kill him."[26] The Spanish interlocutor responded that "here one cannot because His Majesty had appointed him and ordered that they obey him."[27]

On the occasions when colonial powers tried to promote a more centralized government among their Indian neighbors, Creeks resisted. In 1752, for example, an Upper Creek named Tunape traveled to Coweta on the Chattahoochee River to present papers he had obtained in England making him the king of all the Creeks. He told his audience that the British monarch would build forts in their towns, well supplied with arms, munitions, and troops, to defend them against their enemies, and that they would enjoy "all the freedoms, benefits, liberties, distinctions, and privileges" of other English subjects. The Cowetas responded that they wanted nothing to do with the English and gave the pretender a dose of poisonous herbs, leaving him crippled, "unable to move."[28] Similarly, when the governor of French Louisiana promoted the leader of Coweta as the head of the Indians along the Alabama River, they objected, "claiming that one chief over each village was enough." "In brief," noted a French officer in 1759, "they were unwilling to make any changes at all in their form of government."[29]

Though the observations of Europeans are cloaked in the rhetoric of liberalism (and likely tinctured by the association between Native Americans and the "state of nature" posited by philosophers such as John Locke), Creeks were not liberals in any sense. In the late seventeenth century, Locke had argued that humans were naturally in a state of "perfect Freedom," but across the Great Water, in the Deep South Interior, Creeks understood their law quite differently.[30] In fact, southeastern Indians believed just the opposite. Only people with kin relations within a larger clan network – and hence with a number of reciprocal obligations – were considered human.[31] Others, free of these relations, were "dunghill fowl," as Creeks and other Indians put it.[32] In fact, the opposition between slavery and freedom is peculiar to European thought; for many other peoples, the opposite of slavery is kinship, a status that brings a host of mutual obligations.[33] Within their own understanding of kinship and of political order, Creeks found good reason to object to the oppressive society developing in South Carolina.

For Creeks, the emerging slave society on their northeastern border must have been an alarming development.[34] In 1711, some Creeks checked the power of South Carolina by concluding a peace treaty with the French in Mobile.[35] Then, in 1715–16, neighboring Indians, including the Creeks, joined together in the Yamasee War and nearly destroyed the colony.[36] The overture to the French and the uprising against the British may in fact have been responses to the rapid expansion of slavery that had occurred over the preceding few years. In 1708, the slave population for the first time had surpassed the free population in South Carolina, and in the seven years before the outbreak of war, annual slave imports grew by a factor of eight (to 419 in 1714).[37] In addition, between 1711 and 1713, White Carolinians had enslaved hundreds of Native Americans in the Tuscarora War. Referring to the Indian conflict, one observer reported in 1712:

Our Traders have promoted Bloody Warrs this last Year to get slaves and one of them brought lately 100 of those poor Souls. . . . As for our free Indians – they goe their own way and bring [up] their Children like themselves with little Conversation among us, I generally Pceive something Cloudy in their looks, an Argumt. I fear, of discontent. I am allso Informed yt. our Indien Allyes [the Yamasees] are grown haughty of late.[38]

The defeat of the Indian alliance in the Yamasee War led some Creek towns to move closer to the French and open up relations with their former Spanish enemies in Saint Augustine.[39] Individual Creeks favored France, Britain, or Spain for a variety of reasons, but the relative presence or absence of plantation slavery in the southeastern colonies of these empires was certainly a significant consideration. Historians have failed to recognize its importance, instead emphasizing political factionalism and the drawing power of trade.[40]

Various sources indicate that Creeks had conflicting views of slavery. Though as early as 1717 some Creeks had agreed with Carolina officials to apprehend and return fugitive slaves, White Carolinians did not always obtain the results they wanted.[41] A few years later, one English agent accused Lower Creeks of "Robbing and Plundering us or our Slaves and Goods." He complained, "This has been practis'd several years against my King."[42] Some Creeks probably were motivated only by the lucrative market for slaves, but others surely saw these attacks as blows against the slave colony they had failed to dislodge a decade earlier.

Other resistance was more explicit. In 1725, South Carolina agent Tobias Fitch set out for the Creeks with the partial goal of securing the return of stolen slaves. In Coweta, he captured one fugitive, telling the residents, "The Negro is a Slave and tho he has Been Taken by the Yamasees and Lived among the Spanyards Yet that dos not make him free."[43] But when the slave escaped while being transported back to South Carolina, an Indian named Squire Mickeo "Imediatly assisted him with Cunnue and provissions sufficient to Carry him to Saint Mallagoes." An angry Fitch later accused, "Now there Sitts the Squire. Let him Denie it if he dares."[44] Squire Mickeo apparently had other concerns. He did not want the social oppression of the colonies to contaminate the square ground, the physical and symbolic center of Creek towns. Fitch was foiled again when a Creek leader from Palachuckaly on the Chattahoochee untied another fugitive slave captured under the agent's direction. The "King of the Town Cutt the Rope and threw it into the fire," Fitch wrote, "and the King of sd Town Told the White men that they had as good Guns as they, and could make as good use of them."[45] If some Creeks clearly opposed the South Carolina agent, Fitch could take consolation in the opposing views of a different Creek leader, who told him, "I have heard that the Chocktawes makes as good slaves as Negroes; if you think it will be good I will soon have some of them here."[46] Years later one of Fitch's successors would run into similar problems. In 1752, when a party of White South Carolinians captured a fugitive slave "sculking about" a Creek town, the bondsman escaped and made his way back to Coweta, where he disappeared, likely with the assistance of Indians.[47]

Spanish documents give a more complete voice to those Creeks who opposed the bondage practiced by British colonists. These sources must be read with the same care given English-language records; like Carolina settlers, Spanish Floridans selectively wrote down the words of their Indian allies. Moreover, Creeks surely manipulated the Spanish as well as the English by telling them what they wanted to hear. And the Spanish in turn manipulated the Creeks, explaining that the British intended to enslave them.[48] Nevertheless, Creeks who allied with the Spanish made a conscious choice to do so. When they praised Spanish Florida in contrast to the slave colony of Carolina, they perhaps even intended their words to be prescriptive as well as descriptive.

In the mid-1730s, Governor Francisco del Moral y Sánchez in Saint Augustine learned from eight Creek visitors that "trade with the English was not what they most desired, nor did it agree with them that they went in their towns, fearing that with the passage of time they could subjugate them, resulting in the injury of enslaving them."[49] According to the 1745 testimony of one Spanish officer familiar with the Creeks, they believed that the English encouraged them in war with the end of "subjugating the few who remain and enslaving their women and children."[50] Similarly, Laureano Solana, another Spanish officer conversant in Muskogee, reported that the Creeks believed that the English intended to "enslave them and their women and children and assume control of their land" after encouraging warfare to reduce their numbers.[51] These fears explain the behavior of a party of Spanish Indians who captured a "settlement Indian" from Georgia in 1742. The captive reported that "they kept him

Prisoner five days but as he spoke Indian and pretended to be a Slave they intrusted him with Arms telling him they were Freinds to all Slaves and He under pretence of hunting made his escape."[52]

At times, Creeks revealed a deeper, inner fear of slavery. In August 1739, Quilate, a leading warrior from the town of Apalachicola, informed the Spanish commandant at Fort San Marcos in Apalache that "the English had gone with more than 100 Negroes to construct a fort; that these had risen up and killed all the English."[53] In fact, there had been no such uprising.[54] But Quilate's report reflected the anxieties swirling through the towns of the Deep South Interior. South Carolina was at that time rife with rumors of slave conspiracies and would in a few weeks experience its most serious slave uprising ever.[55] When they had visited settlers during their winter hunts, Creeks had likely been exposed to the climate of fear that had settled on the White colonists in 1739. Quilate's story of a gruesome slave uprising reflected his fear of being put in chains by the English.

The objection of some Creeks to slavery manifested itself more generally as a fear of the forms of social control common to the colonial settlements. In 1735, during a visit to the Deep South Interior, Indian agent Patrick MacKay had written to the storekeeper of Savannah, "Please Send by my Express 4 pair Cuffs with Small Padlocks. I find a great many Saucey Villians in this Country that dont incline to Submitt to any Government, and their is an absolute Necessity to make Examples of some for the Terror of others."[56] MacKay intended the cuffs for disobedient traders, but his "Examples of some for the Terror of others" frightened the Creeks as well. In 1756, an English officer commanding at Fort Prince George outside the Cherokee town of Keowee, roughly twenty-five miles west of present-day Greenville, South Carolina, reported: "The large Quantity of Iron that is come from Charles Town at the different Times which is enough to build any Citadel has struck a great Terror amongst many of the [Cherokee] Indians they imagine they are brought up on Purpose to put them in Irons and make them Prisoners and the same News was sent to the Creeks and to the French."[57] A few months earlier, the Mortar of Ockchoy had returned from the Cherokees with a talk "which is that the English has now a Mind to make Slaves of them all, for [they] have already filled their nation with English Forts and great Guns, Negroes and Cattle."[58] Rumors reportedly had the Creeks in an uproar by the end of the year.[59] Most Creeks "look upon the Words Fort and Slavery as Synonomous Terms," an English agent wrote.[60] Nearly fifty years later, a Creek leader named Hoboithle Micco, who may have been old enough to remember stories of Patrick MacKay's "Cuffs" and "Padlocks," would insist that he did not want a "Blacksmith in the nation or weavers to bring them into slavery, no plough or any plantation tools."[61]

The division over slavery that emerged among Creeks in the early 1700s grew deeper in midcentury. In 1763, when Britain assumed control of Florida from Spain, the enslaved population in the region began to expand significantly.[62] Georgia, too, which had begun permitting slavery in 1751, witnessed dramatic growth in the number of slaves. Between 1760 and 1775, the unfree population in Georgia and Florida more than quadrupled from scarcely four thousand to roughly eighteen thousand, rapidly exceeding the entire number of Creeks in the area.[63] Georgia and Florida planters emulated their more successful counterparts in South Carolina, where the slave population numbered over seventy-one thousand in 1775.[64] Plantation slavery now threatened to engulf the heart of Creek hunting grounds.

Creeks not only faced the reality of an expanding slave society but also confronted related changes in their own towns. Traders, who had once used individual slaves as packhorsemen and factors, began establishing slave plantations in the Deep South Interior in the 1760s and 1770s. In 1771, a Creek warrior named Emistesigo explained, "I am now far advanced in life, and this is the first time I ever saw plantations settled in my nation."[65] A few months after Emistesigo lodged his complaint, Wolf King also objected to the plantations owned by traders.[66] Indian agent David Taitt noted visiting one such establishment, owned by trader James Germany, on the Tallapoosa in 1772.[67] That same year, Upper Creeks decided to forbid traders from establishing additional plantations.[68]

Despite Creek resolve, the reassuring line between the social organization of Creek towns and the oppressive establishments operated by resident Whites began to dissolve during and after the American Revolution when the traders' mestizo children rose to power.[69] Full members of their mothers' clans, yet comfortable with the political ideology and economic practices of their fathers, they brought into the heart of Creek society the plantation slavery and social oppression that Creeks had so long abhorred. Trader George Galphin, for example, left sixteen adult slaves and their children to each of his mestizo sons, George and John.[70] An uncle of the Galphin brothers, mestizo John Cannard, worked slaves as well and had plantations on Pensacola Bay and later near the Spanish Fort San Marcos in Apalache.[71] In 1791, he would reportedly own forty "valuable negroes" and some Indian slaves.[72] The naturalist William Bartram visited another mestizo in the 1770s, whom he identified as Boatswain, by birth one James

Latson (Lachin). Bartram described Boatswain's "villa" with one hundred fenced acres worked by fifteen slaves and other members of his "family."[73] In addition to these men, after the Revolution a number of mestizos descended from deerskin trader Lachlan McGillivray established plantations on the Alabama River and on the Little River north of Mobile.[74] Slave owner Alexander McGillivray, Lachlan's son by an Indian named Sehoy, would figure prominently in post-Revolutionary Creek history. To a greater or lesser degree, each mestizo introduced new economic and social practices into Creek lands.

Once plantation slavery began expanding in Creek towns, it became linked to broader developments in the Deep South Interior, especially to the consolidation of power and the rise of a political and economic hierarchy. Africans and African Americans consequently found themselves at the center of the Creek conflict over unfree labor and social oppression. (Creeks occasionally enslaved White and Indian peoples, too, but in general, plantation slavery in the Deep South Interior conformed to the model provided by European colonies.) In the late eighteenth century, Blacks in the Deep South Interior probably numbered fewer than six hundred, or about four percent of the population; yet their association with and resistance to the rise of a coercive political order gave them a far greater role in Creek history than their numbers would seem to indicate.

In the 1790s, there were two populations of Africans and African Americans in Creek lands. One was centered among the Upper Creeks around the fork of the Coosa and Tallapoosa Rivers, where Alexander McGillivray and his relatives kept many of their slaves. There, Blacks were consigned with ever greater frequency to the plantations of the few wealthy residents. The other population center was in outlying Lower Creek and Seminole settlements on the Chattahoochee and Lake Miccosukee and in Alachua near present-day Gainesville, Florida. In these towns, Blacks often became important and respected (though not always equal) members of their communities.

About three hundred Black slaves lived among the Upper Creeks in the 1790s, most of them on plantations owned by traders such as Robert Grierson and Richard Bailey and by wealthy mestizos such as McGillivray.[75] Many mestizos and White traders had accumulated slaves during the Revolution or in border raids thereafter. Between 1787 and September 1789, Creeks were said to have stolen 110 slaves and killed 10 others in attacks on the Georgia border. During the same period, in contrast, they allegedly killed 72 Whites and wounded 29, taking only 30 as prisoners, indicating that Creeks singled out slaves as war booty.[76] Many such prisoners were later sold in Pensacola, but others remained in the Deep South Interior.[77] In addition, some men occasionally bought slaves in colonial settlements and transported them into the Deep South Interior. McGillivray, for instance, arranged to purchase slaves from Jamaica, and John Cannard traveled to the slave market in Savannah.[78]

As part of their efforts to establish themselves as planters, McGillivray and others worked with Spanish authorities to limit the freedom of Africans. In January 1784, for example, McGillivray wrote Commandant Arturo O'Neill of Pensacola, "The nation is now pretty well drained of Negroes what few there is, don't answer the description you wish."[79] Similarly, in February 1786, he secured the return of Ciro to his master in New Orleans.[80] In fact, McGillivray's correspondence is full of instances in which he oversaw the return of fugitive slaves to colonial settlements.

Despite the efforts of men such as McGillivray, slaveholders in the Deep South Interior could not re-create to their satisfaction the conditions in European-American settlements that allowed for expansive slave plantations. The landscape and diffuse political geography simply were not conducive to an extensive system of social control. A slave who was despondent over his or her lot could always run away, especially because the nearby forests offered an escape and there were no overseers keeping guard. Moreover, the tools of control had to be imported. In 1799, when one Georgian volunteered to go to the Creek nation to recover stolen slaves, he explained, "I have in my employ a very good blacksmith which I would take on with me and place in the most central part of the nation where he could take care of negroes as we would collect them, and place irons on them to prevent their escape."[81] McGillivray, acknowledging this reality, regretted that, although he owned slaves, he "could not use them in this country."[82]

In the Seminole and outlying Lower Creek towns, where the other center of Black population lay, Indian residents distanced themselves from the coercive social order expanding in main Creek towns. Language (many of them spoke Hitchiti, a dialect related to yet distinct from the dominant Creek tongue) and geography led these people to identify with the dissident Creeks known as Seminoles rather than with the new "national" leaders.[83] Products of imperial warfare and the deerskin trade, Seminoles and their allies embraced the diffuse distribution of power that these pursuits had encouraged, and they objected in words and action to the new forms of social control promoted by would-be planters such as McGillivray.[84] Moreover, the mostly marginal land they occupied in the pine barrens of southern Georgia and northern Florida discouraged the development of plantation slavery.[85] Consequently, African American residents in the Seminole and outlying Lower Creek towns enjoyed far more autonomy than their counterparts elsewhere in the Deep South Interior.

Near the end of 1790, Julian Carballo, an interpreter for the Spanish, wrote a brief note to Arturo O'Neill, the commandant of Pensacola. In Chiaja, he informed his superior, "free and maroon negroes, from the Americans and a few from Pensacola, are forming a type of palisade. They number more than 110."[86] By necessity, the Black community at Chiaja (a Creek-Seminole town on the Chattahoochee River some thirteen miles below the site of present-day Columbus, Georgia) developed outside the purview of literate observers, but beginning in early 1793, a series of frontier raids brought the settlement to the attention of Whites. In February of that year, a group of Indians stole some slaves on the south side of the Altamaha River, and a month later, George Galphin led a raid on the Saint Marys River, stealing seven slaves along with some horses and cattle.[87] In early May 1793, Creeks raided William Smith's rice plantation in Liberty County, Georgia, and carried off thirteen more slaves.[88] Later that same year, perhaps aware of the palisade at Chiaja, a "horrid banditti of negroes" fled from South Carolina for the Creek nation, though there is no record that they made it successfully.[89] In fact, between 1793 and 1796, Chiaja and the neighboring towns of Hitchiti and Usiche were involved in several more slave raids.[90] The palisade Carballo noted at the opening of the decade had become the hub of African and Indian relations in the Deep South Interior.

It is clear that Blacks were more than passive objects in these raids. One slave, for instance, reportedly was not stolen but "got with the Indians" on his own accord and later stated to an agent hired to secure his return "that he would not go back if he could help it."[91] The Georgia militia encountered stronger evidence that some slaves conspired with their kidnappers. Marching against Chiaja "where they expected a large booty in negroes and other property," they were rebuffed by sixteen Indians and four Blacks.[92]

At least one of the leaders of the raids was in fact of African descent, though he lived and identified himself as an Indian. Ninnywageechee, also known as the Little Negro Factor and the Black Factor, was an "Indian and negro mestizo, [a] trader among the Lower Creeks."[93] White traders noted that he owned a "plantation," but it probably resembled less a regimented plantation in coastal Georgia than a small Seminole settlement populated by Creeks, Africans, and mestizos.[94] Philatouche was also of African descent, and though not directly involved in the raids, he was a prominent leader in Chiaja, perhaps explaining in part why this town became the center of the Black population among the Lower Creeks in the 1790s.[95] In addition to Philatouche, another Creek leader who lived in Chiaja or nearby Usiche also appears to have been of African ancestry.[96] His name, "Cudgomicco," likely was derived from "Cudjo," a common West African day name meaning Monday, and "micco," roughly translated from Muskogee as "chief."[97]

In 1795, an African American named Peter surfaced to spread news among slaves in East Florida of the "good life" enjoyed by Blacks living with the Seminoles and Lower Creeks. Early that year, Spanish officials complained that ten Indian men, women, and children had been in the area for some time "burning forests and pastures and even introducing themselves into the houses of the residents." A Spanish officer named Carlos Howard reported that "they have in their company two negroes stolen in past years from the then Governor of Georgia, Houston." The Blacks praised "to the residents' slaves the good life that people of their color enjoy in the nation where they eat the same as their masters and work only when they wish without fear of punishment."[98] The Spanish officer clearly feared the potential danger of the situation, noting that the Indians had already visited John McQueen's plantation, where nine fugitive slaves were temporarily imprisoned.[99]

Howard noted with certain anger that Peter, the Indians' Black translator, met his orders to desist from "bribing the slaves to flee to the nation" by brazenly laughing in his face.[100] When slave owner John McQueen later reprimanded Peter and the Indians for assisting in the escape of some slaves, Peter responded "with much haughtiness," stating that "his master and every other Indian there were as good" as McQueen.[101] Peter and his Indian allies remained in East Florida throughout May, June, and July 1795, dancing with the local slaves, preaching the good life to them, and "daily inconveniencing the settlers by conspiring with their negroes and . . . persuading them to flee."[102] They eventually disappeared from the watchful eyes of literate European Americans into the Deep South Interior, where the relationship between Blacks and Indians continued to evolve and expand.

The example of Peter must be balanced with stories of Blacks who did not fare as well. Like the central towns of the Upper and Lower Creeks, these peripheral towns also had their would-be planters. John Cannard, a mestizo with forty bondsmen and bondswomen, was the largest slaveholder in the area. One visitor wrote, "He is a despot, shoots his negroes when he pleases, and has cut off the ears of one of his favorite wives, with his own hands, in a drunken fit of suspicion."[103] Nevertheless, other evidence suggests that Cannard had an ambiguous relationship with his slaves. A White traveler noted meeting Cannard's bondsmen in the woods on their way to Saint Marys with a drove of horses for sale, suggesting that Cannard could trust them with a fair amount of independence.[104] Ten years later, a Georgian reported meeting a slave of Cannard's named Sam in the town of Tallassee. Sam had been "seduced and taken away" from Savannah by the Creeks during the Revolution, and he apparently decided it was worth staying in the Deep South Interior.[105] Cannard also had a "negro servant . . . whom he always brings with him, and he serves him as an interpreter to treat with the whites."[106] All of these slaves worked independently without any supervision, and Cannard especially entrusted his "confidential negro Joe" with significant authority.[107]

At the beginning of 1796, Cannard established a small plantation about twelve miles from the Spanish fort at Apalache, at the head of the Wakulla River.[108] At this establishment, slaves worked unsupervised, producing corn for the nearby Spanish fort and for the Seminole town of Mikasuki, near the lake of the same name (Miccosukee). Corn demanded little labor compared to export crops such as rice or sugar, and most of the year, especially from November to April, Cannard's slaves probably only worked occasionally for their master, though at times Cannard rented them out to work at the Spanish fort.[109] Though Cannard was more attuned than most Indians in the area to the plantation economy, his marginal land, remote from market towns, worked against his ambitions.

Cannard was perhaps the most severe slave owner in the region. Kinache, the head of Mikasuki, and Payne, the head of the Alachua Seminoles near present-day Gainesville, Florida, practiced a different type of slavery. In Alachua, Blacks possessed and traded their own property. Visitor John Hambly purchased a horse from "Payne's Joe" in January 1794, for example. Later that same year Hambly bought two more horses from "Payne's negro Pompey" and paid "Payne's Jose" for a horse he had rented, giving them promissory notes payable by Mrs. Hambly for $56 and $12.50, respectively.[110] Payne, who had succeeded Cowkeeper as the head of the Alachua Seminoles, probably used his slaves as cowboys, as did Kinache.[111] Kinache's slaves lived about a mile and a half above the Indian settlement at Mikasuki.[112]

Other Blacks were adopted directly into Creek families.[113] The initial step to adoption might be ownership by the clan rather than the individual. Such was the case of Sambo, who in 1788 was owned by the Tiger or

Panther Clan in Chiaja.[114] Sambo's role as clan property derived from the Creek practice of taking captives in war. Creeks who were not interested in benefiting from the surplus labor of African Americans welcomed them for other reasons. In adopting or owning slaves, clans increased their power. While living among the Creeks, Mary, for instance, stolen in 1793 from Liberty County, Georgia, gave birth to four children whom "the Indians kept because they were born upon their hands."[115] Fanny, stolen in 1796 also from Liberty County, contributed eighteen children and grandchildren to the Creek population in a little more than twenty years.[116] Other African Americans offered needed manpower to a people who valued warriors. In the late 1790s, a group of slaves who found themselves for sale by their White owner to Indians in the Deep South Interior explained that "they did not know how to work but give them guns and go to war they knowed how to do that."[117] In the coming years, as the expansion of the United States threatened the social order of the region, they would be true to their word.

The contrast between the status of Blacks among the Creeks and among the Seminoles (including residents of such towns as Chiaja) became a distinguishing feature of Seminole identity by the beginning of the nineteenth century. While Creek leaders increasingly adopted elements of centralized government urged on them by U.S. officials, the Seminoles insisted on the preservation of the dispersed power that had characterized the Muskogee peoples earlier in the eighteenth century. Among other methods of social control, Creek leaders and wealthy mestizos continued to discipline slaves. Their plantations held most of the African Americans in the region. Big Warrior, the leader of the Creek national council, reportedly "cultivated a fine plantation with 70 or 80 negroes near Tuckabatche,"[118] and mestizo Samuel Moniac owned two plantations with a total of thirty-eight slaves.[119] Along the Alabama River, mestizos expanded the slave plantations their forebears had established. In 1874, for example, a number of elderly freedmen and freedwomen recalled working some sixty years earlier on the river plantation of David Taitt, a relative of Alexander McGillivray's.[120] Other mestizos, such as Dixon Bailey, owned small numbers of slaves who worked in cotton fields.[121]

In 1813, the accumulated stress of years of contested and difficult change gave way in the Redstick War. Fought mainly among Upper Creeks, the war pitted the "idle" against the "industrious," as one Indian put it.[122] The industrious kept cattle and spun cotton, and the most successful among them owned slaves. Redsticks targeted slave owner Big

Warrior as their main opponent, destroying twenty thousand dollars' worth of his property.[123] They also razed the two plantations of Samuel Moniac and those of other mestizos living along the Alabama River.[124]

Though one report suggests that the Redsticks killed some of the slaves belonging to their enemies, evidence indicates that they spared most.[125] One Black man stated that a Redstick had told him not to fear because the Master of Breath, as the Creek supreme being was known in English, had "ordered us not to kill any but white people and half breeds."[126] Moreover, Blacks played key roles in the conflict, fighting alongside the dissident Redsticks. In an attack on Fort Mims, one African American named Siras cut down the pickets.[127] "The blacks were the first in," a Redstick leader later recalled.[128] According to a mestizo Creek writing in the 1830s, when Redstick confidence had flagged, "the negroes they had would not cease urgeing them on, untill they saw their mettle was raised, by reciting that they thought it interested them to have the Fort people destroyed."[129] In another engagement, a U.S. officer reported that the "negroes were the last to quit the ground."[130] Only two years before the outbreak of the war, memories of the Haitian Revolution had inspired slaves in Louisiana to march on New Orleans, burning plantations along the way.[131] Such recollections (and personal experience in some cases) may have also encouraged Blacks in the Deep South Interior. Refugees such as Laurent and Dominique, "French" slaves who had been stolen in East Florida by Lower Creeks in 1800, may have given the Creeks wider knowledge of the Atlantic world revolutions of the late eighteenth century.[132]

After the Redsticks' defeat at the hands of their Creek and U.S. enemies, they fled into the swamps of Florida with their Black allies.[133] With the assistance of fugitive slaves from Pensacola, Saint Augustine, and Georgia, and with the support of the British navy (then engaged in the War of 1812), Redsticks constructed a redoubt in early 1815 some fifteen miles from the mouth of the Apalachicola River. Food scarcities as well as threats of invasion from U.S. troops eventually led most of the two thousand Indians to abandon the fort for nearby Seminole towns. The three hundred or more Blacks in the area soon followed suit. By late July 1816, when Creek and U.S. forces surrounded and destroyed the redoubt (called the Negro Fort by Americans), most of its inhabitants had already settled in nearby Seminole towns.[134] The Redsticks shared with the Seminoles a mutual dislike for the coercive order of the main Creek settlements. All "idlers" alike, they rejected the economy of the "industrious" and the plantation slavery of its main proponents. Mikasuki, the closest Indian town to the Negro Fort, absorbed many of the refugees. As Spanish commandant Francisco Caso y Luengo wrote, it had become a "refuge for those who don't belong elsewhere."[135]

Creeks, historians tell us, carefully evaluated the relative cost of Spanish, French, and English trade goods, tested the temper of British-forged guns, and examined the fastness of India dyes. But the slave labor camps and skewed hierarchy of their trading partner between the Savannah and Santee Rivers weighed at least as heavily on their minds. Spanish documents allow us to recover, if not Creek debates about slavery, the deep divisions that these debates rent. These divisions indicate that though we explain, and in some sense naturalize, historical developments such as plantation slavery, from the perspective of the Creeks, the forced labor of the Southern colonies was a bizarre and threatening innovation. White Carolinians called their labor camps "plantations," a word historians have adopted, but many Creeks knew better. Beneath this benign term lay a system of compulsion and inequality that threatened the core of the Creek peoples.

NOTES

1. Peter H. Wood details this transformation in South Carolina in *Black Majority: Negroes in Colonial South Carolina from 1670 through the Stono Rebellion* (New York: Norton, 1974). See especially chap. 2, "Black Labor – White Rice."

2. Peter H. Wood, "The Changing Population of the Colonial South: An Overview by Race and Region, 1685–1790," in *Powhatan's Mantle: Indians in the Colonial Southeast*, ed. Peter H. Wood et al. (Lincoln: University of Nebraska Press, 1989), 38. For portraits of the Black population in Spanish Florida in the First Spanish Period, see Jane Landers, "Gracia Real de Santa Teresa de Mose: A Free Black Town in Spanish Colonial Florida," *American Historical Review* 95 (1990): 9–30; and Landers, "Traditions of African American Freedom and Community in Spanish Colonial Florida," in *The African American Heritage of Florida*, ed. David R. Colburn and Jane L. Landers (Gainesville: University Press of Florida, 1995), 17–41.

3. Wood, "The Changing Population of the Colonial South," 38; Daniel H. Usner, *Indians, Settlers, and Slaves in a Frontier Exchange Economy: The Lower Mississippi Valley before 1783* (Chapel Hill: University of North Carolina Press, 1992), chap. 4.

4. Governor of Havana to Secretary Torrenueva, 18 May 1738, Stetson Collection (hereafter ST), bnd. 5731, 87–1–3/48, Santo Domingo 2593, P. K. Yonge Library of Florida History, University of Florida, Gainesville (hereafter PKY).

5. Literature on Indian slavery or Indian-Black relations in the Southeast includes Laurence Foster, *Negro-Indian Relationships in the Southeast* (Philadelphia: University of Pennsylvania Press, 1935); several articles by Kenneth Wiggins Porter scattered in the *Florida Anthropologist*, the *Journal of Negro History*, and the *Florida Historical Quarterly*, republished in a Kenneth Wiggins Porter collection, *The Negro on the American Frontier* (New York: Arno Press, 1971); John M. Lofton Jr., "White, Indian, and Negro Contacts in Colonial South Carolina," *Southern Indian Studies* 1 (1949): 3–12; William S. Willis, "Divide and Rule: Red, White, and Black in the Southeast," *Journal of Negro History* 48 (1963):157–76, republished in *Red, White, and Black: Symposium on Indians in the Old South*, ed. Charles M. Hudson (Athens: University of Georgia Press, 1971), 99–115; William G. McLoughlin, "Red Indians, Black Slavery, and White Racism: America's Slaveholding Indians," *American Quarterly* 26 (1974): 366–83; Daniel F. Littlefield, *Africans and Seminoles: From Removal to Emancipation* (Westport CT: Greenwood Press, 1977); Daniel F. Littlefield, *Africans and Creeks: From the Colonial Period to the Civil War* (Westport CT: Greenwood Press, 1979); Theda Perdue, *Slavery and the Evolution of Cherokee Society, 1540–1866* (Knoxville: University of Tennessee Press, 1979); James H. Merrell, "The Racial Education of the Catawba Indians," *Journal of Southern History* 50 (1984): 363–84; and Kathyrn E. Holland Braund, "The Creek Indians, Blacks, and Slavery," *Journal of Southern History* 57 (1991): 601–37.

6. On the term "slave labor camp," see Peter H. Wood, "Slave Labor Camps in Early America: Overcoming Denial and Discovering the Gulag," in *Inequality in Early America*, ed. Carla Gardina Pestana and Sharon V. Salinger (Hanover NH, University Press of New England, 1999).

7. Nancy Shoemaker, "How Indians Got to Be Red," *American Historical Review* 102 (1997): 625–44, has argued compellingly that the indigenous beliefs of southeastern Native peoples made them comfortable with European racial categories.

8. The history of the Seminoles and Creeks has long attracted the attention of historians interested in Black-Indian relations, not least because the three Seminole wars of the nineteenth century provide dramatic examples of Black-Indian interaction and a plethora of government reports documenting the subject. Predictably, the historiography is slanted toward the nineteenth century, after Spain ceded Florida to the United States. Those few historians who consider the earlier period in detail do not take advantage of the vast archives of the Spanish empire. See, for example, Littlefield, *Africans and Seminoles* and *Africans and Creeks*; and Kevin Mulroy, *Freedom on the Border: The Seminole Maroons in Florida, the Indian Territory, Coahuila, and Texas* (Lubbock: Texas Tech University Press, 1993). J. Leitch Wright Jr., *Creeks and Seminoles: The Destruction and Regeneration of the*

Muscogulge People (Lincoln: University of Nebraska Press, 1986), chap. 3, uses Spanish materials but not systematically.

9. For an overview of Creek and Seminole history, see Wright, *Creeks and Seminoles*; Angie Debo, *The Road to Disappearance: A History of the Creek Indians* (Norman: University of Oklahoma Press, 1941); and James W. Covington, *The Seminoles of Florida* (Gainesville: University Press of Florida, 1993).

10. David Corkran, *The Creek Frontier, 1540–1783* (Norman: University of Oklahoma Press, 1962), 49; Wood, *Black Majority*, 38–40; and J. Leitch Wright Jr., *The Only Land They Knew: The Tragic Story of the Indians in the Old South* (New York: Free Press, 1981), 137–50.

11. Perdue, *Slavery and the Evolution of Cherokee Society*, 3–15.

12. Wright, *The Only Land They Knew*, 148–49; Braund, "The Creek Indians, Blacks, and Slavery," 608. Carolina officials apparently preferred women and children for the same reasons that Creeks did: men proved troublesome.

13. Wood, *Black Majority*, chap. 4.

14. Wright, *The Only Land They Knew*, 138–39, 148. Wright suggests that most Indian slaves were not exported, but other historians argue more convincingly that White Carolinians, faced with the prospect of disciplining Native Americans who knew the region and often had nearby allies, found that exporting Indian slaves was more profitable. Wood, *Black Majority*, 38–39; Peter H. Wood, "Indian Servitude in the Southeast," in *History of Indian-White Relations*, vol. 4 of *Handbook of North American Indians* (Washington: Smithsonian, 1988), 407–9; and Verner W. Crane, *The Southern Frontier, 1670–1732* (1928; reprint, with a preface by Peter H. Wood, New York: Norton, 1981), 112–14.

15. Wood, *Black Majority*, 35–55.

16. Wood, *Black Majority*, 152.

17. Quoted in Wood, *Black Majority*, 262 n. 85.

18. Talk of Creek leaders, 11 June 1735, *Colonial Records of the State of Georgia*, ed. Allen D. Candler (Atlanta, 1904–16) (hereafter CRG), 20:386. This citation is to the 1982 edition. Volumes 27–39 are in typescript in the Georgia Department of Archives and History (hereafter GDAH).

19. Edmond Atkin, *The Appalachian Indian Frontier: The Edmond Atkin Report and Plan of 1755*, ed. Wilbur R. Jacobs (University of South Carolina, 1954; reprint, Lincoln: University of Nebraska Press, 1967), 10.

20. Karl Kroeber, a scholar of ethnopoetics, argues convincingly that myths, and more generally spoken stories, foster rather than constrain the reassessment of "tradition." Kroeber, "Unaesthetic Imaginings: Native American Myth as Speech Genre," *Boundary 2* 23 (1996): 171–98.

21. James Grant to the Board of Trade, 30 August 1766, Public Records Office

(hereafter PRO), Colonial Office (hereafter CO) 5/541, 125. British Colonial Office Records, 1:256, typescript in the PKY.

22. Thomas Causton to his wife, 12 March 1733, *CRG*, 1982 ed., 20:15–18, GDAH. Archaeological evidence confirms Causton's observation that Indians "maintain very little Distinction." See Gregory A. Waselkov, "The Macon Trading House and Early European-Indian Contact in the Colonial Southeast," in *Ocmulgee Archaeology, 1936–1986*, ed. David J. Hally (Athens: University of Georgia Press, 1994), 194–95.

23. Quoted in Charles C. Jones, *Historical Sketch of Tomo-chi-chi, Mico of the Yamacraws* (Albany: J. Munsell, 1868), 45.

24. William Bartram, "Observations on the Creek and Cherokee Indians, 1789, with Prefatory and Supplementary Notes by E. G. Squier," *Transactions of the American Ethnological Society*, vol. 3, pt. 1 (New York: American Ethnological Society, 1853), 24.

25. Information of George Johnston, 2 October 1754, *Documents Relating to Indian Affairs, Colonial Records of South Carolina*, ed. William L. McDowell Jr. (Columbia: South Carolina Archives Department, 1958) (hereafter *DIASC*), 2:10.

26. Juan Joseph Solana to Secretary Arriaga, 9 April 1760, ST, bnd. 6447, 86-7-21/91, Santo Domingo 2584, PKY.

27. Juan Joseph Solana to Secretary Arriaga, 9 April 1760, ST, bnd. 6447, 86-7-21/91, Santo Domingo 2584, PKY.

28. Copy of letter from Alonzo de Arrivas to Fulgencio García de Solis, 17 July 1754, Historia, Archivo General de la Nación, Mexico City (hereinafter AGN), v. 436, exp. 4, f. 6, reel 144G, PKY; Fulgencio García de Solis to Conde de Revillagigedo, 27 July 1754, Historia, AGN, v. 436, exp. 4, f. 1, reel 144G, PKY.

29. Jean Bernard Bossu, *Jean Bernard Bossu's Travels in the Interior of North America, 1751–1762*, ed. and trans. Seymour Feiler (Norman: University of Oklahoma Press, 1962), 152–53.

30. Locke, *The Second Treatise of Government*, sec. 4.

31. Perdue, *Slavery and the Evolution of Cherokee Society*, 12, 16–18.

32. Saunt, "A New Order of Things," 253; Merrell, "The Racial Education of the Catawba Indians," 365. For the Cherokees, see Thomas Hatley, *The Dividing Paths: Cherokees and South Carolinians through the Revolutionary Era* (New York: Oxford University Press, 1993), 162–63. Many Native American groups identified outsiders as nonhumans. Among the Kato Indians of northern California, for example, the phrase "na nesh" originally meant "human, not animal." Later, it came to distinguish Indians ("na nesh") from Europeans. Karl Kroeber, "An Introduction to the Art of Traditional American Indian Narration," in *Traditional Literatures of the American Indian*, ed. Karl Kroeber (Lincoln: University of Nebraska Press, 1981), 7.

33. Igor Kopytoff and Suzanne Miers, "Introduction: African 'Slavery' as an Institution of Marginality," in *Slavery in Africa: Historical and Anthropological Perspectives*, ed. Igor Kopytoff and Suzanne Miers (Madison: University of Wisconsin Press, 1977), 3–84. For an opposing view, see Claude Meillassoux, *The Anthropology of Slavery: The Womb of Iron and Gold* (London: Athlone Press, 1991).

34. The sentiments of Creeks in the eighteenth century mirrored those of the Osage in the early nineteenth century. In 1820, Big Soldier, an Osage, stated to his American audience: "You are surrounded by slaves. Everything about you is in chains, and you are slaves yourselves. I hear I should exchange my presents for yours. I too should become a slave." Quoted in Willard H. Rollings, *The Osage: An Ethnohistorical Study of Hegemony on the Prarie-Plains* (Columbia: University of Missouri Press, 1992), 67.

35. Corkran, *The Creek Frontier*, 56–57.

36. Wright, *The Only Land They Knew*, 122. For a general account of the war, see Crane, *The Southern Frontier*, 162–86. See also Richard L. Haan, "The 'Trade Do's Not Flourish as Formerly': The Ecological Origins of the Yamasee War of 1715," *Ethnohistory* 28 (1982): 341–58.

37. Wood, *Black Majority*, 143, 151.

38. Quoted in Wood, *Black Majority*, 143 n. 48.

39. Crane, *The Southern Frontier*, 183; Corkran, *The Creek Frontier*, chap. 3.

40. See, for example, Corkran, *The Creek Frontier*; and Braund, *Deerskins and Duffels*.

41. Corkran, *The Creek Frontier*, 64; Willis, "Divide and Rule," 103, 106–9.

42. Charlesworth Glover to Lower Creeks, 8 February 1728, Sainsbury Transcripts, 13:109, South Carolina Department of Archives and History, Columbia. Partially quoted in Wood, *Black Majority*, 261. For an example of a plantation raid, see Jno. Sharp to Gov. Nicholson, 12 November 1724, Sainsbury Transcripts, 2:266–69, South Carolina Department of Archives and History, Columbia (these citations courtesy of Peter H. Wood). See also Willis, "Divide and Rule," 110.

43. Tobias Fitch, "Journal of Captain Tobias Fitch's Mission from Charleston to the Creeks, 1726," in *Travels in the American Colonies*, ed. Newton D. Mereness (New York: Macmillan, 1916), 186.

44. Fitch, "Journal," 211.

45. Fitch, "Journal," 205–6.

46. Fitch, "Journal," 207.

47. Second Journal of Thomas Bosomworth, October–December 1752, DIASC, 1:272, 320.

48. See, for example, Fitch, "Journal," 193.

49. Governor of Florida to the King, 17 February 1745, ST, bnd. 6151, 58-2-13/17, Santo Domingo 862, PKY.

50. Governor of Florida to the King, 17 February 1745, ST, bnd. 6151, 58-2-13/17, Santo Domingo 862, PKY.

51. Governor of Florida to the King, 17 February 1745, ST, bnd. 6151, 58-2-13/17, Santo Domingo 862, PKY.

52. The Declaration of Nottoway a Settlement Indian in Georgia, 22 November 1742, CRG, 36:54, GDAH.

53. Manuel de Montiano to Juan Francisco de Güemes y Horcasitas, 19 August 1739, East Florida Papers (hereafter EF), bnd. 37, 157, reel 15, PKY.

54. Manuel de Montiano to Juan Francisco de Güemes y Horcasitas, 20 November 1739, EF, bnd. 37, 167, reel 15, PKY.

55. Wood, *Black Majority*, 308–14.

56. Patrick MacKay to [Thomas Causton], 27 March 1735, CRG, 1982 ed., 20:290–91.

57. Captain Raymond Demere to Governor Lyttelton, 12 September 1756, *DIASC*, 2:200.

58. Creek Traders to Governor Lyttelton, 31 July 1756, *DIASC*, 2:152.

59. Headmen of the Upper Creek Nation to Governor Lyttelton, 9 August 1756, *DIASC*, 2:153–54.

60. Daniel Pepper to Governor Lyttelton, 21 December 1756, *DIASC*, 2:297–300. Also see Daniel Pepper to Governor Lyttelton, 30 November 1756, *DIASC*, 2:295–97.

61. James Durouzeaux to Vicente Folch, 5 October 1803, Papeles Procedentes de Cuba, Archivo de Indias, Seville, Spain (hereafter PC), leg. 220A, 489, reel 307, PKY. Over two hundred years later, in a mythic story recounted by one Seminole Indian, chains appeared, along with other foreign materials, as exotic items in the "Breath-maker's home," the residence in the sky of the supreme being. Ethel Cutler Freeman, "A Happy Life in the City of Ghosts: An Analysis of a Mikasuki Myth," *Florida Anthropologist* 14 (1961): 27–28, 30.

62. See Wilbur H. Siebert, "Slavery and White Servitude in East Florida, 1726–1776," *Florida Historical Quarterly* 10 (1931): 3–23; and Siebert, "Slavery and White Servitude in East Florida, 1776–1785," *Florida Historical Quarterly* 10 (1932): 139–61.

63. Wood, "The Changing Population of the Colonial South," 38.

64. Wood, "The Changing Population of the Colonial South," 38; Edward J. Cashin, *Lachlan McGillivray, Indian Trader: The Shaping of the Southern Colonial Frontier* (Athens: University of Georgia Press, 1992), 253.

65. "At a Congress of the Principal Chiefs and Warriors of the Upper Creek Nation," 29 October 1771, Lockey Collection (hereafter LOC), PRO, CO 5/589, PKY.

66. David Taitt, "David Taitt's Journal of a Journey through the Creek Country,

1772," in *Travels in the American Colonies*, ed. Newton D. Mereness (New York: MacMillan, 1916), 510.

67. Taitt, "David Taitt's Journal," 501, 535.

68. David Taitt to John Stuart, 4 May 1772, in *Travels in the American Colonies*, ed. Newton D. Mereness (New York: Macmillan, 1916), 552–54.

69. Though many European traders married Creek women, in Creek towns they were still outsiders, without a clan and blood relations. When Creeks threatened to expel trader Charles Weatherford from their lands in 1798, they decided to give him a reprieve on account of his marriage to a Creek woman. Nevertheless, men like Weatherford never were fully accepted as Creeks. Benjamin Hawkins to Edward Price, 29 May 1798, *Letters, Journals, and Writings of Benjamin Hawkins*, ed. C. L. Grant (Savannah: Beehive Press, 1980) (hereafter *LBH*), 1:195.

70. George Galphin's will, dated 1778, Creek Indian Letters, Talks, and Treaties, 1705–1839, ed. Louis F. Hays, typescript in the GDAH, 1:8–15.

71. Arturo O'Neill to Estevan Miró, 3 January 1789, PC, leg. 38, 681, reel 191, PKY; John officio con el S.or Governador de Panzacola, PC, leg. 225B, reel 431, PKY. Cannard himself referred to John Galphin as his nephew. John Cannard to Juan Nepomuceno de Quesada, 13 October 1795, EF, bnd. 115K9, reel 43, PKY.

72. Caleb Swan, "Position and State of Manners and Arts in the Creek or Muscogee Nation in 1791," in *Information Respecting the History, Condition and Prospects of the Indian Tribes of the United States*, ed. Henry Rowe Schoolcraft (New York: Paladin Press, 1855), 260–61.

73. William Bartram, "Observations," 37–39. For Boatswain's birth name, see Arturo O'Neill, 31 May 1783, EF, bnd. 195M15, doc. 1783-1, reel 82, PKY; and Balance, 30 April 1798, Forbes-Innerarity Papers, reel 147 P, PKY.

74. Arturo O'Neill to Governor Miró, 11 May 1783, PC, leg. 2351, 10, reel 436, PKY; Arturo O'Neill to Conde de Gálvez, 4 December 1783, PC, leg. 36, 684, reel 183, PKY; Saunt, "A New Order of Things," 299–303.

75. It is impossible to arrive at an exact number of slaves in the region. We can be sure of the following: McGillivray died with sixty slaves, some but not all of whom would have worked at his residence at Hickory Ground; Robert Grierson, a Scotch trader who lived at Hilibi on the Tallapoosa, owned forty slaves; McGillivray's sister Sophia at one time owned eighty slaves, many of whom would have worked at her residence near the fork; Sehoy, another of McGillivray's sisters, owned thirty slaves. Richard Bailey, who lived in Atasi, owned seven slaves. In addition to these people, there surely were other large slaveholders in the area. Milfort likely owned a number of slaves, and almost every trader owned one or two. See, respectively, the following documents: William Panton to Lachlan McGillivray, 10 April 1794, no. 214, *McGillivray of the Creeks*, ed. John Walton Caughey (Norman: University of Oklahoma Press, 1938); Journal of Benjamin

Hawkins, 11 December 1796, *Letters of Benjamin Hawkins, 1796–1806: Collections of the Georgia Historical Society*, vol. 9 (Savannah: Georgia Historical Society, 1916), 31: Journal of Benjamin Hawkins, 24 December 1796, LBH, 1:24; Benjamin Hawkins, "A sketch of the Creek Country in the years 1798 and 1799," LBH, 1:298–99; Journal of Benjamin Hawkins, 18 December 1796, *Letters of Benjamin Hawkins, 1796–1806*, 39–41.

More difficult to deduce are the number of slaves held in small numbers by other mestizos and Creeks. Efau Hadjo, we know, owned five Black slaves, and Alexander Cornels owned nine. Hawkins reported that in Eufala "several of the Indians have negros taken during the revolution war." See Benjamin Hawkins, "A sketch of the Creek Country in the years 1798 and 1799," LBH, 1:292–93, 316. It seems then that three hundred would be a fair estimate of the number of slaves along the Coosa and Tallapoosa Rivers.

76. Return of depredations committed by the Creek Indians since the commencement of hostilities in the State of Georgia, 5 October 1789, *American State Papers, Class II: Indian Affairs* (Washington, 1832) (hereafter ASPIA), 1:77.

77. In one such case, McGillivray himself sold three stolen slaves in Pensacola, claiming all the while that other Creeks had sold them. See Affidavit of John McKenzie, 22 January 1822, Indian Depredations, 1787–1825: Original Claims in Department of Archives and History of Georgia, vol. 2, pt. 2, ed. Louis F. Hays, typescript in the GDAH, 391b.

78. Alexander McGillivray to the Intendant-General Martín Navarro, 7 November 1785, in D. C. Corbitt, "Papers Relating to the Georgia-Florida Frontier, 1784–1800. Part II," *Georgia Historical Quarterly* 21 (1937): 75; William Laurence to William Panton, 15 August 1798, Cruzat Papers, PKY.

79. Alexander McGillivray to Arturo O'Neill, 3 January 1784, PC, leg. 197, 738, reel 273, PKY.

80. Alexander McGillivray to [Arturo O'Neill], 21 February 1786, PC, leg. 199, 770, reel 383, PKY.

81. Murdoch McLeod to James Jackson, 6 May 1799, Creek Indian Letters, Talks, and Treaties, 1705–1839, 2:558–59, GDAH.

82. Alexander McGillivray to Charles McLatchy, 25 December 1784, EF, bnd. 116L9, reel 44, PKY.

83. Historian J. Leitch Wright Jr., in his last book before his untimely death, argued that the linguistic division between Muskogee and non-Muskogee speakers explains many of the intratribal conflicts in Creek history, including the civil conflict known as the Redstick War. His argument is overstated but still useful. Wright, *Creeks and Seminoles*.

84. For an account of the emergence of the Seminoles, see Saunt, "A New Order of Things," 23–36.

85. Between the Suwannee and Apalachicola Rivers there is a swath of fertile land, but in the eighteenth century, the lack of ports made the transportation of crops unfeasible. John Solomon Otto, *The Southern Frontiers, 1607–1860: The Agricultural Evolution of the Colonial and Antebellum South* (New York: Greenwood Press, 1989), 112–13.

86. Julian Carballo to Arturo O'Neill, [1790?], PC, leg. 39, 1635, reel 162, PKY.

87. J. Houston to Edward Telfair, 18 March 1793, Creek Indian Letters, Talks, and Treaties, 1705–1839, 1:275, GDAH; Richard Lang to Governor of Florida, 19 April 1793, EF, bnd. 123F10, doc. 1793-79, reel 48, PKY; John Forrester to Juan Nepomuceno de Quesada, 23 April 1793, EF, bnd. 123F10, doc. 1793-87, reel 48, PKY.

88. Affidavit of William Smith, 4 June 1821, Indian Depredations, 1787–1825, 2, part 2:628, GDAH; James Jackson to Edward Telfair, 9 May 1793, Creek Indian Letters, Talks, and Treaties, 1705–1839, 1:309–10, GDAH.

89. [James Jackson?] to [the Governor of Georgia], 21 July 1793, Creek Indian Letters, Talks, and Treaties, 1705–1839, 1:334–37, GDAH.

90. "News from the Newspaper of Georgia," 10 May 1794, EF, bnd. 114J9, reel 43, PKY; James Durouzeaux to Henry White, 19 November 1794, PC, leg. 208A, 572, reel 286, PKY. When Upper Creeks promised to secure the return of slaves stolen from Americans, they pointed to Usiches and Chiajas as the culprits. Extract of a letter from Timothy Barnard to James Seagrove, 18 December 1794, Unpublished Letters of Timothy Barnard, 1784–1820, ed. Louise F. Hays, typescript in the GDAH, 241, also *ASPIA* 1:559; translation of talk of Mad Dog to the Governor of Georgia, from the Charleston newspaper of 7 February 1795, 7 February 1795, EF, bnd. 115K9, reel 43, PKY.

91. Affidavit of Nathan Atkinson, 31 October 1802, Indian Depredations, 1787–1825, vol. 2, pt. 1:85, GDAH; affidavit of Richard Carnes, 18 March 1800, Indian Depredations, 1787–1825, vol. 2, pt. 1:87b, GDAH. Apparently, owner Nathan Atkinson never secured the return of his slave. His affidavit was filed in 1802 in an attempt to obtain remuneration.

92. James Seagrove to the Secretary of War, 31 October 1793, *ASPIA*, 1:468–69. Spanish officials had mixed success when they negotiated the return of some of the slaves stolen from East Florida. See Juan Nepomuceno de Quesada to Luis de las Casas, 7 September 1793, EF, bnd. 24, 177, reel 9, PKY; Juan Nepomuceno de Quesada to Francisco Montreuil, 14 November 1793, EF, bnd. 114J9, reel 43, PKY; Carlos Howard to Richard Lang, 3 December 1793, EF, bnd. 124G10, doc. 1793, reel 49, PKY; Francisco Montreuil to Juan Nepomuceno de Quesada, 25 February 1794, EF, bnd. 115K9, reel 43, PKY.

93. John Cannard to Juan Nepomuceno de Quesada, 25 May 1793, EF, bnd. 114J9, reel 43, PKY; John Cannard to the kings, principals, and chiefs of the Lower

Creeks, 25 May 1793, EF, bnd. 114J9, reel 43, PKY; James Burges to Robert Leslie, 1 July 1793, EF, bnd. 114J9, reel 43, PKY.

94. In 1810, Forbes and Co. rented a horse from the "Black Factor's plantation" in order to pursue some fugitive slaves. This Black Factor may have been someone other than Ninnywageechee, but his purchase of a slave in 1810 reaffirms that he owned some sort of plantation. See Appal.a L. purchase for sundry Negroes sent to the Establishment at Prospect Bluff, Negroes purchased there, and other charges incurred in Consequence of that Establishment, 30 September 1804 to 30 November 1814, Greenslade Papers, PKY. Also in April 1814, the following expense is listed in the books of John Forbes and Co.: "To this sum paid the Black factors Negroes and an indian for their services for driving Cattle out of the swamp at the forks of the River at different periods during the high Water in the Winter of 1813." See Land Purchase Appa.la for sundry Cattle purchased there and Expences attending them to John Forbes and Co., 28 February 1813 to December 1814, Greenslade Papers, PKY.

95. Alexander McGillivray identified Philatouche as the leader of Chiaja in his letter to Manuel Vicente de Zéspedes, 3 August 1786, EF, bnd. 114J9, reel 43, PKY. He is identified again as the "gefe muy conocido del pueblo de Chiaja" in Bartolomé Benites y Gálvez to the Governor of Saint Augustine, 6 April 1790, EF, bnd. 385, doc. 1791-2, reel 173, PKY.

96. Payemicco, Cudgomicco, Pohosimicco, and Tustoncos to [?], 21 October 1791, EF, bnd. 114J9, reel 43, PKY.

97. On African naming practices in colonial South Carolina, see Wood, *Black Majority*, 181–86.

98. Carlos Howard to Juan Nepomuceno de Quesada, 16 April 1795, EF, bnd. 128K10, 1795-218, reel 51, PKY.

99. These Indians had been in the area for over two months, since the end of January 1795. See Carlos Howard to Juan Nepomuceno de Quesada, 3 February 1795, EF, bnd. 128K10, 1795-92, reel 51, PKY; and Carlos Howard to Juan Nepomuceno de Quesada, 27 April 1795, EF, bnd. 128K10, doc. 1795-251, reel 51, PKY.

100. Carlos Howard, Report on Indian relations at San Vicente Ferrer, 26 April 1795, EF, bnd. 128K10, doc. 1795-244, reel 51, PKY.

101. John McQueen to Carlos Howard, 24 April 1795, EF, bnd. 128K10, doc. 1795-245, reel 51, PKY.

102. Andrew Atkinson to Carlos Howard, 15 May 1795, EF, bnd. 128K10, doc. 1795-287, reel 51, PKY; Carlos Howard to Bartolomé Morales, 17 May 1795, EF, bnd. 128K10, doc. 1795-282, reel 51, PKY; Carlos Howard to Bartolomé Morales, 26 June 1795, EF, bnd. 128K10, doc. 1795-355, reel 51, PKY

103. Swan, "Position and State of Manners," 261.

104. Swan, "Position and State of Manners," 254.

105. Affidavit of Patrick Mackelmurray, 14 October 1802, Indian Depredations, 1787–1825, vol. 2, pt. 3:784, GDAH; Affidavit of Alexander Shaw Newman, 14 October 1802, Indian Depredations, 1787–1825, vol. 2, pt. 3:784, GDAH.

106. Quesada to Las Casas, 7 December 1792, PC, leg. 1436, 5372, reel 158, PKY. John Galphin also had a Black interpreter.

107. Wiley Thompson to the Governor of Florida, 20 April 1803, EF, bnd. 139H11, 1803-63, reel 57, PKY.

108. John Cannard to Robert Leslie, 21 January 1796, Forbes-Innerarity Papers, 81/13, reel 147P, PKY; Diego de Vegas to Enrique White, 8 February 1796, no. 192, in letterbook Correspondencia de officio con el S.or Governador de Panzacola, PC, leg. 225B, reel 431, PKY.

109. Diego de Vegas to Enrique White, 5 March 1796, no. 197, in letterbook Correspondencia de officio con el S.or Governador de Panzacola, PC, leg. 225B, reel 431, PKY; Vegas to Gelabert, 31 May 1796, PC, leg. 122B, 1201, reel 397, PKY.

110. Diary of John Hambly, 14 January 1794 and 29 June 1794, LOC, New York Historical Society, B. Smith Papers, PKY. José and Joe may have been the same person.

111. Tomás Portell to Vicente Folch, 1 October 1799, PC, leg. 2355, 697, reel 382, PKY.

112. Jacobo Dubreuil to Vicente Folch, 28 March 1801, no. 19, in letterbook Correspondencia de officio con el S.or Governador de Panzacola, PC, leg. 225B, reel 431, PKY.

113. In 1799, for instance, an Indian named Tossicio purchased a slave and adopted him into his family, renaming him Chenapkee. Edward Price to Benjamin Hawkins, 11 January 1799, p183, Records of the Creek Trading House, Letter Book, 1795–1816, U.S. Bureau of Indian Affairs. Originals in the National Archives, Washington, microfilm copy in the PKY, reel 94 O.

114. Chehaw Tiger King noted that Sambo was "one of his family property" and that though he had received five kegs of rum from Arturo O'Neill in exchange for the slave, "he was not the right owner" and could not sell him. John Millar to Arturo O'Neill, September 1788, LOC, AGI, PC, leg. 121, PKY.

115. Affidavit of William Smith, 4 June 1821, Indian Depredations, 1787–1825, vol. 2, pt. 2:628, GDAH.

116. Affidavit of John A. Cuthbert, 8 August 1835, Indian Depredations, 1787–1825, vol. 2, pt. 1:17, GDAH.

117. John Cannard to James Seagrove, 5 June 1803, Creek Indian Letters, Talks, and Treaties, 1705–1839, 2:675–76, GDAH.

118. Absalom Harris Chappell, *Miscellanies of Georgia: Historical, Biographical, Descriptive, etc.* (Columbus GA: Gilbert Printing Company, 1928), 72.

119. United States Serials Set.H.doc. 200 (20-1) 173:8, 11–12. Such devel-

opments run parallel to the appearance of substantial plantations using African American slave labor among the mestizo elite of other southeastern Indians, such as the Cherokees. See Perdue, *Slavery and the Evolution of Cherokee Society*.

120. Richard S. Lackey, ed., *Frontier Claims in the Lower South: Records of Claims Filed by Citizens of the Alabama and Tombigbee River Settlements in the Mississippi Territory for Depredations by the Creek Indians During the War of 1812* (New Orleans: Polyanthos, 1977), 50–51; J. D. Dreisbach to Lyman Draper, July 1874, Draper Mss. 1V62, State Historical Society of Wisconsin, reel 1461, PKY.

121. Journal of Benjamin Hawkins, 18 December 1796, *Letters of Benjamin Hawkins, 1796–1806*, 39–41; H. S. Halbert and T. H. Ball, *The Creek War of 1813 and 1814* (Montgomery AL: White, Woodruff, and Fowler, 1895), 130; Journal of Benjamin Hawkins, 18 December 1796, *Letters of Benjamin Hawkins, 1796–1806*, 39–41.

122. Extracts of occurrences in the agency for Indian affairs, August 1813, in J. E. Hays, ed., Letters of Benjamin Hawkins, 1797–1815 (typescript in GDAH), 238.

123. United States Serials Set.H.doc 200 (20-1) 26.

124. Henry Toulmin to Thomas B. Robertson, 23 July 1813, LOC, State Department, Miscellaneous, 61:2 M, PKY; deposition of Samuel Monac, in Halbert and Ball, *The Creek War*, 91–93.

125. Benjamin Hawkins to John B. Floyd, 26 September 1813, LBH, 2:667; Benjamin Hawkins to John B. Floyd, 4 October 1813, LBH, 2:670.

126. Robert of Benjamin Hawkins, 17 September 1813, enclosed in Hawkins to Armstrong, 21 September 1813, LBH, 2:665.

127. Extract of a communication from the chiefs at Coweta to Benjamin Hawkins, 16 September 1813, Letters of Benjamin Hawkins, 1797–1815, 248, GDAH.

128. Colonel Nicolls to Alexander Cochrane, August through November 1814, Cochrane Papers, MS 2328, p59, reel 65 M, no. 1, PKY.

129. "A historical narration of the genealogy, traditions, and downfall of the Ispocoga or Creek tribe of Indians, written by one of the tribe," Draper Mss. 1V66, State Historical Society of Wisconsin, reel 1461, PKY.

130. United States Serials Set.H.doc 200 (20-1) 173:12.

131. Julius S. Scott, "The Common Wind: Currents of Afro-American Communication in the Era of the Haitian Revolution" (Ph.D. diss., Duke University, 1986), 273–74.

132. Undated document, EF, bnd. 197B16, doc. 1801-33, reel 83, PKY. For information on their theft, see Saunt, "A New Order of Things," 403–4. Julius S. Scott investigates the exchange of revolutionary ideas among Caribbean slave communities in "The Common Wind." On the response of slaves to the ideology of the American Revolution, see Peter H. Wood, "'Taking Care of Business' in

Revolutionary South Carolina: Republicanism and the Slave Society," in *The Southern Experience in the American Revolution*, ed. Jeffery J. Crow and Larry E. Tise (Chapel Hill: University of North Carolina Press, 1978), 268–93.

133. At least two of Samuel Moniac's slaves, for example, accompanied the Redsticks to Florida. United States Serials Set.H.doc. 200 (20-1) 173:11.

134. For a full account of the Negro Fort, see Saunt, "A New Order of Things," chap. 12.

135. Francisco Caso y Luengo to Joseph de Soto, 28 September 1815, PC, leg. 147B, 513, reel 479.

3. "Colored" Seamen in the New England Whaling Industry
An Afro-Indian Consortium

RUSSEL LAWRENCE BARSH

I Jeremiah Pharoah the Bold mariner I saild the world over.

In an important recent revisionist work, Jeffrey Bolster contends that African Americans not only comprised one-fifth of American seamen until 1865 but that seafaring was antebellum African Americans' main opportunity to achieve a modicum of personal freedom, political consciousness, and economic independence.[1] Black and White sailors worked together under conditions of relative equality, moreover, and formed "an occupational identity not dependent on race" in which African Americans could rise by merit and even give orders to Whites.[2]

On the other hand, seamen's wages and whaling shares, or "lays," were barely adequate to support families. With little opportunity to supplement their income by acquiring farmland or business property, African American sailors tended to remain unmarried. "The most stable seamen of color in New England lived among the Indian populations . . . on Martha's Vineyard and at Mashpee on Cape Cod," Bolster explains, where they had access to reservation land. In turn, Indians "were prominent beyond their numbers" in seafaring because they were barred from other occupations.[3] Bolster does not explore the possibility that Black and Indian seamen may have amalgamated through kinship and shared economic interests, however, or that Afro-Indians became distinct from African Americans (as well as Indians) in their outlook and experience.

While Bolster regards all "seamen of color" as essentially Black, there is an old historiographic tradition that New England whaling was dominated by Indians. An early study of American fisheries, published over a century ago, observed that the Indians of Martha's Vineyard and Long Island provided the industry with such "excellent material" that "upon them New Bedford more or less relies for her boatsteerers."[4] As shown below, this assertion is not supported by crew lists, but it has been repeated for a century in popular works on American seamanship. Although Indians were pioneers of New England nearshore, or drift, whaling from the 1650s to 1750s and continued to participate in small numbers in deep-sea whaling until the late nineteenth century, they were never occupationally specialized as boatsteerers or harpooners. Furthermore, a large proportion of Indian seamen were actually Afro-Indian in ancestry. This may have been confusing to scholars who tended to essentialize race, but it is important evidence of a partial socioeconomic consortium of two marginalized communities.

The whaling industry provides an ideal environment for exploring cooperation and competition among Whites, Blacks, and Indians. Working conditions for seamen were particularly miserable in the New England whaling industry, but all crew members regardless of color received equal shares of the profit at the end of a voyage.[5] The four largest whaling centers of New England – Nantucket Island, New Bedford, New London, and Sag Harbor – were all located near large communities of Indians and African American freedmen (see map).

AMERICAN WHALING AND WHALEMEN

Like cowboys, whalemen have symbolized archetypical Americanness: shrewd, freedom-loving, and indomitable. Like cowboys, New England whalemen were never numerous, amounting to no more than ten thousand men at sea or awaiting work on shore during the industry's peak years. Although whaling made small fortunes for some Sag Harbor, New Bedford, and New London merchant families, moreover, its financial output was dwarfed by the China trade before the Civil War and by manufacturing, mining, and meatpacking afterward. American historiography magnified the whaleman as a national archetype nonetheless and, in the process, made him fundamentally *White*, with Tonto-like Indian sidekicks.[6]

Whaling peaked during the decade 1835–45, then went into a steady decline (see Table 1). Although Nantucket pioneered the industry, it was eventually overshadowed by New Bedford, which dominated the last half century of American whaling. In the industry's declining years, Alexander Starbuck argued that the growing scarcity of whales had led to longer, more costly voyages in more hazardous seas and to far greater risk of

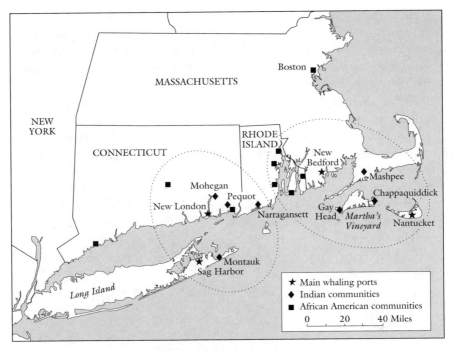

Afro-Indian Population Centers and the Whaling Industry in 1800

returning with an unfilled hold. The final blow was the commercial development of inexpensive petroleum fuels in the 1870s and consequent drop in the price of whale oil.[7]

Starbuck also argued that the American whaling industry had been undermined by "the character of the men engaged" as seamen. "Formerly the crews were composed almost entirely of Americans," he observed in 1878, "but latterly they were largely made up of Portuguese shipped at the Azores, a mongrel set [mestizos] shipped anywhere along the western coast of South America, and Kanakas [Hawaiians and Polynesians] shipped at the Pacific Islands."[8] Starbuck used the term "American" as if it were equivalent to "White" and implied that crews had become *darker* over time. On the contrary, the research presented here indicates that crews had become *whiter* by Starbuck's time, due to a steady replacement of African Americans and Afro-Indians by European immigrants, chiefly Portuguese.

Samuel Eliot Morison synthesized mainstream perceptions of whaling in his *Maritime History of Massachusetts*, originally published in 1921. Ex-

Table 1. Whaleships Returning to American Ports 1815–1875

	Nantucket	New Bedford	New London	Sag Harbor	All Ports
1815	15	2	—	—	17
1825	23	26	4	7	69
1835	30	63	15	17	182
1845	31	83	25	22	257
1855	12	89	12	6	177
1865	5	61	10	1	139
1875	—	56	5	—	103

perienced merchant seamen would never have tolerated the abominable working conditions and meager pay on whaleships, Morison argued, forcing recruiters to target "farmer boys from New England and New York, bitten with the lure of the sea," and to round out whaling crews with several "unemployed immigrants and mill-hands, fugitives from justice, and human derelicts," together with "a few hungry and docile" Portuguese from the Azores. By the 1850s, Morison complained, even these wretched and inexperienced Whites were difficult to keep on shipboard, hence "Kanakas, Tongataboors, Filipinos, and even Fiji cannibals like Melville's hero Queequeg were signed on for a nominal wage or microscopic lay."[9] For Morison, even the White whalers had been a pathetic lot, quickly yielding berths to a growing number of even more miserable Pacific savages.

Morison offered no sources for his characterization of whalemen, but he had almost certainly relied entirely on Herman Melville's great novel of whaling and obsession, *Moby Dick*, in which we learn that, "in New Bedford, actual cannibals stand chatting at street corners" while awaiting their ships.

[B]esides the Feejeeans, Tongataboors, Erromangoans, Pannangians, and Brighgians, and besides the wild specimens of the whaling-craft which unheeded reel about the streets, you will see other sights still more curious, certainly more comical. There weekly arrive in this town scores of green Vermonters and New Hampshire men, all athirst for gain and glory in the fishery. They are mostly young, of stalwart frames; fellows who have felled forests, and now seek to drop the axe and snatch the whale lance.[10]

Here is Morison's source for the predominance of naive White farm boys in the whaling industry.

Queequeg, shipmate and mentor of Melville's alter ego Ishmael, is actually a composite savage, an archetype of all of the tribal peoples who might be found aboard whaleships. Queequeg sports blue facial tattoos, smokes a long-stemmed pipe, wears a beaded poncho, brandishes a toma-hawk, and sells shrunken heads on the New Bedford wharves. Inscrutable and monosyllabic to the end, he is the master harpooner aboard the *Pequod*, a whaleship named for a tribe that in Melville's time lived in Stonington, Connecticut, a few miles east of New Bedford, and produced a score of seamen and whalemen.[11]

Melville's contemporaries would nonetheless have agreed that "for all practical considerations, the Long Island Indian was a creature of the past" by the 1820s.[12] Marriage with African Americans was equivalent to extinction in the thinking of Americans preoccupied with racial taxonomy and color. Amos Daley, of African and Narragansett ancestry, tried to evade the restrictions on Black seamen's liberty in port by arguing that he was actually Indian, which his shipmates heartily affirmed. A Charles-town, South Carolina, judge disagreed, ruling that Daley was obviously a "person of color" and therefore subject to any law applicable to "Negroes."[13] In racist conceptualization, Afro-Indians could not be genuinely Indian.

Recent historiography has brought new biases, with some scholars emphasizing the Blackness of Afro-Indians and other scholars emphasizing their Indianness. While Bolster acknowledges that many "colored" seamen were probably Afro-Indian, or Afro-Portuguese from Cape Verde and Senegambia, he assumes that their identities were mainly determined by Blackness. At the opposite extreme, Montauk historian Philip Rapito-Wyppensenwah concedes only that marriages with African Americans "were not unknown" among Long Island Indians and does not consider the possibility that a prominent Montauk family such as the Cuffees, with its Akan surname, must have had African as well as Indian ancestry.[14] In his groundbreaking study of Black communities in antebellum New England, William Pierson refers to Afro-Indian marriages only to allege that Indian women preferred Black husbands because Black men were better providers than Indian men and did not beat their wives.[15] He implies that Afro-Indians were really Black, because their mothers had deliberately married to escape from Indian culture.

This is reminiscent of a debate a century ago over whether seaman and Boston Massacre victim Crispus Attucks was Black or Indian, when the evidence pointed to mixed African and Indian ancestry.[16] The prominent Westport seaman and merchant Paul Cuffe has generally been described by historians as Black and abolitionist minister William Apess as Indian, although both men had one Black parent and one Indian parent and both were contemporaries who moved in the same mixed social circles.[17]

In reality, African American and Indian communities were so extensively intertwined by kinship and employment that they should be considered together as a single antebellum socioeconomic class, defined by their occupations as well as color. An appreciation of Afro-Indian connections begins with the origins of New England whaling in indigenous whaling practices and the subsequent recruitment of New England's large free Black community to fuel the expansion of whaling ventures into "the deep."

INDIANS AND INSHORE WHALING

Whaling began as a small-scale, seasonal cash pursuit for fishermen and farmers on Nantucket, Cape Cod, and Long Island in the seventeenth century. New England Indians had long made use of any whales that beached during their annual midwinter migrations. Early English settlers traded with neighboring Indians for whale oil and baleen, and as early as 1691 the settlers on Nantucket began purchasing the shorelines and associated whaling rights from the original Indian proprietors.[18] On eastern Long Island, each English town adopted ordinances asserting monopoly rights over whales beached or hunted within their boundaries. The right to hunt whales freely was guaranteed to New York Indians in a 1708 act for "the encouragement of whaling."[19]

The earliest English settlers on Nantucket lived in close and relatively amicable proximity to the island's small indigenous population of Wampanoags, which from the beginning was employed at wages in farming and fishing. In 1672, the settlers organized a joint-stock company to pursue migrating whales offshore, and "the Indians, ever manifesting a disposition for fishing of every kind, readily joined with the Whites in this new pursuit, and willingly submitted to any station assigned to them." Lookouts were posted along the shore, and six-man longboats were dispatched whenever whales were sighted. "Nearly every boat was manned in part, many almost entirely, by natives: some of the most active of them were made steersmen, and some were even allowed to head the boats: thus encouraged, they soon became expert whalemen, and capable of conducting any part of the business."[20]

Elizabeth Little has identified sixty-six individual Indian whalers from

Nantucket business records of the 1700s, including some whose original homes were at Martha's Vineyard and Rhode Island.[21] Several Nantucket Indians were also identified as the masters of whaleboats. Some families were consistently involved in whaling. John Tashama and his sons John and Isaac were all listed as whalemen from the 1730s to 1750s, as were several men from the Micah and Towaddy families. While none of Nantucket's alongshore whalemen were identified as Black, a whale lance was found in the estate of a man named Africa, which suggests that he was an expert harpooner.[22]

Based loosely on Indian customary law for the division of beached whales, acknowledged since the 1670s by the English authorities on the island, Indian crewmen shared in the profits of each season's work. This became the basis for the peculiarly American practice of paying whalemen lays as opposed to the European practice of paying merchant sailors and whalers predetermined wages.[23]

English settlers on eastern Long Island organized joint-stock companies to pursue shore whaling by the 1650s, often recruiting men from Nantucket as masters. The crewmen were mainly Montauk and Shinnecock Indians, and rival companies offered bonuses to secure the services of the most experienced Indian seamen.[24] One of the best surviving records of Long Island shore whaling is the Pigskin Book, a ledger kept by storekeeper William "Tangier" Smith from 1696 to 1721.[25] Smith sold cornmeal, cider, clothing, powder, and shot to his Indian neighbors and accepted furs, feathers, and casks of whale oil in payment of their debts. Some of his customers were already as much as £25 in debt by 1696, and all of them remained in debt despite spending many of their winters whaling in boats Smith outfitted.

Smith's customers let their debts mount for several years before going to sea. Pumpsha already owed Smith £25 in 1697, for example, but accumulated another £21 in debts before he went whaling for five years. He had to pay Smith all of his income. Cownus owed £23 in 1697 and paid Smith back £16 in three successive good whaling seasons. He did not go to sea again until 1703, after his debt had risen again to £23. Townus, who went whaling profitably for ten consecutive years, was still £63 in debt when his account closed in 1706. All but one of Smith's twenty-three regular clients went whaling for him at least once during the twenty-five years covered by the Pigskin Book, and twelve of them went whaling for five or more seasons. Smith evidently extended credit as an incentive for men to accept berths on his whaleboats.[26]

Obed Macy reported that eighteenth-century Nantucket shipowners looked after the families of their Indian crewmen, who were continually in debt or indisposed by hard drink.[27] Nathaniel Philbrick argues that while some merchants may indeed have extended credit generously to secure the loyalty of skilled Indian sailors, others exploited Indian seamen by encouraging them to borrow heavily. Under colonial Massachusetts laws, debt delinquency was punishable by indentured servitude, either on shore or at sea. The Massachusetts General Court agreed in 1718 that Indians were frequently deceived "by reason of their being drawn in by small gifts, or for small debts" or by being persuaded to sign security bonds "when they are in drink, and out of capacity to trade."[28]

Nantucket shore whaling peaked in 1726, when eighty-six whales were taken, but thereafter the whales grew increasingly "shy." By 1760, the islanders were forced to pursue whales into "the deep," requiring much heavier vessels and larger crews. An epidemic devastated the island's Wampanoag population in 1763, however, so that extending the whale fishery offshore depended on recruiting seamen from nearby Cape Cod and Long Island shore-whaling communities.[29]

After the interruption of the Revolutionary War, Nantucket whaling grew rapidly in response to new markets in Philadelphia and Baltimore. As more ships were built, Nantucket again faced a shortage of labor. Sag Harbor and New Bedford were building their own deep-sea whaling fleets and competing for experienced sailors. "It therefore became necessary to resort to the continent [the mainland] for a considerable portion of each crew," Macy recalled, "whence there were brought some Indians and a great number of negroes" as whalers. "Many of the latter took up their residence here, and became the head of families."[30]

Nantucket whaling sloops ventured no farther than the Grand Banks of Newfoundland and the Caribbean archipelago until 1791, when attempts were first made to follow British whalers into largely uncharted South Pacific waters. The expense and duration of voyages increased considerably, as did the strain on whalemen and their families. The transition from shore whaling to "the deep" also changed the nature of relationships between whalemen and shipowners.[31] Alongshore whaling involved individually negotiated contracts between owners and seaman, who were most often neighbors and had long-term economic relationships. Deep-sea whaling involved standard contracts signed by all crewmen and were made with the managers of large joint-stock companies in major seaports with whom seamen had little other social or business contact.

The map suggests two distinct spheres of Afro-Indian interaction in connection with whaling, one along Long Island Sound linking the New London and Sag Harbor areas and the other on Buzzard's Bay linking the New Bedford area with Cape Cod and the islands of Martha's Vineyard and Nantucket. The Pequot and Mohegan reservations anchored the first sphere of interaction, while the Wampanoag Indian township of Mashpee anchored the second.

African American slavery and Indian debt-bondage (under labor contracts or indentures) were practiced throughout colonial New England, together with restrictions on the mobility and occupational choice of free people of color. Although many New Englanders freed their slaves in a burst of idealism during the Revolution, newly independent states like Massachusetts responded anxiously by prohibiting Whites' marriage to "any Negro, Indian, or mulatto" and by authorizing towns to arrest and expel non-White transients.[32] Indian servants worked alongside slaves on early-eighteenth-century plantations, and as more Indians were drawn into towns and wage labor toward the century's end, they found themselves to be residentially, occupationally, and socially segregated with Black freedmen. Many African Americans meanwhile found refuge in Indian communities such as Mashpee, where their skills were regarded as more important than their color.

Although the aboriginal people of Nantucket had disappeared as a distinct community by 1763, identifiable Wampanoag communities survived on the reservations established in the early eighteenth century at Chappaquiddick, Gay Head, and Christiantown on Martha's Vineyard and at Mashpee on Cape Cod.[33] An 1861 report to the Massachusetts state senate concluded that more than one thousand Wampanoags still resided in the region – about 40 percent of them at Mashpee, 33 percent on Martha's Vineyard, and most of the remainder at New Bedford. These figures were "exclusive of the very considerable number at sea in New Bedford ships."[34] The report noted that most Wampanoags had some Black ancestry and argued that this had intensified the "prejudice of caste, social exclusion, and civil disenfranchisement" that had resulted in their impoverishment and dispersal.

When Ezra Stiles, president of Yale College, visited Mashpee in 1762, he found 250 persons in seventy-five households, most of them living in traditional birchbark "wigwams" and subsisting by gardening and hunting deer.[35] Surrounded by non-Indian farms, close to seaports and to the rapidly expanding African American population of Providence Plantations (Rhode Island), Mashpee changed dramatically over the next twenty-five years. Even before the Revolution led to the emancipation of slaves in most of New England, Mashpee's leaders demanded the right "to vote on and receive other Indians or mulatoes [*sic*] to share with us in our privileges or properties." Half of the adult men subsequently perished in the war, and by 1788 three-fourths of the community was reportedly of mixed, chiefly Afro-Indian ancestry.[36] A policy of sending the men into whaling and indenturing their children to White farmers forced the women and youngest children to go "among the white people a beging [*sic*] for the necessaries of life,"[37] where they presumably found shelter and sympathy among free Blacks. It was no coincidence that William Apess, an Afro-Pequot, chose Mashpee to make the great public stand of his career.

"The inhabitants of Mashpee are denominated Indians," a visitor to Mashpee in 1802 explained, "but very few of the pure race are left; there are negroes, mulattoes, and Germans."[38] The women kept gardens and sold baskets and brooms to the White households of Cape Cod and Nantucket, while their husbands fished for subsistence or worked as whalemen. "Several of the young females go to the large sea-port towns for months together, and serve in gentlemen's kitchens, to the great injury of their morals; and others of the women lead a vagabond life in the country, where at last they find negro husbands, whom they bring home to enjoy all the privileges and immunities of Mashpee." Edward Kendall wrote in the mid–nineteenth century that whaling "is a favorite employ, to which they give themselves, and to which they are anxiously solicited. Shipowners come to their cottages, making them offers, and persuading them to accept them," paying them advances in the form of liquor and goods to put them into debt.[39]

As Francis Hutchins has observed, Mashpee became the crucible of Afro-Indian consciousness and solidarity. William Apess played a key role in this development, arriving in 1833 to preach the gospel, then remaining in the community for several years as an advocate for their right to local self-government. Apess's tract, *Indian Nullification of the Unconstitutional Laws of Massachusetts*, not only took the state to task for its mismanagement of Mashpee lands but set out Apess's larger views on race and rights. Adopting a rhetorical style that previewed the writings of Frederick Douglass and later African American leaders, Apess challenged Whites to become genuine Christians by recognizing the equality of all men: "Does the proud White think that a dark skin is less honorable in the sight of God than his own beautiful hide?" Africans and Indians had shared the experience of exploitation and had reason to make common cause; "degradation is degradation," Apess wrote, with the same causes and effects. "Oh, that all men of color thought and felt as I do on this subject."[40]

In 1834 the Mashpees voted to allow any "colored" person to live in their township, and Apess was one of the first beneficiaries of this edict. Many African Americans moved there, not only to marry Mashpee women but to seek refuge.[41] The Civil War held special significance for Mashpee, and nineteen Mashpee men fought on the Union side – seventeen of them, not surprisingly, in the navy. "These people are all my people, all my friends," an African American married to a Mashpee woman told visiting state officials in 1869. "I have lived other places, under what some of us call the White man's law. I lived there, and thought I was a man as well as anybody else. Here, I consider myself a man among my folks."[42]

Relatively isolated at the eastern tip of Long Island, Montauk in 1741 consisted of thirty-four households of 162 persons, most of whom reportedly still spoke their native language.[43] Along with other Indians of eastern Long Island, however, the Montauk were drawn into predominantly non-Indian towns by the late eighteenth century, where they clustered in a few distinctly Indian neighborhoods – Freetown near Sag Harbor, Eastville on the outskirts of Easthampton, and the Bridge Street area of Southold.[44] The population and family composition of these settlements were highly variable because a large proportion of Montauk and Shinnecock men continued to hunt, fish, or work as seamen and farm laborers.

Mohegan seafaring began as early as 1732, when "two Indians from Mohegan died of smallpox as sailors returning from Ireland."[45] Twelve years later, it was reported that an "Indian crew member of [the] government sloop" had died at New London: "While displaying his dexteritty [sic] at the mast head he fell and was killed." The Mohegan minister Samson Occom, later one of the founders of Dartmouth College, received his first parish among the Montauks in 1749. There he met and married Mary Fowler, whose brothers Jacob and David joined Occom's ministry. Jacob returned with Occom to Mohegan, where he married Esther Poquiantups. The Occom and Fowler marriages thereby linked Mohegan and Montauk, and Fowlers continued to be prominent seafarers in both communities. In 1854, one of Jacob Fowler's great-granddaughters married a Niantic seaman, Zaccheus Nonesuch, creating another regional intertribal seafaring link. A tiny colonial-era reservation near Stonington, Connecticut, survived as the Mohegan social and cultural nucleus.

The Pequots, whose extermination had been compassed by the Puritans of Massachusetts Bay in 1637, were dispersed but survived.[46] In 1850, John DeForest reported that while the remaining Pequots "were considerably mixed with white and negro blood," they nevertheless "still possessed a feeling of clanship, and still preserved their ancient national hatred for the Mohegans."[47] Mohegans and Pequots lived scattered, "some on the ocean, chiefly in whale ships," wherever they could find employment. "From a fellow feeling," DeForest added, "they are extremely hospitable to all vagabonds; receiving without hesitation all that come to them, whether white, mulatto, Indian or negro." Although aimed at illustrating Indians' degradation, DeForest's observation suggests that the Pequots and Mohegans had begun to think of themselves broadly in terms of class and color, like the Mashpees.

Two complementary questions arise. To what extent were Indian tribes and African Americans consolidated by kinship? And to what extent were Afro-Indians the "Black Jacks" who filled up to half of the berths on New England whaleships?

IDENTIFYING AFRO-INDIAN SEAMEN

To demonstrate that a significant proportion of American seamen prior to Reconstruction were African American, Bolster relied on the Seamen's Protection Certificates issued to individual sailors and crew lists filed with customhouse officials when ships cleared an American port. Bolster classified the bearers of Seamen's Protection Certificates according to the way issuing officers recorded men's skin color, hair color, and hair texture. This method would not necessarily distinguish between Afro-Indians, African Americans, and Africans from Portuguese colonies, however, and assumes that color was more important than nationality, ethnicity, or social ties in determining men's fates in seafaring trades. There are also gaps in customhouse records, due to fires and other losses, which undermine their utility as a source of industry-level analytical statistics.

It is impossible to distinguish individuals as Afro-Indians or African Americans without recourse to family histories.[48] Fortunately, there is sufficient published data on the African American and Indian families of the New London area to achieve a partial reconstruction of ninety-four Mohegan and Pequot lineages. The data are still incomplete; therefore, no inference should be drawn from the absence of evidence of a family's African American ancestry. Similarly, more complete family data would probably reveal more intertribal kinship ties.[49]

The figure summarizes intertribal and inter-"racial" marriage links among these ninety-four lineages from the earliest records in the early to mid–eighteenth century through 1850.[50] Each connecting line represents one marriage. An additional twenty-nine Afro-Indian marriage links were not included in the figure because either the surname or tribal affiliation of one of the partners could not be determined. This is only an approximate measure of the prevalence of Afro-Indian ties within Indian communities, but these links compare favorably to the prevalence of intertribal ties. Ties within each tribe, or between African American families, are not shown in the figure to avoid confusion.

Afro-Indian ties were often renewed from generation to generation within families, as was the case of the unusually well documented Ross family. Gerant Ross was an Afro-Narragansett slave who won his emancipation after the Revolutionary War. There are complete records of twenty-four marriages of his descendants in the nineteenth century: five to other Afro-Indians from southeastern Connecticut and Long Island, six into African American families that had kinship links to other Indians (such as the Niles and Scotts), and the remaining thirteen to African Americans with no recorded Indian ancestry.[51]

Among the families shown in the figure, there were 20 men identified in their marriage or death records as sailors: 6 Indians, 10 men of Afro-Indian ancestry, and 4 African Americans married to Indians. Southeastern Connecticut vital records as a whole for the period 1750–1850 identified 105 colored seamen: 16 Indians, 10 Afro-Indians, and 79 African Americans. This included 3 Indians married to African Americans and 4 African Americans married to Indians. Occupational notations were not always included in vital records, so that the total number of colored seamen was certainly greater. Some men identified as Indian or Black may have had other, unrecorded ancestors, moreover. At a minimum, then, there was a 16 percent overlap between Indian and African American seamen through ancestry and marriage.

At New Bedford, 357 colored marriages were recorded to 1850. A substantial majority (80 percent) appear to have involved African American men and African American women. The remainder involved African American men and Indian women (9 percent), Indian men and African American women (3 percent), or Indian men and Indian or Afro-Indian women (8 percent).[52] Occupations were identified infrequently in marriage records, so it is hazardous to make any inference from the fact that only five African Americans and none of the Indians or Afro-Indians (not even the famous Bostons of Nantucket) were identified as seamen. What

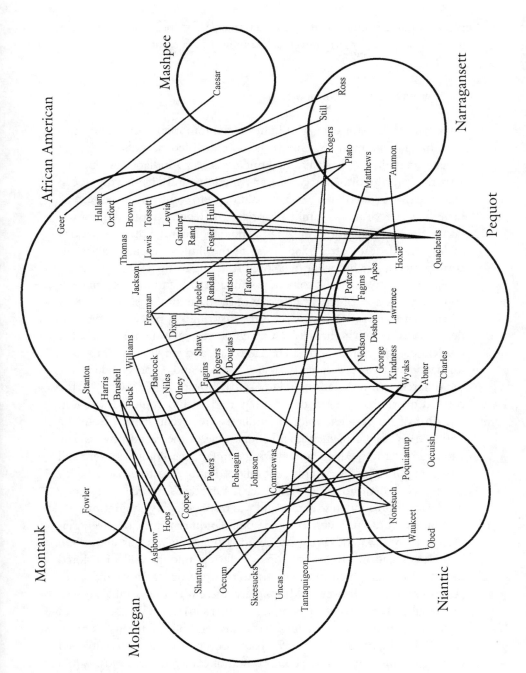

Intertribal and Interracial Marriage Links among Ninety-four Mohegan and Pequot Lineages, Early Eighteenth Century–1850

is indisputable from these records is a tendency for Indian women in this growing seaport to marry into Black families (52 percent).

AFRO-INDIAN SEAFARING

Two main sources of data shed light on the importance of seafaring to Afro-Indian communities. One is the decennial federal census, and the other is crew lists.[53] Each has its limitations. Afro-Indians and Indians were rarely distinguished from African Americans and Afro-Portuguese in federal censuses or company records, although to some extent they can be identified by recourse to family histories. The federal census did not use occupational classifications until 1840 and only recorded the occupations of household heads after 1860. Despite the limitations of the data, it corroborates a steady decline of colored seafaring by the 1840s.

From 1800 to 1840, the colored population of Nantucket remained at approximately 250, or barely 4 percent of the total for the island. In 1840, when occupations were reported for the first time, 94 percent of the resident colored men who held jobs were employed as seamen. By 1860, the resident colored population had fallen to 144, and employment in seafaring had fallen to 65 percent.[54] Unskilled laborers and barbers made up for the difference in occupations. Many of the houses in New Guinea, the colored quarter of the island, were reported as unoccupied. Moreover, one-fifth of the resident colored families were recent arrivals from the South, the Caribbean, Africa, and India. One of the island's two oldest and largest African American seafaring families, the Pompeys, were still represented in 1860 by two resident sailors, but the Bostons had all relocated to New Bedford. As a whole, then, Nantucket's colored community was losing its ground in seafaring and was responding by emigrating.

New Bedford's resident "colored" population remained relatively stable between 1840 and 1860, by comparison, remaining at about 120 households and nearly 500 persons. Seafaring among resident colored men declined sharply from 83 percent of reported occupations in 1840 to 10 percent in 1860, however.[55] In its place, there was considerable growth in day labor (47 percent of occupations in 1860) and in trades such as house construction, shipbuilding, barbering, and blacksmithing (37 percent). This dramatic shift to shore-based occupations was accompanied by a significant change in the composition of colored households. A majority (71 percent) of New Bedford's colored household heads in 1860 had been born outside Massachusetts – half of them south of the Mason-

Dixon line. Indeed, only one-tenth of the household heads enumerated in 1840 could still be found in New Bedford in 1860. They included four men who had been seamen in 1840; three had become laborers. No more than one-third of the colored seamen who had homes in New Bedford in 1840 were still in the city or were represented by their children.

The "colored" population of Sag Harbor and adjoining settlements fell sharply from 328 in 1840 to fewer than 100 in 1860. Seamen accounted for 30 percent of employed colored men in 1840. Another 13 percent worked on Long Island's inland waters as ferrymen or fishermen, and most other men engaged in farming or farm labor. By 1860, seamen had fallen to 18 percent and inland boatman to 9 percent of employed colored men, while employment in casual labor and farm labor had increased. A number of the families that were enumerated in Sag Harbor in 1840 were living in smaller eastern Long Island settlements in 1860, suggesting a gradual dispersal in search of employment on farms.

Crew lists tell the same story. The most complete record of whaling crews shipped from a single American port is from Sag Harbor on Long Island. At its peak in the 1840s, Sag Harbor whaling employed a thousand seamen. "Portuguese sailors, Kanakas, Fijians, Malays and Montauk and Shinnecock Indians, all good whalemen, walked the streets . . . flush with money," an early chronicler remembered, adding that the downtown docks were still known locally in the 1930s as "the Indian jail."[56] The most thorough study of Sag Harbor whaling to date estimated that as many as one-third of all Sag Harbor crewmen in the 1810s and 1820s were Blacks and Indians.[57] In the 1860 and 1870 census schedules, 60 percent of the identifiable Montauk Indian men who were listed as employed were identified as seamen.[58] In the 1880 census, the proportion of seamen among Montauk men fell to 20 percent, and by 1900 it had fallen to zero.

The changing ethnic composition of whaling crews is evident in the shipping ledgers of Charles Dering of Sag Harbor, which include crew lists for twelve whaleships he managed between 1828 and 1855. Table 2 summarizes the characteristics of the crews. Also included in the crews were nine Polynesians (Maori and Hawaiians), a Chinese, and, judging by their surnames, thirteen Irishmen.

The combined colored proportion of crews remained at roughly 10 percent, with Indians and Afro-Indians decreasing within that group between the 1820s and 1830s. The Portuguese proportion of Dering Company's crews nearly doubled between the 1840s and 1850s, by comparison.[59]

Crew lists have also survived for several individual Sag Harbor whale-

Table 2. Composition of Dering Company's Sag Harbor Crews (%)
(Total of 1,477 Seamen on 57 Voyages)

	1820s	1830s	1840s	1850s
Voyages	2	27	24	4
Total crewmen	59	705	611	102
% Indians, Afro-Indians*	6.8	2.0	2.3	3.1
% African-Americans*	3.4	4.4	5.9	5.7
% Portuguese*	10.2	8.9	9.3	17.6
% All others	79.6	84.7	82.5	73.6

*Conservative estimate based on identifiable individuals.

ships, such as the *Thames*, which made six voyages from 1826 to 1832. Of the seamen aboard the *Thames* on its first three voyages, 42 percent were listed as "colored," and almost half (48 percent) of these "colored" seamen were either Indian or Afro-Indian. On its next three voyages, only one-tenth of the *Thames*'s crew were "colored," and nearly as many were Portuguese. By the time the retired whaleship *Sabina* sailed from Sag Harbor to the California gold fields in 1849, there was only one African American and one Afro-Indian among the crew of nineteen.[60]

The 1840 federal census of Nantucket Island included 753 seamen aboard ships anchored in the harbor. More than one-third of them (35 percent) were enumerated as "colored," including three "Kanakas" and eight New England Indians who could be identified from other records. The Indian seamen were from Martha's Vineyard, Mashpee, Montauk, Pequot, and Mohegan, and at least two of them were of Afro-Indian ancestry.[61] Sailors with Portuguese surnames made up 5 percent of the total. Half of them were identified as "colored" and thus may have originated in the Azores and Senegambia, but the other half were described as "white," indicating that they were Europeans. There were also a hundred "colored" seamen enumerated on board ships in New Bedford harbor in 1840. Only five Indians (Mohegan, Pequot, and Wampanoag) and one Afro-Indian can be positively identified among them.

Crew lists for the New London whaleship *Charles W. Morgan* extend from 1841 to the end of the nineteenth century but include only six African Americans and a single Martha's Vineyard Wampanoag who sailed on the *Morgan*'s first voyage. There was only one Portuguese on the *Morgan*'s second voyage (1844–45), but 40 percent of the crew on the *Morgan*'s 1867–71 voyage bore Portuguese surnames.[62] All of these clues suggest that Indians, Afro-Indians, and African Americans were being replaced by Portuguese seamen after 1840.

A decline in Indian seafaring is suggested by applications for Seamen's Protection Certificates. In the New London district, for instance, forty men identified as "Indians" applied for these documents in the period 1795–1809. Only eleven "Indian" men applied during the following thirty-five years. It is possible that Indians and Afro-Indians were still applying for certificates but were simply increasingly perceived and described as "colored" or "black" by customs officials. However, census records also suggest a sharp drop in Indian seafaring after the 1840s, which is to say at the end of the working lives of the men who obtained their certificates around 1800.

The relatively small numbers of Indians on New London and New Bedford whaleships must be interpreted in the light of the very small size of the region's total Indian population. In 1761, there were reportedly 309 Indians and 254 African Americans living among 3,300 English colonists in the town of Stonington, which included the Pequot and Mohegan reservations. By 1850, there were scarcely 200 Pequots and Mohegans in all of southeastern Connecticut, including Afro-Indians who self-identified as Indians.[63] The diminished Pequot and Mohegan population would have produced perhaps twenty-five to thirty-five men of working age, at a time when New London alone operated that many whaleships. New England African Americans were ten times more numerous than Indians by 1850 and, not surprisingly, were more heavily represented on crew lists. Nevertheless, both groups' participation in whaling and other seafaring trades remained somewhat greater than their proportion of the total regional population until the peak whaling decade of 1835–45.

COLOR AND CAPITAL

Why were colored sailors disappearing from New England docks at the time that the whaling industry was approaching its zenith? It is conceivable that masters and recruiters changed their opinion of African American and Afro-Indian seamen and (for whatever underlying reasons) selectively sought out sailors of Yankee and Portuguese origins. Testing this possibility quantitatively is not possible, but there is some suggestive data in a notebook kept by a New Bedford merchant in the 1860s, rating the reputations of mates and boatsteerers from the major New England whaling ports.[64] Among them are a number of men who are identified or identifiable as African-American, Afro-Indian, Indian, Polynesian, and

Table 3. Ratings of White and Colored Whaleship Officers 1860–1869

	AI	Good	Fair/Poor	Unrated	Total
"Colored"	—	4	—	6	10
"Indians"	—	2	—	4	6
"Kanakas"	—	2	—	2	4
Portuguese	5	34	10	88	137
Others*	24	80	4	52	160
Total	29	122	14	152	317

*Ethnicity not identified, presumably mostly white.

Portuguese (Table 3). They include Montauk Indian seaman Stephen Pharoah and a "Mr Indian" of whom the diarist observed, "good whaler fair officer."

One-fifth of the White officers and one-tenth of the Portuguese officers who were rated earned an "AI" assessment. Portuguese made up 43 percent of all officers, furthermore, while only 6 percent of officers were non-Whites.

A recent study of Salem, Massachusetts, a prosperous seaport until the Civil War, reports a sharp decline in the number of African American seamen between 1855 and 1865, accompanied by an exodus of young Salem-born Black men.[65] The large postwar influx of southern Black families merely slowed the economic erosion and political marginalization of Salem's Black community. Although Salem was hobbled commercially by a relatively shallow harbor that grew obsolete in the era of steel and steam, colored seafaring was simultaneously in decline throughout New England. Broader social forces are therefore implicated, including growing solidarity between poor, native-born Whites and new European immigrants such as the Portuguese.

Bolster attributes declining African American seafaring to a wave of racist legislation restricting the freedom of Black seamen in Southern seaports before the Civil War and pressure on labor recruiters to adopt a Whites-first policy after the Civil War.[66] This cannot explain the replacement of Afro-Indian and African American whalers by Portuguese in the 1830s and 1840s, however, because whaleships did not stop at Southern ports. Indeed, racist laws discouraging colored seamen from taking berths on ships carrying freight to Southern ports should have resulted in more colored Northern seamen seeking berths on whaleships. Census records evidence a shift from seafaring to casual labor, however, suggesting that whaling berths were either unavailable or had become far less rewarding for men of color.

The rise of Portuguese and Afro-Portuguese seafaring communities in New England has largely been overlooked by previous studies of the ethnic and social history of American whaling and seafaring. Whaling, nevertheless, was the stimulus for the first wave of 1,055 Portuguese immigrants in the 1850s, most of them destined for New Bedford.[67] The overwhelming majority arrived from Portugal and from the Euro-Portuguese settlements in the Azores. Afro-Portuguese *Bravas* were never more than 15 percent of New Bedford's Portuguese American community and continued to be socially segregated by other Portuguese immigrants.[68]

A small Portuguese nucleus was established at New Bedford by 1840. There were thirty-four recorded marriages of men with Portuguese surnames in New Bedford from 1821 to 1839.[69] Most were identified as foreign-born. Seven of the men and eight of the women were identified as "colored." In the 1840s, twenty-two men with Portuguese surnames were married at New Bedford. Ten were identified as sailors (including harbor pilot Amos Lopez), and only one was identified as "colored." Although nearly half of the Portuguese men married at New Bedford in the 1840s were seamen, they were still barely 5 percent of the seaport's maritime workforce: during the same decade, 221 resident White seamen were married at New Bedford.[70]

By 1871, Boston journalist Edward King wrote of the Portuguese quarter of New Bedford known as Fayal, "They are a prosperous and very generally a peaceable lot; the Portuguese, all along the coast, have an especially good reputation, not only as brave and hardy seamen, but as orderly citizens."[71] Many "colored" sailors were still living in New Bedford and New London, according to census records, but, as noted earlier, they were chiefly employed (if at all) in casual labor. Since whaleships paid all men equal lays, the attraction of Portuguese seaman could not have been any willingness on their part to accept lower wages. According to some early historians of the whaling industry, "ships' masters favored them because of their long-suffering docility under poor food and abuse."[72] We may speculate that the first generation of African American and Afro-Indian seamen had attained a stage of political consciousness that made them unwilling to continue working under such abusive conditions.

Men of color were not particularly successful finding employment ashore in New England towns and cities, however. The data suggests exclusion, both at sea and on the land. Everett Allen has painted the growing parochialism of New Bedford's small Yankee elite in the following strokes: "Labor unions, Democrats, the Irish, people with unfamiliar accents or ideas and, generally, any man who was poor and thought he had a right to get rich if he could (even though this was precisely what New Bedford's founding fathers had done) were privately or even publicly looked upon as ridiculous or dangerous."[73]

The intolerance of New Englanders toward their Indian neighbors was indistinguishable from their treatment of African Americans. William Apess related one of the experiences that convinced him of the shared conditions and rights of all people of color in America:

I was passing through Connecticut, about 15 years ago, where they are so pious that they kill the cats for killing rats, and whip the beer barrels for working upon the Sabbath, that in a severe cold night, when the face of the earth was one glare of ice, dark and stormy, I called at a man's house to know if I could not stay with him, . . . and withal we were both members of one church. My reception, however, was almost as cold as the weather, only he did not turn me out-of-doors; if he had, I know not but I should have frozen to death. My situation was a little better than being out, for he allowed a little wood, but no bed, because I was an Indian.[74]

Paul Cuffe likewise wrote of his mistreatment by fellow passengers on the coach ride from Washington, where he had met with the president, to Baltimore. "When I arrived in Baltimore they utterly refused to take me in at the tavern or to get me a dinner unless I would go back among the servants."[75] For Cuffe, a prosperous Quaker shipowner, and Apess, a widely traveled and widely published Methodist minister, it was plain that education, Christian faith, and material success were less important than one's color.

Indians (largely Afro-Indians) remained involved in whaling the longest at Sag Harbor, where Montauk families such as the Cuffees and Pharoahs were still producing young whalemen in the 1870s. The explanation may be demographic. Sag Harbor was the smallest of the New England whaling ports, and it was only a few miles from a Montauk community large enough to be identified on some late-eighteenth-century maps of Long Island as "Indian Town" (later known as Eastville, near Easthampton). By the 1850s, New Bedford and New London were hosting large numbers of Southern African American and southern European immigrants, who could find employment shoreside as well as shipboard, while Sag Harbor remained chiefly agricultural apart from its whaling industry. Nantucket Island also offered very little shoreside employment other than farm labor and attracted few permanent immigrants. Labor was therefore relatively scarce at Sag Harbor, but New Bedford and New London enjoyed a surplus of fresh workers and could afford to be selective. Although both seaports had large Afro-Indian populations and New London had both the Pequot and Mohegan reservations as neighbors, whaling recruiters evidently preferred the Portuguese.

SEAFARING AND LEADERSHIP

Despite their declining numbers, individual Afro-Indian and Indian seamen continued to play key leadership roles in their communities, as Bolster argues in the case of African American sailors. Several became masters and merchants, competing directly with the New England Yankee elite. Amos Haskins, an Afro-Wampanoag, was given command of the bark *Massasoit* of Mattapoisett in 1851 and made two successful whaling voyages to the Caribbean over the next three years.[76] Absalom Boston, Afro-Indian son of Thankful Micah, became the master of the *Industry* of Nantucket in 1822 and raised a household of sailors.[77] Long Island produced many career Afro-Indian seamen, such as Jason Cuffee, who made at least five voyages on the *Thames* and the *Thorn* between 1826 and 1833, but five other members of the Cuffee family also sailed on Sag Harbor whaleships until the 1830s.[78]

Several of the important nineteenth-century Mashpee leaders had been seamen in their youth. Solomon Attaquin first went to sea at the age of only twelve as the cook on a fishing boat. Two years later he shipped on a whaler and eventually saved enough money to become captain of his own coastal freighter. After retiring from seafaring in 1840, Attaquin served for many years as president of the Mashpee council and operated a resort hotel at Mashpee Pond where he reputedly entertained his guests "with wondrous tales of the ocean."[79] Matthias Amos, a major figure in the fight for Mashpee self-government in the 1830s, as well as his son Matthias Jr., a renowned Indian doctor, had both been whalers.[80]

The best-known and best-studied Afro-Indian seaman of the time is unquestionably Paul Cuffe, the son of an African-born slave, Cuffe (Kofi) Slocum. Slocum purchased his freedom; married a Gay Head Wampanoag, Ruth Moses, in 1746; and cleared a farm on Martha's Vineyard.[81] Born in 1759, Paul was thirteen when his father died and was raised by his mother on Cuttyhunk Island and the town of Westport, a few miles west of New Bedford. At sixteen he made his first voyage on a New Bedford whaler and was two years at sea. At nineteen he replaced his father's slave name, Slocum, with his father's original Akan name, and at twenty-one he joined six other "Negroes and molattoes" in an unsuccessful petition to the Massachusetts legislature for recognition of "the same Privileges" respecting business ownership and voting rights "as the white People."[82] Undeterred, Cuffe began building small coasting freighters and shipping goods to Nantucket, an enterprise that soon made him wealthy enough to purchase larger seagoing vessels for cod fishing, whaling, and more ambitious freighting ventures.

In 1784, with his fortunes rising, Cuffe married Alice Pequit, a Martha's Vineyard Wampanoag like his mother, and then took his Wampanoag brother-in-law, also a seaman, into partnership. He reportedly made a point of employing only African American and Indian seamen on his small fleet, to the dismay of the Southern ports at which his freighters sometimes docked.

A Quaker and philanthropist, Cuffe built Westport's first public school and a new meetinghouse. As he prospered, however, Cuffe became utterly disillusioned by the tenacity of White racism. By 1808, he had embraced the idea of establishing an African American colony in Sierra Leone, and he spent the next two years mobilizing support among the large Quaker congregations of Philadelphia. After an 1811 visit to Sierra Leone (where he was surprised to learn that the people were Muslims) and the disruption of his plans by the British-American war of 1812–14, Cuffe was finally able to carry a first boatload of emigrants to Sierra Leone in 1815. Two years later, he died amid a growing clamor of criticism from Black abolitionists, who accused him of encouraging educated free Blacks to emigrate to Africa rather than to work together to defeat slavery at home.[83]

Until he became engrossed in African colonization projects, Cuffe identified himself as a Black, Indian, or "mustee" (Afro-Indian).[84] As noted earlier, his shipping ventures were Afro-Indian enterprises, from his partnership with his Wampanoag brother-in-law to the recruitment of Black and Indian seamen for his ships. His sister, Freelove, was involved in Samson Occom's project to resettle New England's Christian Indians among the Oneida Nation at Brothertown, New York. At least one of his biographers has accused Cuffe of a repressed desire to be accepted as White, but his balancing of his Akan, African American, and Wampanoag ties is at least as interesting a puzzle for historians.[85] His life and work defy simple classification as "Black" or "Indian."

Men who have been kicked out of all society for their baseness and depravity – with whom no reputable person will associate – very generally show their contempt towards the African and Indian race, in a marked and violent manner; to console themselves, no doubt, with the reflection, that there is still somebody below them.

I. Peirce, *Narragansett Chief*

African Americans and Indians suffered a common fate in New England – social stigmatization and economic marginalization in the most miserable and insecure trades, such as whaling. They might have become competitors on the lowest rungs of Yankee industry, but their experience of common abuse as colored men, and as seamen, appears to have forged a common consciousness. Colored seamen had often participated in the slave trade and witnessed its brutality firsthand.[86] Over time, kinship ties between African Americans and Indians may have reinforced a sense of shared destiny. In the seamless interweaving of African and Indian identities, Paul Cuffe and William Apess were probably not atypical of their less visible and eloquent peers.

The rise of the New England whaling industry created new opportunities for men of color to earn a somewhat more independent living and gain a wider perspective of the world. It provided them with a kind of occupational solidarity and color consciousness as well, when masters and labor recruiters began to favor recent European immigrants over seamen who were American-born but non-White. The growth of competition for berths between the Portuguese and African American, Afro-Indian, and Indian sailors redefined seafaring as "White" and demonstrated the pervasive priority of color in Yankee economics.

Whaling was already in decline everywhere in New England by 1860 – even in front-running New Bedford, which was still operating 75 percent of the fleet it had built in the 1840s. The California Gold Rush and the "opening of the West" to homesteading after the Civil War undoubtedly drained laborers from New England seaports, but immigration from Europe was growing during that period as well. The net effect on the total supply of labor in New England was not great and certainly was not a factor in the eventual collapse of the whaling industry. On the other hand, immigrants replaced men of color on shipboard, and men of color (in turn) replaced westward-bound Yankee laborers in fields and on farms.

The impact of the steady loss of berths for colored seaman varied among seaports. At Nantucket, there were few alternatives for dry-docked seamen, and a large part of the century-old colored seafaring population simply left the island. A majority of colored seamen also abandoned New Bedford, although New Bedford shipbuilding brought an offsetting new influx of African American tradesmen and laborers from New York, Pennsylvania, and the South. Sag Harbor's colored population had been more agrarian from the outset, and it became even more so as Sag Harbor's whaling industry declined after 1860.

Social and economic solidarity between African Americans and Indians did not persist after the occupational foundation of their temporary consortium ceased to exist. Interrelated lineages eventually identified themselves as "Black" or "Indian" once again. It would be tempting to conclude that this is a case in which shared economic interests united communities and where the loss of those shared interests led to a renewal of competitive ethno-nationalisms – and a loss of memory of cultural and kinship bonds.

NOTES

Travel support from the University of Lethbridge Research Fund is gratefully acknowledged. I am indebted to John Strong for sharing his copies of the Pigskin Book and seventeenth-century Long Island whaling contracts and to the Mystic Seaport Library, New Bedford Whaling Museum, and Easthampton Public Library for generous assistance in the use of their archival collections.

The chapter epigraph is from an inscription dated 1798 in a book of Jeremiah Pharoah's that is preserved at the East Hampton Public Library (MM 698). Quoted by Philip Rapito-Wyppensenwah, "Eighteenth and Nineteenth Century Native American Whaling of Eastern Long Island," in *The History and Archaeology of the Montauk,* ed. Gaynell Stone (Mattituck NY: Amereon Limited, 1993), 437.

1. "African American" has been used here to refer to persons of African or mixed African and European descent; "Indian" to refer to persons of indigenous or mixed indigenous and European descent; and "Afro-Indian" to refer to persons of mixed African American and Indian descent. I use the term "seamen of color" to refer collectively to persons of African and/or Native American ancestry and enclose it in quotation marks where it also appears in the historical sources I have cited. This may not be entirely satisfactory terminology, but I hope it serves its purpose here without causing unnecessary offense.

2. W. Jeffrey Bolster, *Black Jacks: African-American Seamen in the Age of Sail* (Cambridge: Harvard University Press, 1997), 91–96.

3. Bolster, *Black Jacks*, 164, citing no sources capable of supporting these con-

clusions. But a similar statement appears (also without references) in Elmo P. Hohman, *The American Whaleman: A Study of Life and Labor in the American Whaling Industry* (New York: Longmans, Green, 1928; reprint, Clifton NJ: Augustus M. Kelley, 1972), 50.

4. George Brown Goode, *The Fisheries and Fishery Industries of the United States; Section 5: History and Methods of the Fisheries* (Washington DC: Government Printing Office for the U.S. Commission on Fish and Fisheries, 1887), 219. See also Hohman, *American Whaleman*, 50.

5. Bolster, *Black Jacks*, 161, 177. See also William R. Palmer, *The Whaling Port of Sag Harbor* (Ann Arbor MI: University Microfilms, 1959), 84-87.

6. Cf. William Loren Katz, *The Black West* (New York: Doubleday, 1971).

7. Alexander Starbuck, *History of the American Whale Fishery from its Earliest Inception to the Year 1876; Report of the Commissioner of Fish and Fisheries for 1876* (Washington DC: Government Printing Office; reprint, Secaucus NJ: Castle Books, 1989), 113.

8. Starbuck, *History*, 112. Unlike Starbuck, Hohman, *American Whaleman*, 51, observed that while as many as half of New England whalemen were African American, Afro-Indian, and Indian before 1820, their numbers thereafter declined.

9. *Maritime History of Massachusetts, 1783–1860* (Boston and New York: Houghton Mifflin, 1921), 322–23. Many retired New England whalemen were still living in Morison's time; hence, his failure to acknowledge the presence of American-born Black and Indian seamen is difficult to excuse.

10. Herman Melville, *Moby Dick* (New York: Dutton, 1907), 33. Morison was not the only historian to rely upon this passage as fact. Hohman, *American Whaleman*, 51–52. Hohman (53–55) also states that there were 500–600 Polynesians on American whaleships in 1844, mainly working under assumed, Americanized names. This is consistent with the crew lists described here.

11. Compare Rennard Strickland's analysis of Hollywood Indians in *Tonto's Revenge: Reflections on American Indian Culture and Policy* (Albuquerque: University of New Mexico Press, 1997), 17–45.

12. Obed Macy, *The History of Nantucket; Being a Compendious Account of the First Settlement of the Island by the English, Together with the Rise and Progress of the Whale Fishery* (Boston: Hilliard, Gray, 1835), 32; Palmer, *Sag Harbor*, 84–87; Hohman, *American Whaleman*, 49–50.

13. Bolster, *Black Jacks*, 195.

14. Rapito-Wyppensenwah, "Native American Whaling," 435–44.

15. William D. Piersen, *Black Yankees: The Development of an Afro-American Subculture in Eighteenth-Century New England* (Amherst: University of Massachusetts Press, 1988), 19–20. Pierson relies on a single letter written by a nineteenth-century observer.

16. Hiller B. Zobel, *The Boston Massacre* (New York: W. W. Norton, 1970), 214; Benjamin Quarles, *The Negro in the American Revolution* (Chapel Hill: University of North Carolina Press, 1961), 4.

17. See Barry O'Connell, ed., *On Our Own Ground: The Complete Writings of William Apess, a Pequot* (Amherst: University of Massachusetts Press, 1992), xxvii–xviii, xxxix, lix, who acknowledges the likelihood that Apess's mother, Candace, freed in 1805 when William was about five years old, was African American but then treats this as peripheral to Apess's identity. Apess identified himself as a Pequot but also as "colored," and he spoke out forcefully against slavery. Paul Cuffe is discussed in detail below.

18. Nathaniel Philbrick, *Abram's Eyes: The Native American Legacy of Nantucket Island* (Nantucket MA: Mill Hill Press, 1998), 149.

19. Harry D. Sleight, *The Whale Fishery on Long Island* (Bridgehampton NY: Hampton Press, 1931), 4–7; Frederick P. Schmitt, *Whale Watch: The Story of Shore Whaling Off Nassau County, New York* (Cold Spring Harbor NY: Whaling Museum Society, 1972). There is a colorful seventeenth-century account of Long Island shore whaling, but it does not mention Indians as crewmen. Charles Wooley, *A Two Years Journal in New York, and Part of Its Territories in America* (1860; reprint, New York: William Gowans, 1679).

20. Macy, *History of Nantucket*, 28.

21. Elizabeth Little, *Indian Whalemen of Nantucket: The Documentary Evidence* (Nantucket MA: Nantucket Historical Association, 1992). Based on a questionable eighteenth-century observation that each Nantucket whaleboat had an English master and crew of five Indians, Little estimated that shore whaling occupied 30 Englishmen and 150 Indians, or most of the adult men on the island. Elizabeth Little, *The Indian Contribution to Along-Shore Whaling at Nantucket* (Nantucket MA: Nantucket Historical Association, 1981), 30.

22. Little, *Indian Contribution*, 32–33. Probate records indicate that Englishmen owned all the boats and nearly all of the lances and other gear.

23. Little, *Indian Contribution*, 31–33; Philbrick, *Abram's Eyes*, 148.

24. Rapito-Wyppensenwah, "Native American Whaling"; Palmer, *Sag Harbor*, 83–85; John A. Strong, "Shinnecock and Montauk Whalemen," *Long Island Historical Journal* 2(1): 29–41. Strong found evidence that at least one all-Shinnecock whaling company was organized in the 1670s.

25. The original is in the Bellport-Brookhaven Historical Society. John A. Strong, "The Pigskin Book: Records of Native American Whalemen 1696–1721," *Long Island Historical Journal* 3(1): 17–29.

26. Smith's customers were not enthusiastic about going to sea on these terms, as suggested by a number of Smith's marginal notes. Will Bean "like a base Rog[ue] Run a way after he had his Close [clothes] & Cost me 35 s[hillings] in

sending for him." Natutamy "got nothing this season but went away [and] left the Beach like a Villen pretended he was sicke & never came back againe." Sacutace "stayed away 10 dayes at a on[e] time when he went to se[e] his squa[w]."

27. Macy, *History of Nantucket*, 42–44.

28. Philbrick, *Abram's Eyes*, 157–59.

29. Macy, *History of Nantucket*, 50.

30. Macy, *History of Nantucket*, 138. Macy adds that Black seamen "built a cluster of houses near the south part of the town, which is called New Guinea. Their inebriety, and want of economy, generally kept them poor, *although they made great voyages*" (my emphasis). See also Hohman, *American Whaleman*, 50.

31. Rapito-Wyppensenwah, "Native American Whaling," 437.

32. Francis G. Hutchins, *Mashpee: The Story of Cape Cod's Indian Town* (West Franklin NH: Amarta Press, 1979), 96–97; and William D. Piersen, *Black Yankees: The Development of an Afro-American Subculture in Eighteenth-Century New England* (Amherst: University of Massachusetts Press, 1988).

33. Laurie Weinstein-Farson, *The Wampanoag* (New York and Philadelphia: Chelsea House, 1989), 55.

34. Much of Earle's 1861 report is available in Milton A. Travers, *The Wampanoag Indian Federation of the Algonquin Nation; Indian Neighbors of the Pilgrims*, rev. ed. (Boston: Christopher Publishing House, 1957), 193–98.

35. Jack Campisi, *The Mashpee Indians: Tribe on Trial* (Syracuse NY: Syracuse University Press, 1991), 86.

36. Weinstein-Farson, *Wampanoag*, 57. Most leading families probably were Afro-Indian by 1800. See Earl Mills Sr. and Alicja Mann, *Son of Mashpee; Reflections of Chief Flying Eagle, A Wampanoag* (North Falmouth MA: Word Studio, 1996), for genealogies of the Pocknett-Webquish, Bearse-Jones, and Attaquin-Oakley (Ockree) lineages.

37. Campisi, *Mashpee Indians*, 88–91.

38. "A Description of Mashpee, in the County of Barnstable. September 16th, 1802," *Collections of the Massachusetts Historical Society* (2nd series) 3 (1815): 4–5.

39. Quoted in Weinstein-Farson, *Wampanoag*, 63. William Apess complained that Mashpee whalers' lays being were paid to the state-appointed White overseers of the Indian township rather than to the whaleman. Apess, *Indian Nullification of the Unconstitutional Laws of Massachusetts Relative to the Marshpee Tribe: Or, The Pretended Riot Explained* (Boston: Jonathan Howe, 1835), 78.

40. Apess, *Indian Nullification*, 79, 96, 104; Hutchins, *Mashpee*, 103–4.

41. Hutchins, *Mashpee*, 114, 121–24; see also Campisi, *Tribe on Trial*, 89, 91.

42. Hutchins, *Mashpee*, 134. Hutchins (147–54) persuasively argues that Whites' romanticism triggered both cultural revival and racism among the Mashpees after 1900, leading to this "tribe's" denial of its African roots.

43. Harold Blodgett, *Samson Occom* (Hanover NH: Dartmouth College, 1935), 37–40.

44. Philip Rapito-Wyppensenwah, "'Town' Montaukett Economic Survival, 1860-1910," in Stone, *History and Archaeology of the Montauk*, 445–54. The Pharoahs and Fowlers lived in Freetown, the Cuffees in Eastville.

45. Barbara W. Brown and James M. Rose, eds., *Black Roots in Southeastern Connecticut, 1650–1900* (Detroit: Gale Research Company, 1980), 604–5.

46. Alden T. Vaughan, *New England Frontier: Puritans and Indians 1620–1675* (Boston: Little, Brown, 1965), 122–54.

47. John W. DeForest, *History of the Indians of Connecticut from the Earliest Known Period to 1850* (Hartford CT: William James Hamersley, 1852), 443–45, 488. Although DeForest stated that "national hatred" continued to prevent intertribal marriage between Pequots and Mohegans, the figure shows that such unions had indeed occurred during the century prior to DeForest's study.

48. I avoid the use of the term "genealogy," which implies the tracing of blood relationships, as opposed to "kinship," which is constructed socially. My mother's close friends may be my "aunts," for example, although they are not my mother's sisters by blood, by marriage, or in law.

49. The term "tribe" is always problematic because it implies explicit social boundaries between groups. Most neighboring groups intermarry, however, so that some proportion of each group's population can claim ancestry from other groups. Present-day New England and Long Island Indians are organized into "tribes" with restrictive, nonoverlapping memberships, and their own self-definition is adopted here for convenience of reference.

50. Data chiefly from Brown and Rose, *Black Roots*; Campisi, *The Mashpee Indians*; Mills and Mann, *Son of Mashpee*.

51. A number of surnames, such as Babcock, Tobey, and Watson, were shared by Indian and African American families that have no documented relationship. It is possible that their ancestors worked for the same English masters in the eighteenth century and therefore took the same names, or they may have been related through undocumented marriages. None of these families have been included as Afro-Indian in the figure.

52. Henry Edwards Scott, ed., *Vital Records of New Bedford Massachusetts to the Year 1850* (Boston: New England Historic Genealogic Society, 1932).

53. Census data has been taken from National Archives Microfilms M32 (roll 18), M33 (roll 52), M704 (rolls 178, 193, 343), and M653 (rolls 489, 513, 865).

54. Half as many colored women were employed as men on Nantucket, mainly as domestics. In New Bedford, by comparison, one-third as many women were working as men, but more than half of them were engaged in skilled trades such as millinery and dressmaking.

55. Some of the 1860 census schedules for New Bedford have faded to illegibility, although coverage of New Bedford's principal "colored" neighborhood (consisting of seventy-two households) appears to be complete.

56. Sleight, *Whale Fishery*, 16. Note once again the echo of Morison and Melville. I have thus far been unable to identify any Fijians or Malays on crew lists or census schedules (I speak Fijian and can easily recognize Fijian names), although Maori and Hawaiians do indeed appear frequently.

57. Palmer, *Sag Harbor*, 84–87.

58. Rapito-Wyppensenwah, "Native American Whaling," 445.

59. Since it is somewhat easier to identify Portuguese seamen, the "colored" percentage may have been much higher, perhaps a third rather than a tenth.

60. H. D. S., "Crews of the Old Sag Harbor Whalers," 28 May 1925, in the Whaling Scrapbook, East Hampton Library, 99.

61. Three other "colored" seamen also bore common Wabanaki surnames (Basque and Battiste) and may have been Penobscots or Míkmaqs (Micmacs). Boston has been home to a Wabanaki community since the 1720s. Only 10 percent of the African American sailors could be identified with families residing historically on Nantucket Island.

62. Crew Lists, *Charles W. Morgan*, Mystic Seaport Library, MS No. HFM 144; Andrew H. German, "Racial and Ethnic Diversity aboard the Charles W. Morgan" (MS No. RF 633, Mystic Seaport Library, 1995).

63. Brown and Rose, *Black Roots*, 616; DeForest, *Indians of Connecticut*, 442-46, 488; Melissa Jane Fawcett, *The Lasting of the Mohegans* (Uncasville CT: Mohegan Tribe, 1995), 40. Connecticut death records suggest that Indians were disproportionately likely to die from violence such as falls, fights, and drowning. A similar mortality pattern developed on western Indian reservations in the late nineteenth century. Russel L. Barsh, "Ecocide, Nutrition, and the 'Vanishing Indian,'" in *State Violence and Ethnicity*, ed. Pierre van den Berghe (Niwot: University Press of Colorado, 1990), 221–51.

64. "Memorandum of Captains officers cooper Boatsteerers &c. that came home in Whalers from 1860 to Jan 1st 1870," Miscellaneous vol. 37, Mystic Seaport Library.

65. Michael Sokolow, "'New Guinea at One End, and a View of the Alms-House at the Other': The Decline of Black Salem, 1850–1920," *New England Quarterly* 71(2): 204–28. Salem's African American community included Afro-Indians of Fall River Wampanoag ancestry.

66. Bolster, *Black Jacks*, 194–98, 224–27.

67. Urban Tigner Holmes Jr., "Portuguese Americans," in *Our National and Racial Minorities: Their History, Contributions, and Present Problems*, ed. Francis J. Brown and Joseph Slabey Roucek (New York: Prentice-Hall, 1937), 394–405.

New Bedford remained the center of Portuguese American population through-out the nineteenth century, producing composer John Philip Sousa and novelist John Dos Passos, among others.

68. A bibliography of major Portuguese sources on Azorean fishing and whal-ing can be found in Grace M. Anderson and David Higgs, *A Future to Inherit: The Portuguese Communities of Canada* (Toronto: McClelland and Stewart 1976). As described by Alec Wilkinson in *The Riverkeeper* (New York: Alfred A. Knopf, 1991), the Cape's Portuguese fishing communities as a whole largely remain so-cially isolated.

69. Three White seamen were recorded as marrying Portuguese American women. Occupations were only included in marriage records after 1840. Scott, *Vital Records*.

70. Only six men with Portuguese surnames were identified as "colored" in New London vital records, all of them after 1820. Four were seamen, including Antonio Ferrara, who married the widow of Black seaman Samuel Parker, and John Francisco, who became the business partner of Black seaman and merchant Prince Beaumont in 1831. No marriages of Beaumonts with Indians are recorded, but Prince's wife, Esther, born circa 1797 in Rhode Island, made her living as a basket maker, suggesting that she had Narragansett or Niantic ancestors. Brown and Rose, *Black Roots*.

71. Everett S. Allen, *Children of the Light: The Rise and Fall of the New Bedford Whaling and the Death of the Arctic Fleet* (Boston: Little, Brown, 1983), 99.

72. Hohman, *American Whaleman*, 54; see also, Morison, *Maritime History*, 322-23.

73. Allen, *Children of the Light*, 113. See also Hohman, *American Whaleman*, 57, on the continued control of capital and management of the increasingly multi-ethnic whaling industry by a very small Yankee elite.

74. O'Connell, *On Our Own Ground*, 304–5.

75. Kaplan and Kaplan, *Black Presence*, 158–59. Compare the testimony of another Afro-Indian seaman: "to find, in every tavern where I halted, from every passenger who I encountered on my road, a similar expression of dislike and contempt – this almost tempted me to conclude, that there was some foundation for such conduct, and that, in endeavoring to oppose and elude it, I was warring against human nature itself." [I. Peirce?], *The Narragansett Chief; Or, The Adven-tures of a Wanderer; Written by Himself* (New York: J. K. Porter, 1832), 18.

76. Haskin's photograph and biographical notes may be found in the New Bedford Whaling Museum.

77. Philbrick, *Abram's Eye's*, 223.

78. Palmer, *Sag Harbor*, 88. They were alternately identified on crew lists as "Indian" or "colored." The East Hampton Library has photographs of Stephen

Pharoah, a Montauk whaler, which is reproduced in Philbrick, *Abram's Eyes*; and of Jeremiah Pharoah, MM 698. Sam Talkhouse Pharoah was on Sag Harbor crew lists as a mate. Indeed, a Pharoah (no surname) was shore whaling at Nantucket in the 1720s. Little, *Indian Whalemen*.

79. Hutchins, *Mashpee*, 115, 130.

80. Bolster, *Black Jacks*, 184, also speaks of "uncle" Jimmie Axum and his Narragansett wife, Hannah, who ran a Providence boardinghouse for seamen.

81. See Sheldon H. Harris, *Paul Cuffe; Black America and the African Return* (New York: Simon and Schuster, 1972); Lamont D. Thomas, *Paul Cuffe: Black Entrepreneur and Pan-Africanist* (Urbana and Chicago: University of Illinois Press, 1986); and Sidney Kaplan and Emma Nogrady Kaplan, *The Black Presence in the Era of the American Revolution*, rev. ed. (Amherst: University of Massachusetts Press, 1989), 151–63. Paul Cuffe's papers have been preserved at the New Bedford Free Public Library.

82. Kaplan and Kaplan, *Black Presence*, 153.

83. Kaplan and Kaplan, *Black Presence*, quoting Cuffe's letter to William Allen. Indeed, Cuffe's Wampanoag wife did not want to go to Africa with him.

84. Harris, *Paul Cuffe*, 37–38.

85. Thomas, *Paul Cuffe*, 25–27. Cuffe opposed miscegenation, and his two daughters married Black freedmen.

86. If the author of *The Narragansett Chief* is to be believed (his identity remains uncertain, and his tale is sufficiently melodramatic and improbable to challenge credulity), he was one seaman of Indian ancestry who learned to deplore slavery on the deck of a slave ship.

4. Strategy As Lived
Mixed Communities in the Age of New Nations

DANIEL H. CALHOUN

In one neighborhood of Parras, in the province of Coahuila, there lived in 1820 a household that made its own statement about relations between Native and African Americans. The oldest person in the group was a *mulata* widow of forty, María Josefa Reyna. The next oldest person was a married *mulato* shoemaker, Nicolás Soto. The only other married person, and apparently Soto's wife, was an *india*, María Salomé Adriano. Then came her sister, a widow at thirty-two, and her single younger brother who was a *labrador* (a farmer or farmworker, presumably on some property out in the country). Finally came Francisco Rios, a single *indio* of twenty-one, a shoemaker, probably taken on by Soto as a helper and by the household as something between boarder and servant. There were no children.[1]

Here were the pieces of two families, brought together by whatever emotional need, and by the process of maintaining an artisan operation – or by the simple urgency of not living alone. The situation was neither urban nor rural. While the household was biracial, it was not at all clear who led, whether the *mulato* Soto as young patriarch or the *india* Adriano who had the leverage to bring her relatives into the household along with her. Perhaps the younger-brother *labrador* had inherited some small land-right, into which Soto was marrying. With variations, and up to the end of the colonial period, something like this household could have appeared as far afield as Louisiana or Veracruz.

All this was recorded in a special census taken for Parras in that last year of Spanish rule. Soon, the laws of a newly independent Mexico would prevent the reporting of racial distinctions. The Parras census of 1820 marks a triple point of inflection: between the old regime and the new, between the *campesino* life of central Mexico and the nomadic life of the plains to the north, and between indio and *mulato*. According to some English-language usage, this last would be "Indian and Black," since there was no person listed as *negro*, or African, for all of Parras. Whatever the terminology, many people there could trace their origins to some kind of Indian community on the one hand, and to some kind of slave labor on the other. At the moment, in this one household, they were simply individuals who had group needs – like most people anywhere.

If we pull back, though, from the little world of Soto and Adriano, we can find in Parras more about the "big" groups that history teaches us to see. Among the 10,625 individuals in that Parras census, there were certain neighborhoods that were almost wholly Indian, as if the remains of some closed corporate community. The Pueblo of Parras acted in some legal cases as if it were a traditional community, with interests different from those of the non-Indian *vecinos* who were part of the pueblo. According to some accounts, the autochthonous population of the immediate area had died off or been exterminated and had been replaced by Tlaxcalan Indians brought in from central Mexico. Other, unattached Indians then called themselves *tlaxcaltecas* when they joined that settlement and claimed its privileges. For uncomplicated or "pure" Indian groups, though, there was no need to look farther than ten miles or so to the north, where began the territories dominated by raiding "*bárbaros*."[2]

Parras also had haciendas. There were three, two of them the properties of the family of the Marqués de San Miguel de Aguayo. On one of the Aguayo properties, most of the labor force was mulatto, descendants of slaves who had once been brought in to work the neighboring mines or to feed the miners. On the other two haciendas, the labor force was more mixed in race, and largely mestizo, though four families on the largest hacienda were still slaves. About 40 percent of Parras lived on the three haciendas together. These great establishments "dominated" life in the way that standard history says they did. In much, to be sure, the Parras of the census was a nuanced version of that conventional wisdom. The haciendas were considerable, but not everything. The 2,893 persons in the towns were more than in any one hacienda, and over a third of the whole 10,000 lived in scattered ranches and small settlements. So, too, with the data on race. The 1,011 Whites (called *españoles* in the report) included *administradores* of the haciendas, the *cura* in town, some tradesmen, and many people living on individual ranches. Though two-thirds of all the 1,761 mulattoes lived on the three haciendas, they formed a majority of the workforce on only one. Of the 3,728 Indians, some lived on the haciendas, but many resided in separate family units that were listed in the census as if they were independent. The mestizos, numbering 4,008, were scattered through all the settlement patterns and almost all the occupations.

Parras was too much a microcosm to be typical of anything, even while it exemplified "everything." Within a few miles there were nomadic Indians, and there were Christian village Indians. There were haciendas; there were hamlets and ranches. There was one hacienda that looked like an old-time plantation; there were other haciendas that looked more like the conventional image of patriarchal Mexico. There were legal complaints between *naturales* and *vecinos* and by *naturales* against their *cura*.[3] There were expeditions being organized against the *bárbaros*.[4] There were segments of the community as complex as anybody's "middle ground"; there were other segments almost as homogeneous as somebody's ethnic "ideal types." Observers then and historians since have oversimplified and generalized.

One of the hacendados of a century earlier, a previous Marqués de San Miguel de Aguayo, had served as governor of Coahuila and Texas, had fought to keep the French out of Texas, and had then undertaken cattle-raising in the area around San Antonio de Bexar.[5] Through his example, the social composition of Parras hints to what Texas might have become if it had remained a Hispanic society.[6] The racial groups did have distinct historical origins, even if individuals diverged from mechanical group patterns. Their lives moved in two broad currents that, however distinct as types, flowed close enough to mingle. One stream consisted of a population, heavily indigenous, distributed in small units. The other consisted of the various groups who had been taken into the dependent workforces of the haciendas, some of them originally as slaves. The hacienda with many mulattoes reported most of them as *labradores*. Another, with large numbers of mestizos and Indians as well as mulattoes, called many of its workers vaqueros. On this cattle ranch, there were vaqueros who were mestizos, vaqueros who were mulattoes, and vaqueros who were Indians. On all three haciendas, the necessary worker types (farmworker, cow-hand, mule-skinner, artisan) included all of the major racial types (*indio, mestizo, mulato*), without any obvious segregation.

Just as in central and southern Mexico in earlier generations, a once enslaved group was being transformed into something very like the general mestizo population.[7] At the same time, many neighboring Indians and even mestizos remained external to this structured hacienda population of Whites and mixed-race families. It would have been easy for an outside observer to tag the two streams with racial terms, seeing the external population as "Indian," the internal hacienda workers as mixed-race but rooted in slavery.

In the midst of it all, Soto and Adriano, and the other members of their household, managed to work together to feed themselves and make shoes for people. Whatever the claims and conflicts that swirled around them, there was a potential there for cooperation.

There persisted a strategic distinction between external and internal populations but along with it a trend toward assimilation in work patterns. External families and hacienda families were not invisible to each other. The contrast carried with it the potential for some kind of mutual support between the two poles, possibly even a military transaction, or just some interaction that would escape any easy oversight by hacienda interests. Our imaginary outside observer (coming, say, from a segregated society such as the United States) might have felt reassured at first by the fact of polarization, then disturbed by the signs that various racial groups were living together. In a mining area not too far west of Parras, as recently as the 1770s, a Maroon community of "rebels, mulattos, *lobos, coyotes*, Tarahumaras, and other wild Indians" had gathered into one miscellany much the same kinds of people who lived in Parras.[8] Because the settlement patterns of Parras made it a microcosm for much of North America, the potential for local cooperation raises questions about any grand strategic visions in which statesmen imagined alliances and mobilizations among the peoples of the continent.

The geopolitical frame for those questions was recognized as early as 1792, in a different kind of multi-ethnic community – the Glaize, Ohio. There, separate villages of Shawnees, Mohawks, Miamis, and Delawares lived, along with a settlement of métis traders. At that time Britain was trying to mobilize local resistance against U.S. influence, and worldwide resistance against France. This question reached into diplomatic consultation among Native leaders gathered at the Glaize: one participant from the east told the council about the troubles afflicting European powers and about slaves who had "cut off many of their masters" (apparently meaning in Jamaica and Santo Domingo). The assembled leaders were audibly pleased by this last; it was a sign that the White powers were vulnerable. Local concerns slipped into a global frame.[9]

The emblematic character of the Parras case makes it part of a borderlands history that, its critics say, ignores the obvious cultural differences between Hispanic and Anglo thought. For some critics, the failure to draw proper distinctions may derive from the outdoor Pan-Americanism of Herbert Bolton. Precisionists like Lewis Hanke insist that an empiricist culture, spreading over the North Atlantic, nourished in the social relations of an emerging industrial capitalism, has differed from a cosmic and spiritual culture, spreading over southern latitudes, nourished in a precapitalist drive to conquer lands from the infidel.[10] A messy intermediate case, like Parras with its variety of northern and southern social relations, becomes intellectually invisible if it has to conform to this exactness.

Arguments like Hanke's also make it easy to stereotype people. Labor systems north and south of some line are then seen as different developments: those to the north growing out of the displacement of indigenous populations, whose place is filled by African slaves; those to the south, out of a succession of paternalistic controls over indigenous peasants. The slaves and segregated ex-slaves of the north become something distinct from the peasants of the south, even while indigenous warriors (north) become distinct from indigenous peasants (south). The peasant type then treads the historical stage as indigenous, the warrior type as Indian, the slave type as Black.

Both academic thought and social pressure have worked toward that simplification. The more finely distinguished racial mixtures of Mexico came to be lumped as *castas; castas* merged, over the years, into the category of mestizos – even if the mestizos were supposed to be defined as a simple mixture of Indian and White. In the process, this simplification has obscured the specificity of relations among Native American and African American groups. As Gonzalo Aguirre Beltrán came to complain, a linguistic and ideological preoccupation with *lo indio* blinded many people to the reality of Black or mulatto life in communities like the Cuijla he described in the Costa Chica.[11] And Jack D. Forbes has argued that, from the standpoint of specific racial history, the north-south distinction should be replaced by an east-west distinction, between the mixed-race populations predominantly African to the east and the mixed-race populations predominantly American to the west.[12]

The search for specificity may continue, though, at the level of particular communities. Whether in Jalisco or Florida or Sonora or the Missouri country, many a community in North America can be classified internally into roles that are relevant to the political and intersystem conflicts of the early nineteenth century. Examples for such classification can be found wherever people realized the complementary action that was potential in Parras. Maroons, dog soldiers, "young man" groups, social bandits – many such types have enough in common to fit into a generalized three-part system:

1. The military cohorts within many communities, from the Caribbean to Oaxaca to the High Plains, where activism as soldiers or merchants set some persons in opposition to older leadership or to outside domination

2. The stable leadership groups into which soldiers sometimes graduated and which allocated formal prestige

3. The crop-tending population, sometimes making autonomous decisions about production but sometimes bound in auxiliary relations to soldiers or elders

The division here between soldier and farmer points to a boundary relation, common in resistance situations, between warrior-Maroon groups and sedentary-subsistence groups. While this relationship has sometimes differentiated indigenous and African American, it could also distinguish social roles within a single racial group.[13]

The interaction between the Seminoles and the Black Maroons of Florida – and therefore between them both, as a group, and the neighboring slave population – has served as a guiding example for scholarship on Native-Black relations.[14] Reduced to popular terms, it becomes the relation between the Indian warrior and the fugitive slave. Planters of the Southeast saw Indian identity as a threat to their need for obedient slave labor. Traced out in realistic detail, among various peoples who migrated to Oklahoma, Texas, and northern Mexico, the Native-African symbiosis was a shifting connection among some families seeking agricultural subsistence and others pursuing military action. It was not always clear which ethnic group was driven to which social goal. One by-product was the confused, deadly, and only occasionally well-intentioned effort by U.S. authorities to distinguish between Seminole slaves and White-owned slaves.[15]

The soldier-fieldworker nexus was hardly confined to an interaction among different races but could also reflect different levels of experience within some one group. It appeared within African American populations, in the form of the relation between Maroons and slaves, in Jamaica, Surinam, and Haiti. It appeared as a significant political choice within groups like the Comanches and the Cheyennes. It also marked at times the dealings between Lakotas and Arikaras in the upper Missouri region.[16] Soldier groups in many situations were drawing on food-producers for provisions or recruits. Sometimes soldiers came from a younger age-cohort; sometimes they were newer arrivals or migrants to an area. Whether they were also trying to mobilize farmworkers into a larger military movement depended very much on local social politics.

In one case, that of the Yaquis, the soldier-farmer relation within a single descent group has cut across the great north-south boundary insisted on by the critics of Bolton. It therefore raises indirect questions about the racialism implicit in any facile intellectual distinctions between north and south. As described by Evelyn Hu-Dehart, the Yaquis were for several generations divided into interacting segments. One segment worked in their pueblos, visibly useful not only to their own subsistence but also to their occasional employers among the White-Mexican population. Another segment, taking refuge in the backcountry, drew on the pueblos for provisions and information while fighting to preserve autonomy for the whole group of Yaquis. One result was the confused, deadly, and only occasionally well-intentioned effort by Mexican authorities to distinguish between "wild" Indians and "tame" Indians.[17] In the Yaqui country, Maroons and food-producers supported each other right across a contested geographical boundary between a northern system where Indians were *bárbaros* and a southern system where they were *campesinos*. What appears as an interracial connection in the Florida case is an inter-system case in Sonora.

Florida, though, is not the only biracial case. In at least one other, sometimes misrepresented in works influenced by the north-south paradigm, the "warrior" side of the relation was taken by mulatto or *pardo* forces. During the decades after Mexican independence, the part of Mexico called "the South" (that is, the present state of Guerrero) went several times into rebellion, led sometimes for political purposes by Vicente Guerrero or Juan Alvarez but driven often by communities resisting encroachment on their lands. The working populations of this region were sometime indigenous pueblos but sometimes communities derived heavily from earlier Black slaves. Vicente Guerrero, whom one indigenous historian from the U.S. has called mestizo, was described by those who drove him from the presidency as "*el negro Guerrero*."[18] The fighters whom Alvarez sponsored, and led in combat from time to time, were the "*pintos*," so designated because of the skin markings that were supposed to derive from African ancestors. Proper people in the capital saw in these fighters a threat to the notion that *campesinos* were deferential Indians. The frequent, anxious talk of a *guerra de castas* was a White or mestizo fear of another Haiti, a fear that need, hatred, or the Black example would drive even passive Indians into action.[19] The racial identities ascribed to the passive worker and the corrupting warrior were the reverse of what they were in Florida.[20]

The soldier-farmworker relation could involve either Black or indigenous person as soldier, or either as farmworker, in any combination. Sometimes, racial distinctions were used to label this relation. But the basics within the relation were matters of political economy: the efforts of farmworkers to produce food, the efforts of soldiers ("warriors" or "bandits" in conventional vocabulary) to control the movement of hostility or goods through an area. This was an alternative kind of mercantile system, hardly less militarized than the European mercantile system but tied more closely to subsistence communities.[21]

The Seminole diaspora offers, then, one example of a common articulation between military assertion and sedentary tillage.[22] The contrast between the two types of activity carried many of the meanings often ascribed to racial distinction. In the case of the Yaquis, the distinction that Mexicans made between *bronco* and *manso* paralleled the supposedly cultural distinction between *indios bárbaros* and *gente de razón*, which was used to replace a literally racial discrimination. Any surreptitious cooperation across this line threatened the emerging Mexican national ideologies of the nineteenth century. If any *gente de razón* were actual kin of *bárbaros* with whom they cooperated, the alliance would affirm a racial solidarity outside the official nation. On the other hand, if the *gente de razón* who did the cooperating were "renegade" Whites, the resulting transracial border community would be a local rival to the multiracial identity of the nation-state. In transnational class terms, any cooperation between external soldiers and internal farmworkers constituted a threat to the criollo, or White-settler world.

Several features of this articulation kept it from settling into a series of disconnected cases. Settlers and hacendados had long imposed geographical changes on local labor forces by congregating indigenous towns, or pushing some indigenous groups to settle against others, or importing slave labor on top of indigenous, or imposing slaves from new sources on top of old. Even if the result was at first a neat layering of ethnic groups, the process of aggregation tended to make each local productive community into its own kind of microcosm, sharing some patterns with other microcosms.[23] Further, when some young men pulled away to take up as Maroons, soldiers, or bandits, they were not necessarily fighting only against overlords. Nor was it only local people who might have to worry about being exploited by their own defenders. While these soldiers were often concealed and subsisted by friends and family, they also supported themselves by raiding the commerce between units or by drawing subsistence from communities outside their own. And as individuals they moved about, by their own will or otherwise. The African intermediaries and functionaries who moved across the Atlantic world were paralleled within North America by such groups as the Shawnees – who defied easy attempts to locate them, as they turned up in the Southeast, in the upper Ohio valley, on the Texas border, and along the trail left by Santiago Kirker's mercenaries from Chihuahua to Taos to California.[24] From one generation to the next, the ethnic identity of such individuals became complex. In their economic activity, they imposed regulatory checks on the flow of goods and people through an emerging system.

The "essence" of such a system was that it had no essence but was a network of adopted and transmuted identities, protean "all the way down." Dichotomous relations between soldier and farmer were aspects of an alternative mercantile system anchored partly in once-autonomous regional economies (as far apart as central Africa and the Pacific Northwest), partly in the way European mercantile penetration provoked defensive echoes, partly in the ways non-Europeans actually participated in the European mercantile system – but partly also in the converging efforts of autonomous, non-European "soldier regulation." Since the securing of material support for soldiers is a determinant in any strategy, these conditions were also producing a general strategic context. The soldier-farmer relation, interwoven with the indigenous-African relation, was one element in that context.

Some twentieth-century vanguard thinkers are always unhappy with the idea that such a system can emerge from the actions of individuals or local groups, independent of any shared or central strategic consciousness – that is, independent of the *vanguardista* as leader. The danger is that this criterion may be applied selectively, only against outsider or subordinate peoples. When it comes to merchants venturing out of Bristol, or slave traders out of Bordeaux, or whisky salesmen out of Santa Fe, scholars have little difficulty seeing these operators as part of a larger mercantile system, even if the individual operators did not see it whole. Scholars assume, easily, that rival European nations can constitute a single imperialist movement. Only peasant rebels, it would seem, have to be described as lacking a "global vision."[25]

This judgment is a form of exoticism, as is confirmed by the very real exoticism of those nineteenth-century observers who did react – from the outside – to the potential of a non-European system. Such observers were ever offering themselves as White chieftains to an indigenous-African world. The Texas border attracted, or spewed up, several of these people.[26]

Sam Houston traced the beginnings of the reflex, even if he did not carry the fancy very far. Fleeing from his own disorders in Tennessee, he thought that he could offer himself as agent to migrant Cherokees west of Arkansas, working as trader even while he sought new lands for them, eventually across the international border. Although most of this romanticizing disappeared into his later role as Texas politician, a little survived whenever he was playing the "good cop" opposite to Mirabeau Lamar's "bad cop."[27] A more comprehensive vision turned up in the plans of the

Fredonia rebels in 1826: themselves renegade border Whites rather than respectable slave owners, they assembled what were supposed to be the leaders of many immigrant tribes, frustrated in their land needs by both the United States and Mexico. To these leaders they offered all of Texas north of a line from Nacogdoches toward El Paso, reserving for the Whites in the alliance anything else that might be conquered from Mexico.[28] Just as fanciful was the project of James Dickson in 1836, who turned up on the East Coast, first as a poet-propagandist for the Texas revolution, then recruiting soldiers of fortune whom he took to the métis country northwest of the Great Lakes. There he proclaimed an "Indian Liberating Army" that would go overland to Santa Fe, where he as Moctezuma II would set up a vast secessionist realm in which only Indians could own land. Running into Hudson's Bay Company opposition, he lost what resources he had and disappeared off into the Rockies. Whether he himself was métis was not established.[29]

Dickson's initial appearance in the East intersected with a statement of global vision by a man whose identity was not obscure at all: John Quincy Adams. Adams saw the racial bearings of his own questions, filtering it all through irony and intellect rather than through self-indulgent adventure. Even while he was putting Dickson's stories into his file of newspaper clippings, he was picking up on reports from the campaigns against the Florida Seminoles and on the indications that the Jackson administration was dallying with Sam Houston and the Texas revolution. His response was to deliver a geopolitical analysis on the floor of Congress, which he then wrote out for newspaper and pamphlet distribution. Taking off from debate on relief for victims of Creek attacks, he warned that the United States risked a multifront war: slave rebellion was always possible; the army was already having trouble with Seminoles and fugitive slaves in Florida; Mexico had reason to ally with Indians on the western border; and over all loomed the possibility that European powers might intervene. The United States would find itself fighting a "Mexican, Indian, negro and English war." But he concluded the analysis by announcing that he would vote in favor of the relief bill, since it would demonstrate the ability of Congress to adopt a social measure under cover of its war powers. Specifically, it would vindicate the right of Congress to act against slavery, in case the war he prophesied did break out.[30]

While Adams's U.S. followers saw his speech as a domestic partisan coup, publicists in Mexico received it as a global statement, supporting their cause against U.S. expansion. They distributed a pamphlet translation.[31] The Mexican military had already been making halfhearted attempts to recruit support from immigrant tribes and fugitive slaves in Texas.[32] In the long run, the development of a Mexican nationality would require that even criollo leaders endorse some kind of indigenism. As of the 1820s and 1830s, however, this kind of recruitment ran into two problems: the government's lack of resources to offer much support to any peripheral group, whether Indian or anti-Indian; and the reluctance of Mexican leaders to take alien Indian nations into Mexican society. Lucas Alamán, minister of foreign relations in 1825, responded to a Shawnee request for land in Mexico by insisting that the migrants should come in as a "peaceful, industrious and useful" part of Mexican society, not a separate nation with their own culture.[33] In other words, they should become, within Mexico, what the various races of workers were within the haciendas of Parras. The Mexicans who reprinted the John Quincy Adams speech were operating somewhere on a trajectory that ran from Alamán's conservative brand of social mobilization to the more open indigenism of later years. What they did not see was the extent to which Adams was mapping a quite different road to mobilization. He had abandoned none of his old distaste for non-Yankee cultures, at home or abroad. Rather, his strategic vision operated in combination with his Yankee patriotism to suggest that Congress, if it was to head off the interethnic and international threat, might have to use its war powers to mobilize Black populations in the U.S. interest – that is, as elements in the modern, New-Englandish social evolution for which he was a long-term spokesman.[34] Though he censured the Jacksonians for how they behaved toward Indians and Mexicans, he was not suggesting any move to include those other groups in a U.S. coalition.

Explicit global visions of the Black-indigenous interaction were thus available in the early nineteenth century, in the form of "well-intentioned" efforts to co-opt local alliances for some metropolitan purpose, as imagined by White, criollo planners. It was characteristic of such strategists, even when they looked beyond formal political categories, that they wanted to mobilize whole races or whole classes in the cause of some national society. Those visions took little account of concrete social relations.

In contrast, local efforts were establishing personal connections across the gap between social systems. These efforts drew on two realms of discourse. One was an explicit language of racial, ethnic, and local identities, persisting through much actual mixture. The other was an evolving variety of economic and proprietary roles, including a tactical repertory offered by the distinct soldier and farmer types. On a day-to-day basis, there was no guarantee that neighboring communities would cooperate with each other in the way elite groups feared; they might, or they might fall into the disputes over land and water that have been common in the Americas. Neighboring groups, distinguished by race, did sometimes react with mutual hostility but sometimes united against a common outside enemy. Similarly with the interactions between soldier and farmer. What was at work was not some vast conspiratorial alliance nor some great sentimental support network. It was a network of people having varied, concrete dealings with each other, converging toward whatever common end was potential in their circumstances.

Warrior and peasant responded to each other in a relation that was sometimes protective, sometimes exploitative, developing over time. If "warrior" took the form of "bandit" ("social" or otherwise), bandits did not have to rein in at community boundaries. Neither did the muleskinners who moved products between markets. The negotiating of alliances within communities was also a slow but fluid process of reassortment and realignment between communities. Shifting identities like those within the Shawnee-Creek-Seminole-Maroon network can be seen also among the evolving Cheyenne identities argued by John H. Moore or among the shifting Carib soldier identities described by Neil Lancelot Whitehead.[35] These networks developed in open, fluid ways. They reached across considerable distances. And they produced groups that had great and serious import for the lives of their members.

This seriousness of identity was sometimes expressed in an essentialist vocabulary of ethnic labels, which has found echoes in other kinds of formalistic analysis. One formal European system was that of adjudicated property right. This system of legal criteria, when offered by the Spanish crown, required that communities acquire evidence of titles enjoyed from "time immemorial" – thus requiring that community identity be expressed in a form that denied historical change. A second formal system, similar in style to that of legal property right but more recent in its intellectual vogue, has been that of "modes of production." In modes-of-production debate, the emergent American networks might have been described as a tributary mode, incompletely articulated to an expanding mercantile capitalism. Such language would assume, though, that each mode is governed by a single dominant essence. The vocabulary has much the same simplifying, abstracting character as did the strategic projections of an Adams or an Alamán – or as did the static criteria of juridical property. For working historical purposes, research on concrete social relations serves better than that kind of abstraction.

This does not mean that ideological implications can be evaded. The bare posing of questions about the Black-indigenous relation carries with it the more recent political debate about the relation between "indigenous" and "popular" roles in movement ideology. While any all-embracing relation between indigenous and Black would reinforce the "popular" emphasis, and while any immediate interpretation here is a matter for people active in those movements, there are certain observations to be made about historical cases. First, the system toward which soldier-peasant relations converged was always based on local units. Each such unit included some group or groups identified by racial category, whether African, indigenous, or fictively indigenous. Indigenous categories have often provided a model for the rights that such units would claim or seek – whatever their real or supposed racial identity. Second, the dubious character of the blood-quantum criterion has demonstrated that all these categories are better defined by the actual participants in local life.[36] Any externally imposed definition is at best a dogmatic vanguard form.

But third, the events of the late nineteenth century showed that the growing strategic coherence of criollo society threatened to overwhelm and fragment any alternative network. This new power worked through a reconciliatory merger between victorious investment interests and the defeated, military-minded landowners. Each set of interests was active across some wide expanse of the continent. Their civil wars of the 1860s were the bloody but ritualistic negotiation into which they diverted their rivalries in order to determine what internal relations would govern the eventual coalition. The kind of blow that this coalition could strike was demonstrated in 1877, when U.S. troops, withdrawn from any effort to check planter control in the South, took advantage of railroads and interior lines to operate alternatively against labor in the East and indigenous peoples in the West.

The social power of this landed-industrial complex was also imposed on the consciousness of individuals. One among many cases was that of Lucy Parsons, who responded to the racial pressures of her time by leaving a confused record about whether the non-White part of her ancestry was Indian, Mexican, or African. It was hardly an accident that she married a man, Frank Parsons, whose identities also spanned a broad range, in his case from Confederate boy soldier to anarchist agitator. The marriage took her into organizing work on behalf of the condemned Haymarket anarchists, and her moral example served in the evolving political consciousness of José Martí. Those decades brought also a convergence between indigenous and anarchist consciousness in Mexico, toward the Ayala movement.[37] Often, the "popular" category, like its kin the "anarchist" category, has been associated with efforts to whistle away the defeats imposed by landholder-industrial success. Much of the indigenous thrust, within the recent indigenous-popular debate, amounts to an effort to reassert identities defeated in those repressive movements around 1877.

But the communities of the earlier nineteenth century did not exist just to provide healthy warnings for later tacticians. They undertook moves of their own, which had a distinct strategic character, whether or not they amounted to "movements" directed by "activists." Soldier-farmworker interaction, when it worked as an immunological reaction against criollo power, sought control over relations among local units, gathering them into a tougher tissue. If the criollo intrusion had eased off, the efforts to maintain connections might have grown less sharply defensive, leaving a less tense situation, revealing more of how that tissue was evolving on its own terms. Between the crises of obvious intrusion, there did come some intervals when the saner of criollo agents seemed to deal with local soldiers and producers as given systems, more to be used than shattered. Those spaces, like the Green River rendezvous system in the 1820s or Bent's Fort in the late 1830s, are intellectually useful now because they were not opaque blanks in history. Rather, they were spaces of reduced turbulence, through which we can see how indigenous agents continued to build the connections that suited their own purposes.[38]

That kind of historical rhythm also marked indigenous or mulatto communities in the south of Mexico, as it did the nonhacienda side of life in those parts of Mexico where transport and herding work was a source of local soldiering.[39] Though such communities may have become less contentious during less stressful intervals, their assertive, transformative outreach was never trivial.[40] It sought constantly to subject external commerce to a tributary obligation, even while it weakened or commandeered the coercion that neighboring elites might impose on agricultural labor. It moved toward decision patterns of its own, not in terms of prices and formal market relations but in terms of the active social relations that produced the means of subsistence, power, and prestige.

NOTES

1. "Padron General de ambos sexos de la Jurisdiccion de esta Villa de Parras . . . Año de 1820," expediente 723, Coahuila Microfilms, Roll 17, Instituto Nacional de Antropología e Historia México. The census gave only maiden names for wives.

The small number of *castas* (117) in the census report would indicate, if literally correct, that there had been little racial mixing of the indigenous and slave populations. On one Parras hacienda, larger numbers of slaves were held as late as 1761, when most of their marriages were to persons described as *"libres"* (María Vargas-Lobsinger, *Formación y decadencia de una fortuna: Los mayorazgos de San Miguel de Aguayo y de San Pedro del Alamo, 1583–1823*, México: UNAM, 1992). Ida Altman, "A Family and Region in the Northern Fringe Lands: The Marqueses de Aguayo of Nuevo León and Coahuila," in *Provinces of Early Mexico*, ed. Ida Altman and James Lockhart (Los Angeles: UCLA Latin American Center, 1976), 261, says, "A small number of Black slaves worked on the estates in addition to the hired laborers, holding skilled or supervisory positions as overseers of obrajes, weavers, or shoemakers." In fact, almost all the *labradores* on the Aguayo hacienda in Parras in 1820 were mulattoes and were presumably descendants of earlier slaves. These figures vary, but not materially, from the 1819 census used in Héctor Barraza, "La población negra en el sur de Coahuila," in Agustín Curruca Pelaez et al., *El sur de Coahuila antiguo, indígena y negro* (Parras: Museo y Archivo Histórico MATHEO, 1991), 181–94.

In some towns of Durango, almost all mulattoes were *libres* by 1779. Michael M. Swann, *Tierra Adentro: Settlement and Society in Colonial Durango* (Boulder CO: Westview, 1992). Peter Gerhard, *The North Frontier of New Spain*, rev. ed. (Norman: University of Oklahoma Press, 1993), 27. Carlos Manuel Valdés and Ildefonso Davila, *Esclavos negros en Saltillo: Siglos XVII–XIX* (Saltillo: Ayuntamiento de Saltillo y Universidad Autónoma de Coahuila, 1989). In most of New Spain, emancipation was carried out by ordinary social process, by the early seventeenth century in some areas, by the late eighteenth in most – in any case, long before the formal acts of emancipation ascribed to particular leaders in the early years of Mexican independence. Adriana Naveda Chávez-Hita, "Veracruz en el Caribe: Esclavitud y cimarronage en el siglo XVIII," *El Caribe Contemporáneo* 21 (1990): 45–51.

The distribution of races between ranchos and haciendas was not peculiar to Coahuila, according to Adriana Naveda Chávez-Hita, "Esclavitud en Córdoba: Composición y distribución racial, 1788," in *Jornadas de homenaje a Gonzalo Aguirre Beltrán* (México: Instituto Veracruzano de Cultura, 1988), 289. In patriarchal moments, of course, hacendados might use mulatto cowhands as retainers in their conflict with indigenous peasants. See the Huasteca tensions described by Frans J. Schryer, *Ethnicity and Class Conflict in Rural Mexico* (Princeton NJ: Princeton University Press, 1990), 81–84. The detail of analyses like Schryer's should be taken as a caution in any quick interpretation of census results like those of Parras.

2. Ernesto de la Torre Villar, ed., *Coahuila: Tierra anchurosa de indios mineros y hacendados* (México: SIDERMEX, 1985), 239–42, 249–50, 270, 296, 399–406, 449.

Juan Agustín de Morfi, *Viaje de indios y diario de Nuevo México*, ed. Vito Alessio Robles (México: Porrua, 1935), 127–43, 149, 153–69. Gildardo Contreras Palacios, *Parras y La Laguna* (Torreón: Editorial del Norte Mexicano, 1990), 32–35, would infer from the occasional artificiality of the *"tlaxcalteca"* designation that there had been no real displacement of *chichimecas*. Gerhard, *North Frontier of New Spain*, 219–24.

In the Parras *padrón*, while the designation of anyone as mulatto is probably correct (barring clerical error in the lists), such classifications as *indio* may reflect this particular ethnogenesis.

3. Registro de expedientes, Coahuila Microfilms, INAH, reel 2: 1790/402; 1794/447; 1795/1, 467; 1801/524; 1804/539; 1807/585, 590, 591; 1813/664; 1814/670; 1815/683 (on San Francisco Vizarrón); 1823/742.

4. Registro de expedientes, Coahuila, 1796/475; 1807/597; 1809/620. Proclamation by Nemesio Salcedo y Salcedo, governor of the Provincias Internas, 16 February 1804 (Coahuila Microfilms, INAH, reel 17), specified the arms to be carried by each person traveling through the countryside: shotgun, pistol, or lance for those who could afford them; sling and stones for those who could not; and bow or lance for *indios de pueblo*. He required that Indians not leave the pueblo without government permission and that they return from the countryside as soon as their business was over. His order was not well observed.

5. Donald E. Chipman, *Spanish Texas 1519–1821* (Austin: University of Texas Press, 1991), 119–28, 246. Sandra L. Myres, *The Ranch in Spanish Texas* (El Paso: Texas Western Press, 1969).

6. Alicia V. Tjarks, "Comparative Demographic Analysis of Texas, 1777–1793," *Southwestern Historical Quarterly* 77 (1974): 291–338.

7. As recently as the census records of 1777 and 1791, and baptismal records of the same period, mulattoes formed over 40 percent of the population in parts of the Parras area. During the intervening years, largely those of the War of Independence, social transformations seem to have included a reclassification of many mulattoes as mestizos. Carlos Manuel Valdés, "Negros y mulatos en el noreste de México," *Review of Latin American Studies* 4 (1991): 252–63. See the arguments of Patrick James Carroll, "Los mexicanos negros, el mestizaje y los fundamentos olvidados de la 'raza cósmica': Una perspectiva regional," *Historia mexicana* 44 (1995): 403–38 (that the openness of Afro-mestizos and mulattoes to exogamy broadened the process of *mestizaje*, even though they made themselves invisible in the process); Miguel Angel Gutiérrez Avila, "Negros e indígenas: Otra historia que contar," *México indígena* 3 (1987): 53–56; Robert McCaa, Stuart B. Schwartz, and Arturo Grubessich, "Race and Class in Colonial Latin America: A Critique," *Comparative Studies in Society and History* 21 (1979): 421–33; Robert McCaa, *"Calidad*, Class, and Marriage in Colonial Mexico: The Case of Parral, 1788–90,"

Hispanic American Historical Review 64 (1984): 477–501; and David A. Brading, "Grupos étnicos: Clases y estructura ocupacional en Guanajuato (1792)," *Historia Mexicana* 21 (1972): 460–80.

Some studies assume that Black slaves, or African Americans generally, simply disappeared from central Mexico in the face of the renewed availability of indigenous labor. Alfonso Toro, "Influencia de la raza negra en la formación del pueblo mexicano," *Ethnos* 1 nos. 8–12 (1920–21): 215–18; Woodrow Borah, "Race and Class in Mexico," *Pacific Historical Review* 23 (1954): 331–42; Ward J. Barrett and Stuart B. Schwartz, "Comparación entre dos economías azucareras coloniales: Morelos, México y Bahía, Brasil," in *Haciendas, latifundios y plantaciones en América Latina*, comp. Enrique Florescano (México: Siglo XXI, 1975), 532–72; Colin A. Palmer, *Slaves of the White God: Blacks in Mexico, 1570–1650* (Cambridge: Harvard University Press, 1976), 4. But see the much stronger argument, for a coherent transition from African slaves to free mulattoes, in Dennis N. Valdés, "The Decline of Slavery in Mexico," *The Americas* 44 (1987): 167–94; and in Patricia Seed, "Social Dimensions of Race: Mexico City, 1753," *HAHR* 62 (1982): 569–606; and compare the circumstantial narrative in Jonathan I. Israel, *Race, Class, and Politics in Colonial Mexico 1610–1670* (London: Oxford University Press, 1975), chap. 2. R. Douglas Cope, *The Limits of Racial Domination: Plebeian Society in Colonial Mexico City, 1660–1720* (Madison: University of Wisconsin Press, 1994), 83, as cited in Dennis N. Valdés, "The Decline of the Sociedad de Castas in Mexico City" (Ph.D. diss., University of Michigan, 1978) supports the virtual-disappearance interpretation. For bibliography, see Gabriel Moedano Navarro and Emma Pérez-Rocha, *Aportaciones a la investigación de archivos del México colonial y a la bibliohemerografía afromexicanista* (México: INAH, 1992), 37–64.

See also Lester G. Bugbee, "Slavery in Early Texas," *Political Science Quarterly* 13 (1898): 389–412, 648–68; Edgar F. Love, "Negro Resistance to Spanish Rule in Colonial Mexico," *Journal of Negro History* 52 (1967): 89–103; Love, "Legal Restrictions on Afro-Indian Relations in Colonial Mexico," *Journal of Negro History* 55 (1970): 131–39; Marcelo Carmagnani, "Demografía y sociedad: La estructura social de los centros mineros del norte de México, 1600–1720," *Historia Mexicana* 21 (1972): 419–59; Vincent Mayer Jr., *The Black on New Spain's Northern Frontier: San José de Parral, 1631–1641* (Durango CO: Center of Southwest Studies, 1974); John K. Chance, *Race and Class in Colonial Oaxaca* (Stanford CA: Stanford University Press, 1978); María Elena Cortés J., "Negros amancebados con indias, siglo XVI," in *Familia y sexualidad en Nueva España* (México: Fondo de Cultura Económica, 1982), 285–93; Cheryl English Martin, *Rural Society in Colonial Morelos* (Albuquerque: University of New Mexico Press, 1985), 199–200; Gisela von Wobeser, "Los esclavos negros en el México colonial," *Jahrbuch für Geschichte von Staat, Wirtschaft und Gesellschaft Lateinamerikas* 23 (1986): 145–71; Silvia Soriano

Hernández, "Aportes sobre el mestizaje de esclavos africanos en Chiapas colonial," *Cuadernos Americanos* nueva época no. 43 (1994): 80–93; and the census-based essays in Carmen Blázquez Domínguez et al. coords., *Población y estructura urbana en México, siglos XVIII y XIX* (Xalapa: Universidad Veracruzana, 1996), especially Adriana Naveda Chávez-Hita, "El censo de 1788, análisis poblacional de ranchos y haciendas en la villa de Córdoba," and Antonio Escobar Ohmstede, "La población en el siglo XVIII y principios del siglo XIX ¿Conformación de una sociedad multiétnica en las Huastecas?"

8. William L. Merrill, "Cultural Creativity and Raiding Bands in Eighteenth-Century Northern New Spain," in *Violence, Resistance, and Survival in the Americas: Native Americans and the Legacy of Conquest*, ed. William B. Taylor and Franklin Pease G.Y. (Washington: Smithsonian Institution Press, 1994), 124–52. Morfi uses similar terms for a 1692 list of 147 families in Parras: Torre Villar, *Coahuila*, 249, 270. Peter A. Stern, *"Gente de color quebrado*: Africans and Afromestizos in Colonial Mexico," *Colonial Latin American Historical Review* 3 (1994): 202–4.

9. Helen Hornbeck Tanner, "The Glaize in 1792: A Composite Indian Community," *Ethnohistory* 25 (1978): 15–39. Michael Mullin, *Africa in America: Slave Acculturation and Resistance in the American South and the British Caribbean, 1736–1831* (Urbana: University of Illinois Press, 1992), chap. 9. Hendrick Aupaumut, "A Narrative of an Embassy to the Western Indians," *Memoirs of the Historical Society of Pennsylvania* vol. 2, pt. 1 (1827): 89. Richard White, *The Middle Ground* (Cambridge: Cambridge University Press, 1991), 454–68.

10. Lewis Hanke, ed., *Do the Americas Have a Common History? A Critique of the Bolton Theory* (New York: Knopf, 1965). One clue to Herbert Bolton's intellectual stance was his preoccupation with the paths of hero imperialists, whom he treated collectively as the linkage through the borderlands. This sentimentalism, which to some extent justified any attack on his homogenizing impulse, did ignore hard asymmetries between north and south. Lewis Hanke, less the scholar "gent" and more the intellectual, was more interested in earlier intellectuals, such as Las Casas, people who like himself were makers of exact distinctions. Both Bolton and Hanke, however, slighted the broader populations about whom the explorer and scholar stories said little. Adele Ogden and Engel Sluiter, eds., *Greater America: Essays in Honor of Herbert Eugene Bolton* (Berkeley: University of California Press, 1945), 537–48. John Francis Bannon, *Herbert Eugene Bolton: The Historian and the Man, 1870–1953* (Tucson: University of Arizona Press, 1978). Bannon, ed., *Bolton and the Spanish Borderlands* (Norman: University of Oklahoma Press, 1964). *Selected Writings of Lewis Hanke on the History of Latin America* (Tempe: Center for Latin American Studies, Arizona State University, 1979). David J. Weber, "John Francis Bannon and the Historiography of the Spanish Borderlands," *Journal of the Southwest* 29 (1987): 331–63. David Bushnell and Lyle N. McAlister, "An Inter-

view with Lewis Hanke," *HAHR* 68 (1988): 653–74. For a recent criticism of borderlands history, with specific application to the haciendas of Coahuila, see José Cuello, *El norte, el noreste y Saltillo en la historia colonial de México* (Saltillo: Archivo Municipal, 1990). Hanke's inclination to write from the point of view of social "authorities" can be seen in his *History of Latin American Civilization: Sources and Interpretations*, vol. 1 (Boston: Little, Brown, 1967), 464.

11. Gonzalo Aguirre Beltrán, *Cuijla: Esbozo etnográfico de un pueblo negro* (México: Fondo de Cultura Económica, 1958). Even Aguirre Beltrán, like some other writers, would at times treat the Black population of Mexico as a picturesque or statistical category, not as an element acting or employed in dynamic ways in an evolving economy. Aguirre Beltrán, *La población negra de México, 1519–1810: Estudio etnohistórico*, 2nd ed. (1946; reprint, México: Fondo de Cultura Económica, 1972); Aguirre Beltrán, "La integración de la población negra en la sociedad mexicana," *Economía y ciencias sociales* (Caracas) 10 (1968): 5–21; Miguel Angel Gutiérrez Avila, "Los pueblos afromestizos de México: Su tradición oral," *Plural* 14, no. 165 (1985): 43–48; Gabriel Moedano Navarro, "El arte verbal afromestizo de la costa chica de Guerrero: Situación actual y necesidades de su investigación," *Anales de Antropología* 25 (1988): 283–96.

12. Jack D. Forbes, *Africans and Native Americans: The Language of Race and the Evolution of Red-Black Peoples*, 2nd ed. (Urbana: University of Illinois Press, 1993), 64, 270. Suggestions of this view can be found in James H. Johnston, "Documentary Evidence of the Relations of Negroes and Indians," *Journal of Negro History* 14 (1929): 21–43; Kenneth Wiggins Porter, "Relations between Negroes and Indians within the Present Limits of the United States," *Journal of Negro History* 17 (1932): 287–367; Peter B. Hammond, "Afro-American Indians, and Afro-Asians: Cultural Contacts between Africans and the Peoples of Asia and Aboriginal America," in *Expanding Horizons in African Studies*, ed. Gwendolen M. Carter and Ann Paden (Evanston IL: Northwestern University Press, 1969), 275–90; Darrell A. Posey, "Origin, Development and Maintenance of a Louisiana Mixed-Blood Community: The Ethnohistory of the Freejacks of the First Ward Settlement," *Ethnohistory* 26 (1979): 177–92; and J. Leitch Wright Jr., *The Only Land They Knew: The Tragic Story of the American Indians in the Old South* (New York: Free Press, 1981), chap. 11. Compare Forbes, "El concepto de mestizo-metis," *Plural* 13, no. 145 (1983): 21–32. Where Forbes argues from *mestizaje* and fragmentation to the emergence of larger "meta" races, Herman L. Bennett argues, from the New World persistence of African local identities, that scholars should replace the concept of a single Black identity with a more "nuanced" and pluralistic view: Bennett, "Lovers, Family and Friends: The Formation of Afro-Mexico, 1580–1810" (Ph.D. diss., Duke University, 1993); Bennett, "A Research Note:

Race, Slavery, and the Ambiguity of Corporate Consciousness," *Colonial Latin American History Review* 3 (1994): 207–13; and Bennett, review of *Blacks in Colonial Veracruz*, by Patrick James Carroll, in *The Americas* 49 (1992): 95–96. While much of this distributional question can be traced also in Claudio Esteva Fabregat, *Mestizaje in Ibero-America* (Tucson: University of Arizona Press, 1995), Esteva provides detailed analysis only for Central America and northern South America, adopting a priori pictures for Mexico and Argentina.

13. For a major alternative perspective on this pattern, see Cynthia Radding, "Ethnicity and the Emerging Peasant Class of Northwestern New Spain, 1760–1840" (Ph.D. diss., University of California San Diego, 1990), 468–76. The matter is treated briefly in Radding, "En la sombra de la sierra: La etnicidad y la formación del campesinado en el noroeste de Nueva España," HISLA: *Revista latinoamericana de historia económica y social* 11 (1988): 13–44.

14. Kenneth W. Porter, "Florida Slaves and Free Negroes in the Seminole War, 1835–1842," *Journal of Negro History* 28 (1943): 390–421. Porter, "Osceola and the Negroes," *Florida Historical Quarterly* 33 (1955): 235–39. Porter, "Negroes and the Seminole War, 1835–1842," *Journal of Southern History* 30 (1964): 427–50. Porter, *The Negro on the American Frontier* (New York: Arno, 1971). Daniel F. Littlefield Jr., *Africans and Creeks: From the Colonial Period to the Civil War* (Westport CT: Greenwood Press, 1979). Kevin Mulroy, *Freedom on the Border: The Seminole Maroons in Florida, the Indian Territory, Coahuila, and Texas* (Lubbock: Texas Tech University Press, 1993). In Mexico, the Seminole experience can be compared with that of other migrant groups: Felipe A. Latorre and Dolores L. Latorre, *The Mexican Kickapoo Indians* (Austin: University of Texas Press, 1976), including 220–22 on Kickapoo resentment against Seminole Maroons as successors to the Mexican lands of Seminole Indians.

15. John K. Mahon, *History of the Second Seminole War 1835–1842*, rev. ed. (Gainesville: University of Florida Press, 1985), 251–52. Joshua Giddings, *The Exiles of Florida* (1858; reprint, Gainesville: University of Florida Press, 1964), 120–214. The Seminole case was one stream within the broad question of how African Americans related to the nations that were relocated west. For a recent review of extension of this literature, see Katja Helma May, "Collision and Collusion: Native Americans and African Americans in the Cherokee and Creek Nations, 1830s–1920s" (Ph.D. diss., University of California Berkeley, 1994).

16. Jean Louis Berlandier, *The Indians of Texas in 1830*, ed. John C. Ewers (Washington: Smithsonian Institution Press, 1969), 70–72. Roy Willard Meyer, *The Village Indians of the Upper Missouri: The Mandans, Hidatsas, and Arikaras* (Lincoln: University of Nebraska Press, 1977), 39–40.

17. Evelyn Hu-DeHart, *Missionaries, Miners and Indians: Spanish Contact with*

the Yaqui Nation of New Spain 1533–1820 (Tucson: University of Arizona Press, 1981). Hu-DeHart, *Yaqui Resistance and Survival: The Struggle for Land and Autonomy 1821–1910* (Madison: University of Wisconsin Press, 1984).

18. Todd Downing, *The Mexican Earth*, 2nd ed. (Norman: University of Oklahoma Press, 1996), 153. This foreshortening of perspective reflects the fact that much "American Indian history" has operated subliminally as a subdivision of Anglo-American history, with a closed intellectual boundary at the Rio Grande but a somewhat more open boundary to the north: See the important query by Evelyn Hu-DeHart, reviewing *Violence, Resistance, and Survival in the Americas*, by Taylor and Pease, in *Ethnohistory* 42 (1995): 516. For a recent survey of the literature that operates within conventional nation-state boundaries, see R. David Edmunds, "Native Americans, New Voices: American Indian History, 1895–1995," *American Historical Review* 100 (1995): 717–40.

19. José María Bermúdez, *Verdadera causa de la revolucion del sur* (Toluca: Matute y González, 1831). Juan Suárez y Navarro, *Historia de México y del general Antonio López de Santa Anna* (México: Cumplido, 1850), 207–8, 290, 374–75. J. MacGregor C., "El levantamiento del sur de Michoacán, 1830–1831," *Estudios de historia moderna . . . de México* 13 (1990): 61–80. Nicolás Bravo, Parte oficial al secretario de la guerra, 25 de abril de 1830, in José María Bocanegra, *Memorias*, vol. 2 (México: imprenta del gobierno federal, 1892), 247–50. Lorenzo Zavala, *Ensayo histórico*, vol. 1 (New York: Elliott and Palmer, 1832), 160–61. Moisés González Navarro, "La venganza del sur," *Historia Mexicana* 21 (1972): 679. Moisés González Navarro, "Las guerras de castas," *Historia Mexicana* 26 (1976): 80. Peter Guardino, "Barbarism or Republican Law? Guerrero's Peasants and National Politics, 1820–1846," *HAHR* 75 (1995): 185–213. Peter F. Guardino, *Peasants, Politics, and the Formation of Mexico's National State* (Stanford CA: Stanford University Press, 1996). Romana Falcón, "Descontento campesino e hispanofobia: La tierra caliente a mediados del siglo XIX," *Historia mexicana* 44 (1995): 461–98. On the mixed role of Black soldiers in the war between Spain and the Insurgency, see Gabriel Moedano Navarro, "Notas etnohistóricas sobre la población negra de la Costa Chica," in *Arqueología y Etnohistoria del Estado de Guerrero* (México: INAH, 1986), 553–54. One of the few studies that connects the demographic developments of the colonial period to the anti-elite political movements of the 1820s is Patrick J. Carroll, *Blacks in Colonial Veracruz: Race, Ethnicity, and Regional Development* (Austin: University of Texas Press, 1991), chap. 8.

20. For other examples of this reversal, from both the southwest and the northwest of New Spain, see Lolita Gutiérrez Brockington, *The Leverage of Labor: Managing the Cortés Haciendas in Tehuantepec, 1588–1688* (Durham NC: Duke University Press, 1989); and Rafael Valdez Aguilar, *Sinaloa: Negritud y Olvido* (Culiacán: sin

editorial, 1993). In both areas the prototypical cowhand was free Black or mulatto. This could lead toward a co-opted definition of group identity: the sixteenth-century Presidio de San Juan Bautista de los Negroes, described by Valdez, mobilized Black soldiers against rebellious Indians. Cattle-raising, together with the demographic collapse of the indigenous population in the early colonial period, put serious strains on the ability of all groups to live according to "community" standards. Guatemalan Indians, as described by Murdo MacLeod, resisted the intrusion of mulattoes into village affairs and their employment as majordomos of cattle *fincas*. MacLeod, "Extensive Landholdings by Indian Corporate Groups and Individuals in Colonial Guatemala: Some Little-Known Reasons and Uses" (paper presented at the meeting of the American Society for Ethnohistory, November 1997). Bernardo García Martínez, *Los pueblos de la sierra: El poder y el espacio entre los indios del norte de Puebla hasta 1700* (México: Colegio de México, 1987), 227, describes a situation in which vaqueros of all races (*negros* or *mulatos* in the low country, *ladinos* or mestizos or rootless *indios* in the upcountry) were so involved in transhumancy that they slipped through the constraints of the law: The *naturales* of one village complained that the migratory herdsmen stole women and children, "enticing them with gifts of money and clothing."

For an account of Black "contributions" to the defense of the Spanish empire, see Joseph P. Sanchez, "African Freedmen and the 'Fuero Militar': A Historical Overview of 'Pardo' and 'Moreno' Militiamen in the Late Spanish Empire," *Colonial Latin American Historical Review* 3 (1994): 165–84; and Ben Vinson III, "Las compañías milicianas de pardos y morenos en la Nueva España: Un aporte para su estudio," in Blázquez, *Población y estructura*, 239–50; and see Peter M. Voelz, *Slave and Soldier: The Military Impact of Blacks in the Colonial Americas* (New York: Garland, 1993), which combines the "contribution" interpretation and the "resistance" interpretation. Compare Thomas William Dunlay, "Indian Allies in the Armies of New Spain and the United States: A Comparative Study," *New Mexico Historical Review* 56 (1981): 237–58.

There is a large controversial body of literature on whether the slavery practiced among some Native American peoples was "real" slavery or a "family" institution. For two poles of this argument, see Kenneth W. Porter, "Wild Cat's Death and Burial," *Chronicles of Oklahoma* 21 (1943): 41–43; and Daniel F. Littlefield Jr., *Africans and Seminoles: From Removal to Emancipation* (Westport CT: Greenwood Press, 1977), 80–82, amplified in Daniel F. Littlefield Jr. and Lonnie E. Underhill, "Slave 'Revolt' in the Cherokee Nation, 1842," *American Indian Quarterly* 3 (1977): 121–31.

21. Patricia Albers, "Symbiosis, Merger, and War: Contrasting Forms of Intertribal Relationship among Historic Plains Indians," in *The Political Economy of*

North American Indians, ed. John H. Moore (Norman: University of Oklahoma Press, 1993), 94–132; Alan M. Klein, "Political Economy of the Buffalo Hide Trade: Race and Class on the Plains," ibid., 133–60.

22. This military process, typical of the early nineteenth century, was structured differently from the *regiones de refugio* conceptualized by Gonzalo Aguirre Beltrán in the twentieth century. The soldier groups of the nineteenth century sought to determine, from a point of view internal to the indigenous community, the controls that they might assert toward other groups. To Aguirre Beltrán, the indigenous countryside or backcountry was an area dominated by town mestizo interests, whose influence might be circumvented by a state-sponsored cadre, that provided enough modern development to the indigenous people that they could take advantage of the services offered by social workers and bureaucrats. Aguirre Beltrán's sophistication was taken up and diluted in more conventional academic literature; for just one example, see Lucio Mendieta Núñez, *México indígena* (México: Porrua, 1986), with its complaint that there had not been "sufficient" *mestizaje* or *aculturación*. This outlook resembled the ideology offered by liberals like Mora and J. Q. Adams a century earlier. Gonzalo Aguirre Beltrán, *Regiones de refugio: El desarrollo de la comunidad y el proceso dominical en mestizo América* (México: Instituto Indigenista Interamericano, 1967). Aguirre Beltrán, *El indigenismo en acción: XXV aniversario del Centro Coordinador Indigenista Tzeltal-Tzotzil, Chiapas* (México: Instituto Nacional Indigenista, 1976). Aguirre Beltrán, *Obra polémica* (México: Centro de Investigaciones Superiores, INAH, 1976). Eduardo Medina Cárdenas, "El modelo 'región de refugio' de Aguirre Beltrán: Teoría, aplicaciones y perspectivas," *Cuadernos de historia* (Universidad de Chile) 7 (1987): 175–92. Andrés Aubry, "Indígenas y movimientos populares," *Boletín de antropología Americana* 8 (1983): 59–62.

23. Cynthia Radding, "Población, tierra y la persistencia de comunidad en la provincia de Sonora, 1750–1800," *Historia Mexicana* 41 (1992): 566. Compare the phrase "la nación como palimpsesto" in Salvador Rueda Smithers, *El diablo de Semana Santa: El discurso político y el orden social en la ciudad de México en 1850* (México: INAH, 1991). At the same time, the preserved identity of such a community is easily made a subject for literary sensitivity and style, rather than exact analysis. Consider Enrique Krause, *El amor a la tierra: Emiliano Zapata* (México: Fondo de Cultura Económica, 1987), 39, on the "verdadera patria de Zapata . . . que en términos raciales, formales y lingüísticos había dejado de ser una comunidad indígena, pero seguía constituyéndola en zonas del ser más profundas." Compare the analyses in Mary Helms, "Negro or Indian: The Changing Identity of a Frontier Population," in *Old Roots in New Lands: Historical and Anthropological Perspectives on Black Experiences in the Americas*, ed. Ann M. Pescatello (Westport

CT: Greenwood Press, 1977), 157–72; and in Schryer, *Ethnicity and Class Conflict*, chap. 5. Schryer implies, but does not answer, the question of what happened to mulatto cowhands during the social differentiation that was experienced in the Huasteca both by haciendas and by indigenous communities. See also María Luisa Herrera Casasus, *Presencia y esclavitud del negro en la Huasteca* (México: Porrua, 1989).

24. John K. Thornton, "African Soldiers in the Haitian Revolution," *Journal of Caribbean History* 20 (1991): 58–80. Ira Berlin, "From Creole to African: Atlantic Creoles and the Origins of African-American Society in Mainland North America," *William and Mary Quarterly* 3rd ser., vol. 53 (1996): 251–88. David Barry Gaspar, *Bondmen and Rebels: A Study of Master-Slave Relations in Antigua* (Durham NC: Duke University Press, 1993), chap. 11. John A. Witthoft and William A. Hunter, "The Seventeenth-Century Origins of the Shawnee," *Ethnohistory* 2 (1945): 42–57. The geographical and social mobility of Maroons caused some vulnerability to being recruited as scalp-hunting or slave-catching mercenaries. Octaviano Corro R., *Los cimarrones de Veracruz y la fundación de Amapa* (Veracruz: Comercial, 1951). Neither, of course, did common exploitation guarantee a sense of common cause among slaves of different races; compare the actions of some Indians deported to Cuba, where they escaped from bondage and resorted to surviving at the expense of Black slaves. Christon Archer, "The Deportation of Barbarian Indians from the Internal Provinces of New Spain," *The Americas* 29 (1973): 376–85. Ralph A. Smith, "Scalp Hunting: A Mexican Experiment in Warfare," *Great Plains Journal* 23 (1984): 41–81. Smith, "Mexican and Anglo-Saxon Traffic in Scalps, Slaves, and Livestock," *West Texas Historical Association Year Book* 36 (1960): 98–115. William Cochran McGaw, *Savage Scene: The Life and Times of James Kirker, Frontier King* (New York: Hastings House, 1972). McGaw, "James Kirker," in *The Mountain Men and the Fur Trade of the Far West: Biographical Sketches*, vol. 5, ed. LeRoy R. Hafen (Glendale CA: A. H. Clarke, 1965), 125–43.

25. This discriminatory label exerts a strong attraction on intellectuals, even on scholars who cannot possibly be called antipeasant: Leticia Reina, *Las rebeliones campesinas en México, 1819–1906*, 3rd ed. (México: Siglo XXI, 1986), 34.

26. The more realistic of these exoticists were the people like the fur traders, who have inspired a complex literature on the interplay between commerce and ethnic identity. Besides the materials cited below on the middle-ground theme, see Tanis Chapman Thorne, "Marriage Alliance and the Fur Trade: Bent, St. Vrain and Co., 1831–1849" (master's essay, UCLA, 1979).

27. Anna Muckleroy, "The Indian Policy of the Republic of Texas," *Southwestern Historical Quarterly* 25 (1922): 228–60; 26 (1922): 1–29, 128–48, 184–206.

28. A different interpretation of the boundary offered in the "treaty" can be

found in Expediente de la rebelion del pueblo de Nacogdoches, apollada por varias tribus de indios, tratando de declararse independientes y demarcando el territorio que deben ocupar, 1827, Coahuila Microfilms, Reel 19, INAH. Vito Alessio Robles, *Coahuila y Texas . . . hasta . . . Guadalupe Hidalgo*, vol. 1 (México: Antigua Librena Robredo, 1945), chap. 13.

29. James Dickson proclamation, Washington, 17 May 1836, newspaper clipping in Adams Family Papers, microfilm reel 503. George Simpson to Alexander Christie, 4, 18 September, 10 November 1836; to J. D. Cameron, 18 September 1836; and to C. S. Fox (British Minister, Washington), 22 April 1837, Hudson's Bay Company Archives, Winnipeg. Marcel Giraud, *The Métis in the Canadian West*, vol. 2 (Edmonton: University of Alberta Press, 1986), 229–30. Elizabeth Arthur, "Dickson, James," *Dictionary of Canadian Biography*, vol. 7 (Toronto: University of Toronto Press, 1988), 249–50. Arthur, "General Dickson and the Indian Liberating Army in the North," *Ontario History* 62 (1970): 151–62. Grace Lee Nute, ed., "The Diary of Martin McLeod," *Minnesota History Bulletin* 4 (1921–22): 351–439. Nute, "James Dickson: A Fili-buster in Minnesota in 1836," *Mississippi Valley Historical Review* 10 (1923): 127–40; and "Documents Relating to James Dickson's Expedition," ibid., 173–81. Margaret MacLeod and W. L. Morton, *Cuthbert Grant of Grantown: Warden of the Plains of Red River* (1963; reprint, Toronto: McClelland and Steward, 1974), 117–21. Jennifer S. H. Brown, *Strangers in Blood: Fur Trade Company Families in Indian Country* (Vancouver: University of British Columbia Press, 1980), 190–92.

30. John Quincy Adams, *Speech . . . on the Joint Resolution for Distributing Rations to the Distressed Fugitives from Indian Hostilities . . . May 25, 1836* (Washington: National Intelligencer Office, 1836). Adams, *Memoirs*, vol. 9 (Philadelphia: Lippincott, 1876), 297. John Quincy Adams to Charles Francis Adams, 15 May and 24 May 1836, Adams Family Microfilms, Reel 503. In these letters to his son, Adams was explicitly concerned about a Jacksonian effort to use "Massachusetts" as a whipping-boy in the electoral game.

31. John Quincy Adams, *Discurso del ex-presidente de los Estados-Unidos, . . . en la Cámara de Representantes de Washington, miércoles, mayo 25 de 1836* (Méjico: sin editorial, 1836).

32. Diana Everett, *The Texas Cherokees: A People between Two Fires, 1819–1840* (Norman: University of Oklahoma Press, 1990), chap. 4.

33. Lucas Alamán to Governor of State of Coahuila and Texas, 16 April 1825, Coahuila Microfilms, Reel 18, INAH.

34. Letters from constituents and supporters to John Quincy Adams, May and June 1836 passim, Adams Family Microfilms, Reel 503. R. R. Stenberg, "J. Q. Adams: Imperialist and Apostate," *Southwestern Social Science Quarterly* 16, no. 4 (March 1936): 37–50, interprets Adams's 1836 moves as a shift motivated

narrowly by his political ambitions, much as does Ernest R. May, *The Making of the Monroe Doctrine* (Cambridge: Harvard University Press, 1975). The other extreme, seeing only antislavery idealism, can be found in Leonard Richards, *The Life and Times of Congressman John Quincy Adams* (New York: Oxford University Press, 1986), and in William Lee Miller, *Arguing about Slavery: The Great Debate in the United States Congress* (New York: Knopf, 1996). None of these takes into account the consideration that the relation between an intellectual politician and his constituency may reflect his sense for the long-term economic and geopolitical needs of that same constituency.

35. John H. Moore, *The Cheyenne Nation: A Social and Demographic History* (Lincoln: University of Nebraska Press, 1987), 191–204. Neil Lancelot Whitehead, "Carib Ethnic Soldiering in Venezuela, the Guianas, and the Antilles, 1491–1820," *Ethnohistory* 37 (1990): 357–85. These two cases reflect on each other. There is no need to take the imperialistic creation of client "tribes" as some basic model for ethnogenesis, nor to exclude it from the variety of forms that ethnogenesis can take. See the flexibility of Nancie L. Solien Gonzalez, *Sojourners of the Caribbean: Ethnogenesis and Ethnohistory of the Garifuna* (Urbana: University of Illinois Press, 1988), 51–73. For other network descriptions, often with implications for ethnogenesis, see Brooke S. Arkush, "Yokuts Trade Networks and Native Culture Change in Central and Eastern California," *Ethnohistory* 40 (1993): 619–40; George Harwood Phillips, *Indians and Intruders in Central California, 1769–1849* (Norman: University of Oklahoma Press, 1993); Angelo Anastasio, "The Southern Plateau: An Ecological Analysis of Intergroup Relations," *Northwest Anthropological Research Notes* 6 (1972): 109–207; José Luis Mirafuentes Galván, "Seris, apaches y españoles en Sonora. Consideraciones sobre su confrontación militar en el siglo XVII [i.e., XVIII]," *Históricas*, 22 (1987): 18–29; William B. Griffen, *Utmost Good Faith: Patterns of Apache-Mexican Hostilities in Northern Chihuahua Border Warfare, 1821–1848* (Albuquerque: University of New Mexico Press, 1988), 7; James Brooks, "Captives and Cousins: Violence, Kinship and Community in the New Mexico Borderlands" (Ph.D. diss., University of California Davis, 1995).

36. The matter of who defines ethnic identity has long been a question in local politics, often affecting economic claims. Father Juan Agustín de Morfi, who was no friend to novel ethnogenesis, noted about his visit to Parras in 1777, "The commissioner told me of the abuse [committed] by the Indians, who are all *castas*; and he demonstrated it to me by the voluntary declaration of their governor, who admits to having no known father. That they did not want to give water to the *vecinos* unless paid one peso for every day and another for every night, as is the Marqués, since between the two of them they own all the water. That they count as *tlaxcaltecas* those whom they like, and exclude those at odds with them; the *cura*

says the same thing." Morfi, *Diario y derrotero (1777–1781)*, ed. Eugenio del Hoyo and Malcolm D. McLean (Monterrey: Instituto Tecnológica y de Estudios Superiores, 1967), 63. See also Torre Villar, *Coahuila*, 296.

37. José Martí, *Nuevas cartas de Nueva York*, ed. Ernesto Mejía Sánchez (México: Siglo XXI, 1980), 78–81, 86, 228. Antonio Díaz Soto y Gama, *La revolución agraria del sur y Emiliano Zapata su caudillo* (México: El Caballito, 1976), 17–73, 272–74. John Womack Jr., *Zapata and the Mexican Revolution* (New York: Knopf, 1969), 193. John M. Hart, *Anarchism and the Mexican Working Class, 1860–1931* (Austin: University of Texas Press, 1978), deals with formal anarchist organizations that were less friendly to the convergence of rural and urban concerns.

38. One such semitransparent window was the rendezvous system described in Paul Chrisler Phillips, *The Fur Trade*, vol. 2 (Norman: University of Oklahoma Press, 1961), 395–429. It can be argued, though, that microconfrontations in such a space were much of what precipitated later wars and transfers of sovereignty. Another alternative is the epistemological model at work behind much of the recent métis or middle-ground literature, suggesting an imperfect utopia that for a time held essentialism at bay. Jacqueline Peterson and Jennifer S. H. Brown, *The New Peoples: Being and Becoming Métis in North America* (Lincoln: University of Nebraska Press, 1985). Tanis Chapman Thorne, *The Many Hands of My Relations: French and Indians on the Lower Missouri* (Columbia: University of Missouri Press, 1996). Richard White, *The Middle Ground: Indians, Empire, and Republics in the Great Lakes Region, 1650–1815* (Cambridge: Cambridge University Press, 1991).

39. Salvador Rueda Smithers, "Oposición y subversión: Testimonios zapatistas," *Históricas* 3 (1983): 3–32; and Rueda, *El diablo de Semana Santa*, 84.

40. The reality of this proactive component is often foreclosed in otherwise valuable discussions that are framed only in terms of "resistance." Gilbert M. Joseph, "On the Trail of Latin American Bandits: A Reexamination of Peasant Resistance," *Latin American Research Review* 25, no. 3 (1990): 7–53.

PART TWO   The Legacy of Slavery

5. Uncle Tom Was an Indian
Tracing the Red in Black Slavery

TIYA MILES

The story of Uncle Tom in Harriet Beecher Stowe's nineteenth-century best-selling novel *Uncle Tom's Cabin* has been read and reread, told and retold, on stages and in classrooms. In it, Uncle Tom, a steadfast and guileless African American slave, remains kindhearted to the end toward the White people who sell and persecute him. As his final and harshest owner, Simon Legree, leans over Tom intending to kill him, Tom whispers: "I'd give ye my heart's blood; and, taking every drop of blood in this poor old body would save your precious soul, I'd give 'em freely, as the Lord gave his for me. Oh, Mas'r! don't bring this great sin on your soul! It will hurt you more than 't will me."[1] The Christ-like character of Uncle Tom was so compelling for nineteenth-century readers, who, as literary critic Jane Tompkins has argued, were steeped in a culture of Christian sentimentalism, that the book launched a wave of popular antislavery feeling.[2] In the years since the abolition of slavery in the United States, the image of Uncle Tom continues to resonate, though with negative connotations. His character has become symbolic of the institution of American slavery, so that to call a contemporary African American person an "Uncle Tom" is to brand that person with the insult of servile and accommodationist behavior.

Yet Cora Gillam, a former slave who was interviewed in the 1930s as part of the Works Progress Administration (WPA) Federal Writers' Project, offers a very different picture of a man she refers to as "Uncle Tom." In a lengthy statement, Gillam informs her interviewer: "Now I want to tell you about my uncle Tom. Like I said, he was half-Indian. But the Negro part didn't show hardly any. There was something about uncle Tom that made both White and Black people be afraid of him."[3] Though Cora Gillam is speaking of an actual person and Harriet Beecher Stowe of a fictional character, I am quoting Gillam here to introduce another image –

a competing image – of a slave called Uncle Tom. In Stowe's imagination, Tom is Black and benevolent, "full glossy Black" with "truly African features."[4] In contrast, Gillam's Tom is more Indian than Black and is decidedly strong. Considering these Toms side-by-side, we see not only two persons but also two versions of the model American slave: one kind, the other fierce; one Black, the other part-Indian. Gillam's remembrance of a man who was of Black and Native ancestry challenges the familiar version of slavery in which everyone is either Black or White. Her narrative is a window into a complex understanding of American slavery, an understanding that includes Native Americans in this critical national drama.

The association between Black people and enslavement in American culture has become instinctive, natural. Consider recent films on the subject, such as *Amistad* and *Beloved*, that have won large audiences or critical acclaim. These stories offer no surprises about slavery's main characters: the slaves are Black or of Black and White ancestry, and the slave owners are White. But as historian James Walvin has argued in his book *Questioning Slavery*, this second-nature correlation of enslavement with Black people is a correlation that rewrites history. It was not always the case in the United States, and the British colonies that preceded it, that enslavement applied only to African Americans and that slavery involved only Blacks and Whites. As Walvin observes: "Looking back, the association between black slavery and the Americas seems so natural, so much a part of the historical and economic development of the region, that the two seemed obvious partners. Quite the contrary, it was no such thing."[5]

Walvin goes on to explain that American slavery was birthed out of an intimate triangular relationship between Europe, Africa, and the Americas. Necessarily, Europeans, Africans, and people indigenous to the Americas became enmeshed in the developing phenomenon. The transatlantic slave trade was indiscriminate, catching up anyone and everyone in its net. Still, the popular story of slavery in America, the one told in novels, films, and even high school and college classrooms, is a story without American Indians in it.[6] Worse yet, it is a story that has been reproduced by respected scholars in African American and Native American histories who have painted slavery with a narrow brush. In *Race and History*, John Hope Franklin writes Native people out of the South, ignoring the many Native nations that occupy that region and have contributed to shaping its history. Franklin states: "My field of concentration has been the South, where I have studied intensively the two great racial groups, black and white, the principal actors in the drama of Southern history. (Even before most of them were expelled from the South by Andrew Jackson, Native Americans played only a limited role in the region.)"[7] And in his classic *Custer Died for Your Sins: An Indian Manifesto*, Vine Deloria Jr. says about Native Americans: "It is fortunate that we were never slaves. We gave up land instead of life and labor."[8] The misperceptions in these statements by otherwise erudite scholars are reflective of many Americans' views. As historian Jack Forbes has urged: "The existence of a large group of 'Red-Black People,' part-American and part-African, has been largely overlooked. . . . Still further, the former existence of comparatively large numbers of Native American slaves has also been ignored generally, with great consequence for both early Native and Afroamerican history."[9] These exclusions and inaccuracies must be addressed if we are ever to stretch ourselves toward a richer understanding of American slavery. Perhaps what we need to move toward this goal is what historian Ronald Takaki has called "a fresh angle, a study of the American past from a comparative perspective."[10] If we look at African American history and Native American history side-by-side rather than in isolation, we will see the edges where those histories meet and begin to comprehend a fuller and more fascinating picture. At the intersections of Black and Native experiences, we gain greater understanding of the histories of both groups.

This essay is an exploratory contemplation of the multiple and varying experiences as well as the legacy of Native Americans in slavery. I begin with a brief historical overview of Indians as slaves and slave owners, followed by a discussion of Black and Native kinship ties grounded in this past. Next, through an account of Black Indian women's experiences in slavery, I consider the potential for slave history to impact scholarship on Native American women. Finally, I delve into the vagaries and contradictions of Black Indian identities that emerge out of the history of Native enslavement.

BACKTRACKING: INDIANS AND SLAVERY

In the New World, Native Americans and imported Africans were the planters' laborers of choice.

Ira Berlin, *Many Thousands Gone*

If the association between Black people and slavery is by now a natural one, how do we disrupt it to grasp a different reality? One method is to backtrack and revisit the beginnings of slavery in North America. A number of scholars have taken on this task, tracing out the slow and cumbersome development of institutionalized slavery as an economic, cultural, racial, and gendered system that grew out of the European quest for empire. Sociologists Michael Omi and Howard Winant have argued that race as we understand it, with all of its concomitant categories, hierarchies, and meanings, began with the European project to colonize the Americas. As European explorers encountered Native American peoples who were unlike themselves, they sought to assess and categorize them. Defining Native people as different, heathen, and inferior meant it was possible for European settlers to treat them poorly, to value territory and wealth over the dignity and rights of the people who occupied the land. Omi and Winant write:

The conquest, therefore, was the first – and given the dramatic nature of the case, perhaps the greatest – racial formation project. Its significance was by no means limited to the Western Hemisphere, for it began the work of constituting Europe as the metropole, the center, of a group of empires which could take, as Marx would later write, "the globe for a theater." It represented this new imperial structure as a struggle between civilization and barbarism, and implicated in this representation all the great European philosophies, literary traditions, and social theories of the modern age.[11]

As momentous as this movement proved to be, it was also far-reaching, stretching into Africa to pluck free laborers and pillage natural resources. What followed was a complex and high-stakes system: the movement of capital, products, and persons across continents for national and personal gain.

The single-minded vision of "empire as a way of life" did not discriminate between Black and Red people. Both groups, representing multiple nations and tribes, were seen as ripe for the picking. Indigenous Americans in South America, Central America, North America, and the Caribbean, as well as Africans, were coerced and pressed into labor by the British, Dutch, Spanish, Portuguese, and French. Omi and Winant argue that "the seizure of territories and goods, the introduction of slavery through the *encomienda* and other forms of coerced native labor, and then through the organization of the African slave trade – not to mention the practice of outright extermination – all presupposed a worldview which distinguished Europeans, as the children of God, full-fledged human beings, etc., from 'Others.'"[12] As this statement intimates, Native Americans were the first slaves in the Americas. With the majority of the indigenous population in Central and South America decimated by European diseases, the remaining population was weakened and vulnerable. In the

Portuguese colony of Brazil, which would become a shining success in its production of sugar and wealth, indigenous people were the original slaves. In the Spanish-controlled North American Southwest, Native people were also forced into servile labor, carrying Spanish supplies and even Spaniards on their backs like packhorses. In Jamestown, Virginia, the first successful British colony in what would become the United States, Native people were likewise pressed into laboring for European interlopers.

In order to persevere, Jamestown required more agricultural workers than it had, and this demand only increased with the eventual success of the colony's tobacco crop on the British market. In response to this need, Virginia gentlemen and colonial leaders used White indentured servants, transplanted Africans, and American Indians as a captive and inferior labor force.[13] By 1660, Virginians were so well pleased with the enterprise of African slave labor that they solicited Dutch captains to sell them shiploads of Africans. Soon after, in 1676, Virginia colonists legalized the enslavement of Native people by enacting that "soldiers who had captured Indians should 'reteyne and keepe all such Indian slaves or other Indian goods as they either have taken or hereafter shall take.'"[14] As Africans' and Indians' role as slaves solidified, White indentured servants, who had comprised the first work gangs on Virginia plantations, appeared in the fields less and less.[15] This was in part because fewer White servants were choosing to move to the colony and also, importantly, because a rigid color line had begun to emerge. Whiteness became synonymous with freedom and nonwhiteness with slavery. From this point onward, Virginians did not take care to distinguish between Africans and Indians. Indeed, as historian Edmund Morgan notes: "Indians and Negroes were henceforth lumped together in Virginia legislation, and white Virginians treated black, red, and intermediate shades of brown as interchangeable . . . as Virginians began to expand their slaveholdings, they seem to have had Indians as much in view as Africans."[16] Non-White people of any variety were seen as suitable for enslavement because their color was the mark of their difference and, in the view of Whites, their inferiority. The British saw Blacks and Indians as equally debased, equally defunct of moral virtue. By the mid–seventeenth century, the project to colonize the Americas had developed into a pervasive ideology and system of White supremacy in which all people of color were viewed as subordinate and suspect.

This system of White supremacy was nourished by an ideology of White superiority that pervaded the rhetoric and writing of the seventeenth- and eighteenth-century English. Historian Winthrop Jordan has written extensively on the image of Africans and Indians in the British mind, arguing that the English saw Africans as "black," a descriptor that, for them, connoted evil, bestiality, and filth. Upon encountering Native Americans in North America, people with brown skin who exhibited "savage" behavior and were known to be enslaved in the West Indies, English colonists associated them with the dark and "uncivilized" Africans. Jordan asserts that "it is easy to see why: whether considered in terms of religion, nationality, savagery, or geographical location, Indians seemed more like Negroes than like Englishmen."[17] Seeming "more like Negroes" meant that Native people were located "on the losing side of a crucial dividing line," which, along with Africans, "set them apart for drastic exploitation, oppression, and degradation."[18]

Though European colonists in North America heartily adopted the enslavement of Indians in the late 1600s and early 1700s, they decreased this practice over time. The poor logic of enslaving people in their own homeland soon became clear to Euro-Americans as runaway Indian slaves continually found their way back home. In addition, Native Americans proved highly susceptible to the foreign diseases that had already decimated hundreds of African slaves in the Middle Passage. And Indian slaves, the colonists claimed, were just poor workers. Increasingly, colonists favored and sought African slaves over Native American ones, and the relative value placed on African slaves was evident in their high purchasing price.[19] At the same time, Indian people who found themselves displaced from Native communities or who chose to remain close to Black relatives continued to be swept up by slavery. Their presence within slave communities was rarely documented, however. As blackness became synonymous with bondage, it seemed like commonsense for planters to define enslaved persons as Black, regardless of their possibly complicated racial backgrounds. Ira Berlin explains that "the massive influx [of African slaves] overwhelmed the Native-American population, and Indian slaves were swallowed in the tide. . . . Native-American slaves soon vanished from the census enumerations and plantation daybooks, as planters simply categorized their Indian slaves as Africans."[20]

Though absent from the written record, Native American slaves are remembered in the oral testimony of their relatives. Mary Allen Darrows, a former slave from Arkansas, explained that her grandmother was "a little full-blooded Indian girl" who was captured and enslaved by White men in the "Indian Nation (Alabama)."[21] In another example, Sweetie Ivery Wagoner, a former slave from Oklahoma, reported: "My father was a slave, but he wasn't a Negro. He was a Creek Indian whom the Cherokee

Indians stole long years ago and put in slavery just like he was a Negro, and he married with a slave woman and raised a big family."[22] To some historians, Indian enslavement has seemed incidental and unimportant in comparison to more than two centuries of institutionalized Black enslavement in the United States. However, as historian J. Leitch Wright has argued, no experience of slavery is insignificant, especially to those who were enslaved. Wright contends: "Readers usually get the impression that this [Indian slavery] was a transitory and not particularly significant phenomenon. The aboriginal perspective was quite different."[23] Slavery as an aspect of Native American history is meaningful, both in what it tells us about the range of Native experiences and in what it signifies for the status of Native people in early America.

Equally important to the story of Native Americans and slavery is the fact that Indians owned slaves in the Southeast and in the western Indian Territory. Native American acceptance of slavery was slow to develop and continually contested by the majority of Native people. Still, some Indians bought, sold, and worked Black slaves – in several cases, hundreds of them. Practices of slaveholding differed from tribe to tribe, with some tribes (like the Seminoles and Creeks) maintaining relatively loose and lenient systems and others (like the Cherokees and Choctaws) developing harsh and controlled systems over time. Native slaveholders hoped and believed that by owning land and Black slaves they could demonstrate their level of "civilization" to American federal and local powers and thus gain a measure of protection from impending displacement. Despite this and other concessions, however, the Native nations collectively known as the Five Civilized Tribes, were forced west in the 1830s to make way for White settlement.[24] Slaveholding in Indian country persisted until the American Civil War.

BLOOD TELLS: THE REVELATIONS OF KINSHIP

If you'll believe it, this [bed]spread took first prize. Look, here's the blue ribbon pinned on yet. What they thought was so wonderful was that I knit every stitch of it without glasses. But that is not so funny, because I have never worn glasses in my life. I guess that is some more of my Indian blood telling.

Cora Gillam, WPA Interview

In her interview with a Federal Writers' Project employee, former slave Cora Gillam claims that "blood tells." By this she means that "blood," or

Indian ancestry, explains something about her that is otherwise inexplicable. Her prizewinning bedspread appeared to the judges to have been sewn by an African American woman, but Gillam complicates this initial impression by highlighting her Native American heritage and connecting that heritage with the quality of good eyesight. It is, she reveals, her Native "blood," present but unseen, that has facilitated the creation of the beautiful textile. Though clearly essentialist in its attribution of good health to Native ancestry, Gillam's statement points to fruitful directions for inquiry. Following Gillam's lead, what can "blood" tell us? What can we learn by looking at family lineage that would not otherwise be obvious in a study of Native Americans and slavery?

In the Southeast, where most Native Americans and Africans encountered one another, the intricate constellations of Native kinship systems shaped social interactions, political agendas, and crime and punishment within Native communities. For southeastern tribes, kinship was a primary determinant of social and ceremonial relations.[25] A person without kinship ties was hardly a person at all, and a person with kinship ties was an integral part of an extended family, or clan. Information about clan membership determined the trajectory that any encounter or relationship would follow.[26] A person could expect to be received hospitably by a clan member even if that clan member was a personal stranger or lived in a distant town, and a person could be punished or killed for a crime committed by a clan member whom he or she had never met.[27] Kinship was the web that knit Native people together as tribes, and Native people viewed the world through the intricate netting of that web. Given the centrality of kinship to Native definitions of peoplehood, tracing bloodlines across Black and Indian communities seems both a fitting and effective means of locating further dimensions of Native Americans' experience with slavery. In the absence of reliable historical records, cartographies of kinship can serve as guides to the complex ways that Native people were drawn into slavery's matrix.

Anthropologist Melville Herskovits of Howard University found in studies conducted between 1926 and 1928 that over 25 percent of the African American population reported having Native American ancestry.[28] Even allowing for misrepresentation or imprecise memory, this figure suggests that significant numbers of Black Americans have one or more Native American forebears. Jack Forbes has argued that "by the nineteenth century it seems quite certain that Afroamericans, whether living in Latin America, the Caribbean or in North America, had absorbed considerable amounts of Native American ancestry."[29] In the 1600s, 1700s, and 1800s, when many of these interracial links were forged, the descendants of a Native American and African American would have been defined as Indian by other Indians of their tribe. Native nations in the Southeast tended toward matrilineality and reckoned clan membership through the mother's family line. Within the framework of a matrilineal kinship system, a person was Cherokee, Creek, Seminole, and so on if the person's mother was Cherokee, Creek, or Seminole. Race as we understand it now was not the determining factor in a person's tribal identity or tribal membership. Instead, lineage determined belonging. A person who appeared "Black" and had a Native American mother would have been defined and accepted as Indian. Later, in the early 1800s, as southeastern tribes began to incorporate aspects of the Euro-American patrilineal kinship system, mixed-race descendants of Native mothers or Native fathers could be considered Indian by their Native relatives and associates. The prevailing understanding was consistent: if your relatives were Indian, so were you.[30]

The children and grandchildren of Indian and Black families were considered Native by their Native relatives and Black by their Black relatives. They belonged to dual and overlapping tribal/racial communities and were most likely fluent in the values and cultural practices of both. Because of phenotypical characteristics that marked them as "Black" and because of their location in Black families, children of Native and Black couples were especially vulnerable to enslavement. Whether by birth, trade, or capture, they could easily fall prey to slave dealers and slave owners. Even as Native Americans were enslaved outright in early America, Black Indians, or people of both Black and Native descent, were enslaved in large numbers along with African Americans into the nineteenth century.

Interracial marriage in the slave quarters and in free communities of color meant that the Black population and Indian population were overlapping and expanding and that the slave population included more and more persons of Black and Native descent. Advertisements for runaway slaves in eighteenth-century newspapers indicate the mixed-race heritage of many slaves and also show the ambivalence of White slave owners in describing slaves of Black and Native ancestry. Repeatedly in these advertisements, slaves are defined as "Negro" or "Mulatto" with "claims" of Indianness or the ability to "pass" as Indian, but rarely are slaves designated as "Indian" or both Black and Indian.[31] A survey of advertisements for escaped Black Indian slaves from several newspapers follows:

a Mulatto slave named David, about twenty two years of age, five Feet eight or nine Inches high, a cunning artful Fellow with a sly Look, slim made, a little knock-kneed, says he is of the Indian breed[32]

a mulatto servant man, named John Newton, about 20 years of age, an Indian by birth, about 5 feet 6 inches high, slender made, has a thin visage, sour look, remarkable projected lips, and wears his own black hair tied behind[33]

a tall thin Mulatto slave, looks very much like an Indian, and will endeavour to pass as such when it suits him[34]

a Mulatto slave named Dan, much the Colour of an Indian, is a lusty Fellow about 25 Years of Age[35]

a negro man of the name Tom, about 5 feet 6 inches tall, of a yellowish complexion, much the appearance of an Indian. . . . His hair is of a different kind from that of a Negro's, rather more of the Indian's, but partaking of both[36]

a Mulatto man named Jim who is a slave, but pretends to have a right to his freedom. His father was an Indian . . . he is a short well fed fellow, about Twenty seven Years of Age, with long black Hair resembling an Indian's.[37]

In these examples, slave owners deflect the right of Black Indians to be Indian by reducing Indianness to a list of "traits" such as hair, attitude, skin color, and known relatives. The authenticity of Black Indians' Indianness is called into question by the circumlocutory language of many of these advertisements.[38] In some cases, slave owners misclassified Black Indians because they were sloppy, in other cases because it made no difference exactly what racial background a colored, enslaved person claimed. In still other cases, persons who were both Black and Indian were misidentified because Whites stood to gain at the reduction of the Native American population. "Black" people did not have the rightful claim to American land that Native people had. To define Indians as Black meant there would be fewer "real" Indians with whom land deals and treaties had to be negotiated.[39]

The intricate and even paradoxical means of defining racial categories in the United States has meant that enslaved Black Indians have not been defined as Indian but instead as solely Black. The simplification of mixed-race ancestry and resulting misclassification of people have contributed to the fiction that Native Americans did not play a role in slavery past the eighteenth century. Given the prevailing understanding of racial categories, many of us find the notion of Indians who are also Black difficult to accept. The logic within which we operate when defining Blacks and

Indians is governed by the dialectic of the "one-drop rule" and blood quantum ratio. The "one-drop rule," which holds that a person who has one drop of Black blood is Black, was devised by Euro-American slave owners. It ensured an ever-growing slave population fattened by the children of Black slaves and White masters, even as it protected White people from legitimizing "mulattoes," "quadroons," and "octoroons" as White. Likewise, the blood quantum ratio method of defining Native Americans was developed by White policy-makers in the late nineteenth century. It holds that a person can only be Indian if he or she demonstrates a particular ratio of Native forebears to non-Native forbears.[40] Because it was difficult for some Native people to meet this criterion due to intermarriage in their families, there were fewer Indians whom federal and state officials had to recognize as having rightful claims to their homelands and to political sovereignty as tribal nations. The "one-drop rule" ensured that there would be more Black laborers for slavery's human machine, while the blood quantum ratio ensured that there would be more available land for White settlement and development.

For people of both Black and Native descent, these two rules interface in a way that makes it difficult for Black Indians to be considered Indian. Anthropologist Circe Sturm confronts this dilemma in this volume, arguing that "the rules of hypodescent played out in such a way that people with any degree of African American blood were usually classified exclusively as Black. . . . multiracial individuals with Black ancestry were always 'Black.' "[41] Sturm notes that, given this logic, it has been much easier for Indians with White ancestry to be defined as "Indian" than it has been for Indians with Black ancestry. What is important to recognize here is that these means of defining group membership for Blacks and Native Americans originated outside of Black and Native communities. Though many African American and Native American people subscribe to these definitions today, during the antebellum period Blacks and Indians regularly defined the members of their families and tribes in accordance with their own values. Black Indian people were viewed as Indian by Native community members. And just as important, many Black Indian people constructed biracial identities for themselves.

The WPA interviews with Black Indians who were former slaves include self-descriptions that suggest a biracial and bicultural consciousness. In the next two essays in this volume, Celia Naylor-Ojurongbe and Laura Lovett look closely at these interviews to assess the specific aspects and meanings of biracial Black Indian cultures, with particular attention to material culture and language.[42] Here I will simply offer examples of

Black Indian slaves' self-descriptions as a means of indicating their self-conceptualizations as Black Indian people. Former slave Sweetie Ivery Wagoner states that her father was an enslaved Creek man who married a Black woman. She also describes her parents' dress as an indicator of their Indian identity: "My folks was part Indian alright; they wore blankets and breeches with fur around the bottoms. My father's own daddy was Randolph Get-a-bout."[43] R. C. Smith, like many Black Indians who were interviewed, traces out his Native lineage: "My father was half Cherokee Indian. His father was bought by an Indian woman and she took him for her husband. . . . My father played with Cornelius Boudinot when he was a child. Cherokee Bill was my second cousin."[44] This gesture of naming Native relatives, common in interviews with Black Indians, might be understood as a habit grounded in Native kinship customs. Alternately, or simultaneously, the gesture could be read as an attempt to authenticate the speaker's Indianness in the face of skepticism, a bicultural characteristic grounded in the particular experience of Black Indians.

Cornelius Neely Nave, a Black-Cherokee man who was the slave of Cherokees, described himself as follows: "I wasn't scared of them Indians for pappa always told me his master, Henry Nave, was his own father; that makes me part Indian and the reason my hair is long, straight and black like a horse mane."[45] As Nave's statement implies, Black Indian slaves owned by Native people experienced their Indianness in complex and contradictory ways, as their relationship to Native cultures would have been filtered through and constrained by the fact that their enslavers were Indians. In a final example, a Black-Creek healer explains his talent as bicultural in nature: "Cross blood means extra knowledge. I can take my cane and blow it twice and do the same thing a Creek full blood doctor does in four times. Two bloods makes two talents. Two bloods has more swifter solid good sense. I is one of them."[46]

Defined on the most literal level of blood ties, Black Indians were Indians as well as Blacks. Additionally, beyond this literal interpretation, Black people could become Indian through adoption. The experience of Molly, a Black slave adopted into a Cherokee clan, points to the ways that racial categories were malleable in Native communities. Molly was purchased in the late 1700s by a White man named Sam Dent who had been an Indian trader in Cherokee territory. Dent gave Molly to the Deer clan as retribution for having beaten to death his Cherokee wife, a Deer clan member. The Deer clan accepted Molly as a family member in place of the deceased woman and gave her the name Chickaua.[47]

Molly lived with her new family as a free woman until her liberty was challenged in 1833 by the White daughter of Sam Dent's associate, who claimed ownership of Molly and her son, Cunestuta (or Isaac Tucker). The Deer clan refused to give Molly and Isaac up to the agents who had been sent to retrieve them. Instead, clan members challenged the White claimant, whose name was Molly Hightower, before the Cherokee Supreme Court. They urged the "Council and authorities of the Cherokee nation" to protect Molly and her son, insisting: "[We] ask and require of our Council and headmen for assistance and for Council to resist this oppression and legal wrong attempted to be practiced on our Brother and Sister by the Hightower in leasing into slavery two of whom have ever been considered native cherokee [sic]. We feel that the attempt is one of cruel greavance [sic]."[48] In this document, the petitioners refer to Molly and Cunestuta as "brother and sister" and "native Cherokees" and argue that as adoptees into the Deer clan, the former Black slaves were now Cherokee citizens. The Cherokee Supreme Court agreed and protected the mother and son's status as Cherokees. In the words of historian William McLoughlin, the court concluded that "the slave, Molly, had become a Cherokee, had always been treated as a Cherokee, and still retained the rights of Cherokee citizenship by virtue of her adoption into the Deer clan, regardless of her race, complexion, or ancestry. By this same right, her son was also a Cherokee citizen."[49]

THE WAY IT IS: BLACK INDIAN WOMEN IN SLAVERY

I was a Cherokee slave and now I am a Cherokee freedwoman, and besides that I am a quarter Cherokee my own self. And this is the way it is.

Sarah Wilson, WPA Interview

As evidenced by the customs of Native kinship systems, the accounts of Black Indian slaves, and the outcome of a representative Native court case, Black Indians were Indians. When taken as a presupposition, this conclusion opens up new questions in the study of Native American history. Take, for instance, the history of Native women in the United States – a topic that has been neglected within the broader field of Native American studies. Scholars like Bea Medicine, Patricia Albers, Theda Perdue, and Nancy Shoemaker have addressed this absence in their own work on Native women. Anthropologist Patricia Albers points out that attention to the Native American past has focused on men, particularly chiefs and warriors. She argues that "native women rarely appear" in historical writings and are "conspicuous by their absence."[50] Laura Klein and Lillian Ackerman make a similar case, asserting that the textures and meanings of

Indian women's lives are left unexplored in ethnographic works: "Silence surrounds the lives of Native North American Women. . . . The wives, sisters, and mothers of Native nations do appear in traditional ethnographies but only where they are expected, and the meanings of their lives are left to the readers' imagination."[51]

In addition to the lack of attention to Native women, there is the equally problematic issue of sparse and compromised sources for research. Historian Nancy Shoemaker explicates the problem of locating reliable sources for Native women's history. Particularly in colonial and early America, records were kept by White men who, if they noticed Native women at all, viewed them through a Eurocentric and masculinist lens that did not allow for clear vision of Native women's experience. Shoemaker explains: "From Columbus's initial descriptions of 'India' up through the twentieth century, most of the available written records have been produced by Euro-American men – explorers, traders, missionaries, and government policymakers. . . . Historical accounts of Indian women usually depict them as 'squaw drudges,' beasts of burden bowed down with overwork and spousal oppression, or as 'Indian princesses,' voluptuous and promiscuous objects of white and Indian men's sexual desire."[52] As Theda Perdue argues, even when White men were intimate and careful observers, they could not accurately describe Native women's lives. Perdue notes that "male European observers had virtually no access to the private lives of women or to women's culture. Even those who married Native women usually had only scant insight into the most basic matters."[53]

The historical experience of Native women has been difficult to unearth, even for scholars who are versed in and committed to the subject. Presupposing that Black Indians are Indians has the potential to reveal new sources of information for this crucial work. A number of Black Indian women lived as slaves in the American colonies and the United States. Thus themes and arguments that scholars of Black women's history have explored in their studies of slave women can now be read as intersecting with Native women's history. Topics like sexual abuse, breeding, and physical brutality, key in the experience of Black slave women, now become meaningful and illuminating in the study of Indian women's lives. More, the firsthand experience of Black Indian women as recorded in slave interviews and narratives is an untapped source of primary material for Native women's history. As personal accounts that delve into the everyday happenings and key issues in the lives of a specific set of Native women, these narratives are valuable and rare.

For instance, slave interviews reveal that the threat of rape clouded the lives of Black Indian women, as it did for all enslaved Black women. As scholars of Native women's history address the misrepresentation of Native women's sexuality and the particularities of culturally specific understandings of sex, they might broaden their studies by attending to the issue of sexual abuse in Black Indian women's experience. In one interview, former slave Hannah Travis painfully recounts her mother's abuse. The daughter of a "full blooded Indian" woman and a Black French man, Travis's mother worked in the kitchen of her master and mistress.[54] The inhumane treatment she endured is apparent in the punishment she received if she missed a spot while washing the dishes. Her master would "make her drink the old dirty dishwater [and] whip her if she didn't drink it."[55] In addition, Hannah Travis's mother was raped by her master, Hannah's father. Hannah Travis says of this incident: "I hate my father. He was white. I never did have no use for him. . . . He was my mother's master. My mother was just forced. I hate him."[56]

Ellen Cragin, the daughter of a Black woman and Indian man, explains that her father was conceived during a period when her enslaved grandmother had run away: "My father was an Indian. Way back in the dark days, his mother ran away, and when she came up, that's what she come with – a little Indian boy. They called him 'Waw-hoo'che.'" Cragin continues: "They used to call me 'Waw-hoo'che' and 'the Red-Headed Indian Brat.' I got into a fight once with my mistress' daughter on account of that."[57] The "dark days" of slavery were riddled with violence in the experience of this young Black Indian girl. She saw her mother forced to breed for the master and repeatedly witnessed her mother being whipped. While a child, Cragin watched as her pregnant mother was beaten with a technique that was developed to protect the valuable offspring of slave women while brutally punishing the women themselves. The master or overseer would dig a hole for the protection of the woman's extended belly, while leaving her back and hips exposed.[58] Cragin recounts: "One day, Tom Polk [her master] hit my mother. That was before she ran away. He hit her because she didn't pick the required amount of cotton. . . . I don't know how many times he hit her. I was small. . . . I went to see. And they had her down. She was stout, and they had dug a hole in the ground to put her belly in. I never did get over that."[59] Cragin says further of her master: "He would have children by a nigger woman and then have them by her daughter." In an effort to protect her mother, Cragin once took up arms: "I went out one day and got a gun. I don't know whose gun it was. I said to myself 'If you whip my mother today, I am going to shoot you.' I didn't know where the gun belonged. My oldest sister told me to take it and set it by the door, and I did it."[60]

Mamie Thompson, born after emancipation, described the life of her enslaved mother. Thompson's mother was "mixed with Cherokee Indian and Negro," resulting from her father's status as "a full blood Indian."[61] When she resisted the sexual advances of a White overseer, she was placed on the auction block: "Master Redman had her in the field working. The overseer was a white man. He tried to take her down and carry on with her . . . He was mad cause he couldn't overpower her. Master Redman got her in the kitchen to whoop her with a cowhide; she told him she would kill him; she got a stick. He let her out and they came to buy her – a Negro trader."[62] Thompson's mother was later recovered and brought home by her mistress.

Sarah Wilson, the woman whose words begin this section of the essay, was a Black-Cherokee slave owned by a White-Cherokee family. Her story is both illuminating and compelling in the ways that it details the experience of one Black Indian girl and indicts that girl's own Cherokee relatives for their cruelty. Sarah Wilson's master, whom she describes as "a devil on this earth," was a White man married to a Cherokee woman.[63] The couple's son was Wilson's father. Though Wilson does not describe the sexual encounter between her African American mother and the master's son, it is probable that her mother was forced. Wilson says of her father, "Young Master Ned was a devil too."[64] She also reports that her master practiced breeding and sold female slaves who did not have babies. Wilson describes her mistress, who was also her grandmother, as being equally harsh: "Old Master wasn't the only hellion either. Old Mistress just as bad, and she took most of her wrath out hitting us children all the time."[65] Wilson reveals that she learned from her Black grandmother the reason for the mistress's venom: "When I was eight years old, Old Mistress died, and Grandmammy told me why Old Mistress picked on me so. She told me about me being half Mister Ned's blood."[66] Clearly, Sarah Wilson's experience adds another dimension to the meaning of blood ties for Black Indians. The depravities and ideologies of slavery, when adopted by Native people, had the potential to warp kinship ties between Indians and Black Indian relatives. Being part Cherokee made Sarah Wilson a threat to her Cherokee grandmother. And Wilson only received minimal protection from her father. In much the same way as White owners who fathered Black babies, he casually defended her against her grandmother's beatings. Wilson reports that on these occasions her father would say, with a laugh, "Let her alone, she got big blood in her."[67]

These accounts and others of sexual abuse and violence reveal the ways that Black Indian women experienced slavery. They were raped, beaten, and threatened, and their children witnessed their vulnerability and violation. Whole families were affected, and sometimes implicated, by the abuse of their relatives and the inhumanity of enslavement. As the experiences of women who were Indian as well as Black, these happenings have a place in the history of Native American women. In the early 1980s, pathbreaking slavery studies began to ask how the particularities of an interrelated gendered and raced experience shaped Black women's lives.[68] With attention to the untapped sources of slave women's interviews and narratives, scholars of Native women's history might now ask: How did Black Indian women experience slavery *as Native women*? What new issues if any arose out of the complex configuration of this specific slave experience? Did Black Indian women understand their enslavement and resistance in ways that were culturally specific? Did they locate their experience within broader tribal and Native group histories? Did they develop biracial identities and bicultural communities? Historian Nell Irvin Painter has observed in her essay "Soul Murder and Slavery: Toward a Fully-Loaded Cost Accounting" that the prevalence of violence and sexual abuse during slavery indelibly stained Black women's lives.[69] Certainly, this history has shaped Black women's ideas about themselves and their sexuality, even in the present day. As historian Paula Giddings has argued, "The issues of gender and sexuality have been made so painful to us in our history that we have largely hidden them from ourselves. . . . Consequently, they remain largely unresolved."[70] Might similar arguments about sexual abuse and the persistence of historical memory be made for Native women, once this aspect of Black Indian women's experience is taken into account? Or does the distinctive historical shape of Native women's experience, when complicated by Black Indian women's voices, offer fresh paradigms for understanding both Black and Native women's history? These questions and more emerge when we tell a story of slavery with Indians in it and recognize Black Indians as Indians.

BLACK INDIAN IDENTITIES:
CONTRADICTIONS AND CONCLUSIONS

Constructing a history of slavery that includes Native people contributes to a richer picture of the American, Native American, and African American pasts. But a richer picture is at the same time more complicated, characterized by contradictions and contestations of the familiar and comfortable. The narrative of Cora Gillam, the former slave from Mississippi whose description of "Uncle Tom" introduces this essay, exemplifies some of the contradictions inherent in this endeavor. I presented Gillam's words at two junctures in this chapter – at the start to illustrate dual images of "Uncle Tom" and in the body to demonstrate the importance of attending to Black and Native kinship networks. However, I deferred until now a discussion of the ways that Gillam's representation of her uncle raises intriguing and challenging questions about her representation of a Black Indian identity.

As Laura Lovett has demonstrated, African Americans' invocation of Native ancestry is a motif in the WPA narratives. Lovett defines these recurring rhetorical moments as attempts on the part of interviewees to resist the hierarchies of segregation by muddying the waters of racial categorization. In other words, interviewees challenged fixed notions of biological blackness and Black inferiority by highlighting Native American family legacies. Lovett posits that in referencing Native kin, interviewees enacted "genealogical performances" that operated as ideological and political disruptions of the racial status quo.[71] Gillam's "genealogical performance" traces Native heritage to contextualize her own personal strengths. But even as Gillam's narrative challenges fixed racial categories, it privileges Indianness over Blackness, imbuing Indian "blood" with an essentialized array of special qualities. Gillam's account lends specificity to the history of Black Indians in slavery. At the same time, it reveals the contested issues of racial hierarchy and racial prestige with which Black Indian slaves and their descendants have wrestled.

Cora Gillam is a confident and purposeful interviewee. She aims to shape her own story and informs the interviewer of this intent when she interrupts the framework the interviewer has imposed by exclaiming: "Wait a minute lady." Gillam explains that she is the child of a Black-Cherokee woman and White man. The mixed-race aspect of her identity, particularly her Indianness, is central to the story she tells about herself. She explains early in the interview when asked if her father was a slave: "No ma'am, oh no indeedy, my father was not a slave. Can't you tell by me that he was white?" She goes on to explain her racial identity further:

My grandmother – on mother's side, was full blooded Cherokee. She came from North Carolina. In early days my mother and her brothers and sisters were stolen from their home in North Carolina and taken to Mississippi and sold for slaves. You know the Indians could follow trails better than other kind of folks, and she tracked her children down and stayed in the south. My mother was only part-Negro; so was her brother, uncle Tom. He seemed all Indian. You know, the Cherokees were peaceable Indians, until you got them mad. Then they was the fiercest fighters of any tribes.[72]

At this point in the narrative, Gillam directs her attention to the valiant story of her uncle Tom, devoting considerable time to chronicling his accomplishments:

Now I want to tell you about my uncle Tom. Like I said, he was half-Indian. But the Negro part didn't show hardly any. There was something about uncle Tom that made both white and black be afraid of him. They say uncle Tom was the best reader, white or black, for miles. That was what got him in trouble. Slaves was not allowed to read. They didn't want them to know that freedom was coming. No ma'am! . . . That Indian in uncle Tom made him not scared of anybody. He had a newspaper with latest war news and gathered a crowd of slaves to read them when peace was coming. White men say it done to get uprising among slaves. A crowd of white gather and take uncle Tom to jail. Twenty of them said they would beat him, each man, till they so tired they can't lay on one more lick. If he still alive, then they hang him. . . . The Indian in uncle Tom rose. Strength – big extra strength seemed to come to him. First man what opened that door, he leaped on him and laid him out. No white man could stand against him in that Indian fighting spirit. They was scared of him. He almost tore that jailhouse down, lady. Yes he did.[73]

Gillam's account of her uncle's bravery is certainly moving. But what does it mean that her uncle "seemed all Indian" and that "the Negro part didn't show hardly any"? Gillam does not describe Tom physically, and it seems that these references reflect Tom's character rather than his phenotype. Gillam's description of the Indian "rising" in Tom when he is forced to defend himself against a lynch mob suggests that she sees her uncle's Indianness as the source and encapsulation of his strength. Like a genie in the bottle of embodied Blackness, Tom's Indianness is invested with a power and magnificence that can be conjured in times of need. More, the strength that Tom derives from his Indianness stands in implicit opposition to his Black heritage, which Gillam never designates as the source of positive or special qualities. Laura Lovett has argued insightfully that WPA interviewees invoked (often stereotyped) Indian characteristics to demonstrate a legacy of resistance in their families. In the case of Gillam and others, however, this rhetorical act of protest can simultaneously be read as an act of negation, coding Black Indian resistance as solely Indian and thereby rendering invisible an accompanying tradition of Black resistance.

This reading of Cora Gillam's narrative challenges more celebratory views of Black Indian historical identities and Black and Native relations. However, the project of reimagining the history of slavery in America, of weaving Native experiences into that history, brings with it the responsibility of complicating our findings. Just as the popular version of slavery is incomplete, a version in which Indians and Black Indians appear is like-wise unfinished unless we continually push the boundaries of our knowledge and expectations. Constructing a complex story of American slavery, and of Black and Native relations, means exploring what is disconcerting and contradictory, even as we seek what is liberatory and luminous.

NOTES

1. Harriet Beecher Stowe, *Uncle Tom's Cabin* (1852; reprint, New York: Signet, 1966), 440.

2. Jane Tompkins, *Sensational Designs: The Cultural Work of American Fiction, 1790–1860* (New York: Oxford University Press, 1985).

3. Interview with Cora Gillam in Works Progress Administration: Oklahoma Writers Project, *Slave Narratives: A Folk History of Slavery in the United States from Interviews with Former Slaves* (Washington DC: Government Printing Office, 1932 [microfilm]), 28. I am grateful to Patrick Minges for compiling and sharing many of the WPA interviews used in this essay. The WPA interviews, structured by specific questions, reveal details of everyday slave life such as diet, housing, work, child-birth and childrearing, methods of punishment, and degree of mobility. While rich as source material, these interviews must be read closely and critically, as many of them were conducted by White workers, creating a dynamic that led some inter-viewees to mask their actual feelings about slavery. Perhaps the most reliable approach to reconstructing a picture of slave women's experience from these inter-views is a comparative analysis that teases out common themes and shared experi-ences across a range of interviews. This type of reading can glean major aspects of slave women's experience without wholly depending upon the complete veracity and forthrightness of single interviewees. For more on the use of the WPA mate-rials, see Melvina Johnson Young, "Exploring the WPA Narratives: Finding the Voices of Black Women and Men," in *Theorizing Black Feminisms*, ed. Stanlie James and Abena Busia (New York: Routledge, 1993), 55–74.

4. Stowe, *Uncle Tom*, 32.

5. James Walvin, *Questioning Slavery* (New York: Routledge, 1996), 1.

6. I borrow this phrasing from Colin Calloway, who commonly describes his historical work as "writing American history with Indians in it."

7. John Hope Franklin, *Race and History: Selected Essays 1938–1988* (Baton Rouge: Louisiana State University Press, 1989), 71.

8. Vine Deloria Jr., *Custer Died for Your Sins, an Indian Manifesto* (1969; reprint, Norman: University of Oklahoma Press, 1988), 7.

9. Jack Forbes, *Africans and Native Americans: The Language of Race and the Evolution of Red-Black Peoples* (Urbana: University of Illinois Press, 1993), 190.

10. Ronald Takaki, *A Different Mirror: A History of Multicultural America* (Boston: Little, Brown, 1993), 7.

11. Michael Omi and Howard Winant, *Racial Formation in the United States: From the 1960s to the 1990s* (New York: Routledge, 1994), 62.

12. Omi and Winant, *Racial Formation*.

13. Edmund Morgan, *American Slavery, American Freedom: The Ordeal of Colonial Virginia* (New York: W. W. Norton, 1974).

14. Quoted in Morgan, *American Slavery*, 329.

15. Morgan, *American Slavery*, 308.

16. Morgan, *American Slavery*, 329.

17. Winthrop Jordan, *The White Man's Burden: Historical Origins of Racism in the United States* (London: Oxford University Press, 1974), 48. See also Jordan, *White Over Black: American Attitudes Toward the Negro 1550–1812* (New York: W. W. Norton, 1968).

18. Jordan, *White Man's Burden*, 46; Walvin, *Questioning Slavery*, 75.

19. Walvin, *Questioning Slavery*, 4–5, 10.

20. Ira Berlin, *Many Thousands Gone: The First Two Centuries of Slavery in North America* (Cambridge: Harvard University Press, 1998), 145.

21. Interview with Mary Allen Darrows in Works Progress Administration, *Slave Narratives*, 95.

22. Interview with Sweetie Ivery Wagoner in T. Lindsay Baker and Julie Baker, eds. *The WPA Oklahoma Slave Narratives* (Norman: University of Oklahoma Press, 1996), 442.

23. J. Leitch Wright, *The Only Land They Knew: American Indians in the Old South* (Lincoln: University of Nebraska Press, 1981), 126.

24. The "Five Civilized Tribes" was a label assigned to the Cherokees, Creeks, Choctaws, Chickasaws, and Seminoles by White officials and reformers in the nineteenth century.

25. Charles Hudson, *The Southeastern Indians* (Knoxville: University of Tennessee Press, 1976), 193; Duane Champagne, "Institutional and Cultural Order in Early Cherokee Society: A Sociological Interpretation," *Journal of Cherokee Studies* 15 (1990): 3–26, 12.

26. William Gilbert, "Eastern Cherokee Social Organization," in *Social Anthropology of North American Tribes*, ed. Fred Eggan (Chicago: University of Chicago Press, 1937), 296.

27. Champagne, "Institutional and Cultural Order," 11; Hudson, *Southeastern Indians*, 192.

28. Melville Herskovits, *The American Negro: A Study in Race Crossing* (New York: Knopf, 1928).

29. Forbes, *Africans and Native Americans*, 270.

30. Slaveholding and a related acceptance of racial hierarchy among tribes of

the Southeast meant that this rule of thumb concerning kinship was sometimes challenged. Mixed-race Black-Native people could be legally defined as belonging outside of the tribal group. However, the majority of Native people ignored exclusionary laws against Blacks and continued to view Black Indian relatives as kin.

31. In *Africans and Native Americans*, Jack Forbes details the terminology that was developed for racial classification.

32. *Virginia Gazette*, 15 July 1773, 3. I am grateful to Alex Bontemps for compiling and sharing his collection of newspaper advertisements describing Black Indian slaves.

33. *Virginia Gazette*, 19 July 1776, 4.

34. *Maryland Gazette*, 21 May 1752, 3.

35. *Maryland Gazette*, 1 February 1749, 3.

36. *Virginia Gazette*, 11 November 1773, 2.

37. *Virginia Gazette*, 26 November 1772, 3.

38. There are examples in which slave owners describe runaway slaves as "half Indian" or "mustee," a term used to designate people of Black and Indian descent; however, the majority of the ads I reviewed did not clearly designate Black Indians. In an example of an advertisement that is clear, the subscriber seeks "a half Indian fellow who calls himself Jack Brown." *Virginia Gazette*, 10 March 1774, 3.

39. Ira Berlin concludes that the danger of recognizing a Black Indian person's Indianness became apparent in the 1790s, when a new Spanish governor of Louisiana showed a measure of support for free people of color. In response to this chink in the institutionalized armor of state oppression of colored people, mixed-race Black Indians sued the colony for their freedom on the grounds that they were descended from legally free Indians. Louisiana planters responded venomously, forcing the governor to abandon his alliance with free people of color. Berlin, *Many Thousands Gone*, 352–53.

40. The Bureau of Indian Affairs generally defines this ratio as one full-blood Native grandparent out of four, though individual tribes have varying ways of determining citizenship.

41. Circe Sturm, "Blood Politics, Racial Classification, and Cherokee National Identity: The Trials and Tribulations of the Cherokee Freedmen," this volume.

42. See also Celia Naylor-Ojurongbe, "Contested Common Ground: African American Slaves and Freedpeople in the Cherokee Nation, Indian Territory, 1838–1907" (Ph.D. diss. in progress, Duke University).

43. Interview with Sweetie Ivery Wagoner in Baker and Baker, WPA *Oklahoma Slave Narratives*, 443.

44. Interview with R. C. Smith in Baker and Baker, WPA *Oklahoma Slave Narratives*, 398.

45. Interview with Cornelius Neely Nave in Baker and Baker, WPA *Oklahoma Slave Narratives*, 301.

46. Quoted in Sigmund Sameth, "Creek Negroes: A Study of Race Relations" (master's thesis, University of Oklahoma, 1940), 62.

47. Cherokee Supreme Court Docket, 1833, Tennessee State Library and Archives. For additional accounts of Molly's case, see William McLoughlin, *Cherokee Renascence in the New Republic* (Princeton NJ: Princeton University Press, 1986), 347; and Rennard Strickland, *Fire and the Spirits: Cherokee Law from Clan to Court* (Norman: University of Oklahoma Press, 1977), 54.

48. Cherokee Supreme Court, 1833.

49. McLoughlin, *Renascence*, 347.

50. Patricia Albers and Bea Medicine, eds., *The Hidden Half: Studies of Plains Indian Women* (New York: University Press of America, 1983), 4.

51. Laura Klein and Lillian Ackerman, eds., *Women and Power in Native North America* (Norman: University of Oklahoma Press, 1995), 3.

52. Nancy Shoemaker ed., *Negotiators of Change: Historical Perspectives on Native American Women* (New York: Routledge, 1995), 2–3.

53. Perdue, *Cherokee Women*, 4.

54. Interview with Hannah Travis in Works Progress Administration, *Slave Narratives*, 350.

55. Interview with Hannah Travis, 351.

56. Interview with Hannah Travis, 352.

57. Interview with Ellen Cragin in Works Progress Administration, *Slave Narratives*, 42, 43.

58. Historian Angela Davis discusses this method of punishment in the first chapter of her book, *Women, Race and Class* (New York: Vintage Books, 1983).

59. Interview with Ellen Cragin, 44–45.

60. Interview with Ellen Cragin, 44–45.

61. Interview with Mamie Thompson in Works Progress Administration, *Slave Narratives*, 319.

62. Interview with Mamie Thompson, 319.

63. Interview with Sarah Wilson, 493.

64. Interview with Sarah Wilson, 495.

65. Interview with Sarah Wilson, 494.

66. Interview with Sarah Wilson, 495.

67. Interview with Sarah Wilson, 495.

68. Studies in the 1980s by Deborah Gray White, Angela Davis, bell hooks, Paula Giddings, Jacqueline Jones, Elizabeth Fox-Genovese, Catherine Clinton, and others were the first to explore major themes that apply widely to the experiences of Black slave women. See Deborah Gray White, *Ar'n't I a Woman: Female Slaves in the Plantation South* (New York: W. W. Norton, 1985); Davis, *Women, Race and Class*; Jacqueline Jones, *Labor of Love, Labor of Sorrow* (New York: Vintage, 1986); bell hooks, *Ain't I a Woman: Black Women and Feminism* (Boston:

South End Press, 1981); Elizabeth Fox-Genovese, "Strategies and Forms of Resistance: Focus on Slave Women in the United States," in *In Resistance: Studies in African, Caribbean and Afro-American History*, ed. Gary Okihiro, (Amherst: University of Massachusetts Press, 1986); Fox-Genovese, *Within the Plantation Household* (Chapel Hill: University of North Carolina Press, 1988); Catherine Clinton, *The Plantation Mistress: Woman's World in the Old South* (New York: Pantheon, 1982).

69. Nell Irvin Painter, "Soul Murder and Slavery: Toward a Fully Loaded Cost Accounting," in *U.S. History as Women's History: New Feminist Essays*, ed. Linda Kerber, Alice Kessler-Harris, and Kathryn Sklar (Chapel Hill: University of North Carolina Press, 1995), 125–46.

70. Paula Giddings, "The Last Taboo," in *Race-ing Justice, Engendering Power*, ed. Toni Morrison (New York, Pantheon, 1992), 441–70, 442.

71. Lovett, "'African and Cherokee by Choice': Race and Resistance under Legalized Segregation," this volume.

72. Interview with Cora Gillam, 27–28.

73. Interview with Cora Gillam, 28.

6. "Born and Raised among These People, I Don't Want to Know Any Other"

Slaves' Acculturation in Nineteenth-Century Indian Territory

CELIA E. NAYLOR-OJURONGBE

Questions concerning interactions between African Americans and Native Americans emerge in the pages of many articles and books on slavery within Native American nations. For the most part, though, scholars who have described Native American owners and their slaves in nineteenth-century Indian Territory have presented a limited analysis of slaves' views of themselves, outside of the usual descriptions regarding the conditions of servitude. One vital issue that is often ignored or scarcely addressed by historians concerns what could be described as acculturation or transculturation between African American slaves and Native American owners.[1] In their Works Progress Administration (WPA) Oklahoma interviews, ex-slaves explicate their processes of acculturation within nineteenth-century Native American communities based on their racial, cultural, and national identities. Ex-slaves of combined African and Native American descent portrayed their "mixed-blood" racial identity as a way of emphasizing their cultural connection to Native Americans.[2] Slaves of African descent, who did and did not identify themselves as "mixed-blood," also presented their cultural ties to Native American nations in terms of specific cultural markers – namely clothing, language, food, and knowledge of herbal remedies. Moreover, after emancipation, recently freed slaves in Indian Territory reconstructed their identities as freedpeople by creating and exhibiting a national identity and nationalism in connection with specific Native American nations.

BLOOD AS A BODY OF EVIDENCE

Recent research has generated an intensive discussion centering on self-identification and self-consciousness and complementary notions of group identification and group consciousness, especially as these dimensions pertain to persons exhibiting biological (read: blood) and cultural connections to African and Native American heritages.[3] During the WPA Oklahoma interviews, ex-slaves of African and Native American descent spoke openly about their "mixed-blood." At his home in Gibson Station, Oklahoma, eighty-year-old Milton Starr reminisced about his life in his 1938 WPA interview. Starr stated that he was born "right in [his] master's house" on 24 February 1858. Starr was born in the Flint District of the Cherokee Nation on the farm of Cherokee Jerry Starr, relative of renegade Tom Starr. Living among the Cherokees during his childhood, Milton Starr remembered that though he was born a slave, he "was not treated like other slaves and [his] folks never told [him] anything about slavery." He inherited preferential treatment partly because, as he stated, "half-breed Cherokee" Jerry Starr "was my master and father."[4] After the Civil War, Starr did not leave the Cherokee Nation. Instead, young Milton Starr decided to remain with his father and his stepmother, Millie, especially since they "never whipped me, always treat like I was one of the family, because I was."[5]

Although recognizing that he was treated differently because of his connection to Jerry Starr, Milton Starr did not indicate any special treatment toward his mother, Jane Coursey. His mother, a slave from Tennessee, was "picked up by the Starrs when they left that country with the rest of the Cherokee Indians. My mother wasn't bought, just stole by them Indians."[6] Neither born nor raised in Indian Territory, Jane Coursey was what other interviewees called a "crossland Negro."[7] Although Milton Starr favorably described his master and father, Jane Coursey may not have embraced such positive feelings about Jerry Starr. As Milton Starr recalled, when his mother was freed she returned to Tennessee. Like so many other recently freed people, Coursey's return to Tennessee may have been motivated by her desire to reconnect with family from whom she had been separated. Moreover, her interactions with the Cherokees, and with Jerry Starr particularly, may have influenced her decision to leave the Cherokee Nation. Perhaps the Starrs did not treat her like family, or perhaps she did not desire to be part of their family.

Cornelius Neely Nave, who, like Milton Starr, was born and raised in the Cherokee Nation, also explained his blood connection to the Cherokees. Since he was born in 1868, after the Civil War, Nave clarified that what he "knows about slave times is what my pappa told me." As his mother died when he was only two years old, Nave's interview focused on his life and his recollection of his father's stories concerning life in the

Cherokee Nation. Nave's father, Charley Nave, was owned by Cherokee Henry Nave.[8] Cornelius Nave remembered "setting in the yard watching the river (Grand River) go by, and the Indians go by. All Indians lived around there, the real colored settlement was four mile [*sic*] from us."[9] Living mostly among Cherokees, Cornelius Nave "wasn't scared of them Indians for pappa always told me his master, Henry Nave, was his own father; that make me part Indian and the reason my hair is long, straight and black like a horse mane."[10]

Cornelius Nave's interview presents the generational separation between Cherokee ex-slaves/freedpeople and the descendants of Cherokee freedpeople. Even though Cornelius Nave recalled stories his father and others told him about slavery, his stories of slavery are not based on his own personal experiences. Partly because of this generational distance from slavery, Cornelius Nave is able to speak fondly of his childhood during post–Civil War times in the Cherokee Nation. Moreover, Nave's statement regarding his visible blood connection to the Cherokees reinforces his overall connection to the Cherokee Nation.

In addition to the Cherokees, other nations in Indian Territory included slaves and freedpeople of African and Native American descent. Some historians have argued that Choctaws and Chickasaws felt an "aversion" toward African Americans.[11] However, the interviews of freedwoman Peggy McKinney Brown and her son, Charley Moore Brown, illustrate a different reality.[12] Peggy Brown stated that her master, Jesse McKinney, was "one half Choctaw blood." Yet the connection between Brown and her master was not solely that of a slave and a master. During her 1937 interview, Brown disclosed that Jesse McKinney was "her father and also her master."[13] She did not discover that McKinney was her father, however, until he released his slaves after the Civil War. Peggy Brown described her master/father as "a very hard master. He had no regard for himself or any of the slave women, especially if they were of pleasant looks. He did not hesitate to bring half-breed children into the world."[14]

Peggy Brown's son, Charley Moore Brown, did not speak about his mother's family at all; instead, he described living in the Choctaw Nation and his personal interaction with the other residents in Choctaw territory.[15] In his interview, Charley Brown identified himself as a "freedman citizen of the Choctaw Tribe, quarter blood Choctaw Indian and three quarter negro."[16] Not only was Charley Brown part-Choctaw, but he was also born and raised in the Choctaw Nation where, he stated, "there were hardly any real white people." Charley Brown thought the "Choctaws were reasonable to get along with." In fact, he believed "if you treated the

Indian in this country good he would always be your friend and would help you anytime he was able to."[17] Unlike comments made by his mother, Charley Brown painted a positive portrait of the Choctaws with whom he interacted in the post–Civil War era.

Though ex-slaves like Milton Starr, Cornelius Nave, and Charley Brown were raised among Native American kin, others recalled more tenuous connections to such relatives. In their WPA Oklahoma interviews, five freedpeople only briefly mentioned that one of their parents or grandparents was of Native American descent without expanding upon that point.[18] Although the majority of ex-slaves who referred to their mixed racial heritage identified whether they were Black-Cherokee, Black-Choctaw, or Black-Creek, former slave Lucinda Vann made no specific references to her Indianness. While discussing her experiences during the Civil War, she simply stated that "a bunch of us who was part Indian and part colored" left the Cherokee Nation and headed to Mexico.[19]

Although Vann limited her description of her racial ancestry, she nonetheless provided information on various dimensions of life on one of the largest plantations in the Cherokee Nation. Intertwined in her description of life on Joe Vann's plantation, Lucinda Vann explained that with "five hundred slaves on that plantation," the workers were divided into different classes.[20] Thus "the slaves who worked in the big house was the first class. Next, came the carpenters, yard men, blacksmiths, race-horse men, steamboat men and like that. The low class work in the fields." Vann noted that she was not the only member of her family working as a house servant; her "mother, grandmother, aunt Maria and cousin Clara, all worked in the big house."[21] Vann's categorization of house slaves as "first class" and field slaves as the lowest class is certainly not a new idea in the history of slavery in the United States. However, Lucinda Vann implied a correlation between the fact that she and her people were "part Indian and part colored" and their position in the big house. Vann thus associated her "mixed-blood" to her social status and class on the Vann plantation. Being "part Indian and part colored" factored into her placement within the hierarchical construction of the slave society on the Vann plantation.

For the most part, ex-slaves who claimed Native American ancestry in their interviews did so without implying any correlation to class or status. It is feasible, however, that by merely stating their blood connection to Native Americans they believed they were also claiming their association to a group of slaves whose "mixed-blood" qualified them as persons of a higher social status and class than slaves of African descent, who had no identifiable or alleged Native American ancestry.

African American ex-slaves living in Oklahoma clearly invoked the notion of "blood" during their WPA interviews. A number of freedpeople of Native American and African American ancestry carefully detailed their blood associations to Native Americans.[22] The idea of "blood" has shaped the histories of both African Americans and Native Americans in the United States. Tribal or national affiliation often revolves around the question of blood quantum or the amount of Indian ancestry indicated in fractions.[23] Blood quanta have become inextricably linked to degrees of acculturation and assimilation. Thus it is not surprising that ex-slaves frequently articulated notions of blood as literally the "body of evidence" for their physical and biological identification with, and connection to, Native American nations.

CULTURAL PATHWAYS

Was "blood" the deciding factor linking African American ex-slaves to Native Americans in Indian Territory in the decades immediately before and after the Civil War? There were, however, ex-slaves born and raised in Indian Territory, living among Native Americans for all or a significant part of their lives, who closely identified themselves with Native Americans and their customs yet did not mention a "blood" connection.

An illuminating way to understand how such a nonbiological bond was forged and conceptualized is to cast the connection as an example of what A. Irving Hallowell calls the "phenomenon of transculturalization." Hallowell defines transculturalization as "the process whereby *individuals* under a variety of circumstances are temporarily or permanently detached from one group, enter the web of social relations that constitute another society, and come under the influence of its customs, ideas, and values to a greater or lesser degree."[24] The degree to which an individual undergoes transculturalization depends on a number of factors – "the age at which the process begins; the previous attitude toward the people of the second culture; length of residence; motivational factors; the nature of the roles played, and so on."[25] Cultural signs of acculturation or "Indianization" of enslaved African Americans occurred in nineteenth-century Indian Territory. In their WPA interviews, Oklahoma ex-slaves spoke of a number of ways that such acculturation took place.

Clothing

For some ex-slaves living in nineteenth-century Indian Territory, clothing represented one of the most visible signs of their cultural identification with Native Americans. Clothing often represents layers of cultural meaning and significance. It is not only a form of basic protection and adornment but also a form of self- and group expression.[26] Viewed as historical documents, "clothes always signify more than they appear to, like the words of a language which need to be translated and explained."[27] For Native American cultures, clothing has historically revealed social status, group membership, and spiritual connotations.[28]

Descriptions of slaves' clothing, as well as notions of what their clothing represented, appear in the WPA Oklahoma interviews. One hundred-year-old ex-slave Henry Clay presented one of the most telling descriptions of clothing worn by "Indianized" African American slaves. Although born in North Carolina, Clay lived in the Creek Nation, Indian Territory, for the majority of his adult life. Even so, he stated that he "never did get along good with these Creek slaves out here. . . . In fact I was afraid of these Creeks and always got off the road when I seen Creek negroes coming along." Clay explained that he could always identify them for "they would have red strings tied on their hats or something wild looking."[29] Henry Clay distinctly used clothing as a cultural marker that associated "Indianness" with "wildness." For Clay, the Creek slaves' affiliation with Creek Indians made Creek slaves look and dress "wild."[30] Clay's description of the "wild" nature of Creek slaves was also perhaps a way of distinguishing himself as different and possibly more "civilized" than those slaves owned by and associated with Creeks. In this instance, it is unclear what the red strings signified to the Creek slaves who wore them. It is possible that Creek slaves wore these items as markers of their distinctive Creekness and as a way of expressing their group identification with Creeks.[31]

Although Henry Clay used clothing to distinguish himself from Creek slaves, Sweetie Ivery Wagoner used clothing to reinforce her connection with Creeks. When Wagoner claimed that her father was a Creek slave and her mother was a slave of African descent, she emphasized that "my folks was part Indian alright; they wore blankets and breeches with fur around the bottoms."[32] Her statement concerning her father being a Creek slave and her people being "part Indian" verified her blood connection to the Creeks. For Wagoner, what her people wore served as the cultural link to her claimed Creek connection.

For "crossland" slaves, like Henry Clay, the type of clothing worn by Creek slaves represented one way of marking or identifying "natives" as different from himself and other "crossland" slaves. For Sweetie Ivery Wagoner and other "natives," the material manifestation and representation of what they perceived and identified as "Indian" clothing were instrumental to their personal claim to Native American heritage and to their individual and familial acculturation within Native American nations.

Language

Scholars have long recognized that African American slaves often served as interpreters for their Native American owners.[33] When Oklahoma ex-slaves discussed their connections to Native Americans, they also described their ability or their relatives' ability to speak a Native American language. Raised on the Taylor farm in the Cherokee Nation, Patsy Taylor Perryman mentioned that her mother, who had "always been with Mistress Judy Taylor," was "raised by the Indians and could talk Cherokee."[34] Perryman recalled "nobody around the place but Indians and negroes; I was a full grown girl before I ever saw a white man." Perryman's brother, Lewis, "married a full-blood Indian woman and they got lots of Indian children on their farm in the old Cherokee country around Caney Creek. He's just like an Indian, been with them so much, talks the Cherokee language and don't notice us negroes any more." Her brother decided to associate only with Native Americans exclusively because as he told his sister, he was "darn tired looking at negroes!"[35]

Like Patsy Perryman, Betty Robertson did not know a Native American tongue but asserted that those close to her had some knowledge of the Cherokee language. Robertson claimed that her "mammy was a Cherokee slave, and talked it good," and that "her husband was a Cherokee born negro, too, and when he got mad he forgit all the English he knowed." On the other hand, Robertson's father, who "come from across the water when he was a little boy, and was grown when old Master Joseph Vann bought him . . . never did learn to talk much Cherokee."[36] Robertson clearly described how her mother's and her husband's connection to the Cherokees and the Cherokee language, specifically being "native" Cherokee slaves, differed from her father's disconnection with the Cherokee language having been a "crossland" slave.

Not all ex-slaves who were born in Indian Territory and learned Native American languages when they were young continued to remember the languages. Ninety-five-year-old Henry Henderson was born on the Martin Vann plantation in the Cherokee Nation in 1843; he was raised on the Vann place for many years but then later lived among the Creeks. After he moved to the Creek Nation, he recalled that he "done forgot my Cherokee that I heard when I was young. I been living around with the Creeks so long that I picked up some of their words, like 'Lag-ashe' when they mean to set down or take a chair; 'Hum-buc-sha' is the call for meals or come eat; 'Pig-ne-dee' is the Creek way of saying good morning, and 'Car-a-she' is corn bread."[37] Half of the words Henry Henderson remembered were quite similar to the pronunciation of actual Creek words.[38]

Being raised among Creeks who primarily spoke their own language, ex-slave Lucinda Davis spoke only Creek when she was a little girl. She belonged to "a full-blood Creek Indian and . . . didn't know nothing but Creek talk long after de Civil War." Even though her mistress was "part white and knowed English talk . . . she never did talk it because none of de people talked it." Davis heard English sometimes, "but it sound like whole lot of wild shoat in de cedar brake scared at something."[39] While describing her master, Davis claimed that she did not know if her master had a "white name" as "lots of Upper Creeks didn't have no white name. Maybe he have another Indian name, too, because Tuskayahiniha mean 'head man warrior' in Creek, but dat what everybody call him and dat what de family call him too." She also informed the interviewer that they called her master's son "Istidji," which meant "little man" in Creek. All the slaves were called "Istilusti," which meant "Black man" in Creek.[40] Davis also recalled the Creek names and descriptions of particular dances.

Davis's recollection of Creek words was very similar to actual Creek words. "Tvsekvyv" sounded like the Creek words "Tvsekiybv" and "he-nehv," which mean "citizen" and "chief," respectively, and are pronounced "tasikaya hiniha."[41] "Istidji" was similar to "estuce," pronounced "istootsi," which means baby. The Creek word for "little man" is "estelotocke," pronounced "istilotoski."[42] Davis's word "Istilusti" is extremely similar to the Creek word for Black person, "estelvste," pronounced "istilasti."[43]

It is not surprising that the spelling was incorrect in both Henderson's and Davis's interviews, as the Creek alphabet is not the same as the English alphabet; many letters are pronounced differently in the two languages (the "v" in Creek sounds more like an English "a," and the Creek "e" sounds like an English "i").[44] Both Henderson and Davis remembered Creek words in their interviews. They did not simply call out random words and label them Creek; they actually remembered the words and recalled them as best they could for the interviewers. It is also possible that Henderson and Davis correctly pronounced the words and that the WPA interviewers incorrectly transcribed the words they heard during these interviews.

Mary Grayson, who was also born and raised in the Creek Nation and owned by Creeks, recalled, however, a more limited knowledge of the Creek language. Her master, Mose Perryman, as well as other Creek masters in the area, "talked English nearly all the time except when they were talking to Creeks who didn't talk good English, and we Negroes never did learn very good Creek."[45] Grayson "could always understand it, and can yet, a little, but I never did try to talk it much. Mammy and pappy used English to us all the time."[46] Grayson's claim that African Americans "never did learn very good Creek" is challenged by Henry Clay's recollection that "them Creek negroes was so funny to talk to." Clay's comment may have regarded not only the manner in which Creek slaves spoke but also the language they used to express themselves. It is possible that Creek slaves, as well as slaves of the Cherokee, Choctaw, and Chickasaw Nations, created a kind of patois or creole based on a mixture of a Native American language and the English language.

Whether ex-slaves became proficient in Native American languages or created a patois or creole infused with Native American words, they used the spoken word as another means of expressing their cultural connection to Native Americans and their inclusion within Native American nations. Ex-slaves' abilities to communicate in Native American languages symbolize an additional dimension of acculturation. Although representing a discernible marker of cultural identity, the use of language is not one limited to communication solely; language also embodies other aspects of culture, namely mores, values, oral history, and tradition.

Food and Herbal Medicine

Eating food represents more than physical sustenance; it involves a complex "eating culture."[47] What people eat, who prepares meals, how meals are prepared, and how people take in their food are all aspects of a group's cultural identity. Within many traditions, including Native American cultures, food has represented one of the symbolic markers of cultural and national identity.

Ex-slaves responsible for preparing meals presented detailed gendered accounts of the hunting of animals and the preparation of specific Native American meals. Such recollections also reveal their connection to a significant aspect of Native American culture and tradition. By speaking about specific processes of preparing Native American meals, Oklahoma ex-slaves served as cultural agents through which Native American traditions are remembered and passed on. Indeed, a number of ex-slaves spoke of Native American meals as their own. Kiziah Love, an ex-slave of "full-blood" Choctaw Frank Colbert, briefly described the preparation of certain Choctaw meals.[48] She explained that "one of *our* choicest dishes was 'Tom Pashofa', an Indian dish. We'd take corn and beat it in a mortar with a pestle. They took out the husks with a riddle and a fanner. The riddle was a kind of a sifter. When it was beat fine enough to go through the riddle we'd put it in a pot and cook it with fresh pork or beef. We cooked *our* bread in a Dutch oven or in the ashes."[49]

During her interview, Choctaw freedwoman Polly Colbert also discussed various Choctaw dishes.[50] She recalled cooking "all sorts of Indian dishes: Tom-fuller, pashofa, hickory-nut grot, Tom-budha, ash-cakes, and pound cakes besides vegetables and meat dishes. Corn or corn meal was used in all de Indian dishes. We made hominy out'a de whole grains."[51] Colbert vividly described the preparation of specific meals. "Tom-fuller," she explained "was made from beaten corn and tasted sort of like hominy. We would take corn and beat it like in a wooden mortar wid a wooden pestle. We would husk it by fanning it and we would den put it on to cook in a big pot. While it was cooking we'd pick out a lot of hickory-nuts, tie 'em up in a cloth and beat 'em a little and drop 'em in and cook for a long time. We call dis dish hickory-nut grot." In order to make "pashofa we beat de corn and cook for a while and den we add fresh pork and cook until de meat was done. Tom-budha was green corn and fresh meat cooked together and seasoned wid tongue or pepper-grass."[52] Colbert explained that they "cooked on de fire place wid de pots hanging over de fire on racks and den we baked bread and cakes in a oven-skillet. We didn't use soda and baking powder. We'd put salt in de meal and scald it wid boiling water and make it into pones and bake it. We'd roll de ash cakes in wet cabbage leaves and put 'em in de hot ashes and bake 'em. We cooked potatoes, and roasting ears dat way also. We sweetened our cakes wid molasses, and dey was plenty sweet too."[53]

Although born in the Cherokee Nation near Tahlequah, Jane Battiest also remembered preparing food like the Choctaws after she had lived among them for many years. In order to prepare one dish, "we beat our corn to make meal just like the Choctaws did, as there was no grist mills in the country. The only way to get bread was to beat the corn in the bowl made on one end of the block of wood. We made hominy as well as corn meal."[54]

Information concerning hunting animals for meals was presented only by freedmen. Jefferson L. Cole, who was born and raised among the Choctaws, remembered that "there was lots of game; deer and turkey, and I don't know what all. Everyone hunted some; some of the Indians made their living that way. After I got older I hunted now and then myself." Cole especially recalled "a way of hunting deer called 'fire huntin.' " This type of hunting occurred "at night. You took a pan with a long handle and set pieces of rich pine afire in the pan. You'd go where deer were thick; the light blinded them, and you could shoot them as they stood looking into the light."[55] In order to prepare beef, they would "cut it up into slices and put [it] on top of the house to dry. Now and then we would turn the meat over so it would dry evenly. Then we'd build a fire under the scaffold and dry the meat some more. We would barbecue the chunks of meat that clung to the bones."[56]

Cole not only remembered the ways to prepare game, but he also knew what was involved in cooking game. "One way of preparing the dried meat for eating," he stated, "was to make a sort of hash. We put the meat in a mortar and beat it into small pieces. Then we boiled it in an iron pot. When it was done we poured grease over it, and it was good." Cole described Hickory Ta-fula, which was "made with hickory nuts and corn. First we dried the nuts. Then we beat them into a sort of mush in a mortar. We beat corn in a mortar, and sifted it. We mixed the corn and hickory nuts in a pot and boiled them."[57]

Freedman Daniel Webster Burton, born near Old Shawneetown in the Choctaw Nation, mentioned his participation in the fur trade economy in nineteenth-century Indian Territory. He described the "abundance of game in this country at that time, such as deer, wild turkey, bear, wolves, panther and small game too numerous to mention." There was so much that they "never knew what it was to want for fresh wild meat of our own choice." Hunted animals provided not only meat to be eaten but also hides and fur to be sold. Burton proudly claimed that he had "sold as much as $90.00 worth of hides and furs to fur buyers at one time. We had everything we wanted. . . . I have tanned many a deer skin which could be used for coats and jackets and other purposes."[58]

In addition to their discussion of meal preparation, Oklahoma ex-slaves spoke of their knowledge of herbs to cure certain ailments. They discussed the doctoring of people through the use of herbal medicine as a talent revered within their respective communities. Born in 1846 in the Choctaw Nation, ex-slave Ed Butler indicated that "our mammies made all the medicine used from herbs gathered from the woods. We would take baskets into the woods and dig and gather herbs enough to last for months."[59] Ninety-one-year-old Cherokee freedwoman Rochelle Allred (Rachel Aldrich) Ward admitted that persons of her own generation "didn't know what doctoring was." However, "some of the older men and women used to dig roots and get different herbs for medicine; them medicines cure the chill fever and such."[60] Ninety-six-year-old R. C. Smith, who was of Cherokee and African descent, recalled how he "used to get a weed called hoarhound [*sic*], it grows everywhere wild. I'd make a tea and drink it and it would cure the worst kind of kidney ailment. Peach tree leaves tea and sumac seed tea also were good kidney medicines. These were Indian remedies."[61]

During a few interviews, ex-slaves described themselves or relatives as persons who were knowledgeable enough about herbs to be called "herb doctors" or "Indian doctors." Victoria Taylor Thompson, a Cherokee freedwoman, remembered that "for sickness daddy give us tea and herbs. He was a herb doctor, that's how come he have the name 'Doc.' He made us wear charms. Made out of shiny buttons and Indian rock beads. They cured lots of things and the misery too."[62] In his interview with Choctaw freedwoman Irena Blocker, field-worker Gomer Gower summarized Blocker's description of her aunt Penny's special skills. He stated that Irena Blocker portrayed her aunt, Penny Brashiers, "as an 'herb doctor' whose practice it was to use a 'horn cup' in the cure of certain 'miseries' which would not yield to treatment through the virtues of herb concoctions, such as rheumatism or neuralgia. In some instances she would use a piece of glass to make an abrasion in the skin over the seat of the 'misery', then place the horn cup over the abrasion and suck until a vacuum was formed, thus bringing about profuse bleeding of the affected parts and the elimination of the poison which had caused the pain."[63] The horn cup itself "was made from the small end of a cow's horn. The large end would be trimmed until it was made smooth and straight so as to fit snugly and encompass the abrasion, while a small hole would be made in the other and through which air would be extracted and a powerful vacuum created." In addition to this particular treatment with the horn cup, "her herb remedies brought ailing people of all races to the door of Aunt Penny, many to die after their arrival and many more through the ministrations of the good old doctor were cured of their ills and enabled to return to their homes to sing the praises of this colored medicine woman."[64]

Freedman Jack Campbell, who was of Choctaw and African descent, proudly claimed his position as an "Indian doctor" among the Choctaws. Campbell stated that he "was an Indian doctor when I was grown and when an Indian would get sick he would send for me. I would always go and see the sick Indian, if this sick Indian was a real sick fellow. The Choctaw tribe in those days called their sick spells after some of the animals that roamed the woods and some of the fowls."[65] The fact that Choctaws would come to see Campbell to treat various illnesses strongly suggests a level of trust and connection between Campbell and the Choctaws who sought his help. Campbell indicated how serious he considered being an Indian doctor as he declared that he "never would tell the names of the roots and herbs that I dug up and cooked down for the sick." Interviewer Bradley Bolinger noted that Campbell "refused to tell [him] yesterday when [he] was talking to him. He said it was against his belief." The only information about the herbs and roots that Campbell disclosed was that "he always gathered his herbs and medicine in the Spring and in the Fall, and he is able to make many kinds of medicine."[66]

Campbell's resolve to withhold information about the herbs and roots he used as medicine even in the 1930s suggests the significance he associated with the particular knowledge he possessed. As interviewer Bolinger pointed out, Campbell "in some instances as late as today, is called to see a sick Indian."[67] The precious nature of this information makes sense with Campbell's admission that he still treated other persons even at that time of his interview. His knowledge about the herbs and roots still involved Native Americans, and perhaps African Americans, in his community and thus could not just be offered to Bolinger – a stranger to Campbell. By refusing to speak openly about his herbs / root knowledge, Campbell also expressed his allegiance to the culture out of which he gained the knowledge.

NATIONAL IDENTITY AND NATIONALISM

Are "Black Indians" defined according to biological and sociocultural criteria, or is there also a political and national dimension to their identity formation? When speaking about the Reconstruction era during their interviews, some ex-slaves expressed notions of national identity and nationalism as well as a multifaceted connection to their homes and communities in Indian Territory. Although the disruption of the Civil War provided opportunities for many slaves to leave their owners' farms and plantations – of their own volition or as a result of their masters' orders – a number of them desired to return to Indian Territory after the war came to an end. Ex-slaves of the Cherokee Nation specifically expressed their connection to the Cherokee Nation in Indian Territory.

During the Civil War, many masters in the South, as well as in Indian Territory, forced their slaves to leave with them as a result of actual warfare or the threat of warfare. Some Cherokee slave owners left their homes and belongings and temporarily relocated their families, including their African American slaves, to Kansas, Arkansas, and Texas.[68] For many of those born and raised in Indian Territory, this journey to surrounding areas was the first time they had traveled out of Indian Territory. Some Cherokee slave owners wanted to remain within the limits of Indian Territory and thus chose to relocate to areas in the Choctaw and Chickasaw Nations.

Leaving Indian Territory before and during the Civil War was a decision owners made for their slaves; however, after the Civil War, the desire to return to Indian Territory was a decision many Cherokee freedpeople made for themselves. Such individuals, like other freedpeople throughout the United States, began searching for close kin. The separation of family members during slavery continued throughout the Reconstruction era and often left few records behind, so families had to pursue any slim clues to the whereabouts of lost or sold family members. Many of the Cherokee freedpeople who had been relocated outside Indian Territory made their way back in an effort to find lost relatives. Other Cherokee freedpeople returned to Indian Territory because it represented the only home they knew – the only place they identified as home.

This desire to return home to the Cherokee Nation reverberates throughout the WPA interviews of Cherokee ex-slaves. Charley Nave was born and raised in Tahlequah, and his master, Cherokee Henry Nave, was also his father. Charley Nave's son, Cornelius Neely Nave, born in 1868, recalled his father's need to return to Indian Territory after the war. Cornelius Nave identified the place where he and his father were both raised as "home"; it was "that home after the war [that] brought my pappa back home."[69] After completing his service in the Union army, "pappa took all the family and moved to Fort Scott, Kansas, but I guess he feel more at home with the Indians for pretty soon we all move back, this time to a farm near Fort Gibson," within the boundaries of the Cherokee Nation, Indian Territory.[70]

Although Charley Nave successfully relocated his family to the Cherokee Nation, other freedpeople were not as fortunate and were forced to rely on the generosity of their previous owners for their return. Freedwoman Patsy Taylor Perryman and her mother had been relocated to Texas with their mistress, Cherokee Judy Taylor. However, after the war, their mistress decided that she "wasn't going to take us with her." Patsy Taylor Perryman distinctly recalled how, upon hearing of their mistress's decision to leave them behind, her mother "cried so hard she [her mistress] couldn't stand it and told us to get ready."[71] As a result of her mother's pleas they did in fact return to the Cherokee Nation with their former mistress.

Even though there were owners who were willing to aid in their ex-slaves' return to Indian Territory, not all ex-slaves accepted their previous masters' assistance. Ben Johnson and his Cherokee wife, Annie Johnson, had relocated their family and slaves, including Sarah Wilson and her mother, to Texas during the Civil War. Some time after the war ended, Ben Johnson offered to help his ex-slaves "all get back home" if they "wanted to come." In response to his offer, Sarah Wilson's mother told him "she could bear her own expenses."[72] Determined to be independent, Sarah Wilson's mother also had specific reasons for refusing support from Ben and Annie Johnson; her owners' son, Ned Johnson, was Sarah's father. Because her mother refused Johnson's offer, Sarah Wilson and her mother had to "straggle back the best way we could, and me and mammy just got along one way and another till we got to a ferry over the Red River and into Arkansas. Then we got some rides and walked some until we got to Fort Smith." They rested for some time in refugee camps along the way and then headed for Fort Gibson, located in the Illinois District of the Cherokee Nation. Wilson recalled that the "trip was hell on earth. Nobody let us ride and it took us nearly two weeks to walk all that ways, and we nearly starved all the time. We was skin and bones and feet all bloody when we got to the Fort."[73] Instead of creating a new life for herself and her daughter in Texas or even in another state, Sarah Wilson's mother was determined to make the journey back to the Cherokee Nation no matter what the cost.

As many Cherokee ex-slaves made their way back to Indian Territory, they returned with hopes for a new life in the Cherokee Nation. It is hard to imagine that these freedpeople would have made the long journey back to Indian Territory from Arkansas, Kansas, and Texas without good reason. It could have been the need to reunite with family members in Indian Territory that compelled them to make the journey – a need enhanced by a significant cultural connection to the Cherokees. Perhaps their return to the Cherokee Nation signaled their personal recognition that the Cherokee Nation was indeed their homeland. To the Cherokee freedpeople, freedom meant on some level that their previous association with the Cherokees, as their slaves, had been changed forever. Now they believed they were free to, and had a right to, rebuild their lives in the Cherokee Nation.

After the Civil War, residents in the United States and Indian Territory started the business of reconstructing their lives. It was a challenge even to think about rebuilding in some areas given the extensive devastation, the human losses, and the persistent animosities. In parts of Indian Territory, the range of destruction included the burning of homes and other build-ings, the theft of property, and the damaging repercussions due to the battles fought during the war. According to one report, the war had "thrown them back, so that in a great measure they [had] to do over again the work of years in building up their homes and fortunes."[74] J. W. Dunn, U.S. Indian Agent for the Creeks, described 1867 as "a time of severe and necessary labor – a struggle for existence – and every energy of the people was directed to the cultivation of crops and the building of houses."[75] The Cherokee Nation also suffered in the summer of 1867 due to a cholera epidemic.[76]

For the Cherokee freedpeople, resettling in the Cherokee Nation ini-tially meant finding an available area to build homes and plant crops. Depending on the region in which they settled, the majority of freedpeo-ple planted crops that were suitable for that region; they also chose crops they were familiar with harvesting and useful in nourishing their families, particularly wheat, corn, and various fruits and vegetables. As far as the freedpeople were concerned, they had a right to make improvements upon land in the Cherokee Nation by virtue of Cherokee notions and laws regarding the "public domain."[77] Cherokee freedpeople worked the land as did freedpeople in the southern United States; however, unlike south-ern freedpeople, they were limited only to tenant farming or sharecrop-ping during the first few years of Reconstruction. Yet the Cherokee freed-people, unlike others, did not benefit greatly from the variety of services offered by the Bureau of Refugees, Freedmen and Abandoned Lands, more commonly referred to as the Freedmen's Bureau. Without the exten-sive services of this bureau, Cherokee freedpeople could only rely on the laws and treaties of the Cherokee Nation for some assistance during the post–Civil War period.

Although the question of slavery within the Cherokee Nation was finally laid to rest by the Treaty of 1866, this treaty engendered new ques-tions in the era of Reconstruction related to the status, rights, and citizen-ship of Cherokee freedpeople. Proclaimed on 11 August 1866, the Treaty of 1866 specifically approved the Cherokee freedpeople's inclusion as cit-izens of the Cherokee Nation, their access to land in the Cherokee Nation, and their legitimate claim to "all the rights of native Cherokees."[78] No matter what the Cherokee freedpeople might have construed as their con-nection to the Cherokee Nation, however, their right to claim the Cher-okee Nation as their home, and even the Cherokees as their people, would remain debatable with the Nation for several decades.

Only three months after the Treaty of 1866 had been approved and adopted, the Cherokee freedpeople's claims to Cherokee citizenship, including land settlement, became severely limited by the Cherokee Nation. In November 1866, articles of the Treaty of 1866 specifically related to Cherokee citizenship were included in the Cherokee Constitution as amendments. One of the significant changes to the Cherokee Constitution included the delineation of who would be considered part of the Cherokee citizenry. One amendment specified a time limit for freedpeople of the Cherokee Nation who had left the Nation during the war to return to the Nation if they wanted to claim Cherokee citizenship. The amendment to Article 3, Section 5, of the Cherokee Constitution stated: "All native born Cherokees, all Indians, and whites legally members of the Nation by adoption, and all freedmen who have been liberated by voluntary action of their former owners or by law, as well as free colored persons who were in the country at the commencement of the rebellion, and are now residents therein, or who may return within six months from the 19th day of July, 1866, and their descendants, who reside within the limits of the Cherokee Nation, shall be taken, and deemed to be, citizens of the Cherokee Nation."[79] This and other related amendments were presented, approved, and adopted at a general convention of the people of the Cherokee Nation in Tahlequah on 28 November 1866; the next day, the Cherokee National Committee ratified these amendments.[80]

In the first months following the Civil War, many Cherokee freedpeople returned to the Cherokee Nation; however, for some freedpeople, their return to the Nation took several years. There were others who never made the journey back home at all because of limited resources, illness, and other circumstances. Not all Cherokee freedpeople had heard of the six-month limitation for their return to the Cherokee Nation stipulated by the amendments to the Cherokee Constitution. Those who returned after the six-month deadline, oftentimes referred to as the "too lates," became involved in a lengthy legal process not only with the Cherokee Nation but also with the U.S. government. Beginning immediately following the Civil War and continuing into the next century, this time requirement would become a point of contention in determining which Cherokee freedpeople would be recognized officially by the Cherokee government as Cherokee citizens. Embedded within the question of Cherokee citizenship was the issue of land ownership.

The mythical promise of "forty acres and a mule" popularized during Radical Reconstruction still reverberates throughout scholarly analyses of the Reconstruction era; however, due to the work of the Dawes Commission, land ownership for Cherokee freedpeople was not a myth.[81] After being enrolled by the Dawes Commission through proving they were indeed Cherokee citizens, a significant number of Cherokee freedpeople received land allotments in the Cherokee Nation.[82] For some freedpeople, owning land in the Cherokee Nation represented the only way of declaring their rightful position as members of the Cherokee Nation. For other freedpeople, land ownership signified only part of their struggle to be recognized as legitimate members of the Cherokee Nation.

During their WPA interviews, a few Cherokee freedpeople mentioned receiving land allotments.[83] Although her mother died shortly after their return to the Cherokee Nation, Sarah Wilson resettled in Four Mile Branch in the Tahlequah District and married Oliver Wilson, another Cherokee freedman. Wilson explained that she and her husband participated in the Cherokee enrollment process, claiming that they "both got [their] land on [their] Cherokee freedman blood."[84] From her interview, Sarah Wilson indicated that she received her allotment not only because of her position as a former slave of Cherokee Annie Johnson and Ben Johnson but also because of her "blood" connection to the Cherokee Nation by virtue of the fact that her father, Ned Johnson, was the son of her former owners.

Wilson's reference to her "Cherokee freedman blood" serves to heighten her identity as Cherokee. Moreover, her phrase blends two separate yet often interrelated identities – the first being a Cherokee freedwoman and the second being a person of mixed racial heritage, specifically a person of African and Cherokee descent. Wilson's blended notion perhaps represents the creation of a distinct identity separate from the Cherokees generally and from Cherokee freedpeople who were not of Cherokee descent. It is possible that Sarah Wilson and other "mixed-blood" Cherokee freedpeople conceived of their identity in these terms – a blended identity comprised of status, blood, and nation.

However, the Treaty of 1866 and the subsequent amendments to the Cherokee Constitution in 1866 did not require freedpeople to prove a direct "blood" connection to the Cherokees in order to be enrolled in the Cherokee Nation. The requirement centered around freedpeople proving that they had been formerly owned by Cherokees residing in the Cherokee Nation, Indian Territory, and had conformed to the six-month restriction previously discussed. As a result, Betty Robertson, who did not identify any "blood" connection to the Cherokees, "got [her] allotment as a Cherokee Freedman, and so did Cal [her husband]."[85] Betty Robertson's claim as a former slave of Cherokee Joe Vann satisfied the initial requirement for enrollment. The six-month limitation requirement did not restrict her due to the fact that she and her family had remained within the limits of the Cherokee Nation during the Civil War. Since she was able to prove her status as a former slave to Joe Vann and due to the fact that she had not left the Cherokee Nation at any time, Betty Robertson was readily enrolled as a Cherokee freedwoman and received a land allotment within the Cherokee Nation.[86]

Although neither Sarah Wilson nor Betty Robertson spoke of the formal process of enrolling as Cherokee freedpeople in their WPA interviews, Patsy Taylor Perryman offered some indication of the application process, which included, for many freedpeople, the presentation of several detailed written testimonies. At her home in Muskogee, Oklahoma, Perryman recalled that as a result of her writing skills, "all the writing about allotments had to be done by me." She had "written many letters to Washington when they gave the Indian lands to the native Indians and their negroes."[87] Even after writing letters regarding her family's right to land allotments, no evidence exists indicating that Perryman received land in the Cherokee Nation. Since her owner, Cherokee Judy Taylor, relocated Perryman and other members of her family to Texas during the Civil War, it is possible that they might have returned too late to claim a right to Cherokee citizenship and thus to any Cherokee land.

Patsy Taylor Perryman's sister, Victoria Taylor Thompson, was also interviewed by the WPA. At the very beginning of her interview, Thompson stated that she was about eighty years old, at least "so they say down at the Indian Agency where my name is on the Cherokee Rolls since all the land was give to the Indian families a long time ago."[88] It is possible that Victoria Taylor Thompson and her sister, Patsy Taylor Perryman, were on one of the preliminary rolls conducted by the Cherokee Nation and the United States government. However, like many other Cherokee freedpeople, their connection to the Cherokee Nation was at some later point denied, and as a result their names were not listed on the final Dawes Rolls of Cherokee freedpeople.

Like Patsy Taylor Perryman and her sister, Victoria Taylor Thompson, during the Civil War Morris Sheppard had been relocated outside of his home in the Illinois District, Cherokee Nation, by his former owner, Joe Sheppard. They moved to "a place in de Red River bottoms close to Shawneetown [Choctaw Nation] and not far from de place where all de wagons crossed over to go into Texas. We was at dat place two years and made two little crops."[89] Even though Sheppard and his family returned to the Cherokee Nation after the six-month limitation, he stated that he "got a freedman's allotment up in dat part close to Coffeyville [Kansas]" in the

Cooweescoowee District of the Cherokee Nation.[90] However, as was the case for many Cherokee freedpeople, he "lost [his] land trying to live honest and pay [his] debts."[91]

Not all WPA interviewees who were enrolled Cherokee freedpeople indicated that they had received land allotments. Chaney Richardson was among the slaves of Charley and Nancy Rogers who were relocated to an area in the Choctaw Nation during the Civil War; however, federal troops escorted them back to Fort Gibson in the Cherokee Nation toward the end of the war.[92] Since she returned to the Nation before the six-month deadline, Chaney Richardson and her two daughters were enrolled as Cherokee freedwomen.[93] Chaney Richardson, however, did not indicate in her interview that she had received a land allotment, simply stating that she "didn't git any money that [she had] seen."[94]

Certain ex-slaves who were not Cherokee freedpeople benefited from their familial association to someone who was recognized as a Cherokee freedperson. Although born a slave in Arkansas, Katie Rowe married Billy Rowe, a Cherokee freedman, in Little Rock, Arkansas. After they got married, they moved to an area near Tahlequah because Katie Rowe claimed that her husband "had land in de Cherokee Nation." After Billy Rowe died, Katie Rowe continued to reside in the area and later moved in with one of her daughters, Lula, who lived in Tulsa, Oklahoma.[95] For Katie Rowe and other African Americans who had been raised on plantations in the southern United States, the Cherokee Nation and Indian Territory in general represented a place of new beginnings, without the overwhelming prevalence of racial violence. For the Cherokee freedpeople who were born and raised in Indian Territory, the Cherokee Nation still was the only home they knew and for many the only home they would ever know. Having been born and raised as slaves, the reality of owning land became one of the important symbols of a "free" life.

It is not surprising that many ex-slaves explained in their WPA interviews that they decided to remain in Indian Territory following the Civil War, and they fought to become included as members of the Native American nations with which they had been associated. In their reflections on the post–Civil War period, ex-slaves claimed that they had received their land allotments and recalled the importance of land ownership in Indian Territory.[96] Even those who had been forced to leave Indian Territory during the Civil War chose to return to Indian Territory after the war had ended.[97] Their connection to Indian Territory had not been eliminated with their emancipation. They felt instead a renewed affinity to the only home they knew, to the only communities they knew. For many freedpeople of the Cherokee, Creek, Chickasaw, and Choctaw Nations, it was necessary that they begin their "free" life in Indian Territory.

CONCLUSION

In their WPA interviews, ex-slaves highlighted several layers of connections between themselves and Native Americans in nineteenth-century Indian Territory; they grappled with and embraced their racial, cultural, and national identities within specific nations in Indian Territory. Ex-slaves who had been born and raised in Indian Territory among Native Americans for some time described themselves as close to, rather than separate from, Native Americans with whom they interacted. Ex-slaves of African descent identified areas in Indian Territory as the familiar places of their birth and Native American cultural ways as their own ways. For freedpeople who remembered living among Native Americans in Indian Territory, who recalled the Native American blood that gave them life, who proudly spoke of their bilingual abilities, who carefully prepared Native American meals and herbal medicines, their experiences do not reflect a divided "two-ness"; instead, their recollections portray a reality without such stark divisions.[98]

Within Indian Territory in the nineteenth century, there were slaves whose interactions with slaveholding and nonslaveholding Native Americans shaped their lives on a daily basis. Henry Clay at first distanced himself from those "Creek Negroes" because they had a "funny" way of speaking, and whenever he saw them along the road wearing their strange attire he was afraid and thus kept out of their way. On the other hand, it is precisely because her folks wore "blankets and breeches with fur around the bottoms" that Sweetie Ivery Wagoner claimed her association with Creek culture. We learn from Kiziah Love, Polly Colbert, Jane Battiest, Jefferson Cole, and Daniel Webster Burton that their preparation of basic foods and the hunting of animals were grounded inextricably in Native American cultural traditions – Native American ways of cooking and hunting. For some like Patsy Taylor Perryman, Betty Robertson, Henry Henderson, and Lucinda Davis, what occurred as a result of their interactions with Native Americans was that they or their relatives had the ability to communicate in a Native American language. Utilizing Native American herbal treatments to cure diseases was important to Ed Butler and R. C. Smith; however, in the cases of Victoria Taylor Thompson's father, Irena Blocker's aunt Penny, and Jack Campbell himself, to actually become, or to be known as, a "herb doctor" or "medicine woman" represented an entirely different cultural position within Native American communities. Perhaps the most telling aspect of this interaction occurred when Jack Campbell refused to tell interviewer Bradley Bolinger specifically which herbs and roots he used to prepare various medicines. Transferring this knowledge to Bolinger undeniably symbolized a breach of faith in Campbell's position as an Indian doctor to the Choctaw people – as a person responsible for the healing and continuity of the Choctaw Nation.

What happens in the majority of cases of "native" slaves and freedpeople living in Indian Territory is the creation of communities of Native Americans and slaves of Native Americans who interact on various levels and in numerous ways. Unlike "crossland Negroes" who were relocated to Indian Territory, "natives" were born and raised in Indian Territory. The extent of their cultural interactions, oftentimes intensified by their blood relations, established a group of persons of African descent whose cultural and social ties were with Native Americans. Without disregarding or discrediting the fact that these persons were indeed slaves of Native Americans, one can still talk about the strong cultural connection and identification between slaves of African descent and the community of slaveholding and nonslaveholding Native Americans with whom they interacted in Indian Territory.

On 24 August 1876 in the Delaware District, Cherokee Nation, a group of Cherokee freedpeople organized one of their annual celebrations in recognition and remembrance of emancipation and freedom.[99] At this event, freedpeople participated in a variety of activities, including a grand horseback parade, followed by presentations and a barbecue. The speakers addressed a number of pressing issues during this celebration; they focused primarily on the importance of education, their ongoing concerns with the citizenship requirements within the amended Cherokee Constitution, their legal struggle to be recognized as rightful citizens of the Cherokee Nation, and the necessity of participating in Cherokee national electoral politics. One speaker, Joseph Rogers, specifically focused on how the six-month limitation had prevented him from being rightfully recognized as part of the Cherokee citizenry. As one of the "too lates," he discussed his frustration at not being officially acknowledged by the Cherokee Nation as a Cherokee freedman. Rogers attested:

Born and raised among these people, I don't want to know any other. The green hills and blooming prairies of this Nation look like home to me. The rippling of its pebbly bottom brooks made a music that delighted my infancy, and in my ear it has not lost its sweetness. I look around and I see Cherokees who in the early days of my life were my playmates in youth and early manhood, my companions, and now as the decrepitude of age steals upon me, will you not let me lie down and die, your fellow citizen?[100]

As Joseph Rogers passionately articulated, freedpeople who had been born and raised among Native Americans had developed a keen understanding of their rootedness to specific Native American communities in Indian Territory. Although their affiliation with these communities, specifically their position as slaves, had been previously assumed, their construction of their lives among Native Americans had resulted in tangible and appreciable blood, cultural, and national connections with Native Americans. For them, Indian Territory did not simply represent a place where they had been enslaved, it represented a place where they belonged. Ex-slaves experienced a dual sense of belonging; they were previously slaves who were owned by, and belonged to, Native Americans, but they were also persons who believed that they were part of, and belonged to, Native American communities in Indian Territory. Thus, after emancipation, these ex-slaves chose to live and to settle at home in Indian Territory.

NOTES

1. See A. Irving Hallowell, "American Indians, White and Black: The Phenomenon of Transculturalization," *Current Anthropology* 4 (December 1963): 519–31.

2. Throughout this chapter, I use the term "mixed-blood"; however, other terms have been proposed in order to critique notions of race, language, and meaning. In defining "crossbloods," Gerald Vizenor explains that "crossbloods are a postmodern tribal bloodline, an encounter with racialism, colonial duplicities, sentimental monogenism, and generic cultures. The encounters are comic and communal, rather than tragic and sacrificial; comedies and trickster signatures are liberations; tragedies are simulations, an invented cultural isolation. Crossbloods are communal, and their stories are splendid considerations of survivance." Gerald Vizenor, *Crossbloods: Bone Courts, Bingo and Other Reports* (Minneapolis: University of Minnesota Press, 1990), vii. Sharon P. Holland invokes Vizenor's term "crossblood" instead of "mixed-blood" in order to "make a point about language and terminology; to be a mixed blood African-American is to be counted among the thousands of African-Americans who have the *knowledge* of some European and/or Native ancestry, but to be a crossblood is to *identify* as such, to read the

'racial' categories on the U.S. census as bogus and to consistently cross the borders of ideological containment." Sharon P. Holland, "'If You Know I Have a History, You Will Respect Me': A Perspective on Afro-Native American Literature," *Callaloo* 17 (winter 1994): 335.

3. See, for example, Rebecca B. Bateman, "Africans and Indians: A Comparative Study of the Black Carib and Black Seminole," *Ethnohistory* 37, no. 1 (winter 1990): 1–24; Michael Craton, "From Caribs to Black Caribs: The Amerindian Roots of Servile Resistance in the Caribbean," in *In Resistance: Studies in African, Caribbean and Afro-American History*, ed. Gary Y. Okihiro (Amherst: University of Massachusetts Press, 1986), 96–116; Nancie L. Solien Gonzalez, *Sojourners of the Caribbean: Ethnogenesis and Ethnohistory of the Garifuna* (Urbana: University of Illinois Press, 1988); Mary W. Helms, "Negro or Indian?: The Changing Identity of a Frontier Population," in *Old Roots in New Lands: Historical and Anthropological Perspectives on Black Experiences in the Americas*, ed. Ann M. Pescatello (Westport CT: Greenwood Press, 1977), 157–72; William Loren Katz, *Black Indians: A Hidden Heritage* (New York: Atheneum, 1985); and Virginia Kerns, *Women and the Ancestors: Black Carib Kinship and Ritual* (Urbana: University of Illinois Press, 1997). In addition to questioning the limited nature of terms such as "Indian," "Black," and "African," it is also important to understand the changing definitions and meanings of racial terminology within historical context. See Jack D. Forbes, *Africans and Native Americans: The Language of Race and the Evolution of Red-Black Peoples* (Urbana: University of Illinois Press, 1993).

4. George W. Rawick, ed., *The American Slave: A Composite Autobiography*, vol. 12, Supplement Series 1 (Westport CT: Greenwood Press, 1977), 293.

5. Rawick, *American Slave*, vol. 12, 295.

6. Rawick, *American Slave*, vol. 12, 293. Only a small number of the interviewees actually participated in the forced relocation of Native Americans to Indian Territory; in fact, those who described the migration to Indian Territory did so by recollecting what older relatives had related to them about their experiences. See, for example, the WPA interviews of Eliza Hardrick, Ned Thompson, and Nellie Johnson.

7. Tribal freedpeople often distinguished between themselves and "crossland Negroes" or "state Negroes," as they called those who came to Indian Territory from the United States. They maintained this distinction even after Oklahoma statehood. Booker T. Washington encountered this phenomenon during his visit to the Creek Nation in the fall of 1905. See Booker T. Washington, "Boley: A Negro Town in the West," *Outlook* 88 (January 4, 1908): 28–31. See also Norman L. Crockett, "Witness to History: Booker T. Washington Visits Boley," *Chronicles of Oklahoma* 67, no. 4 (winter 1989–90): 382–91. For a discussion of the tension between Creek freedpeople and "state Negroes," also referred to as "watchina" by

Creek freedpeople, see Sigmund Sameth, "Creek Negroes: A Study of Race Relations" (master's thesis, University of Oklahoma, 1940).

8. Rawick, *American Slave*, vol. 12, 234.

9. Rawick, *American Slave*, vol. 12, 235.

10. Rawick, *American Slave*, vol. 12, 235. Cornelius Nave's description of his hair is particularly effective and telling as hair, especially hair length and texture, is often used as an indicator of racial classification.

11. See Wyatt F. Jeltz, "The Relations of Negroes and Choctaw and Chickasaw Indians," *Journal of Negro History* 33 (January 1948): 24–37; Annie H. Abel, *The American Indian as Slaveholder and Secessionist* (Lincoln: University of Nebraska Press, 1992), 20; Kenneth W. Porter, "Relations between Negroes and Indians within the Present Limits of the United States," *Journal of Negro History* 17 (July 1932): 352.

12. Evidence of "mixed-blood" Black-Choctaws and Black-Chickasaws also appears in the Choctaw-Chickasaw Freedmen Census of 1885. A significant number of people on the census identify their parents' nationality as "Red and Black," "Choctaw and Black," and "Chickasaw and Black." See Choctaw-Chickasaw Freedmen Census of 1885, Archives and Manuscripts Division, Oklahoma Historical Society, Oklahoma City.

13. Rawick, *American Slave*, vol. 12, 74.

14. Rawick, *American Slave*, vol. 12, 74. Neither Peggy McKinney Brown nor her interviewer, Bradley Bolinger, directly mentioned the circumstances or interactions between Brown's mother and Jesse McKinney.

15. The published version of the interview notes Charley Moore Brown as the primary interviewee. The interviewer, Bradley Bolinger, included Peggy Brown's comments within the transcribed interview of Charley Moore Brown. Peggy McKinney Brown lived with her son on his farm; as a result, when Bolinger arrived to conduct his interview, he spoke with Charley Moore Brown and his mother. It is not certain whether the interviews occurred simultaneously or if they were arranged separately.

16. Rawick, *American Slave*, vol. 12, 73.

17. Rawick, *American Slave*, vol. 12, 75–76.

18. The five interviewees who briefly spoke of their Native American ancestry were Rachel Aldrich Ward, Agnes Walker, R. C. Smith, C. G. Samuel, and Richard Franklin.

19. Rawick, *American Slave*, vol. 12, 351. Having been born and raised on Cherokee Jim Vann's plantation in Webbers Falls, Cherokee Nation, if Lucinda Vann were "part Indian" she most likely would have been part Cherokee.

20. Rawick, *American Slave*, vol. 12, 342. The kind of social stratification Lucinda Vann described on the Vann plantation was probably not widespread. It

would only have been deemed necessary on significantly larger plantations, of which there were very few in Indian Territory. Lucinda Vann overestimated the slave population on Joe Vann's plantation. After removal, Joe Vann had approximately three hundred slaves on his plantation at the time of his death in 1844.

21. Rawick, *American Slave*, vol. 12, 344.

22. Furthermore, a few ex-slaves distinguished between Native American "mixed-bloods" and "full-bloods," as well as separating those who were more "civilized" from those who remained "wild." See, for example, the WPA Oklahoma interviews of Jefferson Cole and Ned Thompson. Rawick, *American Slave*, vol. 12.

23. See Terry P. Wilson, "Blood Quantum: Native American Mixed Bloods," in *Racially Mixed People in America*, ed. Maria P. P. Root (Newbury Park CA: Sage Publications, 1992), 108–25.

24. A. Irving Hallowell, "American Indians, White and Black: The Phenomenon of Transculturalization," *Current Anthropology* 4 (December 1963): 523. Along the continuum of transculturalization, at one extreme are persons "who become permanently identified with the second culture. In such cases there is more than a cultural readaption – typically, there is a psychological transformation. At the other extreme, readjustment may be relatively superficial and have little psychological depth. Manners and speech may be affected but not basic attitudes and values. In between, we have cases where historical circumstances combined with unusual personality characteristics have motivated some individuals to play a dual role effectively" (Hallowell, "American Indians," 523).

25. Hallowell, "American Indians," 523.

26. See Daniel Roche, *The Culture of Clothing: Dress and Fashion in the "Ancien Regime,"* trans. Jean Birrell (New York: Cambridge University Press, 1996), 45. See also Roland Barthes, *The Fashion System*, trans. Matthew Ward and Richard Howard (Berkeley: University of California Press, 1990).

27. Roche, *Culture of Clothing*, 43.

28. For information on the symbolic nature of Native American clothing, see, for example, Evan M. Maurer, "Symbol and Identification in North American Indian Clothing," in *The Fabrics of Culture: The Anthropology of Clothing and Adornment*, ed. Justine M. Cordwell and Ronald A. Schwarz (The Hague: Mouton, 1979), 119–42; Virginia More Roediger, *Ceremonial Costumes of the Pueblo Indians: Their Evolution, Fabrication and Significance in the Prayer Drama* (Berkeley: University of California Press, 1991); Paul M. Raczka, "Sacred Robes of the Blackfoot and Other Northern Plains Tribes," *American Indian Art Magazine* 17, no. 3 (1992): 66–73; Betty Issenman, *Sinews of Survival: The Living Legacy of Inuit Clothing* (Vancouver: UBC Press, 1997); and Donald Sizemore, *Cherokee Dance: Ceremonial Dances and Dance Regalia* (Cherokee NC: Cherokee Publications, 1999).

29. Rawick, *American Slave*, vol. 12, 115.

30. Although Clay discussed his notions of wildness in relation to Native Americans in his interview, none of the ex-slaves from Oklahoma who were of Native American ancestry stated that their blood relationship to Native Americans made them potentially wild.

31. Like Henry Clay, other visitors to the Creek Nation noticed the distinctive style of clothing worn by Creeks. While traveling through the Creek Nation, Indian Territory, in 1845, Lieutenant James W. Abert expressed his delight with the Creek style of dress. Abert also specifically remarked on the clothing worn by African Americans living among the Creeks. John Galvin, ed., *Through the Country of the Comanche Indians in the Fall of the Year 1845: The Journal of a U.S. Army Expedition led by Lieutenant James W. Abert of the Topographical Engineers* (San Francisco: John Howell, 1970), 62, 64.

32. Rawick, *American Slave*, vol. 12, 355.

33. See Theda Perdue, *Slavery and the Evolution of Cherokee Society, 1540-1866* (Knoxville: University of Tennessee Press), 106; Rudi Halliburton Jr., *Red Over Black: Black Slavery among the Cherokee Indians* (Westport CT: Greenwood Press), 143; Daniel F. Littlefield Jr., *The Chickasaw Freedmen: A People without a Country* (Westport CT: Greenwood Press), 9.

34. Rawick, *American Slave*, vol. 12, 249.

35. Rawick, *American Slave*, vol. 12, 250–51.

36. George W. Rawick, ed., *The American Slave: A Composite Autobiography*, vol. 7, Supplement Series 1 (Westport CT: Greenwood Press, 1973), 266.

37. Rawick, *American Slave*, vol. 12, 178.

38. According to Tim Thompson and David Skeeter at the Creek Nation's office in Okmulgee, Oklahoma, "lag-ashe" is similar to the Creek word "lvkvs," pronounced "lakash," which is the Creek word for sit down. Henderson's "Hum-buc-sha" is similar to the Creek word "hompvshe" pronounced "hombashe," which is the greeting for inviting someone to eat. However, "Pig-ne-dee" did not sound like the most popular Creek word for good morning, nor did it sound like any other word with that meaning. "Car-a-she" did not sound like the Creek word for corn bread, which is "vce-tvklike." The Creek word "licetv," pronounced "leyc-ita," means "to seat, set and make (one) sit." The Creek saying "Likepvs ce," pronounced "leyk-ipa-s ci" is a familiar way of welcoming someone but literally means "have a seat." Jack B. Martin and Margaret McKane Mauldin, *A Dictionary of Creek/Muskogee: With Notes on the Florida and Oklahoma Seminole Dialects of Creek* (Lincoln: University of Nebraska Press, 2000), 71.

39. Rawick, *American Slave*, vol. 7, 53.

40. Rawick, *American Slave*, vol. 7, 54.

41. Translation from Thompson and Skeeter. The Creek word "tvsekvyv," pro-

nounced "tasikaya," means "citizen." However, it was also previously used in combination with other words to form war names. The Creek word "henehv," pronounced "hiniha," is currently defined as the "second chief of a tribal town." Martin and Mauldin, *Dictionary of Creek/Muskogee*, 126–27, 49.

42. Translation from Thompson and Skeeter. The Creek word for baby is "estuce," pronounced "ist-oci." Martin and Mauldin, *Dictionary of Creek/Muskogee*, 35.

43. Translation from Thompson and Skeeter. Martin and Mauldin, *Dictionary of Creek/Muskogee*, 34.

44. See Martin and Mauldin, *Dictionary of Creek/Muskogee*, xix–xx.

45. Rawick, *American Slave*, vol. 7, 121.

46. Rawick, *American Slave*, vol. 7, 121.

47. I borrow this expression from Ron Scapp and Brian Seitz, eds., *Eating Culture* (Albany: University of New York Press, 1998).

48. Rawick, *American Slave*, vol. 7, 193–94.

49. Rawick, *American Slave*, vol. 7, 194, my emphasis.

50. Rawick, *American Slave*, vol. 7, 33–38.

51. Rawick, *American Slave*, vol. 7, 34.

52. Rawick, *American Slave*, vol. 7, 34–35.

53. Rawick, *American Slave*, vol. 7, 35. Kiziah Love and Polly Colbert accurately described the preparation of the Choctaw dish "pishofa" and other Choctaw meals. In addition to describing the fundamental purpose of the mortar and pestle, they also mentioned how baskets, specifically called the riddle and fanner, were used for sifting and cleaning ground corn. For detailed information on these instruments, as well as Cherokee, Creek, Seminole, and Quapaw recipes for preparing corn-based dishes, see Muriel H. Wright, "American Indian Corn Dishes," *Chronicles of Oklahoma* 36 (summer 1958): 155–66. See also Peter J. Hudson, "Choctaw Indian Dishes," in *A Choctaw Source Book*, ed. John H. Peterson Jr. (New York: Garland, 1985): 333-35.

54. Rawick, *American Slave*, vol. 12, 42.

55. Rawick, *American Slave*, vol. 12, 123.

56. Rawick, *American Slave*, vol. 12, 123.

57. Rawick, *American Slave*, vol. 12, 124.

58. Rawick, *American Slave*, vol. 12, 83–84.

59. Rawick, *American Slave*, vol. 12, 88.

60. Rawick, *American Slave*, vol. 12, 364.

61. Rawick, *American Slave*, vol. 12, 281.

62. Rawick, *American Slave*, vol. 12, 322.

63. Rawick, *American Slave*, vol. 12, 67–68.

64. Rawick, *American Slave*, vol. 12, 68.

65. Rawick, *American Slave*, vol. 12, 92.

66. Rawick, *American Slave*, vol. 12, 92–93.

67. Rawick, *American Slave*, vol. 12, 92.

68. See Sarah Wilson's experiences in Rawick, *American Slave*, vol. 7, 350–51.

69. Rawick, *American Slave*, vol. 12, 234.

70. Rawick, *American Slave*, vol. 12, 236.

71. Rawick, *American Slave*, vol. 12, 252.

72. Rawick, *American Slave*, vol. 7, 351–52.

73. Rawick, *American Slave*, vol. 7, 352. Daniel Littlefield explained that "when the freedmen had begun to return to the Cherokee Nation, the federal troops had offered a source of refuge to them. Fort Gibson was the hub of activity, and most of the main routes of travel into the Nation ended there." Littlefield, *Cherokee Freedmen*, 28.

74. Department of the Interior, *Report on Indian Affairs by the Acting Commissioner for the Year 1867* (Washington DC: Government Printing Office, 1868), 22. In addition to the effects of the war, the summer of 1866 proved to be a particularly harsh one for the Creeks, when an onslaught of grasshoppers destroyed a great deal of their fruit and vegetable crops.

75. Department of the Interior, *Report on Indian Affairs*, 321.

76. Department of the Interior, *Report on Indian Affairs*, 319. This epidemic also severely affected the Seminole Nation.

77. See Cherokee Nation, *Laws of the Cherokee Nation Passed During the Years 1839–1867*, vol. 6 of *The Constitutions and Laws of the American Indian Tribes* (Wilmington DE: Scholarly Resources, 1973), 75–76.

78. Charles J. Kappler, ed., *Indian Treaties 1778–1883* (New York: Interland Publishing, 1972), 944.

79. Cherokee Nation, *Constitution and Laws of the Cherokee Nation Published by Authority of the National Council*, vol. 7 of *Constitutions and Laws of the American Indian Tribes*, 25.

80. Cherokee Nation, *Constitution and Laws*, 25.

81. For a thorough examination of the creation and utilization of the Dawes Rolls within the Cherokee Nation, see Littlefield, *Cherokee Freedmen*, 214-48. See also Kent Carter, "Deciding Who Can Be Cherokee: Enrollment Records of the Dawes Commission," *Chronicles of Oklahoma* 69, no. 2 (summer 1991): 174–205. Chickasaw freedpeople were never adopted into the Chickasaw Nation; nonetheless, they were enrolled by the Dawes Commission. See Littlefield, *Chickasaw Freedmen*.

82. Even though one of the important aspects of Article 4 of the Treaty of 1866 concerned the right of Cherokee freedpeople, recognized as such by the Cherokee Nation, to settle on land in the Nation, Cherokee freedpeople were not officially

granted land allotments until they were enrolled as citizens of the Cherokee Nation by the Dawes Commission.

83. Although the WPA interviews highlighted in this section relate to the Cherokee Nation specifically, there are interviews of freedpeople from other nations who mentioned owning land in their respective nations. See the interviews of Choctaw freedwomen Frances Banks, Polly Colbert, and Kiziah Love and Creek freedwomen Lucinda Davis, Mary Grayson, and Nellie Johnson.

84. Rawick, *American Slave*, vol. 7, 353. Sarah Wilson and her children were enrolled by the Dawes Commission. See Cherokee Freedmen Census Card Number 60 for Sarah Wilson and her five children (Lelia, Thomas, Bertha, Allie, and Robert). The enrollment application for Sarah Wilson and her children to the Dawes Commission was dated 3 April 1901. Their citizenship certificate was issued on 6 March 1905. National Archives, Southwest Region in Fort Worth, Texas. See also Land Allotment Record Numbers 182–87, for Sarah, Lelia, Thomas, Bertha, Allie, and Robert Wilson. National Archives, Southwest Region in Fort Worth, Texas.

85. Rawick, *American Slave*, vol. 7, 269.

86. Betty Robertson was enrolled as a Cherokee freedwoman by the Dawes Commission as Belle Roberson with her husband, Calvin, and her children. See Cherokee Freedmen Census Card Number 117 and Land Allotment Record Numbers 356–60 and 3076–77, for Calvin, Belle, Bertha, Watie, Amanda, Arthur Roberson, and Minnie Ivory. National Archives, Southwest Region in Fort Worth, Texas.

87. Rawick, *American Slave*, vol. 12, 251–52.

88. Rawick, *American Slave*, vol. 12, 320. I have been unable to find any census card or application testimony stating that Victoria Taylor Thompson was enrolled as a Cherokee freedwoman.

89. Rawick, *American Slave*, vol. 7, 290.

90. Rawick, *American Slave*, vol. 7, 292. Although Morris Sheppard stated he had received an allotment, his census card indicates that his enrollment application was rejected, and thus he should not have received an allotment. See Cherokee Freedmen Census Card Number FR 186 and Cherokee Freedmen Enrollment Application Testimony, File Number 186, for Morris Sheppard. National Archives, Southwest Region in Fort Worth, Texas. However, Morris Sheppard's wife, Nancy Hildebrand Sheppard, former slave of Joe Hildebrand, was enrolled as a Cherokee freedwoman. She and their children were enrolled by the Dawes Commission. See Cherokee Freedmen Census Card Number 186 for Nancy, Fannie, Emma, Annie, Thomas, and Claud Sheppard. National Archives, Southwest Region in Fort Worth, Texas.

91. Rawick, *American Slave*, vol. 7, 290. Other ex-slaves mentioned that they,

too, had received land in Indian Territory but no longer owned it. See Rawick, *American Slave*, vol. 12, 135, 354, 356.

92. Rawick, *American Slave*, vol. 7, 257–62.

93. See Cherokee Freedmen Census Card Number 134 for Chaney Richardson and her two daughters, Mish Lovely and Nannie Daniels. National Archives, Southwest Region in Fort Worth, Texas.

94. Rawick, *American Slave*, vol. 7, 261.

95. Rawick, *American Slave*, vol. 7, 283.

96. See the interviews of Mary Grayson, Nellie Johnson, Mary Lindsay, Kiziah Love, Betty Robertson, Katie Rowe, Morris Sheppard, and Sarah Wilson. Rawick, *American Slave*, vol. 7. See also the interviews of Richard Franklin, Ned Thompson, Sweetie Ivery Wagoner, Agnes Walker, and Eliza Whitmire. Rawick, *American Slave*, vol. 12.

97. See the WPA interviews of Matilda Poe, Jack Campbell, John Harrison, Moses Lonian, Chaney McNair, R. C. Smith, and Lucinda Vann.

98. See W. E. B. DuBois, *The Souls of Black Folk* (1903; reprint, New York: New American Library, 1982), 45.

99. Information regarding this particular celebration was provided in an editorial article in the *Cherokee Advocate*, 9 September 1876.

100. *Cherokee Advocate*, 9 September 1876.

7. "African and Cherokee by Choice"
Race and Resistance under Legalized Segregation

LAURA L. LOVETT

Zora Neale Hurston once boasted that she was "the only Negro in the United States whose grandfather on the mother's side was *not* an Indian chief."[1] In the same breath, Hurston confessed that she was of mixed-blood but differed "from the party line in that I neither consider it an honor or a shame." This difference from "the party line," as she referred to African American perspectives on Native American ancestry, must have been especially striking to Hurston as she had helped to document race mixture during her brief stint as a research assistant to anthropologist Melville Herskovits. Hurston participated in a 1928 study of the ancestry and physical traits of African Americans that surveyed 1,551 Howard University students and found that 27.2 percent claimed to have some Native American ancestry.[2] Herskovits reports that he went to great lengths to adjust for the "distinct prestige value" of having Native American ancestry within African American communities, but neither he nor Hurston explained why Native American ancestry would have bestowed prestige.[3]

Herskovits's study was aimed at a long tradition of scientific research on the nature of racial difference.[4] Strongly influenced by the work of anthropologist Franz Boas, Herskovits wanted to explain the achievement of those African Americans with lighter skin and European features in terms of the dominant system of values in American culture. Since the 1860s, Social Darwinists and later hereditarian eugenicists had sought to explain racial differences in terms of the value of innate biological traits possessed by what were considered to be separate and distinct races. Indeed, the perception that all characteristics were biologically determined and maintained in bloodlines, which were then regulated by "blood quantum" standards, formed an important part of how family identity was constructed.[5] Herskovits questioned the biological framework of "racial integrity" by appealing to cultural and social differences to explain differences ascribed to races. However, this scientific attack did not work its way into American racial ideology for quite some time. In the interim, people renegotiated what were understood to be scientific racial categories in various ways, pointing to places where biological classificatory schema denied the historical realities of interracial relations.[6]

The project of contesting growing notions of racial fixity became increasingly important to African Americans as scientifically backed theories of inherent racial difference were used to justify the implementation of segregation. Designed to disenfranchise African Americans and other peoples of color, legalized segregation eventually regulated racial distinctions and interracial contact from the moment a child was born in a segregated hospital or at home on a segregated city block to the time he or she died and was buried in a "colored" cemetery.[7] These boundaries began to be defined legally beginning in the 1880s with the enactment of "Jim Crow" railroad car laws in Tennessee (1881), Florida (1887), Mississippi (1888), and Texas (1889).[8] At the heart of segregation was an attempt to delineate who should be considered "white" and who should be considered "colored."[9] While the 1896 Supreme Court decision in *Plessy v. Ferguson* claimed that segregation created separate but equal opportunities, for people of color, life under segregation was at its best one of discrimination and at its worst one of racial violence and terror.

Herskovits's study exemplifies how the discourses of scientific racism and legal segregation both reified racial difference and influenced the construction of racial identity. His interview subjects made claims of Native American ancestry in a severely segregated society divided into two races, a "superior" white race and an "inferior" Black race. Their pride in their Native American heritage, I argue, should be understood as an effort to negotiate an alternative positive identity within the then-dominant discourses of segregation and scientific racism. More generally, Native American ancestry, identities, and history provided African Americans, Native Americans, and peoples of mixed descent with ways to address and question an imposed system of segregation and its effects.[10]

In this essay, I consider how African American citizens and intellectuals, peoples of mixed ancestry, and Native Americans each challenged different aspects of segregation in the late nineteenth and early twentieth centuries by invoking Native American ancestry. For individuals and families classified as "colored," appealing to Indian ancestry in family histories or public pageantry used Indianness, as they understood it, to undermine the very definition of the racial category assigned them by segregation.

African American social scientists presented a different kind of challenge as they defied the biological presuppositions behind a biracial system. Where anthropologists and eugenicists made claims about the traits of pure races and the dangers of race mixing, African American historians documented a long history of intermixture, calling into question the ideas of pure, and therefore separable, races. A third type of challenge to segregation came from Native American communities, such as the Lumbee tribe of North Carolina. At the turn of the twentieth century, proponents of legalized segregation used purported Lumbee intermixture with African Americans to challenge the Lumbees' claim to Native American identity.[11] For the Lumbee and other tribes, reasserting Native American identity denied the universal applicability of the biracial categories of "white" and "colored." Whether they were reasserting Native American identity, passing on tales of Native American ancestors, or rethinking the scientific and historical basis for racial categories, African Americans, Native Americans, and mixed peoples challenged local enforcement of the system of discriminatory segregation that assigned to them a singular status.

INVOKING ANCESTORS

In her book about her family, writer Kathryn Morgan resisted any singular definition of racial identity when she noted that her great-grandmother, her great-uncles, and great-aunt were "white by nature, black by law, African and Cherokee by choice. They called themselves the 'children of strangers.' "[12] Labeling themselves "African and Cherokee by choice" allowed her relatives to reconstruct for themselves and others the racial categories assigned them "by law" as residents of legally segregated Lynchburg, Virginia. Remembering Native American and African ancestry became part of a way of resisting a simplistic legal definition of themselves as "colored."

Morgan's account of her family's negotiation of their racial identity falls within a tradition of African American autobiography, where writers used their personal experiences to address the larger social, political, and economic context for their place in a segregated society.[13] While scholars often associated this tradition with African American intellectuals, I want to examine how other accounts of Native American ancestry addressed the context of segregation.

The Federal Writers' Project of the Works Progress Administration (WPA) sought to create work for up to five thousand writers in a year by commissioning travel guides, historical markers, and projects such as interviews with millworkers, immigrants, and former slaves. Although interviewers were often given racist guidelines for representing southern Black dialect, these materials provide a unique glimpse into popular perception of scientific ideas about race and racial inheritance.[14] In the same way that Morgan's anecdote revealed an acceptance of the categories of science and law as creating parameters within which her family reconstructed its identity, the WPA narratives offer a way to gauge the effects of the project of biracial classification that was inherent in segregation.[15]

Many of the former slaves interviewed as part of the WPA project remembered legacies of Native American ancestry. My survey of 2,193 narratives revealed that nearly 12 percent of the narratives contained some reference to the interviewee being related to or descended from a Native American.[16] While not all of these individuals elaborated on what significance these relations held for them, the fact that so many testified to such a heritage suggests that it was an important element in many family histories. The body of work written by historians Jack Forbes, R. Halliburton, Daniel Littlefield, and Theda Perdue speaks to the empirical evidence confirming the long history of interrelations and the probability that the family memories are rooted in historical realities.[17]

Underlying this effort to recall Native American kinship was the popularly held assumption that racial characteristics were biological and passed on from one generation to the next. Immediately prior to the challenge to racial classification launched by social scientists in the early twentieth century, Americans – Black, white, and Indian – commonly understood race differences to be a matter of fact. For many of the informants of the WPA ex-slave narratives, this meant that any Native American blood conveyed to its recipient those racial characteristics thought to be innate in Native Americans. In the last quarter of the nineteenth century, the stereotypical racial characteristics most commonly associated with Native Americans by African Americans were those of the "noble savage." To many people at the turn of the century, then, any claim to Native American ancestry could be construed as a claim to the possession of some of the features of the "noble savage," including a heroic (sometimes savage) commitment to liberty, connection to the land, or an aristocratic if doomed opposition to "progress." Persons making such claims often saw themselves as the inheritors of those traits they found distinctively Native American and desirable because of this.[18]

For Anna Baker, an ex-slave from Monroe County, Mississippi, the knowledge of her grandfather's Native American blood was even more significant to her than his name. Close to eighty when she was interviewed,

Baker explained that her mother had left the family when she was very young and that all she knew of her maternal grandparents was that her grandfather had been a "full-blood" Indian.[19] His exploits, according to family legend, had included standing up to the overseer. It seems that he agreed to relinquish part of his freedom and to work for the man who owned Baker's grandmother in order to be near the woman he loved. There were limits to what he would tolerate while in this position, though. When the overseer tried to beat him, the grandfather retreated to his home and barred his door. In turn, the overseer, with others, threatened to break open the door, whereupon the grandfather responded by throwing "a shovel full of red hot coals" at them and then running away while the overseer screamed in pain.[20] The outcome of the tale served as both a moral to whites and a legacy of resistance for the teller: though he had disappeared, his granddaughter claimed that those "white folks" learned that if they were going to whip an Indian, as they had done so many of their slaves, they had better kill him or he would kill them.[21]

Anna Baker's narrative is fairly typical. Often in the WPA narratives, the Indian relative has disappeared, leaving a legacy of resistance to coercion and injustice. This particular narrative implies that the patrimony of free-dom loving manifested itself in the actions of Baker's mother, who, like Baker's father, left familial connections behind. Yet the story does not end there. The white interviewer had noted at the beginning of her report that Baker's "high forehead and prominent cheek bones indicate that there is a strain of other than the pure African in her blood." Baker herself directly attributes her "brown color" to her maternal grandfather. The imprint of his physical characteristics, she implies, mirrors those of his less visible ones. The threat of the lesson for the overseer might well reside in Baker's own self.[22]

The explicit threat of such Indian forebears was often presented not only as a part of the individual giving the oral history but as a separable element of that person's makeup. The example of Rebecca Hooks is typical of one way of perceiving blood and racial character. Hooks noted with some pride that her former mistress blamed her tendency to resist direc-tions on the "cursed Cherokee blood in her." This phrasing, so common it is almost clichéd, suggests that the Native American kinship bestowed separable platelets, each imbued with whatever stereotypically Indian qualities were advantageous to the situation. Hooks could not help her need to assert herself as someone not entirely at the whim of her capricious mistress; it was her "Indian blood."[23]

In his WPA interview, Frank Berry of Jacksonville, Florida, identified himself as a grandson of Osceola, "the last fighting chief of the Seminole tribe."[24] His grandmother had been kidnapped by the Seminoles who, as Berry recalled, often intermarried with captured or escaped slaves. Although eventually retaken by her former slave master, she passed on to her son a characterization of his Native American heritage that celebrated the bravery of the people on his father's side of the family. "The red men," he is quoted as noting, "were credited with inciting many uprisings and wholesale escapes among the slaves."[25]

This direct claim to the legacy of Native American resistance and "Indian royalty," as Osceola is presented, may have influenced the interviewer's perception of Berry. Pearl Randolph's report identifies Berry as holding numerous offices in the Radical Reconstruction Government in the South following the Civil War. An experiment in biracial government that for a time offered the hope of an eventual move toward political and civil equality, Radical Reconstruction was short-lived and not well supported while in effect. During that brief interlude, Frank Berry had served as a state and federal government contractor and, after Reconstruction ended, as a registration inspector in 1879 and a U.S. marshal in 1881. As Randolph commented, Berry, "who in spite of reduced circumstances manages still to make one think of top hats and state affairs," reminded her of "the old days of black aristocracy when Negroes held high political offices in the state of Florida, when Negro tradesmen and professionals competed successfully and unmolested with the whites."[26] There is an implicit equation made in Randolph's account between Berry's Indian ancestry, as the grandson of Osceola, and as a member of what she called the "black aristocracy" of Reconstruction. Both are rendered in her narrative as tragically, and inevitably, disappearing. Yet this does not jibe with the way Berry presents his Indian kinship. His version suggests that the same qualities that inspired "uprisings and wholesale escapes" live on in his veins.

Often the Native Americans who appear in the WPA narratives, whether as relations or simply as people living near the ex-slaves, are described in terms of how they differ from whites. This is exactly the image of "the White Man's Indian," which Robert Berkhofer Jr. characterizes as a "separate and single other . . . always alien to the White."[27] The context here is important, though, because the image is offered in the narratives as both a critique of whites and as a celebratory record of familial attributes, many of them an integral part of the individuals' self-construction.

This kind of laudatory representation can be seen in narratives depicting Indians as living outside of the economic control of plantation society.

Black interviewees remembered Indian kin who preferred living in the woods or who possessed remarkable naturalist skills as well as attributes like innate fierceness. Martha Richardson's father, a Native American, like the "general run of Indians," loved to hunt.[28] She claimed that he passed on his family legacy, telling her many times about the "great Catawba Indians" who "made all of their own medicines and killed bears wearing their skins after roasting the flesh for a feast."[29] She was known locally for her mastery of Indian medical lore. For Millie Ann Smith, her grand-father's stories of running off to stay with his relatives at the nearby Native American camp for weeks at a time seemed to be related to his skill at hunting the deer, wild hogs, turkeys, and raccoons that fed his master's family when they first moved to Texas.[30] The image Robert Scott had of his Native American mother was that she could "row a boat, shoot a bird on the wing, and perform wondrous feats of strength and skill."[31]

All of these images of Native Americans share the memory of resistance to "civilization" as embodied by the slave plantation system. Passed down through the family for generations, these images were remembered as a viable part of their identity in the midst of a cultural project undertaken by scholars, newspaper editors, and government policy-makers to claim that since Native Americans in the West had been entirely subdued, they would soon "vanish," as they had already done in the East.[32] Historian Rayna Green suggests that this context is particularly important because the pervasive American cultural practice of what she calls "playing Indian" by non-Indian people depends upon the "physical and psychological re-moval, even the death, of Indians." It is possible to interpret the WPA stories as genealogical "performances," since so many of the representa-tions echo the stereotypical images of Indians available in cultural forums like novels, pageants, medicine shows, and paintings. Jeffrey Steele, for ex-ample, identifies the features most often ascribed to Indians in nineteenth-century advertising as codifying the four most prevalent images in the WPA narratives: Indian ancestors as vanishing royalty, as possessing a special affinity for nature, as doomed by an innately noble character in the face of white progress, and as possessing an unchangeable savagery. The context of racial ideology at the time, however, prevents these images from func-tioning merely as performative. The Blacks invoking these images indicate that, in light of scientific arguments about racial inheritance, these char-acteristics ran through their blood. Indian traits flowed through their veins.[33]

Claiming kinship with Native Americans provided African Americans in the late nineteenth and early twentieth centuries with a way of rebelling against a system of segregation, discrimination, and "civilization" imposed on them by white society. This can be considered a route of resistance because white and Black Americans with the aid of cultural images, science, and governmental policy defined Indians as living outside of white society. They perceived Indians to be dangerous for having fought the encroachment of society at virtually every step. Native American ancestors could thus be empowering insofar as the Native American embodied the potential in Blacks themselves to disrupt social order and white civilization.

RESISTANCE ON PARADE

African Americans propagated the image of the rebellious Native American in their families as an expression of their own resistance to both slavery and legalized segregation. They also used the image of the savage Indian to resist indirectly ordinances and situations that would have been dangerous for them to oppose openly. One of the most readily apparent instances of this type of resistance was the Plains Indian costume adopted and then modified by African Americans participating in Mardi Gras parades at the end of the nineteenth century.

Beginning in 1880s, groups of African Americans began appearing at Mardi Gras dressed in elaborate, handmade costumes which are never reworn. They ritually confront other such groups, called tribes, with highly regulated invented songs, rhymes, and dances. In these battles, the hierarchy of the tribe is supported by a "second line" of neighborhood residents who urge on the combatants. Scholars have drawn connections between these practices and similar ones in the African-Caribbean carnival tradition.[34] While such cultural connections and continuities are important, so is a detailed understanding of the particular context in which such practices developed.

By invoking Native American ancestry in parade, African Americans symbolically resisted the white consolidation of power and segregation imposed in the city of New Orleans, once considered one of the most fluid racial societies in the United States. As Reconstruction ended, the New Orleans white elite used a biological argument about race to impose racial hierarchies and control; they did this both by civic symbol (the Mardi Gras parade) and by violent action. The same civic symbol, though, could function for those people being disenfranchised as well. This was especially true when there was not much that could be done in the face of the white regime's escalating "Redemptionist" violence. Invoking Indian imagery in terms of ancestry and emblem provided a symbolic avenue for resistance. The historical specificities of the process by which the Mardi Gras Indians developed warrants explication because it provides a model for considering the relationship between identity and segregation.[35]

Though African Americans and Creoles had long dressed in Native American costumes for New Orleans's carnival, the first organized tribes appeared the year that Buffalo Bill's Wild West Show wintered in New Orleans to take advantage of the crowds for the World's Industrial and Cotton Exposition in 1885. The man credited with founding the first Mardi Gras Indian tribe, Becate Batiste, was clearly influenced by Cody's Wild West Show, naming his tribe the Creole Wild West Tribe. Batiste's tribe and others, such as the 101 Wild West Tribe, modeled themselves on Cody's show for a variety of reasons. Folklorist Michael P. Smith argues that the Plains Indians depicted in Cody's show had achieved the status of "a mythic people" among New Orleans Blacks.[36] By reenacting before the audience the methods of Anglo-Saxon manifest destiny, Cody provided a scenario representing both the consolidation of white power and the Indian as the vehicle for resisting that power. This formula was presented to an African American audience in New Orleans well aware of the consolidation of white power and their own disenfranchisement. From the middle of the nineteenth century, first slavery and then segregation in New Orleans had been paraded and resisted in the civic performances of the Mardi Gras carnival.

Beginning in 1857, New Orleans's emerging professional and merchant classes sought to replace the city's old Creole elite by reining in the interclass and interracial revelry associated with the Creole balls and masked parades. The formation of "The Mystic Krewe of Comus" to take over Mardi Gras by non-Creole white professionals signaled that the relationship between the civic display of position and power and the city's racial order would become increasingly intertwined. Significantly, the displacement of Creole ceremonial control by the krewe was soon followed by the outlawing of manumission of slaves by owners and by resolutions urging New Orleans's large population of free people of color to seek masters.

This was only the beginning. The history of the Crescent City Democratic Club, for example, demonstrates a clear connection between the civic rule presented at Mardi Gras and actual civic rule. Formed in 1868, the same year that the Radical Reconstruction Constitutional Convention in Louisiana desegregated public schools and facilities and guaranteed

African Americans the right to vote and the right to hold office, the Crescent City Democratic Club was politically affiliated with the Ku Klux Klan. In conjunction with other clubs, in 1870 they went on to form the city's second krewe, "The Twelfth Night Revelers." Like its Miltonian predecessor, the name of the second krewe paid oblique homage to their English-speaking origins, but their parades would quickly become explicitly racist.[37] In 1873, Comus invoked Darwin with a "Missing Links Parade," and another krewe, Momus, expanded on the Social Darwinist theme by mocking the offspring of interracial families in a parade called The Coming Races. The next year the Crescent City Democratic Club renamed itself the Crescent City White League and brought guns into the city in order to overthrow the Republican government. Claiming that the Democratic governor was the properly elected official, it urged white citizens to "redress grievances." The league's actions were racially motivated and directed at controlling what its newspapers had decried as "the Africanization" of the state. White racial dominance that had been acted out symbolically in the parade was now being enacted at gunpoint.

African Americans openly resisted the actions of the White League. Many fought the White League as part of the state militia led by former Confederate General James Longstreet. Although White League control of New Orleans government was put down by federal troops, the segregation of schools and streetcars remained a flashpoint for racial conflict. Members of the White League took it upon themselves to segregate schools forcibly by removing Black children. African Americans attacked and commandeered white streetcars in Black neighborhoods. Both actions led to rioting, with the African American community usually bearing the brunt of the violence.[38]

If African Americans were faced with such ominous obstacles with federal troops in the city, the Compromise of 1876 removing federal troops guaranteed that the arena for resisting white control would be more limited and fraught with danger. After 1876, the White League (and other organizations) that had so openly controlled the city made no effort to hide its power. The Mardi Gras performance of this consolidation left little to be doubted: the Rex parade performed "The Military Progress of the World," while Comus took as its theme "The Aryan Race." There were no more oblique overtures to English literary themes or to scientific theories; the relationship between racial dominance and military protection of segregation was performed civically.

As Mardi Gras became an attraction for tourists in the early 1880s, the parades became more "Confederate," marrying military and white supremacist causes in a romance about the "Lost Cause." By 1884, when Buffalo Bill's show came to New Orleans, the civic presentation of the relationship between the white elite in the city and its control of the future by invoking the past was rooted in an increasing focus on the Confederacy. A statue of Robert E. Lee, built by the Ladies Confederate Association, was unveiled in 1884, and Comus chose for its first queen Lee's granddaughter, Mildred Lee. The daughters of Jefferson Davis, Stonewall Jackson, and D. H. Hill completed the court. Adding women to the Comus's court also completed the story of ruling power.[39] It became a tale of closed bloodlines and the importance of genealogy as much as one of military control. The performance of lineage for the public spoke to this method of control.

As the "old line" krewes were consolidating their myth about their right to rule the city, organized tribes of Mardi Gras Indians began to appear. Culture critic George Lipsitz has characterized the appearance of the Mardi Gras tribes as a counternarrative to the hegemonic story of the old krewes.[40] Where the old line sought to celebrate an "Aryan" lineage and to demonstrate the interconnections between the closed social world of clubs and old families, the Mardi Gras Indians celebrated a different genealogy. Indeed, Becate Batiste specifically cited his Choctaw ancestry as justification for his founding of the Creole Wild West Tribe and dressing as an Indian.[41]

Opposing the narrative of racial purity was not merely a performative practice for New Orleans Blacks. A number of them orchestrated a similar attack in the courts that paraders attempted in the streets. Though integrated by African American initiative under the Reconstruction government, the city's streetcars had been re-segregated. In 1890, an elite coterie of Blacks selected Homer Plessy to challenge the law insisting on separate accommodations for Blacks. Plessy was chosen because, though classified by the law as Black, his nearest "purely" Black relation had been a great-grandparent. His supporters assumed that Plessy's genealogy would make clear the impossibility of enacting legislation designed to separate races. The choice of Plessy challenged assumptions about purity of races and the separability of races. In the same way, the Mardi Gras Indians symbolically questioned the public parading of pure racial lineage and domination exemplified by "old line" krewes supported by members of the White League.[42]

In an atmosphere of violence and white control, the Mardi Gras Indians were masking in a way that invoked some of their ancestors and mixed lineage, but they did so in a way that also invoked the "danger" associated with the Plains Indians. A white observer in 1900 suggested that African Americans chose the Native American disguise, "doubtless from the facility with which it lends itself to a complete transformation of the personality."[43] For Jelly Roll Morton, born in New Orleans in 1886, the Mardi Gras Indians were real incarnations of wild men: "When I was a child, I thought they really was Native Americans. They wore paint and blankets and, when they danced, one would get in the ring and throw his head back and downward, stooping over and bending his knees, making a rhythm and singing – *T'ouwais, bas q'ouwais* – and the tribe would answer – *Ou tendais.*"[44] The dancing and singing of the "Black Indians" was a means of assuming a more threatening posture toward dominating whites by taking on the characteristics of the Native American, who was outside of segregation and seen as a symbol of defiance in the face of white domination. This choice of symbol and the flouting of racial etiquette remained an annual part of the tradition of New Orleans African Americans.[45]

RETHINKING THE RACIAL HIERARCHY

Where the African American population in general regarded Native Americans in a positive way, some Black intellectuals, including Booker T. Washington, regarded Indians as inferior to Blacks on the "scale of civilization." Although these two groups regarded what they saw as Native American characteristics differently, the Black population and Black intellectuals both used this separate racial category (Indian) to challenge the inferior place assigned to African Americans in a segregated society.

In November 1901, a member of the "vanishing race" of Plains Indian made an appearance at the Hampton Normal and Agricultural Institute, an industrial school founded in 1868 by Samuel Chapman Armstrong to provide a practical education for the children of freedmen.[46] His appearance was not unusual. Native Americans had been coming to Hampton since Richard Henry Pratt had first brought a group of Kiowa and Cheyenne prisoners to Hampton in 1878. Pratt, who would eventually found the Carlisle Institute for Native Americans in Pennsylvania, was convinced that the Native Americans' savageness was the effect of environment rather than heredity. He persuaded Armstrong, the son of a missionary to the natives of the Sandwich Islands, that the school designed to help with the racial uplift of the African American would also be an ideal location to "civilize" the people from the West who insisted upon living like savages, thus delaying the advance of American civilization to the western plains.[47]

Unlike his classmates at Hampton, who dressed in cambric dresses made by their own hands if they were female or gray uniforms with polished buttons if they were male, this member of the "vanishing race" in 1901 looked different.[48] He wore buckskin and feathers and a "proud carriage and alert bearing [that] proclaimed the untamed savage." Altogether, one observer noted of this individual, "with his strong Indian features and picturesque dress he looked for all the world as if he had just stepped out of the pages of some early American history."[49] He was dressed this way because the presence of Native Americans at Hampton had suggested to some of the teachers that it would be appropriate to revive the first Thanksgiving at the Massachusetts Bay Colony, and they had asked one of the Native American students to portray an Massachusetts Bay Native American. The tableau in which this Native American appeared was made more realistic by his "savage" features. Despite Pratt's belief in the civilizing effects of an industrial education, there persisted a perception (made clear in the language in which a *Southern Workman* article described this unidentified American Indian student) that there was something innately savage in every Native American.

This perception was reinforced by Hampton Institute's founder. Samuel Chapman Armstrong fervently believed that African Americans and Native Americans must be understood as races that occupied various rungs on a Social Darwinist "scale of civilization."[50] His experience at Hampton, aiding two of the "despised races" on their "slow, tortuous climb" toward Anglo-Saxon civilization, confirmed for him the appropriateness of this racial delineation.[51] In the "Annual School Report" of 1882, Armstrong noted with some despair that many of the Native American students were unable to resist the customs of their people when they returned to the reservations. As he put it, a Native American student "whose intelligence we have learned to respect surprises us sometimes by a darkness of the mind and superstition which is appalling."[52] Like the anonymous student who appeared in the Thanksgiving pageant with a "carriage" and "bearing" that proclaimed him to be an "untamed savage" as soon as he was stripped of his Hampton uniform, Armstrong's Native American students could not help but revert to their former ways once they were removed from the civilizing influence of the industrial school.

As with Native Americans, Armstrong also believed African Americans needed to acquire more respect for the dignity of labor before they could move further up the evolutionary scale. He often argued that "the great value of slavery for the Negro had been its practical lesson in the performance of disciplined labor."[53] That was why African Americans were closer to whites on the scale of civilization. Still, though slavery had taught African Americans "habits of labor," Armstrong observed, it had not inspired them with "enthusiasm" for it.[54] Both races could thus benefit from the industrial school's civilizing program.

Part of this program included learning and, ideally, internalizing the scale of civilization. This would allow students to understand their place in society and the need to work toward the ideal model. A young Native American girl's uncorrected answers to a geography exam, reprinted in an article in the *Southern Workman*, suggests how widely the scale of civilization was disseminated at Hampton:

9. To what race do we all belong?
9. The Human race
10. How many classes belong to this race?
10. There are five [*sic*] classes belonging to the Human race.
11. Which are the first?
11. The white people are the strongest.
12. Which are the next?
12. The Mongolians or yellows.
13. The next?
13. The Ethiopians or blacks.
14. Next?
14. The Americans or reds.[55]

One Hampton student who particularly seemed to internalize this model was Booker T. Washington.[56] At Armstrong's personal request, Washington put aside his own desires for summer work in West Virginia in order to serve as the Hampton "dorm father" for seventy-five Native American youths.[57] Years later, when Washington reflected on his experience at Hampton, he believed it important to recall this incident and how it addressed the scale of civilization: "I have often wondered if there was a white institution in this country whose students would have welcomed the incoming of more than a hundred companions of another race in the cordial way that these black students at Hampton welcomed the red ones. How often I have wanted to say to white students that they lift themselves up in proportion as they help to lift others, and the more unfortunate the race, and the lower in the scale of civilization, the more does one raise one's self by giving the assistance."[58]

While the scale of civilization promised a future of equality (if only other cultures would emulate whites) and explained a past of inequity, there was one thing it could not explain: the peculiarities of legalized segregation. Washington came face to face with the shortcomings of Armstrong's explanation of racial hierarchy in 1880. During that summer, as he recalled in *Up From Slavery*, he was required to escort one of his Native American charges to Washington DC. The Native American had become ill, and it became Washington's duty to "deliver him over to the Secretary of the Interior, and get a receipt for him, that he might be returned to his Western reservation."[59] On the steamboat, Washington and his charge entered the dining room. The steward informed Washington that the Native American could be served in the salon but that Washington could not be. This incident was repeated when Washington sought a hotel that would accommodate the Native American and himself. In both places, he was excluded because of his race while the Native American, a member of a less civilized race, was not.

Apparently this incident did not cause Washington to reevaluate the scale of civilization. When he recounted it in 1901, he dismissed the incident as an example of the "curious workings of caste in America."[60] Washington did not scrutinize that at Hampton, with the exception of the appointment of Black graduates as dorm advisers and some interracial industrial classes, Native Americans and African Americans were entirely segregated. Yet the fact that they lived in separate dorms, ate in separate dining rooms, drilled in separate companies, and sat separately in school chapel might be explained by a Virginia legislator's appeal to restore $15,000 to a bill to support Native American pupils at Hampton on the grounds that the African Americans and Native Americans were maintained in segregated quarters.[61]

Adhering to Armstrong's scale of civilization, which consistently placed the Native American below the African American, might be viewed as Washington's means of resisting legalized segregation. If his readers and his pupils at Tuskegee could be persuaded of the correctness of the scale, then it could be argued that the exclusion of African Americans but inclusion of Native Americans by segregation ordinances mocked the Christian values of civilized society. Washington was making an appeal to reason: given the scale of civilization, if you do not discriminate against Native Americans, then you should not discriminate against African Americans because they are actually higher on the scale of civilization than Native Americans. Washington's was an intellectual response to the way the color line was drawn and segregation enforced.

While educators such as Booker T. Washington were discussing racial differences in terms of degrees of civilization, a new intellectual milieu for the discussion of race differences was emerging, namely that of eugenics and the nature-versus-nurture controversy. The recasting of race in eugenical terms required a different kind of intellectual response – one that was provided by a growing number of social scientists and African American historians in the United States. Scholars like Carter G. Woodson and Alain Locke responded to eugenics by attacking one of its key presuppositions, the biological conception of race.

One of the most popular and influential books on eugenics, *Applied Eugenics*, written by Paul Popenoe and Roswell H. Johnson in 1918, captured the majority opinion on the "Negro question."[62] Popenoe and Johnson concluded that there were great differences between whites and African Americans with regard to both physical and mental traits. In many respects, they found the Negro race to be inferior by the standards of civilization and progress in North America: "the Negro lacks in his germ plasm excellence of some qualities which the white races possess, and which are essential for success in competition with the civilizations of the white races of the present day."[63] The eugenical inferiority of the Negro race forced them to condemn miscegenation and to support segregation as "a social adaptation with survival value."[64] The existing system of segregation thus received a ringing endorsement from these leaders in the eugenics community. Segregation had become a matter of eugenics and the very survival of the human race.

While eugenics leaders promoted segregation, they rarely did so at the level of specific legislation such as marriage restriction laws. Because they were skeptical of the effectiveness of this legislation, its promotion was often left to local groups such as women's clubs, churches, and physicians.[65] Marriage restriction laws may have done little in general, but action at the local level could have considerable impact, as the case of Dr. Plecker illustrates.

Walter Ashby Plecker, M.D., led a crusade as the registrar of Virginia's Bureau of Vital Statistics to assure the "race purity" of Virginia residents.[66] According to Plecker, there were only two possible racial classifications, "white" and "colored." This angered many of the aristocratic Virginia families, who liked to trace their ancestry to Pocahontas. Though some of these individuals may have fit Zora Neale Hurston's outlandish characterization of "white ancestor-hounds . . . whose folks went to England with William the Conqueror, got restless and caught the *Mayflower* for Boston, then feeling a romantic lack, rushed down the coast and descended from Pocahontas," they felt strongly enough about their Native American ancestor *and* their legal rights as whites to force a legal classification of white that included anyone with one-sixteenth or less Native American blood.[67]

This infuriated Plecker, who thought that definition of white left a "chink in the wall" through which anyone with a dark complexion could pass into the white race by simply claiming that the "suspicious" ancestor had been a Native American.[68] He set out on a campaign to reverse the racially deleterious effects of allowing such intermixture to occur. In 1923, he influenced the adoption of the Racial Integrity Law, which stated that Native American people who wanted to transact legal business had to fill out forms with questions about race in conformity with the records of the Vital Statistics Bureau. To persuade the U.S. Census Bureau that the 1930 census should show no Native Americans living in Virginia, Plecker wrote in 1925 to the census director that he had "absolute proof" that Native Americans were actually African Americans, since "we have their pedigree back."[69] He began collecting old federal censuses and county birth, marriage, and death records, as well as information from "reliable" individuals, to prove that Virginians claiming to be Native American were actually of African ancestry. He seized every opportunity to voice his opinion on such racial "mongrels," including a pamphlet published in 1928 by the Bureau of Vital Statistics with "a warning to the public about the racial machinations of ambitious non-whites."[70] In the same year, Plecker secured legal backing for attaching a warning to Native American birth and death certificates, which noted that anyone registered as a Native American should be classed as "colored" and treated accordingly. These Racial Integrity Law measures remained in place until 1959, with Native American birth and death certificates retaining their warning until 1972.[71]

Plecker's efforts provoked a derisive response from National Association for the Advancement of Colored People NAACP leader W. E. B. DuBois, who commented, "It is with difficulty that one keeps from laughing over the plight of Virginia and its 'race purity' legislation." DuBois's editorial in the NAACP journal the *Crisis* suggested something of the African American intellectual response to eugenics and segregation. When DuBois went on to argue that for some 311 years, whites, African Americans, and Native Americans in Virginia had been intermarrying and intermingling, he drew upon a serious response already formulated by the contributors to Carter G. Woodson's *Journal of Negro History*.[72]

From the time of its first appearance in 1916, the *Journal of Negro History*, under the direction of Carter G. Woodson, began to put into practice what Alain Locke had recently theorized as the best direction from which to approach issues of race. In 1915, Locke, as a member of the Teacher's College at Howard University, delivered a series of public lectures deemed by the Board of Trustees too controversial to be included in the regular Howard curriculum. These lectures laid out Locke's new analysis of race as a historical and cultural phenomenon, not a biological phenomenon. This new generation of Black intellectuals thus differed from their predecessors like Booker T. Washington. Still, they, too, used Native Americans to challenge the biological justification for segregation.[73]

Drawing on the work of anthropologist Franz Boas, Locke argued that racial categories were not innate but were subject to change. Pure races or "purity of blood" was taken by Locke to be "a science fiction." Moreover, Locke doubted that any historical evidence could be obtained to demonstrate that pure races had ever existed.[74] This last comment undoubtedly resonated with Carter G. Woodson and with his vision of the task of "Negro history." Only three years after Locke's lectures, Woodson asserted in the *Journal of Negro History* that "science has uprooted the theory . . . that the white race is superior to others" and may be preserved in its purity and integrity.[75]

In his own work, Woodson challenged the existence of pure biological races by historically documenting white and African American miscegenation in Africa and, significantly, Black-Indian intermixture in the United States. Woodson's article on the historical intermarriage of African Americans and Native Americans in Massachusetts traced their interactions from the first contact through the enfranchisement of the Native Americans in the latter quarter of the nineteenth century.[76] The point of the article was that there had been "extensive miscegenation" of the two races.[77] Such articles undercut the historical basis for claims of racial purity.

Between 1929 and 1933 the *Journal of Negro History* published three major articles on African American–Native American relations. Two of these, by Kenneth Porter, were designed to provide historical substantiation for Melville Herskovits's claim that 27.2 percent of the African Americans he surveyed had some Native American ancestry.[78] Assuming that such intermingling took place, Porter sought to establish the historical circumstances, surveying African American and Native American relations from Coronado in 1541 to the two groups' interaction at Hampton Institute, established in 1878.[79] Although Porter thought that diffusing Native American blood throughout the African American population was healthy, he believed that the development of isolated racially mixed communities in secluded parts of the United States was not. This negative claim is immediately countered by Porter's assertion that "a sufficient number of persons of Negro-Indian blood have attained such positions of usefulness and even distinction as to set at rest any idea that this racial mixture is necessarily a bad one, biologically speaking."[80]

When James Hugo Johnson wrote an account of the interrelations of African Americans and Native Americans from the first settlement of North America, he may have been responding to racial theorists like Plecker, whose account of the founding of America insisted that the Europeans had come to America "bringing their families, the Bible, and high ideals of religious and civic freedom . . . not to mix their blood with the savages of the land."[81] After noting that whites had not succeeded in avoiding racial intermixture, Johnson observed that "the class commonly called the mulatto is the result, in many instances, of the union of the three racial elements."[82] He concluded his survey of African American–Native American relations by claiming, "Where the Negro was brought into contact with the American Indian the blood of the two races intermingled. The Indian has not disappeared from the land, but is now a part of the Negro population of the United States."[83]

With the rise of legal segregation and scientific racism, talk of separate races had a new connotation. Woodson's, Porter's, and Johnston's responses took the concern about mixing races seriously and threw into question the idea that such mixing was harmful. Instead, they suggested that the entire endeavor of categorizing "pure" races and enforcing racial integrity was ridiculous, if not impossible. Responding to the Virginia racial integrity legislation, the *Crisis* asked: "Can't you see the 'pure' Anglo-Saxons of the South ranged about, with a fringe of two million mulattos, not to mention that other and secret million who knowing and unknowing 'pass' for white? Can you not view the Anglo-Saxons of all Christendom who have spread their colored bastards over every continent and island of the sea and who have raped and despoiled black and brown and yellow womanhood under every circumstance of disgraceful fraud and force?"[84] It was important to these intellectuals, just as it had been important to Kathryn Morgan's family, that some of this racial intermixing was between African Americans and Native Americans.

RECLAIMING NATIVE AMERICAN IDENTITY

When his story was collected as part of the Federal Writers' Project oral histories of ex-slaves in 1936, Moble Hopson of Poquoson, Virginia, made sure that the interviewer was aware of his ancestry, "Mammy was uh Injun an' muh pappy was uh white man."[85] When asked why he was "put with the colored people," he responded, "Well, ah ain't white an' ah ain't black, leastwise not so fur as ah know. 'Twas the war done that." After the

Civil War, racial interactions that had been controlled by local custom began to change.

The eradication of the legal category of "free person of color" radically altered the status of the Hopson family. Local whites began to redefine community standing based strictly on a biracial code. Hopson summarized this code succinctly as "whut ain't white is black." In Hopson's case, whites began to enforce racial distinctions that before the war had not affected people who were understood to be descended from Native Americans. Intermarriage between Native Americans and whites was now forbidden, and Native Americans were turned away from the white church school they once had attended.[86] The Hopson family resisted this redefinition. When his children were not allowed to attend the white schools, Hopson's father did not allow them to attend school at all rather than "go to the colored school house." Forbidden by law from marrying white persons, the Hopson family married cousins rather than "marry colored."[87]

In many Native American communities, legalized segregation reinforced the search for differences between Native Americans and African Americans. In fact, between 1880 and 1920 many of the recognized Native American tribes in the Southeast United States established separate schools to avoid sending their children to Black schools.[88] For many unrecognized Native American groups in the Southeast, petitioning for recognition as American Indians was a way of both building community and identity as well as resisting the "white" and "colored" categories of segregation by insisting on the creation of a third legal category, "Indian."

The Lumbee tribe of Robeson County, North Carolina, are a striking case in point of the ongoing struggle for recognition after the Civil War. The Lumbees have a documented history as Native Americans dating back to the 1790 census.[89] Nevertheless, under slavery they were usually classified as "free persons of color" and as a result were denied the "right to keep and bear arms, to vote, to testify against Whites in court, to sit on any jury, to attend state-supported schools, and to select ministers for their churches."[90] Without these rights, keeping possession of their land proved very difficult when local whites would demand it as payment for invented wrongdoings. Moreover, as free persons of color during the Civil War, many Lumbees were pressed into labor building Fort Fisher, leaving their farms untended. The "starving time" of the 1860s was punctuated by the rise of the Lowry band, who took up arms after recruitment officers and the Confederate home guard had killed members of the Berry and Lowry families. The Lowry band was racially mixed and, though considered outlaws in the white community, lived for years among the Indians, African Americans, and poor whites of Robeson County.[91] The injustice of disenfranchisement and the defiance of the Lowry band set the stage for the Lumbees' push for recognition.

With the passage in 1875 of state constitutional amendments requiring separate schools for each race, schools and their control became a key site for Lumbees to assert their autonomy. Reconstruction in Robeson County involved increasing violence against Indians and African Americans partly in reaction to the Lowry band and partly as a result of the introduction of the Ku Klux Klan to the area.[92] In the two years before Congress passed the Ku Klux Klan acts of 1870–71 outlawing Klan terrorism, the Klan in North Carolina was averaging one murder a month.[93] For the Lumbees, refusing to send their children to Black schools was a way both to resist any further disenfranchisement and to assert their own autonomy as Native Americans. Adolph Dial and David Eliades have called the years between 1875 and 1885 the "Decade of Despair" for the Lumbees. In their words, "not only were they denied schools of their own, but they were now made brutally aware of their lack of recognition as a people."[94]

The push for separate schools and recognition was aided by Democratic legislator Hamilton McMillan and his 1888 history of the Lumbees as the Croatan Indians associated with the Lost Colony of Roanoke. According to McMillan, the Lumbees were descendants of Native Americans and members of Sir Walter Raleigh's lost colony. In 1885, McMillan's bill was passed, winning separate schools and recognition of the Lumbees as the "Croatan Indians." McMillan seems to have had a genuine interest in the Native Americans from his district but probably thought that the recognition bill would also help win votes and reduce the threat of another Lowry band emerging.[95]

Recognition by the state as "Croatans" legally established a third racial category for the Lumbees, but in practice white attitudes were not quick to change. To anthropologist James Mooney, the name "Croatan" was a "convenient label" that made clear the mixed racial status of the group. For local whites, "Croatan" was shortened to "Cro," with the implication that these Native Americans, like their Black neighbors, had the same place under segregation, in other words, as "Jim Crow." Rather than resolving issues of Native American recognition, "Croatan" had become a fighting word.[96] In 1911 the Lumbees succeeded in petitioning the legislature to change their name to the "Indians of Robeson County," which removed the offensive reference to "Jim Crow" but did little to aid in the cause of recognition locally or with the federal government. Although the Lumbees did gain separate hospital rooms and jail cells as "Indians of

Robeson County," they changed their name again to the "Cherokee Indians of Robeson County" in 1913. Although distinct from the Cherokee of western North Carolina, as the Cherokee Indians of Robeson County they renewed their efforts for federal benefits. It was not until 1956 that the federal government recognized them as the Lumbee tribe, although it would not extend to them benefits it extended to other Native American tribes.

Throughout their struggle for recognition in the late nineteenth and early twentieth centuries, the Lumbees' status as Native Americans was frequently called into question by white officials because of the Lumbees' history of race mixture. White officials and white neighbors were unwilling to grant the existence of a third racial category that complicated their racial hierarchy. While the Lumbees' struggle for recognition and autonomy speaks to their defiance of the biracial code of segregation, that defiance was limited. The Lumbees resisted their own categorization as "colored" but in doing so did not question the system that maintained a racial hierarchy of "white" over "colored." In fact, after the Civil War, previously open and friendly relationships between the Lumbees and their African American neighbors became much more tense.[97] The Lumbees were seen by their African American neighbors as trying to disassociate from them and so were viewed as complicit in the discriminatory effects of segregation.

Not every Native American community in the Southeast was as successful in its fight for recognition as were the Lumbees, but under legalized segregation many Native Americans took steps to distance themselves from African Americans. In Virginia, the Pamunkeys carried membership cards to assure they would not be forced into the "colored" railway coach.[98] Some of the tribal chiefs of the Pamunkeys made certain to wear their hair long in order to show that it was straight and not kinky.[99] In the Blue Ridge Mountains, the Monacan tribe, previously referred to as the Amherst County Indians or as the WIN tribe in a notorious eugenical study of 1926, would not associate with African Americans and could not associate with local whites.[100] The Monacans' situation reflected the character of the local imposition of legalized segregation. The Monacans were known in their area as a racially mixed group and could not recategorize themselves as white by simply denying that they had any African American ancestry.[101] Their representation as mixed by local white officials and church leaders probably also discouraged them from following a strategy of seeking state recognition as the Lumbees had. Like Moble Hopson's family, some of whom chose to remain illiterate and intermarry rather than attend a colored school or marry African Americans, the Monacans socially isolated themselves in the Blue Ridge county in which they lived. Their refusal to intermingle with local African Americans, however, did not allow them to escape the fate assigned to those classified as "colored" by segregation legislation or local custom. Like their African American neighbors, the Monacans' dark skin color marked them as "inferior" in the eyes of local whites and probably kept them raising tobacco on shares and working as a seasonal labor force for white farmers.[102]

CONCLUSION

At a time when governments in the United States were codifying ways to keep the "white" and "colored" races separate in order to keep them unequal *and* unmixed, articulating African American–Native American interrelations was an important form of resistance for people of mixed and African American ancestry. Claiming Native American identity, Native American ancestry, or simply borrowing Native American costume was a way of defying a demeaning biracial code that imposed its own system of identity. Articulating African American and Native American interrelations thus was not merely a matter of defiance but a matter of reclaiming one's identity.

When James Hugo Johnston wrote his history of African American and Native American intermixture, he celebrated a shared history. Zora Neale Hurston celebrated that same history when she wrote, "it is a well known fact that no matter where two sets of people come together, there are bound to be some in betweens. . . . There is no *The Negro* here. Our lives are so diversified, internal attitudes so varied, appearances and capabilities so different, that there is no possible classification that will cover us all."[103] Legalized segregation was oppressive and its influence was pervasive, but the oversimplicity of its system of racial classification was obvious. Diversity not recognized by law was recognized by people of color and reclaimed in their resistance. Kathryn Morgan's relatives may have been Black by law, but they were African and Cherokee by choice.

NOTES

I am in debt to a number of people for their helpful commentary on various drafts of this paper; they include the members of Leon Litwack's seminar on African American history at University of California at Berkeley, James Brooks, Steven Crum, Michael Dietrich, Margaret Jacobs, Waldo Martin, Valerie Mendosa, Jane

Morrison, Sarah Projansky, Mary P. Ryan, Marcy Sacks, Jill Schlessinger, Laura Schwemm, Linda Song, and Jessica Weiss.

1. Zora Neale Hurston, *Dust Tracks on a Road* (Urbana: University of Illinois Press, 1984), 235.

2. Melville J. Herskovits, *The American Negro: A Study in Racial Crossing* (Bloomington: Indiana University Press, 1928), 9. August Meier's 1949 survey of students at Tougaloo College in Mississippi revealed that 72 percent claimed Native American ancestry. Meier, "A Study of Racial Ancestry of the Mississippi College Negro," *American Journal of Physical Anthropology* 7 (1949): 228–32. See the discussion of Meier in Jack Forbes, "The Manipulation of Race, Caste, and Identity: Classifying AfroAmericans, Native Americans, and Red-Black People," *Journal of Ethnic Studies* 17 (1990): 17–18.

3. Melville J. Herskovits, *The Anthropometry of the American Negro* (New York: AMS Press, 1930), 15. The 1928 study was part of the more comprehensive 1930 study. Hurston assisted on both.

4. Dwight W. Hoover, *The Red and the Black* (Chicago: Rand McNally College Publishing, 1976), 233–53; Hamilton Cravens, *The Triumph of Evolution* (Philadelphia: University of Pennsylvania Press, 1978).

5. See Paul R. Spickard, *Mixed Blood: Intermarriage and Ethnic Identity in Twentieth-Century America* (Madison: University of Wisconsin Press, 1989); J. A. Clifton, ed., *The Invented Indian: Cultural Fictions and Government Policies* (Brunswick NJ: Transaction Publishers, 1990); Terry P. Wilson, "Blood Quantum: Native American Mixed Bloods" in *Racially Mixed People in America*, ed. Maria P. P. Root (Newbury Park CA: Sage Publications, 1992).

6. Following Peggy Pascoe's suggestion in "Miscegenation Law, Court Cases, and Ideologies of 'Race' in Twentieth Century America," *Journal of American History* 83 (1996): 44–69, I approach the racial categories of scientific racism through the social construction of racial categories and identities. On the history of scientific racism, see Elazar Barkan, *The Retreat of Scientific Racism: Changing Concepts of Race in Britain and the United States between the Wars* (Cambridge: Cambridge University Press, 1992); George M. Frederickson, *The Black Image in the White Mind: The Debate on Afro-American Character and Destiny, 1817–1914* (New York: Harper and Row, 1971); Thomas F. Gossett, *Race: The History of an Idea in America* (New York: Schocken Books, 1965); John S. Haller Jr., *Outcasts from Evolution: Scientific Ideas of Racial Inferiority, 1859–1900* (Urbana: University of Illinois Press, 1971); Richard M. Hofstadter, *Social Darwinism in American Thought* (Boston: Beacon Press, 1955); Idus A. Newby, *Jim Crow's Defense: Anti-Negro Thought in America, 1900–1930* (Baton Rouge: Louisiana State University Press, 1965); Joel Williamson, *New People: Miscegenation and Mulattoes in the United States* (London: Free Press, 1980).

7. C. Vann Woodward, *The Strange Career of Jim Crow* (New York, 1955;

reprint, New York: Oxford University Press, 1966), 99–100 (page citations are to the reprint edition).

8. An article from the *Crisis* eloquently described the effect of this first segregation legislation as follows: "This means that in each of these states a Negro passenger pays a first-class fare for second or third class accommodations; is carried in the most dangerous and dirtiest part of the train; is given the least comfort and protection, and is often open to insult and molestation from the occupants of the white smoking car. . . . This legislation is not only discrimination and insult – it is theft." "The Commission of Inter-Racial Co-operation," *Crisis* 37 (July 1930): 243.

9. Neil R. McMillen, *Dark Journey: Black Mississippians in the Age of Jim Crow* (Urbana: University of Illinois Press, 1989), 3–5.

10. On segregation in Washington DC, see Constance Green, *The Secret City: A History of Race Relations in the Nation's Capital* (Princeton NJ: Princeton University Press, 1967).

11. Efforts to determine the terms of their own racial identity, controlled to large extent by categories of race and ethnicity available on the U.S. census, have long been fought over. It was not until the U.S. government ruled that a group of Virginia Indians could determine whether they would be considered "colored" – and so whether they would be placed in segregated military units – during World War II over the assessment by the state of Virginia that they must be considered African American. See Paul T. Murray, "Who Is an Indian? Who Is a Negro? Virginia Indians in the World War II Draft," *Virginia Magazine of History and Biography* 95 (1987): 215–31.

12. Kathryn L. Morgan, *Children of Strangers: The Stories of a Black Family* (Philadelphia: Temple University Press, 1980), 7.

13. V. P. Franklin, *Living Our Stories, Telling Our Truths: Autobiography and the Making of the African American Intellectual Tradition* (Oxford: Oxford University Press, 1995).

14. "Memorandum from Henry Bennett to Mrs. Wharton, Dated February 21, 1941" reprinted in the appendix to the general introduction, George P. Rawick, ed., *The American Slave: A Composite Autobiography*, Supplement Series 1, 6: Mississippi Narratives, Part 1 (Westport CT: Greenwood Press, 1977), lxii–lxiii.

15. Similar interviews conducted by the American Freedmen's Inquiry Commission sixty years earlier do not present the same kind of concerns or categories. No one describes themselves in terms of their racial ancestry. The operative categories for these individuals were "slave" or "free." Since the WPA narratives were conducted in the 1930s, they reflect the post–Civil War scientific project of racial classification that I argue works in conjunction with legalized segregation. For a reprint of some of the American Freedmen's Inquiry Commission interviews, see John Blassingame, *Slave Testimony: Two Centuries of Letters, Speeches, Interviews and Autobiographies* (Baton Rouge: Louisiana State University Press, 1977).

16. While many of the narratives discussed memories of Indians living near the interviewees, for the purposes of this project I considered only those narratives that claimed some kind of kinship relation to Native Americans. See especially the Oklahoma volumes for representations of Native Americans not claimed as kin in Rawick, *American Slave*, 7, Supplement Series 1, 12.

17. See especially Jack D. Forbes, *Black Africans and Native Americans: Color, Race and Caste in the Evolution of Red-Black Peoples* (Oxford: Basil Blackwell, 1988); R. Halliburton Jr., *Red over Black: Black Slavery among the Cherokee Indians* (Westport CT: Greenwood Press, 1977); Daniel F. Littlefield Jr., *The Cherokee Freedmen: From Emancipation to American Citizenship* (Westport CT: Greenwood Press, 1978); Theda Perdue, *Slavery and the Evolution of Cherokee Society, 1540–1866* (Knoxville: University of Tennessee Press, 1979).

18. See Robert F. Berkhofer Jr., *The White Man's Indian: Images of the American Indian from Columbus to the Present* (New York: Vintage Books, 1978); Roy Harvey Pearce, *Savagism and Civilization: A Study of the Indian and the American Mind* (1953; reprint, Baltimore: Johns Hopkins University Press, 1977); S. Elizabeth Bird, ed., *Dressing in Feathers: The Construction of the Indian in American Popular Culture* (Boulder CO: Westview Press, 1996); Richard Drinnon, *Facing West: The Metaphysics of Indian-Hating and Empire-Building* (Minneapolis: University of Minnesota Press, 1980).

19. Rawick, *American Slave*, Supplement, Series 1, 6: Mississippi Narratives, 92.

20. Rawick, *American Slave*, Supplement, Series 1, 6: Mississippi Narratives, 99.

21. Rawick, *American Slave*, Supplement, Series 1, 6: Mississippi Narratives, 99–100.

22. Rawick, *American Slave*, Supplement, Series 1, 6: Mississippi Narratives, 92.

23. Rawick, *American Slave* 17: Florida Narratives, 175.

24. Rawick, *American Slave* 17: Florida Narratives, 27.

25. Rawick, *American Slave* 17: Florida Narratives, 28. On the significance of the legacy and popular perception of Osceola and the Seminoles, see Jay Mechling, "Florida Seminoles and the Marketing of the Last Frontier," in Bird, *Dressing in Feathers*.

26. Rawick, *American Slave* 17: Florida Narratives, 29.

27. Berkhofer, *White Man's Indian*, xv.

28. Rawick, *American Slave* 3: South Carolina Narr. (Part 4), 19.

29. Rawick, *American Slave* 3: South Carolina Narr. (Part 4), 19.

30. Rawick, *American Slave* 5: Texas Narratives (Part 4), 41.

31. Orra Langhorne, "Robert Scott, the Albemarle Minstrel," *Southern Workman* 29 (March 1900): 165–68.

32. The report of the Indian Commissioner of 1901, based on the census of the previous year, was the first to contradict the popularly held belief that Indians were disappearing. Though some tribes were reported to be dying out, others were increasing. "Report of the Indian Commissioner," *Southern Workman* 30 (January 1901): 748–49.

33. Rayna Greene, "The Tribe Called Wannabee: Playing Indian in America and Europe," *Folklore* 99, no. 1 (1988): 30–55; Jeffrey Steele, "Reduced to Images: American Indians in Nineteenth-Century Advertising," in Bird, *Dressing in Feathers*, 45–64.

34. Green, "Tribe Called Wannabee"; Mary P. Ryan, *Civic Wars: Democracy and Public Life in the American City during the Nineteenth Century* (Berkeley CA: University of California Press, 1997); Michael P. Smith, "New Orleans' Carnival Culture from the Underside," *Plantation Society in the Americas* 3 (1990): 11–32.

35. For an explication of the ways in which public pageantry can be seen as consolidating civic power, especially in terms of Mardi Gras, see Ryan, *Civic Wars*; and Green, "Tribe Called Wannabee."

36. Smith, "New Orleans' Carnival Culture"; James Gill, *Lords of Misrule: Mardi Gras and the Politics of Race in New Orleans* (Jackson: University Press of Mississippi), 1997.

37. "The Mystic Krewe of Comus" was named for a poem by John Milton.

38. John Blassingame, *Black New Orleans, 1860–1880* (Chicago: University of Chicago Press, 1973).

39. See Ryan, *Civic Wars*, 243–50.

40. George Lipsitz, *Time Passages: Collective Memory and American Popular Culture* (Minneapolis: University of Minnesota Press, 1990).

41. Indeed, to this day many Mardi Gras tribes cite their Indian blood as determining their right to participate in Indian costume. See Michael P. Smith, *Mardi Gras Indians* (Gretna LA: Pelican, 1994).

42. On Plessy, see Eric Sundquist, "Mark Twain and Homer Plessy," *Representations* 24 (1988): 102–28; Brook Thomas, ed., Plessy v. Ferguson: *A Brief History with Documents* (Boston: Bedford Books, 1997); Charles A. Lofgren, *The Plessy Case: A Legal-Historical Approach* (New York: Oxford University Press, 1987).

43. Richter, *Standard History*, 631.

44. Alan Lomax, *Mister Jelly Roll* (London: Virgin, 1991), 14. Samuel Kinser suggests that what had been described as nonsense, "*T'ouwais, bas q'ouwais, ou tendais*," might possibly be Creole ("*Tu [n']avais pas [de] couilles*") for "You have no balls." Kinser, *Carnival, American Style: Mardi Gras at New Orleans and Mobile* (Chicago: University of Chicago Press, 1990), 363.

45. Lomax, *Mister Jelly Roll*.

46. Brian Dippie, *The Vanishing American: White Attitudes and U.S. Indian*

Policy (Middletown CT: Wesleyan University Press, 1982); J. E. Davis, "Hampton Normal School and Agricultural Institute," *Colored American Magazine* 4 (December 1901): 111.

47. David Wallace Adams, "Education in Hues: Red and Black at Hampton Institute, 1878–1893," *South Atlantic Quarterly* 76 (spring 1977): 159–60.

48. J. E. Davis, "Scenes at a Hampton Anniversary," *Southern Workman* 42 (June 1913): 346–47; Booker T. Washington, *Up From Slavery* (1911; reprint, New York: A. L. Burt, 1967), 47.

49. "Hampton Incidents," *Southern Workman* 30 (January 1901): 779.

50. It was commonly believed at the turn of the twentieth century that Indians were disappearing as evidence of their lack of civilization. See "Wanted – A Brave Black Battalion," *Colored American Magazine* 12 (February 1907), 151; C. H. McAdam, "Booker T. Washington's Recent Trip through the Southwest," *Colored American Magazine* 10 (January 1906).

51. David Wallace Adams, "Education in Hues: Red and Black at Hampton Institute, 1878–1893," *South Atlantic Quarterly* 76 (spring 1977): 159–60, 161–62. See also Pearce, *Savagism and Civilization*.

52. Samuel Chapman Armstrong, "Annual School Report" (1 October 1882), 232, cited in Adams, "Education in Hues," 168.

53. Adams, "Education in Hues," 166.

54. Edith Armstrong Talbot, *Samuel Chapman Armstrong: A Biographical Study* (New York: Doubleday, Page, 1904), 228.

55. "Work and Fun in the Geography Class," *Southern Workman* 14 (February 1885), 20.

56. August Meier, *Negro Thought in America, 1880–1915* (Ann Arbor: University of Michigan Press, 1963), 102.

57. Washington, *Up From Slavery*, 67; Adams, "Education in Hues," 172.

58. Washington, *Up From Slavery*, 68.

59. Washington, *Up From Slavery*, 69.

60. Washington, *Up From Slavery*, 69.

61. Adams, "Education in Hues," 170; "Along the Color Line: Education," *Crisis* 4 (May 1912): 112.

62. Newby, *Jim Crow's Defense*, 35–36.

63. Paul Popenoe and Roswell H. Johnson, *Applied Eugenics* (New York: Macmillan, 1918), 280–85.

64. Newby, *Jim Crow's Defense*, 35–36.

65. Mark Haller, *Eugenics: Hereditarian Attitudes in American Thought* (New Brunswick NJ: Rutgers University Press, 1985), 141–42; Twentieth Century Club Manuscripts, *California Woman's Home and Club Journal, The Club Woman*, Bancroft Library, University of California, Berkeley.

66. Helen Rountree, "The Indians of Virginia: A Third Race in a Biracial State," in *Southeastern Indians Since the Removal Era*, ed. Walter L. Williams (Athens: University of Georgia Press, 1979), 41–43; W. E. B. DuBois, "Postscript," *Crisis* 37 (May 1930): 172. For a detailed account of Plecker's efforts, see J. David Smith, *The Eugenic Assault on America* (Fairfax VA: George Mason University Press, 1993), 59–100.

67. Hurston further joked that "from the number of her children, one is forced to the conclusion that Pocahontas wasn't so poky, after all." Hurston, *Dust Tracks on a Road*, 202.

68. Rountree, "Indians of Virginia," 41; Walter A. Plecker, "Virginia's Attempt to Adjust the Color Problem," *American Journal of Public Health* 15 (1925): 111–15.

69. Personal papers of Calvin L. Beale, letter of 15 January 1926 to U.S. Census Bureau, quoted in Rountree, "Indians of Virginia," 41–42.

70. Rountree, "Indians of Virginia," 42.

71. Rountree, "Indians of Virginia," 45, 42.

72. W. E. B. DuBois, "Virginia," *Crisis* 37 (May 1930): 172; The *Journal of Negro History* was not the only venue for this kind of work. See Laurence Foster, *Negro-Indian Relations in the Southeast* (Philadelphia, 1935; reprint, New York: AMS Press, 1978).

73. Jeffrey C. Stewart, introduction to *Race Contacts and Interracial Relations*, by Alain Locke (Washington DC: Howard University Press, 1992), xx.

74. Locke, *Race Contacts and Interracial Relations*, 86.

75. Carter G. Woodson, "The Beginnings of Miscegenation of the Whites and Blacks," *Journal of Negro History* 3 (1918): 335.

76. Carter G. Woodson, "The Relations of Negroes and Indians in Massachusetts," *Journal of Negro History* 5 (1920): 45–57.

77. Woodson, "Relations of Negroes and Indians," 45.

78. Kenneth Porter, "Relations between Negroes and Indians within the Present Limits of the United States," *Journal of Negro History* 17 (1932): 287–88.

79. Porter, "Relations between Negroes and Indians," 287–88; Kenneth Porter, "Notes Supplementary to 'Relations Between Negroes and Indians,'" *Journal of Negro History* 18 (1933): 317.

80. Porter, "Notes," 321.

81. Plecker, "Virginia's Attempt to Adjust the Color Problem," 111.

82. James Hugo Johnston, *Race Relations in Virginia and Miscegenation in the South, 1776–1860* (Amherst: University of Massachusetts Press, 1970), 172.

83. James Hugo Johnston, "Documentary Evidence of the Relations of Negroes and Indians," *Journal of Negro History* 14 (1929): 43.

84. "The Anglo-Saxon at Bay," *Crisis* 30 (May 1925): 10.

85. Rawick *American Slave* 16: Virginia Narratives, 31. Workers hired to collect

the ex-slave narratives for the WPA were instructed to "preserve" the dialect of the ex-slaves and along these lines were given guidelines on acceptable and unacceptable dialect forms. The result is that published dialogue may not always accurately reflect actual speech patterns. See C. Perdue Jr., T. Barden, and R. Philips, eds., *Weevils in the Wheat* (Bloomington: Indiana University Press, 1976), xxvi–xxviii, 377–82.

86. Rawick, *American Slave* 16, 38. Virginia tax rolls and census from 1780 to 1850 almost universally classified Indians as "free people of color" or "mulattoes." Jack D. Forbes, *Black Africans and Native Americans*, 89. A biographical sketch of another man described as white and Indian corroborates Hopson's experience: "All the children attended a white school in Charlottesville, the Virginia law at that time permitting free colored children to attend white school. In telling me of this, Mr. Scott said that the prejudice between the races was not so great then as now, and that he had never heard that any objection was made to the presence of colored children in the schools." Langhorne, "Robert Scott." See also Joel Williamson, *After Slavery: The Negro in South Carolina During Reconstruction, 1861–1877* (Chapel Hill: University of North Carolina Press, 1965), 209–10.

87. Perdue, Barden, and Philips, *Weevils in the Wheat*, 148; On legal issues of racial intermarriage, see Pascoe, "Miscegenation Law."

88. George Roth, "Overview of the Southeastern Indian Tribes Today," in *Indians of the Southeastern United States*, ed. Anthony Paredes (Tuscaloosa: University of Alabama Press, 1992), 186; Karen Blu, *The Lumbee Problem: The Making of an American Indian People* (Cambridge: Cambridge University Press, 1980), 62.

89. Blu, *Lumbee Problem*, 39.

90. Blu, *Lumbee Problem*, 46–48; Gerald Sider, *Lumbee Indian Histories: Race, Ethnicity, and Indian Identity in the Southern United States* (Cambridge: Cambridge University Press, 1993), 159.

91. For a detailed history of the Lowry band, see W. McKee Evans, *To Die Game: The Story of the Lowry Band, Indian Guerillas of Reconstruction* (Baton Rouge: Louisiana State University Press, 1971).

92. Blu, *Lumbee Problem*, 61.

93. Evans, *To Die Game*, 265.

94. Adolph Dial and David Eliades, *The Only Land I Know: A History of the Lumbee Indians* (San Francisco: Indian Historian Press, 1975), 89.

95. Blu, *Lumbee Problem*, 63–64.

96. Blu, *Lumbee Problem*, 77–79; Dial and Eliades, *Only Land I Know*, 94; Brewton Berry, *Almost White* (New York: Macmillan, 1963), 33;

97. Blu, *Lumbee Problem*; see also "Race Relations" Notes and "Caste Ranking" Notes (7–29–37), Guy B. Johnson Papers, Southern Historical Collection, Wilson Library, University of North Carolina at Chapel Hill.

98. Rountree, "Indians of Virginia," 39

99. Christian Feest, "Pride and Prejudice: The Pocahontas Myth and the Pamunky," in *The Invented Indian: Cultural Fictions and Government Policies*, ed. James Clifton (New Brunswick NJ: Transaction Publishers, 1990).

100. Arthur Estabrook, *Mongrel Virginians* (Baltimore: Williams and Wilkins, 1926).

101. Where biologists and social scientists looked at "marginal Indians" as fruitful sources of racial and cultural information, the neighbors of these Indians held a slightly different view of them. The names used to refer to these traditional groups by others, and often by themselves, were usually ethnically derogatory. Anthropologist Brewton Berry collected a list of such labels that included: "Brass-Ankle," "Melungeon," "Guinea," "Wesort," "Red Bone," "Red Leg," "Bushwhacker," "Pondshiner," "Buckhead," "Sabine," "Cuban," "Turks," "Jackson White," "Issue," "Red-nigger," "Half-nigger," "Marlboro Blues," "Yellow Hammers," and "Free Jacks." Social scientists from the 1890s to the 1930s referred to Moble Hopson's "people" in a number of ways, including: "mixed-bloods," "American isolates," "triracial isolates," "folk societies," "racial islands," "marginal peoples," "raceless people," "mystery people," "half-breeds," and "Half-Castes." See Berry, *Almost White*, 33, 36, 39.

102. Smith, *Eugenic Assault*, 102.

103. Hurston, *Dust Tracks*, 236–37.

8. Blood Politics, Racial Classification, and Cherokee National Identity

The Trials and Tribulations of the Cherokee Freedmen

CIRCE STURM

In the spring of 1996, in Tahlequah, Oklahoma, the heart of the Cherokee Nation, I interviewed a Cherokee freedman, one of many phenotypically Black descendents of Cherokee slave owners and their African American slaves.[1] Of the questions that arose in the course of our conversation, the one that elicited the most impassioned response was, "What do you think I should write about?" He responded:

I think you should write about the racism that permeates these Indian programs [re: tribal benefits and who qualifies for them]. And point out that many of the so-called Indians running the Oklahoma tribes are exclusive if the hyphenated Indian is black and inclusive if the hyphenated Indian is white. I think you should go back to the Dawes process and point out how degree of Indian blood was ignored among black people just as degree of European blood did not and does not today affect one's status if one is Black. I think you need to argue that these programs need to be made realistic. . . . It is ridiculous to allow white people to take advantage of Indian programs because they have blood on a tribal roll 100 years ago, when a black person who suffers infinitely more discrimination and needs the aid more, is denied it because his Indian ancestry is overshadowed by his African ancestry. Few Blacks are 100 percent African, and to be frank about it, few Europeans whose ancestors come from the South are 100 percent European. . . . Either the descendents of freedmen should be allowed to take advantage of benefits, or the federal government, not these cliquish tribes, should set new standards for who is an Indian – and save [themselves] some money.[2]

While this statement might be considered angry or even inflammatory in Cherokee County, Oklahoma, it is also supported by the historical record and my own ethnographic observations.

The Cherokee freedmen continue to be one of the most marginalized groups in Native North America, and their story has never received the attention it deserves, in part because many people would prefer that it remain buried. To understand how this came to be, I have sought to unearth contemporary freedmen perspectives like the one above and to situate them within the local political dynamics of the Cherokee Nation. Only then can we begin to examine how Cherokee identity is socially and politically constructed around hegemonic notions of blood, color, race, and culture that permeate discourses of social belonging in the United States. In this essay, I explore how racial ideologies have filtered from the national to the local level, where they have been internalized, manipulated, and resisted in different ways by Cherokee citizens and Cherokee freedmen. I argue that as a result of this continuing dialectic between the national and the local, many Cherokees express contradictory consciousness because they resent discrimination on the basis of race and yet use racially hegemonic concepts to legitimize their social identities and police their political boundaries.

At the center of this story is an absence, an exclusion, a silence where the Cherokee freedmen might have been. The reason for this absence is clear: when Cherokee citizens conflate blood, color, race, and culture to demarcate their sociopolitical community, they often exclude multiracial individuals of Cherokee and African ancestry, who are treated in both discourse and practice in qualitatively different ways from multiracial individuals with Cherokee and White ancestry. This bias against African ancestry has a long history that took root with the advent of plantation slavery among certain sectors of the Cherokee population in the early 1800s.[3] Several centuries of social, political, and economic relations with Euro-Americans engendered Cherokee color prejudice, whose legacy means, among other things, that Cherokee identity politics has never been simply a question of blood or culture. Cherokee freedmen and other multiracial individuals who choose to identify as both Indian and Black challenge the prevailing racial ideologies that ask us to "choose one" racial or ethnic identity, often at the expense of another.[4]

To understand how racial ideologies constrain various multiracial identities, it is necessary to examine the historical process of what Omi and Winant call "racial formation" and the ways in which historically situated "racial projects" give rise to local interpretations of racial hegemony.[5] To that end, I have used a variety of sources, including contemporary interviews, field notes, tribal and federal court documents, and other archival records to trace the legal and political struggles of the Cherokee freedmen over the past century and a half in their efforts to gain recognition as Cherokee citizens. Interweaving ethnohistory, legal history, and ethnography, I follow this largely untold story into the present, focusing on how ideologies of race and culture affect the identity formation and the social and legal classification of multiracial Native and African American people.

Cherokee expressions of contradictory consciousness and racial hegemony reveal the human side of a painful history of racial irresolution, originating in the Cherokee adoption of African slavery. The nature of this slavery continues to be a matter of dispute. Some scholars and many contemporary Cherokees argue that the relationship of Cherokee masters to their Black slaves was more lenient than that of White Southerners to their slaves. One reason for this interpretation is that Cherokees did not indulge in mob violence as Southern Whites often did: there is no record of mass lynching in the Cherokee Nation, and one historian suggests that Cherokee-owned slaves did not fear for their personal safety as much as their bonded counterparts in Alabama or Mississippi.[6] But the fact remains that "the Cherokees held a greater number of slaves than any other tribe in Indian Territory," and despite claims to the contrary, most "historians agree that slavery among the Cherokee was little different from that in the white South."[7]

By the middle of nineteenth century, Black slavery was one of many issues dividing Cherokee citizens along the lines of race and class. Just as in Euro-American society, class divisions among Cherokees tended to fall along racial lines, but not according to separate racial groupings ("White" versus "Black") as much as degree of racial mixture ("fuller-blood" versus "lesser-blood").[8] Slaveholding and nonslaveholding Cherokees were divided "not only in an economic sense but also in terms of values and world views."[9] Complicating these cultural and racial divisions was the growing hostility in the United States between the North and the South, which exacerbated tribal factionalism between slaveholding and nonslaveholding Cherokees.[10] Despite these conflicting pressure groups, the majority of Cherokees remained sympathetic to the Confederacy for the duration of the war.[11]

After a series of Confederate victories, Cherokee Chief John Ross signed a treaty with the Confederacy in 1861 but repudiated this alliance two years later in 1863.[12] Ross's shifting loyalties reflected his confused response to the growing antagonism among his own people. The Cherokee national leadership was divided between pro-Confederate and pro-

Union factions, and when Ross was captured by Union forces in 1862, Thomas Pegg became acting principal chief of the pro-Union Cherokees. Pegg decided to follow the precedent of President Lincoln's emancipation proclamation of 1 January 1863, calling "an extraordinary session of the Cherokee National Council. . . . On February 19, 1863, the body passed an act to become effective on June 25, 1863, emancipating all slaves within the limits of the Cherokee Nation."[13] Although this was two years before the United States formally ended slavery with the Thirteenth Amendment, most of these "freed" Cherokee slaves belonged to masters who were still a part of the Confederacy.[14]

Even though slavery no longer existed after 1863 as a legal institution within the Cherokee Nation, its legacy of social and economic inequality endured along with political division.[15] After the end of the Civil War in 1865, the factionalism that existed among the Cherokees was ignored by federal officials who made no distinction between Union and Confederate Cherokees in the Reconstruction process. In negotiations, the southern faction "thought the United States government should remove the freedmen from the Cherokee Country at its own expense. The northern Cherokees . . . wanted them adopted into the tribe and given an area of land for their exclusive use."[16] But federal officials went even further: they offered a plan for the adoption of the Cherokee freedmen into the tribe, granting them citizenship, land, and annuities in the same amount as Indian tribal members.[17] On 19 July 1866 the Cherokee Nation signed a treaty with the United States extending Cherokee citizenship to the freedmen and their descendents. Article 4 of the treaty set aside the Canadian District, a large tract of land extending southwest of the Cherokee Nation proper, for those freedmen who desired to settle there; Article 5 entitled them to citizenship, to elect their own officials, and to enact their own laws as long as they were not inconsistent with those of the Cherokee Nation. But Article 9 was the crucial point, for it stated: "They [Cherokee Indians] further agree that all freedmen . . . and their descendents, shall have all the rights of native Cherokees." This important clause would become the cause of much legal, political, and social controversy for many years to come.[18]

THE LEGAL STRUGGLES AND POLITICAL RESISTANCE
OF THE CHEROKEE FREEDMEN

Despite the promises of the 1866 treaty, the freedmen were never fully accepted as citizens of the Cherokee Nation. In 1876 Cherokee Chief Rev.

Charles Thompson (1875–79), in his annual address to the Cherokee Nation, identified the status of freedmen as a pressing concern. But the National Council struggled with the issue and eventually decided to create a citizenship court to hear claims on a case-by-case basis.[19] The political atmosphere in which this occurred was revealed by John Q. Tufts, the federal agent who negotiated in 1880 with Cherokee officials on the status of Blacks in their nation. Tufts stated that the question of citizenship eluded resolution and was so unpopular that no Cherokee politician was willing to jeopardize his position by advocating equal rights for the Cherokee freedmen.[20]

The Cherokee Nation's resistance to incorporating the freedmen was motivated largely by economic factors. In the 1870s the Cherokee Nation had sold a large tract of land in the Cherokee Outlet, an area extending west from the northern perimeter of the Cherokee Nation.[21] In 1880 the Nation compiled a census for making a per capita distribution of the communal funds received from the sale.[22] In the same year, the Cherokee senate voted to deny citizenship to freedmen who had failed to return to the Cherokee Nation within a six-month period specified by the 1866 treaty.[23] But even those freedmen who had always resided within the Cherokee Nation were passed over for citizenship. The resulting Cherokee census of 1880 did not include a single Cherokee freedman, "it being the position of those of Cherokee blood that the Treaty of 1866 had granted freedmen civil and political rights but not the right to share in tribal assets."[24]

Cherokee Chief Dennis Wolf Bushyhead (1879–87) believed that the provisions of the Treaty of 1866 were violated by these actions, and in the early 1880s he protested vigorously on behalf of the freedmen. In 1883 the Cherokee Tribal Council overrode his veto to pass an act authorizing per capita payments only to citizens of the Cherokee Nation by blood. This act also excluded approximately a thousand Delawares and an even smaller band of Shawnees who had been adopted into the tribe between 1860 and 1867. At this point the federal government became involved in the controversy. Congress passed a bill in 1888 mandating that the freedmen and other adopted citizens share in tribal assets equally (25 Stat. at L. 608–9). In an effort to identify the freedmen, Congress sent out a federal agent, John W. Wallace, to create a roll to be used in a per capita distribution of federal monies to the tribe. That document, known as the Wallace roll, listed 3,524 enrolled freedmen by 1889 (25 Stat. at L. 980, 994).[25]

The Cherokee Nation continued to contest the freedmen's legitimacy, and in October 1890 Congress passed a jurisdictional act authorizing the Court of Claims to hear and determine once and for all "the just rights of the Cherokee freedmen" (26 Stat. at L. 636). In the case that followed, *Whitmire v. Cherokee Nation and United States*, the Court of Claims decided in favor of the freedmen (30 Ct. Clms. 138 [1895]). The court held that the sovereign power of the Cherokee Nation could not be exercised in a way that breached the treaty obligations of the Cherokee Nation to the United States. Thus, when the Tribal Council liquidated the common property of the tribe, as in the case of the Cherokee Outlet, the monetary payments could not be restricted to a particular class of Cherokee citizens, such as those by blood. The court also held that freedmen had the right to recover $903,365 as their portion of the $7,240,000 in question.

But the Cherokee Nation had already distributed the money to Cherokees by blood, which left its codefendant, the U.S. government, standing with the bill. Before the U.S. could pay the freedmen, the Federal Court of Claims decreed that the secretary of interior must first compile a list of freedmen eligible for the distribution of the award. For reasons that are vague at best, the court made no mention of the previous Wallace roll, and a new freedmen roll was completed in 1896. The Kern-Clifton roll, as the second roll came to be known, was named for Robert H. Kern and William Clifton, the bureaucrats in charge of compiling it. The roll listed 5,600 freedmen who received their portion of the tribal funds in the following decade (10 Ind. Cl. Comm. 117–18 [1961]).[26] The freedmen were finally, if temporarily, able to secure their treaty rights, but only after the judicial machinery of the federal government came to their aid in the late 1880s and early 1890s.[27]

During this same period, the groundwork was laid for what would amount to a political coup against Native sovereignty. In the Dawes Act of 1887, Congress adopted a policy of converting tribal lands to individual ownership, hoping this would assimilate Native Americans, diminish their land base, and free the residual land for White settlement. If Indian Territory were to become an American state filled with "civilized" citizens as many White settlers hoped, then the allotment of tribal land to individual Indians was the logical first step. For six years, the Cherokee Nation and the other Five Civilized Tribes within Indian Territory were not subject to the Dawes Act – until the Indian Appropriations Act was passed on 3 March 1893.[28] In that same year, the Dawes Commission was created to negotiate with the Five Tribes for the purpose of extinguishing tribal title to their lands (10 Ind. Cl. Comm. 117–18 [1961]).

For this purpose, the Dawes Commission required yet another roll, and after three years of political resistance on the part of the tribal governments (1893–96), it began taking oral and written testimony from applicants to its rolls. The final rolls of the Five Tribes were to list newborns, minors, and adults in three racial categories – Freedmen, Intermarried Whites, and Indians by blood, with the latter including an Indian blood quantum.[29] The Cherokee Nation responded with an attempt to frustrate the enrollment of the freedmen who were citizens by law but not in the minds of the majority of Cherokees.[30] Nevertheless, over 53,000 people applied for enrollment in the Cherokee tribe. "When the decisions were finally made, there were 41,798 enrolled citizens of the Cherokee Nation, 4,924 of them freedmen."[31] Many of these freedmen enrollees had appeared on the Kern-Clifton roll six years earlier. However, 1,659 Cherokee freedmen listed on the Kern-Clifton roll of 1896 were not included on the Dawes roll of 1902 for reasons that will be explained below. These excluded individuals would later bring their case to court and seek the benefits of Cherokee citizenship (10 Ind. Cl. Comm. 109 [1961]; 161 C. Clms. 787 [1963]; 13 Ind. Cl. Comm. 33 [1964]).

But in 1898, before the Dawes rolls were completed, Congress enacted the Curtis Act, which further complicated matters by authorizing the Dawes Commission to proceed with allotment without the consent of the tribal governments. The Curtis Act dealt one horrible blow after another to tribal sovereignty by extending the jurisdiction of the federal courts over Indian Territory, abolishing the tribal courts, authorizing the incorporation of towns and town lots for survey and sale, and allowing the federal government to assume the collection of taxes from White citizens of the Indian Nations in the territory.[32] Soon after the passage of the Curtis Act, the Dawes Commission completed its work, and in 1902 the final rolls of the Cherokee Nation were closed.

Many, though far from all, Cherokee freedmen were listed on the Dawes roll. By 1907, the same year the Cherokee Nation was officially dissolved and Oklahoma became a state, 4,208 Cherokee freedmen had received allotments.[33] But allotment often brought a new slate of troubles. In an interview in 1996, Idella Ball, a ninety-nine-year-old original Dawes roll freedmen enrollee, explained the situation to me:

IB: When Black people started to own property and land then the whites undermined them, too. I had got property in Ft. Gibson and a small piece of oil land in Nowata County, about fifteen acres. But the taxes were about to eat it up. So, I was gonna sell five acres to clear up the taxes, and this white man he bought it and beat me out of all fifteen.

CS: *You mean you thought you were selling off five and he took the whole thing?*

IB: Yes! He put on the paper fifteen instead of five and I signed.

cs: *But you could read; you didn't see it?*

IB: That's how they got me, sure I can read, but I didn't know nothing about business and all. I just signed the papers and that was it.

What Ball describes is well documented in the work of Angie Debo, *And Still the Waters Run*.[34] Debo demonstrates how those who received allotments were subject to the manipulations of White "grafters," whose greed led them to take advantage of freedmen and Native American ignorance regarding the rapidly shifting system of land title in Oklahoma. The "grafters" were so successful that by 1930 the Five Tribes Indians owned less than 2,000,000 acres of restricted land, down from a total of 19,525,966 acres in 1890.[35] But on the whole, these new freedmen citizens fared better then they had in the antebellum Cherokee Nation. Now, they were able to access the courts, sit on juries, serve as elected officials, have some security in their improvements, and enjoy some limited school facilities.[36]

But what happened to those Cherokee freedmen who never received allotments, who had been on the Kern-Clifton roll but were excluded from the Dawes roll? It appears that the majority of these 1,659 individuals did not meet the residency requirements set forth by the Dawes Commission. They either were no longer citizens because they had not been in the Indian Territory during the Civil War or they were "too lates" who had not returned to the Cherokee Nation within the six-month period set forth by the Treaty of 1866. In 1909, these disgruntled Cherokee freedmen, most of whom lived just outside the boundaries of the Cherokee Nation, filed a supplemental petition in *Whitmire v. United States* to test the right of the Dawes Commission to deny them enrollment (44 Ct. Clms. 453). The United States was the only defendant, because the Cherokee Nation was not held responsible for the actions of the Dawes Commission. In the same year, the U.S. Court of Claims ruled in favor of the freedmen, but by 1912 the Cherokee Nation joined the federal government in an appeal to the Supreme Court, which reversed the decision (*Cherokee Nation v. Whitmire*, 223 US 108).[37]

The Cherokee Nation continued its quest to restrict the freedmen's property rights and to limit the extent of their citizenship. In 1924, using the Supreme Court's decision as a precedent, Congress passed a jurisdictional act allowing the Cherokees to file suit against the United States to recover money that had been paid to the Kern-Clifton freedmen. The Cherokee Nation alleged that the United States had diverted settlement money belonging to the tribe to non-Indians and nontribal members. It was not until 1937 that the Court of Claims reached a decision denying recovery by the Cherokee Nation. The court held that the Kern-Clifton roll was a one-time-only distribution roll that had served its purpose and that its validity had ceased with the 1894 distribution. Thus it would not affect future rolls or distributions of the Cherokee Nation in any way (*Cherokee Nation v. United States*, 85 Ct. Clms. 76 [1937]).[38]

But this did not settle the matter of the Kern-Clifton applicants who were denied Dawes enrollment. Many years later, in 1946, the Indian Claims Commission Act was passed, stirring activity among people claiming to be descendents of the 1,659 Kern-Clifton freedmen who were denied tribal citizenship. In Kansas and Oklahoma, an organization called the Cherokee Freedmen's Association (CFA) came into being sometime in the late 1940s. Inspired by the fate of the denied Kern-Clifton enrollees, the CFA membership included a diverse gathering of about 110 African Americans who could show they were descended from the Wallace, Kern-Clifton, or Dawes Commission enrollees. Its goals were to secure political and economic rights that had been erroneously denied to members by federal and tribal governments. The members collected dues, gathered documentation, and hired a lawyer. They filed their first petition with the Indian Claims Commission (ICC) on 13 June 1951 in Tulsa, Oklahoma (Docket No. 123). The commission did not actually begin to hear the case until early November 1960. Even then, the commissioners had to make numerous inquiries regarding past litigation to get a grasp on the "judicial jungle," as one writer described it in the *Tulsa Tribune* on 12 November 1960. While the case was still in litigation in 1961, the Cherokee Nation received a $14.7 million settlement from the United States as payment for the Cherokee Outlet nonreservation lands in north-central Oklahoma. The members of the CFA took notice, but their hopes were dashed when the ICC denied their collective claim to tribal citizenship on 28 December 1961.[39] The commission decided that the freedmen's claims were individual in nature and that it had no jurisdiction over them.

The CFA appealed the decision in the U.S. Court of Claims, contending that they were entitled to share in the funds paid to the Cherokee Nation because of their 1866 treaty–based citizenship rights. They asserted that their treaty rights superceded the Dawes Commission rolls, which were created for the sole purpose of allotment. But the Court of Claims affirmed the findings of the ICC on two grounds. First, the freedmen's claims were individual and would require a case by case examination; second, the claims were no longer subject to consideration since they had already been adjudicated in the 1912 Whitmire case before the Supreme Court. However, the Court of Claims realized that some new considerations had been raised and suggested that the freedmen intervene in the remaining portion of the Cherokee Outlet case before the ICC.[40]

On 12 November 1964 the ICC granted the CFA's request, allowing it to intervene in Docket No. 173-A. But the outcome was the same as it had been in 1961; ultimately, the ICC determined that it did not have jurisdiction over the freedmen matter at hand, but this time for different reasons. First, the distribution of an award was a political question that needed to be settled by Congress and not by the commission. Second, membership in a tribe was a political controversy to be resolved by the tribe as a fundamental attribute of sovereignty. Finally, the commission had no jurisdiction over intertribal disputes whether they be between two separate tribes or between two factions within a single tribe (22 Ind. Cl. Comm. 417–20 [1971]).[41] The freedmen made a last-ditch appeal to the Court of Claims in 1971, but the court quickly affirmed the ICC's decision. After twenty years of legal struggle and few victories, the CFA finally rested its case with nothing to show for its efforts.

Even in defeat, the courts had treated the freedmen in a way that suggested the potential validity of their quest for citizenship. From the beginning, the CFA's claims to citizenship in the Cherokee Nation were challenged on the grounds that most of its members were not Dawes enrollees. Even before 1951, the Dawes rolls were accepted as the final authority on who was or was not legally and politically Cherokee, regardless of race. Yet ironically, the ICC ruled in part that it had no jurisdiction over the freedmen case because the conflict was an internal tribal matter. This assertion seems to assume that the freedmen had some legitimate claim or were seen in the eyes of the court as possibly falling within the margins of Cherokee citizenship. In fact, thirteen years later a group of elderly freedmen, most Dawes roll original enrollees, would bring the question of their citizenship rights to trial again. But this time the legal arguments would change dramatically, sometimes in complete opposition to statements made in earlier cases, and charges of racial discrimination would become a central focus of the litigation. There was no question that these people were legitimate Cherokee freedmen listed on the Dawes rolls, but did the freedmen and their descendents continue to have "all the rights of native Cherokees," as they had been promised in the Treaty of 1866?

THE STRANGE CASE OF REV. ROGER NERO

On 18 June 1983 Rev. Roger H. Nero and four other Cherokee freedmen went to the Muskogee courthouse to cast their votes in the Cherokee Nation's elections for principal chief. These Dawes enrollees had received allotments and shares in at least two cash land settlements over the past twenty years. When the tribe was finally given back its right to elect its own officials by Congress in 1970, these descendents of Black Cherokee slaves voted in the first tribal elections (*Baltimore Sun*, 29 July 1984). Cherokee freedmen occasionally received certain educational and housing benefits but had not been allowed health care and most federal benefits granted to other tribal members. Although their treatment by the tribe had been inconsistent, Nero and his companions were shocked when Cherokee election officials turned them away from the polls, saying freedmen no longer had the right to vote.

The justification for this denial was based on blood. In an unpublished interview, Ross Swimmer, chief of the Cherokee Nation (1975–85), stated that five years earlier the Cherokee election registration committee had established new rules in 1977–78. These declared that according to the new Cherokee Constitution of 1976, an individual must have a Certificate Degree of Indian Blood (CDIB) to be registered as a tribal member or voter.[42] However, the 1976 Cherokee Constitution specifies in Section 1 of Article III, "All members of the Cherokee Nation must be citizens as proven by reference to the Dawes Commission Rolls." As mentioned earlier, the Dawes rolls were divided into separate categories for Cherokees by blood, freedmen, and intermarried Whites. Presumably, a descendant of any of these three groups would be eligible for tribal citizenship, since the 1976 Cherokee Constitution only refers to the Dawes rolls and does not limit tribal membership to Cherokees by blood.

This would seem to open the door to the Cherokee freedmen, but in practice the Cherokee Nation only grants citizenship to lineal descendents of Cherokees by blood listed on the Dawes rolls. When applying for tribal membership, an individual must simultaneously apply for a CDIB. If individuals are able to document through state and federal records that they are the direct descendent of a "Cherokee by blood" on the Dawes rolls, then Cherokee blood quantum is assigned and tribal membership is automatic. Unlike many other tribes in the United States, the Cherokee Nation has no blood quantum limitation, and the blood quantum of tribal members ranges from "full blood" to 1/2048. Indeed, out of a total tribal enrollment of 175,326 in February 1996, only 37,420 (21 percent) had one-fourth Cherokee blood or more.[43]

This strictly racial definition of Cherokee identity has many precedents. Not only were the Dawes rolls divided along racial lines, but Indian blood quantum was used by the federal government to determine the trust status of land allotments. Following the Dawes Act, if allotees were one-half Indian or more, their allotment was held in federal trust and restricted from sale and taxation; if allottees were less than one-half Native American, including freedmen and intermarried Whites, they had to pay taxes but were free to sell their allotments if they so desired, a mixed blessing that created both greater autonomy and the possibility of land loss. The justification for this division between "fuller bloods" and "lesser bloods" was based on notions of competency assumed to be in direct correlation with degrees of race mixture.

Today, working through the Bureau of Indian Affairs (BIA), the federal government continues to use similar racial criteria to administer to Native Americans. The CDIB is the primary document used by the BIA to determine tribal enrollments and eligibility for federal social services. During the 1934 Indian Reorganization Act, many tribes took steps toward self-government; but considering their long history of bureaucratic relations with the federal government, it is not surprising that many Native American tribes adopted the exact same criteria that had been used by the federal government. Thus the vast majority of tribes have a blood quantum requirement, often set at one-fourth, which must be verified with reference to a federally approved roll.

The Cherokee's more open policy regarding blood has helped create the largest tribe in the United States, which continues to grow at a rapid pace, with over 1,500 applications for tribal citizenship arriving every month.[44] Blood connections have been stretched to the point of "Whitening the tribe" to a controversial level. Because of the sociopolitical implications of Cherokee blood, most Cherokees assign it an ideological meaning. During the course of my fieldwork, the issue of blood quantum was raised numerous times in regards to who was or was not a "real" Cherokee. While opinions varied a great deal, the vast majority of tribal members whom I interviewed mentioned "Cherokee blood" as a potent symbolic medium that connected all Cherokees to one another. People claimed to feel their Cherokeeness "in the blood," which caused them and other Cherokees to behave in a similar fashion.

To most contemporary Cherokees, anyone without Cherokee blood would automatically fall outside the boundaries of the Cherokee community. For this reason, Cherokee tribal leaders deny freedmen claims to Cherokee citizenship. For example, in 1984, Wilma Mankiller, then deputy chief to Ross Swimmer, said that the freedmen "should not be given membership in the Cherokee tribe. That is for people with Cherokee blood." And tribal member Jimmy Phillips said, "Whether they are white, black or red, if they've got the blood then they are tribal members. Without it . . . no" (*Baltimore Sun*, 29 July 1984). When the Cherokee Nation reorganized its government between 1970 and 1976, the resulting changes in blood legislation had important implications for the freedmen and for race relations within the tribe. During that period, the freedmen were quietly disenfranchised and denied their rights to citizenship at the same time, paradoxically, that these rights were extended to tribal members with minimal Cherokee blood. In December 1977, the one-fourth blood quantum limitation for Indian Health Services was successfully challenged by the tribe. New economic incentives, such as free health care, lured many people to return to the tribal fold, particularly those who through a gradual process of acculturation and intermarriage had long since passed into the surrounding communities of Oklahoma. As a result, in the decade between 1970 and 1980 the Cherokee Nation became progressively "Whiter" at the same time that it rejected most of its Black citizens.

These changes occurred without the knowledge or input of the Cherokee freedmen. When Rev. Nero and his companions went to vote in the Cherokee elections in 1983, they found that the definition of a Cherokee citizen had been changed to exclude them, which came as a surprise since Nero had voted in the last tribal election in 1979. What happened between 1979 and 1983? According to Chief Ross Swimmer, the tribal election committee attempted to use the CDIBs to determine eligibility to vote as early as 1975. But the committee had soon realized that the CDIBs were unreliable since the whole process of application had been mishandled under the BIA. Many people had simply purchased membership within the Cherokee Nation or had provided a Dawes roll number that was not verified through any other documentation. In 1975 the tribe began to purge its rolls and to take control over the certification process. Still struggling to straighten out the mess, the tribe decided the election of 1979 would be the last in which people with old registration cards could vote. Ostensibly, this is why Nero voted in 1979 but was turned away in 1983.

This heightened sense of blood as the primary basis of Cherokee national identity began to take hold as early as 1975. Yet only a year before, on 8 October 1974, Chief Swimmer wrote a letter regarding freedmen eligibility for Public Health Service benefits to Jack Ellison, area director of the BIA in Muskogee. The letter stated:

I have been advised by the local Health Service unit that the BIA does not recognize enrolled Freedmen for benefits and that this is carried over to IHS [Indian Health Service]. . . . The IHS says they cannot participate . . . because the people are Freedmen instead of Indians. It would appear that since the government had us include Freedmen on our rolls they should be entitled to similar benefits of other enrolled Indians. I can understand the blood-quantum problem, but again it would appear that the Freedmen would be taken as a class and would have the same status as ¼ blood.

This letter demonstrates that in 1974 the Cherokee Nation considered the freedmen to be citizens and argued that freedmen were eligible for the same benefits given other enrolled Cherokees. But federal benefits come with strings attached to federally imposed, racially discriminatory policies. Between 1975 and 1983 the Cherokee Nation increasingly began to administer to its own members. However, when the Cherokee Nation began processing applications for CDIBs and tribal membership, it had to conform to federal standards. Thus in its own blood-based policies of administration, the Cherokee Nation reproduced many of the racial ideologies that were the basis of federal Indian policy.

These administrative changes did not come into being without a struggle. The Cherokee Nation shifted its stance back and forth, contradicting its own newly derived policies. In 1983 the Cherokee election committee decided to waive the CDIB requirement for any original enrollee including freedmen and intermarried Whites.[45] In a similar vein, federal administrators also debated whether the freedmen were eligible to participate in Cherokee elections. On 21 April 1983 the Muskogee area director of the BIA wrote a memorandum to the deputy assistant secretary of Indian Affairs stating that according to his interpretation of the Cherokee Constitution, "the Freedmen, who have rights of Cherokee citizenship, but who do not possess any degree of Cherokee blood, would not be eligible to participate as candidates, but would be eligible to vote." Therefore, according to the Cherokee election committee's new policy regarding original enrollees and federal interpretations of the Cherokee Constitution, Nero and any other Cherokee freedmen listed on the Dawes Commission rolls should have been permitted to vote in the 1983 elections.

Regardless, the fact remains that Nero and other freedmen were turned away at the polls because of the race-based assumption that they had no Cherokee blood. This set the stage for freedmen resistance, as the freedmen could not believe that blood had become the main criterion for Cherokee citizenship. As Nero put it, "We weren't allowed to vote because we were freedmen. They said that we didn't have Cherokee blood, but when I was born my birth certificate said that I was declared a citizen of the Cherokee Nation" (*Tahlequah Daily Press*, 21 June 1984). He also said, "We had a guarantee we'd have the same rights as the Indian as long as the water flowed and the grass growed. Well, it's still flowing and growing" (*Baltimore Sun*, 29 July 1984). Angered by the delegitimation of his life-long identification as a Black Cherokee citizen, Nero began to stir up resistance among freedmen who were original enrollees and their descendents living in the Fort Gibson area near Muskogee, Oklahoma. His cause was aided by his calling: he was a prominent Baptist preacher who spent much of his time traveling from congregation to congregation.

On 7 July 1983 Rev. Nero and five other original enrollees filed a letter of complaint with the civil rights division of the Department of Justice. It stated that because they had been denied the right to vote, their civil rights had been violated and that it was "humiliating, embarrassing and degrading of Freedmen, such as ourselves, to be treated as second class tribal citizens." And then one year from the date they were denied the right to vote, on 18 June 1984, Rev. Nero and sixteen other freedmen plaintiffs filed a class-action suit against Chief Swimmer, the tribal registrar, a Tribal Council member, the tribal election committee, the United States, the Office of the President, the Department of the Interior, the Office of the Secretary of the Department of the Interior, the BIA, and three BIA employees. They complained that they had been denied the right to vote and tribal benefits from federal funds because their lack of verifiable Cherokee blood prevented them from obtaining registration cards. Because the Cherokee Constitution also restricts office-holding to members of the tribe with Cherokee blood, the freedmen alleged that the tribe had systematically discriminated against them on the basis of race.

These legal actions were the culmination of the long-term frustration of the freedmen, who had been treated as an invisible faction within the Cherokee Nation for decades. At one point Nero said, "We are not using any hatred or trying to put the Council in misery by our actions. All we are trying to do is fight for our rights. We want them to see us" (*Oklahoma Eagle*, 5 July 1984). The freedmen sought almost $750 million in compensatory and punitive damages and wanted the Cherokee election to be declared null and void. This last request seems to suggest in part that, consciously or not, the freedmen may have been political pawns in an ongoing conflict between Ross Swimmer and Perry Wheeler, another candidate for chief. In the 1983 election for principal chief and deputy chief, Ross Swimmer and Wilma Mankiller ran on a ticket against Perry Wheeler and Agnes Cowen. At the polls, Wheeler received 3,300 votes to Swimmer's 2,437, but, on the strength of a large absentee vote, Swimmer came back to win the election by fewer than 500 votes (*Washington Post*, 2 December 1983). The race was so close that Wheeler and Cowen demanded a recount, stoking the fires of controversy. The subsequent recount prompted Cowen to say, "I have never seen such a farce. They had ballots strewn all over the world. They had them open. They didn't know which came from which county. It looked like a bunch of kids playing mudpies" (*Washington Post*, 2 December 1983). Wheeler, Cowen, and their attorney, L. V. Watkins, brought their case before the Cherokee Judicial Appeals Tribunal and the U.S. District Court. They alleged that the election proceedings were corrupt on several counts and that the freedmen were disenfranchised from voting because they were Wheeler party allies. Although their case was defeated in both venues, the freedmen continued to fight, and Watkins brought the situation to the attention of Tulsa attorney Jim Goodwin, a prominent African American leader in the city. Goodwin became the attorney for the freedmen and used their case as an opportunity to raise the charges of election fraud again.

When the Nero case came under public scrutiny, Ross Swimmer was particularly sensitive to the allegation that he and the tribe had discriminated against the freedmen on the basis of race. In self-defense, he stated that the Cherokee Constitution says:

To run for office you must be a Cherokee by blood. I can't argue with that. I think it means what it says. The President of the U.S. must be a natural born citizen. Even a German immigrant or Spanish immigrant . . . who goes before the judge and is naturalized as an American citizen and has all the rights of an American citizen can never be the President of the U.S., because the Constitution specifically requires that the President of the U.S. must be an American by blood. . . . The Cherokee Nation, good, bad or otherwise, specifically says that to be an elected official you must be a Cherokee by blood. . . . The best evidence . . . has been a Certificate of Degree of Indian Blood. . . . We provide services from the federal government using the federal government's guidelines . . . Every program we get comes from the federal government and it comes with strings attached.[46]

This statement is a good example of contradictory consciousness. Here, Swimmer conflates place of birth and nationality with blood and uses this argument to buttress his political stance. In this case, racial hegemony is consciously manipulated, becoming political ideology.

On 10 July 1984 the Cherokee Nation filed a motion to dismiss the Nero suit, arguing that the court had no jurisdiction over the matter at hand without congressional authorization and that they were immune from suit according to the Indian Civil Rights Act, premised in part on sovereign immunity, a keystone of American Indian law. They asserted that their right to determine tribal membership was a fundamental attribute of sovereignty, even if the basis of exclusion or inclusion was deemed unconstitutionally discriminatory. The Cherokee Nation maintained that the only hope was for the freedmen to bring their case before the Cherokee Judicial Appeals Tribunal in Tahlequah, Oklahoma. Furthermore, they argued that the case at hand was an intertribal political dispute and not a question for the courts. Congress might deem at some future date that the freedmen had legal rights to some tribal assets because of the Treaty of 1866, but the Cherokee Nation continued to assert that the freedmen had no political rights as tribal members (892 F. 2d. 1457–63 [10th Cir. 1989]; *Nero v. Cherokee Nation*, Defendant's Reply Brief 1986b, 8–12).

The freedmen countered these claims, arguing that to bring their case before the Cherokee tribunal would be an exercise in futility. In the earlier Wheeler controversy, Watkins had brought the freedmen issue before the tribal court, where the charges had been summarily dismissed. The freedmen believed that the entire machinery of the Cherokee elections had been compromised, and under the influence of the current Cherokee administration they could not get a fair hearing. Since their civil rights had been violated, the freedmen argued that their case belonged in the federal courts. They also alleged that the Cherokee Nation was subject to federal law because of two clauses in its 1976 constitution that arguably waived the tribe's rights to sovereign immunity.[47] Finally, the freedmen asserted that since federal treaties are the supreme law of the land, their 1866 treaty rights superseded the Cherokee Nation's claims to sovereign immunity.

After hearing the arguments from both sides, the District Court in Oklahoma decided that the plaintiffs had failed to establish a claim against the tribe and granted a motion to dismiss. The Cherokee freedmen quickly filed an appeal before the 10th Circuit Court of Appeals. The final decision on the Nero case came down on 12 December 1989; the Court of Appeals affirmed the decision of the District Court, holding that the dispute between the freedmen and the Cherokee Nation was an intratribal affair over which it had no jurisdiction. The decision followed the arguments of the Cherokee Nation closely but added that the Cherokee Nation had a right to remain a culturally and politically distinct entity (892 F. 2d. 1463 [10th Cir. 1989]).

In doing so, the court ignored the freedmen's long history of cultural and political association with the tribe by conflating race with culture and politics. A more accurate statement would have been that the Cherokees had a sovereign right to remain a *racially* distinct community, but the Court skirted this controversial issue.[48] From the beginning, however, the tapestry of Cherokee culture had been woven with efforts of "White, Black, and Red" Cherokee citizens. While racial self-definition may be a sovereign right upheld by the federal courts, in practice the Cherokees are a multicultural and multiracial people; these characteristics, often misunderstood as in the case of the freedmen, have had dramatic effects on the political trajectory of their nation. This reality is reflected by the ongoing litigation between the Cherokee freedmen and the Cherokee Nation between 1889 and 1989.

RACIAL POLITICS IN THE CHEROKEE NATION

Through a century of trials, the Cherokee Nation resisted the incorporation of the freedmen by progressively narrowing their definition of Cherokee identity. In the 1890s, the Cherokee Nation argued that the only legitimate class of Cherokee freedmen were those listed on the Dawes rolls. By the time of the Nero case, the Cherokee Nation had shifted its position, claiming that Dawes enrollment was no longer sufficient. In March 1988, the Tribal Council passed a statute approving the rules and regulations of the tribal registration committee that had been in practice since 1978 (11 CNCA, Section 12). Now, by tribal law, a Cherokee citizen had to be a Cherokee by blood, and that excluded the freedmen, who generally lacked the requisite documentation to prove blood descent. I say "generally" because there is good evidence that many of the freedmen listed on the Dawes rolls did in fact have Cherokee ancestry. At the turn of the twentieth century, the Dawes Commission rolls enumerated 4,208 adult Cherokee freedmen. Of that number, approximately 300 had some degree of Indian heritage, as the census cards indicate in various ways. Some cards say they are "colored" or "Cherokee-Black." Others state that the person is "Cherokee by blood," "part-Indian," or "mixed."[49] This means that as many as 7 percent of the Cherokee freedmen original enrollees had Cherokee blood but were classified solely on the basis of their Black phenotype.

Further evidence for racial "misclassification" is found in the testimony of members of the CFA before the ICC on 14 November 1960. On that day, Gladys Lannagan, a descendent of a freedman and freedwoman, took the stand. "I was born in 1896 and my father died August 5, 1897," she testified before the court. "But he didn't get my name on the roll. I have two brothers on the roll by blood – one on the roll by blood and one other by Cherokee Freedmen children's allotees." Not only was Lannagan not listed on the Dawes roll, even though her siblings were included, but her brothers were enrolled separately in different racial categories – one as a Cherokee by blood and the other as a Cherokee freedmen minor. She also stated that one of her grandparents was Cherokee and the other was Black and that she was seeking whatever rights she was entitled to from them.[50] Lannagan was not alone among the freedmen in her claim to Cherokee ancestry. During a century of litigation, many of the freedmen asserted that they were of Cherokee descent, implying that if blood was to be the primary criterion, then they had enough biological collateral to be legitimate citizens of the Cherokee Nation.

The Nero case offers numerous examples of this sentiment, as almost all the plaintiffs in the case claimed that they had some Indian ancestry. Curtis Vann said that his grandfather was a Cherokee by blood, and Cornelius Nave stated that his father was three-fourths Indian. Although I was unable to verify their statements in the Dawes records, I was able to locate Berry Niven's birth affidavit of 16 October 1903, which provided further clues to a confused system of racial classification. The affidavit showed that Niven's father and mother were both citizens of the Cherokee Nation. The mother was a citizen by marriage and the father by blood, but the father was enrolled as a freedman. Normally (as in the case of Rev. Nero's birth affidavit), if a Cherokee citizen was listed on the freedmen roll, then he or she was a citizen by adoption and not by blood.

People with mixed ancestry fell between the cracks of the triracial system of classification that existed in Indian Territory at the turn of the twentieth century. This system pushed individuals into categories that did not reflect their personal experiences or their familial connections. The rules of hypodescent played out in such a way that people with any degree of African American blood were usually classified exclusively as Black. For example, three out of four possible multiracial ancestries would result in an individual with a "Black" social classification:

Black/White	"Black"
Black/Indian	"Black"
Black/Indian/White	"Black"
Indian/White	"Indian"

As indicated in this generalized chart, multiracial individuals with Black ancestry were always "Black," while those with White ancestry were never "White." As one Cherokee freedmen descendent put it, "This is America where being to any degree Black is the same thing as being to any degree pregnant."[51] In a similar vein, those with Native American and White ancestry were often classified as "Indian" in part because "Whiteness" was seen as an empty cultural and racial category.[52] Whiteness was a "taken for granted," hegemonic identity that was no longer "marked" in any particular way. Using the analogy of mixing paint, a little red paint in a can of white will turn the whole thing pink, implying that one's whiteness is no longer culturally "blank" or racially "pure." At the same time, pink is not red, and to some degree a fourth racial category developed in Oklahoma. People of mixed European and Indian ancestry, who were phenotypically and culturally ambiguous, were usually classified as "mixed-bloods." But this was the exception rather than the rule, and the majority of individuals with multiracial identities were pushed into a single-ancestry classification. The critical point here is that the social and often political reaction to hybridity varied according to the components of each individual identity. Multiracial individuals with African American ancestry were treated in qualitatively different ways from those without it.

This different treatment was the result of a number of factors. Some were economic, as seen in the 1960 testimony of freedwoman Tessie Claggett Payne before the ICC: "My grandfather and grandmother are on the full blood Cherokee roll, the 1880 roll. . . . All of the children, there was six of them, got allotments, and my mother, and it happened to be in the Nowata oil pool, and they changed us to freedmens, from the blood roll to the freedmen roll, and that give them access to handle or change the land or dispose of it, or we could dispose of it, but none of us ever sold it. It wasn't supposed to be taxable but they sold it for taxes." In this instance, the racial classification of this multiracial family changed between the 1880 rolls and the Dawes Commission rolls to open up their allotted land for "grafter" manipulations.

But the motivations for "misclassifying" Red-Black Cherokees went beyond economic greed. For instance, in a recent interview a Cherokee man described a one-time Cherokee citizen named Mary Walker, who was supposedly one-eighth Black, three-eighths Cherokee, and one-half White:

When she went to the Cherokee citizenship commission [Dawes] to enroll, they looked at her face and they saw a Cherokee woman and said, "through whom do you claim," you know, what are your parents names and what is your degree of Indian blood. They put it all down, and then someone comes in and says, "She ain't no Cherokee. She's a nigger. That woman is a nigger and you are going to put her down as a nigger." . . . So the Dawes Commission had to go back and research her family and get all the documentation and tell this poor woman that not only are you going to be on the freedmen rolls but so are your children.

The vocal denial of Walker's Cherokee and White ancestry and the concerted effort to push her into a solely "Black" racial category reflect the level of emotion in controversies over racial classification. After all, multiracial offspring were the undeniable result of a broken taboo, interracial sex. The mere existence of multiracial individuals like Mary Walker demonstrated the widespread practice of illegal sexual unions despite community norms and the Cherokee Nation's own antimiscegenation laws.

Consider the background of Mary Walker: she had Black, Cherokee, and White ancestry as a result of three generations of illicit sexual relations between prominent "mixed-blood" Cherokee masters and their Black slaves. These men were married to Cherokee women, who rarely ignored their husband's dalliances. At the time of the Dawes enrollment, Mary Walker was also having a love affair with a wealthy Cherokee man named James French, with whom she had several children. Their offspring might have been considered a threat to the French family fortune if French's paternity could be established. But because Mary Walker was socially categorized as a freedwoman, the kinship connections between her, her children, and other Cherokees and Whites were probably severed. Emotions ran high when Mary Walker came before the Dawes Commission, because this one individual brought to mind all the issues of illicit sex, matrimonial betrayal, denied love, fatherless children, and economic greed.

But the responses noted in the case of Mary Walker were specific to multiracial individuals with African American ancestry. In general, Native American and White unions were more readily accepted by the Cherokee community. One reason for this differential treatment may have been a long-held Cherokee bias against dark skin. In an interview, one Cherokee man explained this in the following manner:

My wife's grandmother was born in 1897, and she talked about her childhood which was a long time after slavery, but she talked about Black people in terms of them being culturally similar to us, that they were community type people. You know she didn't have any prejudice against them as far as their behavior. Her prejudice all came from the fact that they were Black. Skin color, it was just skin color. And this was a full-blood Cherokee woman who didn't speak any English. She was a very traditional type person.

This implies that, in spite of cultural commonalities, a Cherokee bias against dark skin maintained the social distance between Cherokees and their ex-slaves. Another, more recent story concerned a pregnant Cherokee woman who used Indian medicine to lighten the child she was carrying. When I asked the same man whether this color bias existed among

Cherokees today, he said that in his opinion "Cherokees have always prided themselves in being a light-skinned people." A Cherokee bias against dark skin, resulting from their adoption of a system of African racial slavery, provides the simplest and most direct explanation for their social treatment and racial classification of multiracial individuals with Black ancestry.

The adoption of plantation slavery and several centuries of social, political, and economic relations with Euro-Americans engendered Cherokee color prejudice, whose legacy means, among other things, that Cherokee identity has never been simply a question of blood. Multiracial individuals who choose to identify as both Indian and Black challenge the prevailing racial ideologies of hypodescent. Freedmen with Cherokee ancestry are confronted with questions of racial belonging influenced by ideas associated with blood, color, money, and sex. These symbolically laden objects of repulsion and desire weigh heavily upon most systems of racial classification. To negotiate these at the cost of being named a "race traitor" is almost too much to bear. Thus it is not surprising that today of the over four thousand multiracial individuals of Cherokee and Black ancestry, relatively few seek recognition as Cherokee citizens.[53]

THE CHEROKEE FREEDMEN TODAY

Regardless of their blood ancestry, most Cherokee freedmen identified as Cherokee citizens on the principle that they had been formally adopted by the tribe in the Treaty of 1866. Tribal citizenship meant social and political continuity and economic security for the Cherokee freedmen, and when this citizenship was challenged, the freedmen were willing to fight for full recognition of their treaty rights in the federal courts. While these battles were mostly unsuccessful, they continued to resist because they knew the stakes involved: the older generation of original enrollees feared that if they were not successful, the younger generation would grow up not knowing their rights, and their real history would be lost. As Nero said with uncanny prescience in 1984, "Over the years they have been eliminating us gradually. When the older ones die out, and the young ones come on, they won't know their rights. If we can't get this suit, they will not be able to get anything" (*Oklahoma Eagle*, 5 July 1984). With the death of Nero in 1994 and the passing of the older generation of freedmen, this is exactly what happened. Today, the descendants of Cherokee freedmen rarely identify as Cherokee in any fashion. They may have a dim awareness that their ancestors were enslaved by Cherokee masters, but the details of this relationship are often confused. For example, one descendent said: "Honestly, I don't know much other than we had a link to the Cherokees because both my parents and my maternal grandmother in the mid 1960's received what they called their Indian money. I sort of assumed we were part Indian." Other than vague memories, contemporary descendents of Cherokee freedmen have retained little knowledge of their specific, historical rights to Cherokee citizenship.

During the course of my fieldwork in the Cherokee Nation, I struggled to find freedmen descendents who were willing to talk with me about their "Cherokee heritage." In Tahlequah, where I was based, I asked around to see if anyone knew of freedmen families living in the area. Usually my questions were met with suspicion as to why I would be interested in such a thing, but many people chalked it up to the unaccountable eccentricities of the outsider. Again and again, I was told that there were no freedmen in Tahlequah and that those families had long since moved the twenty miles or so to Muskogee and Fort Gibson, both of which contain a large percentage of African Americans. Eventually, I got a helpful response and was directed toward a section of town locally known as "Nigger Hill." Although the name made me bristle, it was the only neighborhood in Tahlequah where I could locate men and women who appeared to be African American.[54]

Residential communities are de facto segregated along racial lines in northeastern Oklahoma, and it was difficult for me as a "White" woman to cross these boundaries. I tried to overcome this social geography with the telephone, hoping that a phone call would feel less intrusive than a knock on the door and that I would be given the opportunity to explain my intentions. But the phone presented new obstacles. With each call, I awkwardly explained who I was and why I was interested in an interview. But too often I was nervous about the racially sensitive nature of my questions and tried to hide this fact behind academic jargon. Most of my contacts found this confusing, but one thing was clear: as soon as I hid behind the mantle of academia, my class status shifted, creating more social distance between me and whoever I was trying to interview. Because of race and class barriers and my early bumbles on the phone, most freedmen declined an interview, saying that they were too old to get involved in any controversy with the Cherokees.

Although the issues of race and class never faded, sometimes I was able to get around them with a stroke of good luck. When one freedmen descendent finally consented to an interview, a whole network of freed-men families and communities opened up to me. From then on when I called people, I was able to build trust by saying, "Morris, your cousin in Tahlequah, gave me your number and said that I should talk to you." Then, when I met people on a face-to-face basis, I was more comfortable and so were they. My gender and youth worked to my advantage, because I was perceived as less threatening than an older, White male might have been. My own rural, southeast Texas background also weighed heavily in my favor, since my accent and bearing were familiar and reminded people that we had a rural, southern culture in common. As I shared pictures of my family's small farm, with its own outhouse and cypress siding, and as we exchanged stories about milk cows, roosters, winter gardens, butter-milk corn bread, and poke salad greens, the social barriers between us began to crumble, at least in part.

Once I got to know several freedmen families, I was surprised to find that very few cared whether they were recognized by the Cherokee Nation. Adults between the ages of thirty and fifty recalled freedmen elders who spoke Cherokee as children and who later sat around talking about the "glory days" of the Cherokee Nation. Many remembered the court battles against the Cherokee Nation and the important role that Rev. Nero played in their community, but the current generation was frustrated with Nero's lack of success and did not see the point in continuing the fight. However, some sought the occasional concession from the tribal government. One of their most recent efforts had been to take their children, nieces, and nephews to the Cherokee Nation's registration department hoping to get them enrolled so they would be eligible for educational scholarships. Not only were they denied enrollment, but they claimed they were "snubbed" and "snickered at" when they applied for tribal membership.

Wary of such slights, younger freedmen descendents were often unwill-ing to seek tribal membership, even if they were eligible by virtue of their documented blood descent. Another factor was a sense of disconnection from their Cherokee past. As one freedmen descendent said:

I live in this American society and my view of myself is as an African American. The Cherokee history is interesting, but since I have no familial or social links to the Cherokee Indians, I look at them as a people who are admirable but they're not me. I view them and Oklahoma Indians in general as people who share many of the prejudices of Europeans about Black people. However, that's my view. . . . Several years ago, I asked Seminole Tribal Council member, the late Lawrence

Cudjoe, why as a Black man he wanted to be a Seminole. He replied that it wasn't a question of wanting or not wanting, it was just who he was. Were I like him . . . I'd probably feel as he did.[55]

Like the Cherokees, the freedmen have adopted dominant Euro-American racial ideologies that negate multiracial identities. Although my informant's identity is constituted in multiple ways, it is difficult for him to see himself as anything but African American, thereby negating his potential racial, legal, and political identity as a Cherokee citizen.

Some Cherokees are working to change this situation, with the belief that the freedmen's claims are historically valid and politically potent in the present. A current Tribal Council member stated, "If we don't have to keep our treaty, then why should the U.S. government keep theirs. A promise is a promise." One Cherokee who sees the contemporary political impact of honoring such promises is David Cornsilk, managing editor of the *Cherokee Observer*, a local independent newspaper. Cornsilk is also one of the founders of the Cherokee National Party, a grassroots political organization that uses the *Cherokee Observer* to reach a large audience of Cherokee voters. Cornsilk believes that in order for the Cherokee Nation to be successful, it needs to honor its 1866 treaty by recognizing the freedmen as tribal citizens. When I asked Cornsilk why he was interested in raising the issue, he said:

I don't really have a very deep moral drive to give citizenship to the freedmen. I believe that we have a moral obligation to them, but that's not the driving force. My driving force is that the Cherokee Nation has to realize that it has jurisdiction there, and that in order to protect that jurisdiction, it must exert that jurisdiction over as many of the people who reside here as possible, including the freedmen. Whether they are Black or not, whether they have Cherokee blood or not, if we can control their destiny basically by being their government, then they are not going to agitate against us. They are not going to be our enemy.[56]

Cornsilk's motivation is primarily political: if the freedmen were recognized as tribal citizens then the Cherokee Nation would extend its power base and placate, if not silence, some of its most persistent critics.

Cornsilk's realpolitik vision also takes the issue of race into account. Given the current political climate of this country, Cornsilk believes that the Cherokee Nation cannot continue to identify its citizenry on a strictly racial basis; he fears that tribal citizens who are more White than Indian are in danger of being reclassified as non-Indian, thereby diminishing the size and power of the Cherokee Nation:

That's why I think the freedmen are so important to bring them in, because then it's a non-racial issue. We are a nation and we have become a nation that is big enough and moral enough to realize its responsibilities to the people that it held as slaves. It's like what Charlie Gourd [a tribal official] said, "Great nations like great men keep their word." . . . It's to our advantage to separate ourselves as far as possible from the fact that we are an ethnic and racial group, and just stand behind our identity as a political entity. Then we have strength and power beyond any other ethnic group. . . . We can't be sifted out. . . . We have to be dealt with on that level.[57]

Cornsilk understands how racial identities can be manipulated for political purposes and believes the Cherokee Nation must beat the federal government to the punch. The potential exists for the Cherokee Nation to lose over half its citizens if a more conservative definition of "Indianness" were imposed by the federal government. For this reason, he sees freedmen recognition as critical to the Cherokee Nation's self-preservation.

But Cornsilk has encountered a great deal of resistance among the Cherokees, in part because nationalism of any sort is always tied to ideologies about race and culture. Cherokee national identity is based on a unique sense of peoplehood, which is intertwined with primordial notions about blood and cultural belonging that seems to exclude the freedmen in the minds of most Cherokees. This is a misperception since the freedmen in many cases possess as much if not more Cherokee culture as many "White" Cherokees already enrolled in the tribe.[58] But even if a move from race to a legal and political self-definition would not necessarily threaten the cultural identity of the Cherokee Nation, it is precisely because the tribe has a reputation for cultural and racial dilution that most Cherokees find the possibility of freedmen citizenship so threatening.

Individuals like David Cornsilk are exceptional among Cherokees in their desire to put political self-preservation before race or culture. Cornsilk spent the past several years trying to find a freedman descendent who would work with him to seek tribal recognition, and he had the following scenario in mind. First, a freedman descendent of a Dawes enrollee would apply for tribal membership, which would be denied because they did not have any Cherokee blood. Then, Cornsilk and the rejected applicant would take the case before the Cherokee Judicial Appeals Tribunal, where Cornsilk believes they could use the Cherokee Constitution of 1976 to win their case.

Like me, Cornsilk had little luck in finding a contemporary freedman descendent who thought tribal recognition was worth the trouble. One responded to his request saying, "Why would I want to switch races?" Another man agreed to work with Cornsilk but soon backed out after he received threatening telephone calls and began to fear for his life. Finally in 1997, after several years of searching, Cornsilk found the ideal candidate, a seventy-eight-year-old widow by the name of Ethel Boggs (pseudonym). A long-time resident of Tahlequah, Boggs is the offspring of parents and grandparents who were all original Dawes enrollees. In fact, her father spoke some Cherokee, and her grandfather served in the Indian Home Guard of the Union army under Principal Chief John Ross. Boggs herself has a Cherokee Nation voter registration card that dates to 1975, and she voted in the 1975 elections to ratify the current Cherokee constitution. Given these significant social and political ties, Boggs was shocked when she attempted to register as a Cherokee tribal citizen in 1988 and was turned down. Still smarting from the rejection almost ten years later when Cornsilk came to her with his plan, she was open to this proposal to take this issue to the Cherokee courts.

In the summer of 1998, I sat with Ethel Boggs on her front porch while she fed the numerous wild rabbits, pigeons, and wrens that frequent her yard, and I asked why she had agreed to participate in the case. She told me that she "just wants to have the same rights," that all her life she has identified as a Black Indian, and that although it has been tough, she wants to have some acknowledgment of "who she is." She identifies as a Black Indian not only because of her freedmen lineage but also because of her own Cherokee ancestry. Her paternal grandfather was both the offspring and slave of a "full-blood" Cherokee by the name of Will Rogers (not the famous humorist). Although this fact was noted on her grandfather's application for tribal enrollment under the Dawes Commission, he was still enrolled as a freedmen and not as a Cherokee "by blood." As for Will Rogers, he was never listed on the Dawes rolls because he died shortly before they started taking applications. As a consequence, Boggs is one-eighth Cherokee "by blood" but cannot be enrolled as a tribal citizen because she cannot trace her lineage to her Cherokee Indian ancestors, only her freedmen ones.

In the fall of 1996, Boggs, with the help of Cornsilk, filed her case in the Cherokee District Court (DC Case No. CIV 96–09). However, the judge dismissed the case, saying that the Cherokee Judicial Appeals Tribunal was the proper venue for it. Boggs and Cornsilk then enlisted the aid of attorney Kathy Carter-White who, as a member of the Cherokee Bar Association, was familiar with the nuances of Cherokee law. They petitioned the Judicial Appeal Tribunal to review their case on 24 February 1997, but it would be more than a year before the case would go to trial. The main delay was the eruption in tribal politics that occurred a day after their petition, on 25 February 1997, when Cherokee marshals served a search warrant on Principal Chief Joe Byrd. This action precipitated a serious crisis that would interrupt the functioning of all aspects of the Cherokee government, including the judicial branch where the chief justices of the court had been impeached for upholding the actions of the Cherokee marshals in carrying out their duties.

Only in the fall of 1997 did the Cherokee court system become fully functional once again. At that point, the Massad Commission – a special commission authorized by the Cherokee Tribal Council – issued a report upholding the existing Cherokee courts and denouncing the impeachment of the Cherokee justices as an illegal action. However, over a century's worth of Cherokee court records were in complete disarray following a raid on the Cherokee courthouse by Chief Byrd's forces in the summer of 1997. Only with several months of back-breaking work on the part of a handful of people were the records reassembled into a usable form. While the court records were being put back together, the docket for the Boggs case expanded as the Cherokee Nation lawyers filed several motions to dismiss and members of the Tribal Council tried to intervene. As these efforts to dismiss Boggs's case proved unsuccessful, both sides filed for more time so they could gather their evidence, find appropriate witnesses, and hone their arguments before going to trial. Finally, on 12 June 1998, the freedmen's case was heard in the Cherokee Nation's own court system (JAT 97–03-K).

In her opening statements, Carter-White asked that the court uphold Ethel Boggs's rights to Cherokee citizenship, that they disregard any statutes or regulations that might have eliminated her eligibility, and that they base her rights on the Treaty of 1866 and the 1976 Cherokee Constitution. The Cherokee Nation lawyers contended that Boggs's application had never been denied, that the registration department had only asked for further information. In the defense's opinion, Boggs had filed an appeal before exhausting her administrative remedies. However, the specific information that the registrar requested was that Boggs provide the roll numbers of ancestors who were listed on the Dawes rolls with a degree of Cherokee blood. Carter-White argued that because the Dawes rolls listed no blood quanta for freedmen, fulfilling their request was impossible, and all freedmen descendents would eventually be denied their rights to Cherokee citizenship on a categorical basis. She later argued that for the tribal registrar to require a CDIB as a measure of citizenship has the same effect as "requiring a degree of Native American genetic stock ancestry," an act that essentially eliminates the freedmen from tribal participation. As Cornsilk testified before the court, "I think what we're talking about, and this is strictly my opinion, is an apartheid situation." He stated that the freedmen were people that "one day were citizens of the Nation with the rights of suffrage, and the very next day they found themselves disenfranchised and no longer citizens of the Nation in which they had resided and participated for several generations."

The defense then countered, arguing that both the Curtis Act and the Dawes Act had abrogated the Treaty of 1866, because both treated the freedmen as a special class apart from Cherokees by blood. Furthermore, because the Cherokee Nation had a sovereign right to determine its own membership, the registration committee had the authority to limit tribal membership in any way it saw fit. However, Carter-White responded that the practice of limiting citizenship to Cherokees "by blood" was a decision that was made by the rules and regulations of the registration committee, not by the Cherokee people themselves. Because Cherokee citizens were never given the opportunity to vote on whether the freedmen should be categorically excluded from citizenship, the rights of the freedmen had to be based on the 1976 Cherokee Constitution, which had been ratified by the people and did not specifically exclude the freedmen. The upshot of the arguments before the Judicial Appeal Tribunal seemed to rest on whether the Cherokee Nation, as a sovereign entity, had included or excluded the freedmen in its own legislation. On the one hand, the Treaty of 1866 and the current Cherokee Constitution seem to support the freedmen's claim, whereas other legislation, such as the Curtis Act and the Cherokee Nation's own internal statutes, does not.

As of June 2000 the Boggs case had been heard, and the Cherokee justices now have the difficult job of interpreting the convolutions of Cherokee national law. It has been almost two years since the case was brought to trial and still no decision has been reached. In the time that has passed, a new principal chief has been elected, ushering in a new era of tribal administration, and two of the three Cherokee justices who heard the case have now stepped down from the bench. In May 2000 I asked people in the judicial branch of the Cherokee government whether a decision would be made anytime soon. They assured me that the case had come up on several occasions but said the judges were wary of making such a controversial decision, especially because two of them had not heard the case firsthand and had to base their decision on the trial transcript and other supporting documents. Furthermore, so much political controversy had happened over the past several years that many people wanted the tribal government to stabilize for a while before a final decision was made.

David Cornsilk is not one of those people – he feels a great deal of pressure to get the issue settled quickly before other political events muddy the waters. One complication was the Cherokee Nation's constitutional convention in February 1999, which fulfilled a promise to the Cherokee people that their constitution would be subject to revision twenty-five years after its initial passage in 1976.[59] Cornsilk contends that powerful people in the Cherokee Nation wanted to add a clause to the constitution that would specifically restrict tribal membership to Cherokees by blood. With the simple addition of these two words – "by blood" – the issue would have been settled and the vast majority of freedmen (approximately 93 percent) would have been eliminated forever from Cherokee citizenship. However, when the Cherokee constitutional convention was held in February 1999, the delegates decided the freedmen should be eligible for citizenship as descendents of Dawes enrollees but should be precluded from voting or holding office because they do not have Cherokee blood. The new constitution was adopted by the delegates in March 1999 and was sent to the BIA for approval. According to current Cherokee law, any amendment to the Cherokee Constitution is subject to the approval of the president of the United States or the president's agent, in this case the BIA. The BIA reviewed the new Cherokee Constitution but refused to endorse it on several grounds, one of which was its inconsistency regarding the freedmen. The BIA believed that the freedmen could not be citizens and then denied the rights of suffrage or holding office. Though the issue of the freedmen was only one of several concerns, Cherokee officials responded to the BIA's lack of endorsement by invoking their sovereign right to self-government and self-definition. In a motion before the Tribal Council, they moved to strike the amendment in the 1976 constitution requiring presidential approval of their new constitution. Now, the freedmen's fate is up to the Cherokee people, who will have to vote on whether to accept a substantially revised constitution.

Of course, Ethel Boggs will not participate in the vote. Instead, Cherokees with verifiable "blood" ancestry will make the decision, including the justices who interpret the new Cherokee Constitution when deciding the outcome of her case. It is unclear where the future of the Cherokee freedmen will lead. Boggs and Cornsilk might be successful, or the Cherokee Nation might deny the freedmen their claims to citizenship once and for all. Either way, the decision will be made with little input from the freedmen themselves, whose views are rarely offered and never solicited. Their collective silence can be interpreted as a refusal to struggle any longer against barriers of racial discrimination or as a dignified acceptance that where they find themselves located is perfectly comfortable, even happy. Although it might cost the freedmen in an economic sense, they will no longer be buffeted by the political whimsy and prejudice of others; no longer will they have to fight for a place at a table that does not welcome them. Yet the group with the most at stake in this contest is not the freedmen but the citizens of the Cherokee Nation, who shape their own fate as they decide the freedmen's. If they formally choose to exclude the freedmen, then their own blood policies might be turned against them at some future date, giving the Cherokee Nation a painful lesson in racial politics – the same one they have been teaching the freedmen for over a century.

NOTES

I would like to express my heartfelt appreciation to James Brooks, Carol A. Smith, Deborah Cahalen, Norman Stolzoff, Aram Yengoyan, and Randolph Lewis for their detailed, insightful, and thought-provoking comments on earlier versions of this essay.

1. Although the term "freedmen" is gender biased, I have chosen to use it to maintain historical continuity and to avoid the awkwardness of phrases such as "freedmen and freedwomen" or "freedpeople," which might jeopardize meaning. However, when referring specifically to females, I use the term "freedwomen."

2. I have frequently chosen to protect the anonymity of my informants. Many offered to waive that right, preferring to have their name included. But in some cases the material is particularly sensitive and reveals confidential information about other individuals. I have exercised my own discretion in these instances. All quotes are taken from taped interviews during the course of my fieldwork conducted in the Cherokee Nation, northeastern Oklahoma. From 1995 to 1998, I researched Cherokee identity politics, the subject of my forthcoming book, *Blood Politics: Race, Culture, and Identity in the Cherokee Nation of Oklahoma* (Berkeley: University of California Press).

3. For an excellent historical account of Cherokee slavery see Theda Perdue, *Slavery and the Evolution of Cherokee Society, 1549–1866* (Knoxville: University of Tennessee Press, 1979), which provides, among other things, a rare perspective on precontact slavery practices among the Cherokees. For a broader perspective on the Cherokee freedmen, other recommended authors include Rudia Halliburton

Jr., *Red over Black: Black Slavery among the Cherokee Indians* (Westport CT: Greenwood Press, 1977); and Daniel F. Littlefield Jr., *The Cherokee Freedmen: From Emancipation to American Citizenship* (Westport CT: Greenwood Press, 1978). The secondary literature on post-1866 developments is very limited, with the important exceptions of Littlefield, *Cherokee Freedmen*; Walt Wilson, "Freedmen in Indian Territory during Reconstruction," *Chronicles of Oklahoma* 49(2) (1971); and Morris L. Wardell, *A Political History of the Cherokee Nation* (Norman: University of Oklahoma, 1977). However, their work only extends through the first decades of the twentieth century.

4. Throughout this essay I will alternate between the terms "Indian" and "Native American." I believe that of the two, "Native American" is more accurate, but many argue that any native-born citizen is a "Native American," whereas "Indian" is Columbus's misnomer. During my period of fieldwork in Tahlequah, Oklahoma, if I used the term "Native American" I was immediately marked as an outsider. Only then did I realize how completely Cherokee people have adopted the term "Indian" as their own.

5. Michael Omi and Howard Winant, *Racial Formation in the United States: From the 1960s to the 1990s* (New York: Routledge, 1994), 55–61, define racial projects as hegemonic explanations of racial dynamics linked to efforts to redistribute resources along particular racial lines. In the U.S., we are all subject to these racial projects, since everyone learns the rules of racial classification without any obvious conscious inculcation.

6. Littlefield, *Cherokee Freedmen*, 68.

7. Littlefield, *Cherokee Freedmen*, 8, 9.

8. For instance, in 1835 only 17 percent of Cherokees had any degree of White ancestry, but in the slave-owning class, 78 percent claimed White descent (Perdue *Slavery*, 60). Indeed, only 1 percent of all full-bloods owned slaves; see Russell Thornton, *The Cherokees: A Population History* (Lincoln: University of Nebraska Press, 1990), 53.

9. Perdue, *Slavery*, 68.

10. One group of Cherokees, the Knights of the Golden Circle, or, as they later became known, the Southern Rights Party (Perdue, *Slavery*, 129), used Southern proslavery rhetoric in an effort to bring the Cherokee Nation into the Confederate fold and to oust Cherokee Chief John Ross and his more neutral National Party. Opposing the pro-Confederate Cherokees was a smaller group, the Keetoowahs, who "protested the Cherokees' acceptance of slavery as well as other aspects of white man's 'civilization' and who favored Ross's policy of neutrality" (Perdue, *Slavery*, 130). In this passage from Perdue, she says "the Keetoowahs, or Pin Indians" (130). It is a common error to equate the Keetoowahs with the Pins since they were both "full-blood," culturally conservative factions within the Cherokee Nation. But the Pins, who wore crossed straight pins on their lapels, "were a

separate organization of activists that started among the Goingsnake District, and while most of them were Keetoowahs it was not a requirement and there were many Keetoowahs who were not Pins" (Thornton, *The Cherokees*, ch. 4, n.4; Janey E. Hendrix, "Redbird Smith and the Nighthawk Keetoowahs," *Journal of Cherokee Studies* 8 [1983]: 24).

11. Perdue, *Slavery*, 131.

12. William G. McLoughlin, "Red Indians, Black Slavery and White Racism: America's Slaveholding Indians," *American Quarterly* 26 (1974): 383.

13. Littlefield, *Cherokee Freedmen*, 16.

14. McLoughlin, "Red Indians, Black Slavery," 383.

15. Perdue, *Slavery*, 140.

16. Wilson, "Freedmen in Indian Territory," 233.

17. Halliburton, *Red over Black*, 134.

18. Wardell, *Political History*, 225.

19. Wardell, *Political History*, 228.

20. Wardell, *Political History*, 229–30.

21. The Cherokee Nation's historical boundaries lie in the northeastern corner of modern day Oklahoma and comprise approximately one-eighth of the state's area.

22. Bill Sampson, "Justice for the Cherokees: The Outlet Awards of 1961 and 1972" (master's thesis, University of Tulsa, 1972), 125.

23. Wardell, *Political History*, 229–31.

24. Sampson, "Justice for the Cherokees," 125–26.

25. Wardell, *Political History*, 233; Littlefield, *Cherokee Freedmen*, 148; Sampson, "Justice for the Cherokees," 126.

26. Sampson, "Justice for the Cherokees," 126; Littlefield, *Cherokee Freedmen*, 148. I was able to locate a complete legal record of *Cherokee Freedmen and Cherokee Freedmen's Association, et al. v. United States*, 10 Ind. Cl. Comm. 109 (1961), Dockets No. 173-a and 123, in the Earl Boyd Pierce Collection, Archival Box 75, at the Cherokee National Historical Society (CNHS), Park Hill OK. Earl Boyd Pierce was the Cherokee tribal attorney during that period, and the CNHS has his complete papers, which are well indexed and underutilized.

27. Littlefield, *Cherokee Freedmen*, 250–51.

28. The Cherokee, Choctaw, Chickasaw, Seminole, and Creek Nations are commonly referred to as the Five Civilized Tribes, which usually has much to do with assumptions about their degrees of assimilation. I will refer to them as the Five Tribes.

29. As I understand it, the calculation of Indian blood quantum during the Dawes enrollment process was a purely subjective process based in part on earlier tribal rolls and on oral testimony from enrollees and their supporting witnesses.

30. Wardell, *Political History*, 237.

31. Littlefield, *Cherokee Freedmen*, 238.

32. Sampson, "Justice for the Cherokees," 128.

33. Littlefield, *Cherokee Freedmen*, 238.

34. Angie Debo, *And Still the Waters Run: The Betrayal of the Five Civilized Tribes* (Princeton NJ: Princeton University Press, 1940).

35. Debo, *And Still the Waters Run*, 379; Rennard Strickland and William M. Strickland, "Beyond the Trail of Tears: One Hundred Fifty Years of Cherokee Survival," in *Cherokee Removal: Before and After*, ed. W. L. Anderson (Athens: University of Georgia Press, 1991), 124. For a fictional treatment of this phenomenon in Oklahoma, see Linda Hogan's 1990 novel, *Mean Spirit* (New York: Ivy Books).

36. Littlefield, *Cherokee Freedmen*, 249.

37. Sampson, "Justice for the Cherokees," 128, 129.

38. Sampson, "Justice for the Cherokees," 130.

39. Sampson, "Justice for the Cherokees," 131.

40. Sampson, "Justice for the Cherokees," 131–32.

41. Sampson, "Justice for the Cherokees," 133.

42. Ross Swimmer, interview by David Goodwin, 1984. Virtually all of my information on the Nero cases comes from the files of Jim Goodwin, attorney at law, of Goodwin and Goodwin, Tulsa, Oklahoma. Goodwin was the attorney for the freedmen in the Nero case, and he and his staff were very helpful to me during the course of my fieldwork. Goodwin has two sons, Jerry (who runs the *Oklahoma Eagle*, the only newspaper written for the African American community in Tulsa) and David (who has been a contributor to the paper). David and his father conducted a series of important taped interviews with Ross Swimmer, R. H. Nero, and Agnes Cowen in 1984. The tapes and transcripts are located in Jim Goodwin's files.

43. Cherokee Nation of Oklahoma, Registration Department, Monthly Report for February 1996, 6 March 1996.

44. Cherokee Nation of Oklahoma, Registration Department, 1996.

45. Ross Swimmer, interview by David Goodwin, 1984.

46. Ross Swimmer, interview by David Goodwin, 1984.

47. The clauses in the 1975 Cherokee Nation Constitution are as follows: "The Cherokee Nation is an inseparable part of the State of Oklahoma and the Federal Union, therefore the Constitution of the United States is the supreme law of the land" (Article I, Section 1). "The Cherokee Nation shall never enact any law which is in conflict with any State or Federal law" (Article I, Section 2).

48. My analysis of the freedmen controversy employs the same theoretical bridge linking critical race theory to the progressive Critical Legal Studies (CLS) movement of the early 1980s. Today, CLS challenges ahistoricism and insists on a

contextual/historical analysis of the law. Critical race theory, in a similar vein, focuses on race as a social and political construction, arguing that inattention to race flaws critiques of human rights legislation.

49. David Cornsilk, interview by author, tape recording, Tahlequah OK, 12 April 1996. Cornsilk worked for several years in the Cherokee Nation's registration department and has an extensive genealogical knowledge of the Cherokee community. On his own accord, he undertook the project to determine which Cherokee families had African American ancestry.

50. *Cherokee Freedman and Cherokee Freedmen's Association, et al. v. The United States and the Cherokee Nation* (1971). Appeal No. 5–70, U.S. Court of Federal Claims, Washington DC.

51. Sam Ford, interview by author, E-mail, 14 March 1996.

52. Ruth Frankenberg, *White Women, Race Matters: The Social Construction of Whiteness* (Minneapolis: University of Minnesota Press, 1993); Vron Ware, *Beyond the Pale: White Women, Racism and History* (London: Verso, 1992).

53. Thornton, *Cherokees*, 169.

54. Virtually all the families who resided in this neighborhood had prominent "mixed-blood" Cherokee surnames, like Vann, Ross, Nivens, and Downing, marking their unique history and identity.

55. This quote points to the fact that multiracial identity is not a homogeneous experience. Different groups of Native American–African American people, here Black Seminoles and Cherokee freedmen, have very different experiences of "racial formation" and social incorporation.

56. Cornsilk, interview.

57. Cornsilk, interview.

58. Many Cherokees admit that contemporary freedmen descendents share Cherokee foodways, as well as some economic and religious practices. A case in point is that freedmen community churches are usually Baptist, like the sizable Cherokee Baptist community, and these churches hold socioreligious observances on the same days as Cherokee "traditional" holidays. Several Cherokees whom I interviewed said they could relate more easily to freedmen than to whites because the freedmen were also a community-based people.

59. The Cherokee Constitutional Convention was first convened in 1996. However, its progress was seriously impeded by the political controversy involving Principal Chief Joe Byrd and the judicial branch of the Cherokee government. Under the new chief, Chad Smith, the Tribal Council passed an act creating a formal constitutional commission with over seventy delegates.

PART THREE Complicating Identities

9. Blood and Culture

Negotiating Race in Twentieth-Century Native New England

ANN MCMULLEN

On a Saturday afternoon in August 1992, the federally recognized Mohegan tribe began its annual Homecoming Powwow. During the opening procession of dancers, the Mohegan chief asked the master of ceremonies to announce that only recognized "card-carrying" tribal members could enter the dance circle, thus ejecting members of the "Preston Mohegan," a group in Preston, Connecticut, whose identity claims are not recognized by the Mohegan tribe.[1] About a quarter of the people left the circle, including highly respected members of other tribes who believed the powwow, as a celebration of generic Native culture, was open to all Indian people regardless of political or tribal affiliation. In private, members of other tribes voiced disapproval of the Mohegan chief's actions, declaring that "cards" were a federal imposition and no real measure of anyone's Indianness. Others suggested that Mohegan efforts to regulate the powwow were laughable: the Mohegans treated the powwow as a celebration of *their culture*, while those who doubted the survival of Mohegan "culture" saw the powwow simply as an intertribal celebration.

With its emphasis on differentiating those who participate in Indian cultural activities from those who can demonstrate Indian descent, this event highlights the problematic nature of blood and culture within Native societies in southeastern New England. At the same time, it illustrates that primacy of "blood" or "culture" is a matter of disagreement both within and between tribes and may be openly argued. Here, "cards" represent documented descent within federally recognized tribes and are considered "facts," while culture is obviously more abstract.

This essay explores "blood" and "culture" as ethnic symbols in personal and group identity among Native people in southeastern New England, specifically the Mohegans, Pequots, Narragansetts, Wampanoags, and Nipmucs. Physical type, religion, language, and other criteria are also used, but New England Indians emphasize "blood" – genetic descent demonstrated by genealogy – and "culture" – rectitude of cultural practice – as differentially weighted ethnic symbols in defining their group's traditional character and evaluating individuals as members.

Southeastern New England (east of the Connecticut River and south of Boston) has a population of approximately twenty-five thousand who self-identify as Native Americans, about half of whom are indigenous to the region.[2] Organized tribes include the Mashantucket Pequot (Ledyard, Connecticut), Paucatuck Pequot (North Stonington, Connecticut), Mohegan (Uncasville, Connecticut), Narragansett (Charlestown, Rhode Island), Nipmuc (Webster, Massachusetts), and the Wampanoag, which includes five Massachusetts communities: Mashpee, Gay Head, Assonet, Herring Pond, and Nemasket. All are recognized by their states, while the Mohegan, Mashantucket Pequot, Narragansett, and Gay Head Wampanoag are federally recognized tribes.[3] The Pokanokets, along with other Pequot and Mohegan groups, are not recognized by the states but are currently working toward federal recognition.

The groups listed above descend from tribes that inhabited the region at European contact and whose populations were decimated by introduced diseases, the Pequot War (1637), and King Philip's War (1675–76). Remnant populations often intermarried with Whites and Blacks, resulting in dispersed, mixed-descent populations that remained close to tribal homelands. Many disappeared by leaving their homelands to fight in the Revolutionary War, take up whaling, or join other Native communities to the west and north to escape White encroachment. Within the area, interaction and intermarriage fostered a diffuse and increasingly homogeneous regional Native culture, despite outside contacts.[4]

Today, descendants of southeastern New England's Native groups are integrated members of local society, which includes significant populations of Portuguese Americans and Italian Americans, among others. Presence of other "Brown" people locally makes identification of Native people based on physical appearance problematic for non-Natives, as does general assimilation of Native people into American lifeways.[5]

AMERICAN INDIANS, RACE, AND ETHNICITY OVER TIME

In a provocative article on how race, ethnicity, and culture have defined Australian Aborigines, Gillian Cowlishaw asks, "If race is a social construct surely social analysis must begin with the question: who constructs it and why?"[6] This question is equally pertinent to studying Native Americans' position in America, since the race factor remains largely unexplored. American ambivalence about whether Native Americans are racially or ethnically distinct requires analysis, and this ambivalence must also be historicized and regionally contextualized to address blood and culture in southeastern New England.

Obviously, the roots of difference are historically deep. In examining early American slavery, Ronald Takaki concludes that seventeenth-century indentured servitude and changing definitions of racial difference created slavery in the American South.[7] At first, indentured Africans and Irish were treated equally, but this gave way to differentiation based on religion and skin color: all "imported people" who were not Christians in their countries of origin were deemed slaves. Expansion of ideas about "Blackness" included development of the "one-drop rule" and a caste system that separated Blacks and Whites but left Native Americans in an ambivalent position. For some, Euro-Americans and Native Americans were culturally distinct: Native people fell within a skin-color range that could be applied to Whites, and intermarriage of Whites with Indians was seen as less objectionable than with Blacks.[8] Those who saw the nexus of difference as cultural believed Native Americans could be made White via acculturation, while characterizations of Native people as racially distinct implied behavioral predispositions and a place within a racial hierarchy.[9] As skin color became increasingly coded as cultural difference, the gap between Whites and Indians widened, and during the eighteenth century, Indians were variously seen as a separate race or culturally different.[10] The Naturalization Act of 1790 prevented Indians from becoming citizens, thus enforcing their subordinate status.[11] Categorization of western Indians as "varmints" worthy of physical extermination speaks to Indians as part of a developing caste system throughout America and not simply in the South.[12]

In southern New England, ambivalence about American Indian difference was bound to ideas about Black racial difference: in the seventeenth century, local Indians could be indentured, but Caribbean Indians and Blacks could be enslaved. Living with White families sped acculturation but also brought Native people into contact with enslaved and indentured Blacks, among whom they often found marriage partners.[13] Indians could face discrimination in their indentured homes, and even within the same family ideas about Indian cultural and racial difference varied widely. As a child, the Pequot William Apess was perceived differently by adults in his White family: the woman would accept him as a son if he became a

Baptist, while her husband was quick to label Apess's poor behavior part of his Indian heritage.[14]

Children of Indian-Black marriages were often characterized as "colored" or Black, but Indian identification and freedom depended on genealogy: children of Negro women and Narragansett men were not allowed to vote as Narragansetts in the 1790s and, until Rhode Island abolished slavery in 1784, could have been legally enslaved.[15] "Colored" remained a flexible category depending on the classifier, but terms such as "mustee" ignored distinctions between people of color: "Black," "Negro," and "colored" were increasingly applied to all mixed-descent people.[16] The persistence of slavery in some areas and a tendency to see Indian people as Black also caused difficulties: during the 1840s, the Narragansett tribe issued membership certificates lest tribal members be mistaken for escaped slaves.[17]

After the Civil War, "colored" and "Negro" became synonymous both in the South and the North, and racial ideas about slaves were transferred to all those labeled as Blacks.[18] This is evident in legislative changes equalizing Native Americans and Blacks as citizens and voters in Massachusetts.[19] However, despite some Black heritage, Narragansett children went to White schools after their reservation school closed, suggesting that in this situation, Narragansetts were viewed as culturally rather than racially different from Whites.[20]

The second half of the nineteenth century saw changes in the social position of Native people, both nationally and in New England. On a national scale, federal policies had already removed or subjugated tribes east of the Mississippi, while military campaigns and the reservation system attempted the same for western Indians. Absolute recognition as Indian was ordinarily reserved for reservation populations and those who required federal stewardship off reservations.[21] These Indians were subject to federal assimilation policies developed for nineteenth- and twentieth-century European immigrants based on the theory of the "melting pot" and the misdirected sympathies of White reformers.[22]

Because Indians in New England were assumed to be extinct or fully acculturated, federal policies and social reformers had little effect on them. In addition, intermarriage between Native people and both Whites and Blacks made all "Brown" people problematic for race classification in southern New England. The primacy of phenotype as a means of racial and cultural identification – especially skin color and hair texture – and a general belief that there were no longer any New England Indians led non-Natives to identify most Indian people as either White or Black, such as this description of the Narragansett:[23] "The Indians in 1885 were hardly distinguishable as Indians, however. Intermarriage with the negroes, descendants of the slaves which abounded in South County during the gay Colonial days of Rhode Island, has bred a race more African than Indian. So they are today, and as you come across their clearings in the scrubby pines, only the fact that the cabin is surrounded by corn instead of cotton persuades you that you are in New England rather than the South."[24]

Recognition as Indian also might depend on residence: mixed-descent individuals living in cities often joined African American communities and networks and were seldom identified as Indians.[25] Those who remained close to their homelands might be recognized as tribal members, but only individuals who fit stereotypical notions of Indian phenotype or retained Indian surnames were readily identified as Indians when separated from their communities. Even early-twentieth-century anthropologists – who had largely rejected ideas about racial determinism – often believed in a causal relationship between "loss of blood" and loss of culture and based their ideas about cultural survival largely on phenotype. Evaluations based on phenotype and pedigree applied to individuals and to entire tribes. In an article on Mohegans and Niantics, Frank Speck explained why he eliminated the Pequots from his report:

In 1903, a visit was made to the Pequot remnants at Groton and Ledyard, Connecticut, where there are two so-called reservations. About twenty-five individuals were seen, all more or less of mixed negro blood, but inquiry in every direction elicited absolutely nothing of ethnological or linguistic value. The mixed bloods are thinly scattered over the district inland from Stonington, seemingly most numerous near Lantern Hill where they engage in wood-cutting, fishing and small farming. Some Narragansett from Rhode Island, likewise with negro admixture, are intermarried with them.[26]

The Mohegans and Niantics – who had intermarried with Whites rather than Blacks – were deemed worthy of anthropological study.[27] Thus the appearance of Blackness had an overwhelming effect on whether Indian people were recognized as such and how they fit into society.

Native people in southeastern New England understood anthropological and lay public ideas about phenotype and how it affected their perception as Indians. While being considered "people of color" might have been acceptable in the early nineteenth century, the later equation of colored and Black was disadvantageous, especially if Indian children could no longer attend White schools. In addition, between Emancipation and

World War I, the influx of free Blacks into northern labor markets created job competition with White Americans and recent European immigrants. In southern New England, Blacks were limited to the least-skilled jobs, and employers preferred local Blacks over those newly arrived from the South.[28] To avoid job discrimination, Native people may also have taken pains to avoid being mistaken for new immigrants from Mediterranean countries.[29]

Early-twentieth-century Native writings demonstrate that many Native people avoided being linked with Blacks or being identified as "colored."[30] Racial ideologies that reified Blacks' subordinate position were part of the socialization of Whites and Indians and may have been further complicated by race hatred: some Narragansetts may have developed a hatred for Blacks as a result of being mistaken for them.[31] In the 1920s and 1930s, Indian people fighting against these racial ideologies led pan-Indian cultural revivals and built new tribal organizations to reposition Native Americans within a bipolar Black and White society.[32] This movement illustrates that southeastern New England Native people understood that being labeled colored carried a greater social stigma than being called Indian and combined this with their own cultural pride to change perceptions of Indians or at least define themselves as "not Black."[33]

Native peoples' reactions to these situations, and their attempts to counter phenotypic judgments with culture, suggest that historic New England may have been a caste system in the sense that fixed hereditary categories existed.[34] Although castelike phenomena have been identified in the American South, the situation in the North – and its relatively nonviolent continuation – has not been identified as a caste system because of the larger number of component population groups.[35] The entrenched ideological character of such systems – and individuals' inability to move between levels – is equally characteristic of caste systems. Although Native people worked their way out of being perceived as colored in the early twentieth century, we must also ask what social conditions prompted them to act as they did, necessitating examination of historical non-Native attitudes to identify the shifting effects of race, caste, and ethnicity in southeastern New England.

From its colonial beginnings, New England was not a caste system but rather a meeting ground: boundaries between Whites and Indians were somewhat permeable, as illustrated by transformation of White captives into members of Native societies and the movement of Native people into White society through conversion, White education, and intermarriage.[36] In the late seventeenth century, introduction of enslaved Africans – and the growing number of Native people indentured alongside them – brought about a caste system with Indians in an intermediate role: they could pass into either Black or White spheres depending on their marriage choices or remain Indian. Intermarriage between Blacks and Indians became more prevalent after 1750, and abolition of New England slavery in the late eighteenth century and changes in racial labeling led to a revision of the existing caste system into White and non-White, although Indians who married Whites and their children might pass into White society yet still maintain Indian identity.[37]

Within Native communities, intermarriage often caused tensions that appeared to be racial. However, Mandell suggests that racial language masked conflicts over control of tribal resources – especially land – and that the rhetoric of race was used by Indian men to protest the growing influence of Black spouses of Indian women and "foreign Indians" in their communities.[38] Despite some use of racial labeling, overt racism may not have been a part of most Indian communities in southeastern New England before 1880, yet during the following decades, Indian people's evaluations of one another across tribal boundaries increasingly focused on race and specifically African American ancestry. These changes in perception appear to have mirrored racial ideologies in White society, which disallowed Indian self-identification for individuals who appeared to have Black ancestors.

As stated earlier, Native people in southern New England remade this system in the early twentieth century into a three-part system where being Indian might exist independently of phenotypic judgment and was instead based on a combination of hereditary and cultural factors. This is analogous to what are seen today as ethnic groups, defined as "a self-perceived inclusion of those who hold in common a set of traditions not shared by others with whom they are in contact."[39] Outside of New England, the transition of American Indians from a racial to an ethnic group does not appear to have occurred until the 1960s and 1970s.

The 1960s Black Power movement had vast repercussions for other racial and ethnic groups. In part, Black Power transformed Black from a completely racial category to an ethnic group, bound by culture and history and dedicated to concerted political action and individual and group betterment.[40] This new emphasis on "roots" and ethnicity brought about a concomitant rise in ethnicity for other groups, including the rebirth of White ethnic groups in the 1960s and 1970s and similar movements among Hispanics and American Indians.[41] For many, the rise of ethnic identity helped overcome internalized negativity and increased Native

American ethnic pride and political activity in the 1960s and 1970s.[42] What had been a relatively stigmatized identity became less so, allowing Native people to focus attention on changing their status.[43]

Despite these changes, the status of American Indians as a race or an ethnic group remains problematic and depends on geographical, historical, and political contexts, including intermarriage. If, as van den Berghe states, "a race is a group that is racially defined but on the basis of physical criteria," then individually variable physical differences affect perception of American Indians as racially different.[44] In the U.S. census, declaration of American Indian identity is both a racial designation and a way to declare ancestry even where individuals do not identify themselves racially as American Indian; thus American Indians can be considered either a racial or an ethnic group.[45]

The transition from status as a race to an ethnic group is said to be an interpretive switch from judging "fitness" by biological or mental criteria to examining the fitness of culture; however, Glazer and Moynihan argue that America's rise of ethnicity is actually masked racism.[46] Although ethnicity is considered less "emotionally charged" than race, the pervasiveness of ideas about "ethnic character" supports a kind of "racialized ethnicity" that continues to be based on phenotype.[47] This remains problematic because Whites generally do not understand the social costs of non-White identification or that persistence of racialized ethnicity involves the same deeply held assumptions that created and sustained overt racism, including the belief that "different kinds" of people may be identified by physical traits that imply cultural differences.[48]

Alba and Waters propose that frequency of intermarriage can be used to examine racial boundaries between groups. Census data shows that Indian people are as likely to marry Whites as they are to marry other Indians, suggesting that no racial boundary exists from the Indian viewpoint. More Indians marry Blacks than do Whites, but the number of Indian-Black marriages remains low and is only slightly higher than Black-White marriage levels.[49] This indicates a potential racial boundary between Blacks and Indians as deep as that between Whites and Blacks.

Historical Black-White-Indian intermarriage patterns have created generations of individuals who are problematic for race-conscious Americans who classify individuals on phenotype, especially skin color, hair texture, and facial features. The racial boundary between Whites and Blacks makes such classifications important to many, especially given the persistence of the "one-drop rule" in identifying individuals as Black. All of this is bound up in "folk biology" and how people understand genetics and race, at least part of which stems from analogies to "breeds" of dogs and horses.[50] Physical traits play a strong role in identification, especially where mental templates of racial and ethnic groups exist, and the belief in "blood," or the biological basis of difference, outweighs other criteria, including demonstrated cultural identity.[51] Within such a mindset, bi- or triracial individuals are analogous to "mutts" or "mongrels," with all of the concomitant connotations of those categories, including being less desirable than a "purebred." These judgments – and valuations of "pure blood" – are not confined to Whites: explaining the need to regain Native genetic purity today, a Narragansett man stated, "It's a fact. If you breed out four times, for four generations, then you have to breed back in four times to get back to the original. That's what we are doing now" (*Kevin Chance*, 2 / 1991).[52]

As Snipp suggests, racial definitions may be mystical, biological, or administrative, and for American Indians, racial identity is administrated through the concept of blood quantum.[53] Although kinship and community membership are often more important to self-identification, the federal government stresses the "chain of blood" in determining Indian status, and blood quantum is often used to determine degrees of "Indianness."[54] Intermarriage has reduced the importance of blood quantum somewhat, and being Indian is now more often seen as a matter of descent and community participation, or blood and culture.

There is an obvious difference between identifying American Indians by descent versus tribal membership or community participation. Of the 1.8 million people who identified themselves as racially American Indian, only 60 percent were enrolled in recognized tribes; thus descent may be more important than tribal membership for many.[55] A growing number of Americans report Indian descent and maintain "symbolic ethnicity" as Indian analogous to Whites' ethnic self-identifications (for example, Irish or Italian) according to what they perceive as the "most ethnic" or most exotic in their ancestry.[56]

By contrast, Fogelson delineates Indian identity via primary attributes of blood and descent, relations to land, and sense of community and secondary characteristics of language, culture, dress, physical features, foods, and lifestyles. Identity, as "an image or set of images of oneself or one's group," is a social and psychological phenomenon involving communication of the sense of self both to oneself and to others. Identity is also subject to change since "[t]he identity dynamics of presenting self-concepts to others, be they Euro-Americans or other Native Americans, produced counterimages that might be accepted, rejected, or partially assimilated by the individual or group in question."[57] What endures for tribal identity is the sense of shared history and "interdependence of fate" that helps create ethnic group solidarity as interest groups move through time and react accordingly.[58] Like that of other ethnic groups, American Indian identity focuses on the past through emphasis on ancestry and origins, which may include family narratives of discrimination.[59]

Since ethnicity is part of culture – a system of symbols by which individuals adapt to and make sense of their environments – it involves the use of symbols. Unto itself ethnic identity and its proofs include "subjective, symbolic, or emblematic use of any aspect of a culture."[60] Discrimination, and its context within Native history, is part of the constellation of ethnic symbols Indian people use to separate themselves from American society. Ethnic symbols are thus attributes defining and maintaining differences encoded as ethnicity but are used situationally and depend on proximity to other groups.[61] Although being Indian is a recognized legal status, Indians must defend their uniqueness to local, state, and federal governments; local non-Native communities; and Native people (both within their group and outside), simultaneously addressing multiple audiences with different criteria and understanding of symbols. The Narragansetts – although recognized by local audiences, the state of Rhode Island, and the federal government – must defend against statements by western Indians that Narragansetts are not Indians, despite shared frameworks of pan-Indian powwow culture and traditions: when two Great Lakes Indians living in Providence, Rhode Island, viewed photographs of southeastern New England Native people, one declared, "None of these people are Indian."

Use of pan-Indian symbols illustrates that groups must have a shared symbolic basis to communicate successfully with each other and with non-Natives. Individually, Indian people use pan-Indian symbols with members of other groups or talk about shared antagonism toward Whites. Symbols serving members of one tribe gossiping among themselves – detailed individual histories and genealogies – are meaningless to those who do not recognize events, traditions, or individuals, hence recourse to larger Native symbol systems in other situations. Within the larger milieu of powwow culture, one can "pass" by functioning within accepted standards of powwow behavior, and if Native and non-Native audiences fail to recognize specific symbols, the symbols are explained as characteristic of one's own group. *Charles (Red Horse) Waring*'s ability to pass as a Catawba among the New England Indians – despite the Catawba's refusal to recognize him as a member – exemplifies this tactic: New England Indians know little about the Catawba or are too polite to ask pointed questions.[62]

Gossip and scandal are valuable subjects of study, and gossip points out the ethnic symbols being manipulated. Within New England's Native groups, gossip focuses on "blood" and genealogy, followed by criticisms that some behaviors ("culture") are "not our way." As Gluckman discussed for parvenus, adult newcomers to tribal activities are criticized because they cannot just take up "culture" late in life and so are "faking it."[63] In intertribal powwow culture, where blood is largely ignored, pan-Indian values and behavior take precedence and are judged in gossip: "no matter what her blood, she'll always be a little White girl because she just can't dance," or "he bought those eagle feathers." Dancing in the powwow circle is a recognized symbol, but failure to perform within expected parameters yields criticism. Traditionally, possession and display of eagle feathers represent honors or achievements. Traffic in eagle feathers is illegal, and suggesting that an individual purchased them implies that the feathers do not actually symbolize honors and that the individual participates in criminal behavior.

In southeastern New England, the question of "Who is a real Indian?" has become increasingly problematic. Individuals of Indian heritage may search for personal identity and sense of community, but others may be motivated by the success of local Indian gaming. As Franz Wojciechowski suggests, New England's tribal economic renewal has brought about a decrease in self-consciousness about being Indian and a rise in claimed identity.[64] Newly recognized tribes gain access to federal monies, often causing internal divisions over who will be served by these funds.[65] Because these tribes may open gaming facilities, they are inundated with applications from those attempting to reap the economic rewards of membership, what James Clifton has called the "Indian windfall syndrome."[66] When discussions over a planned casino brought on such a rush, the Narragansett permanently closed their rolls in 1993 and incorporated community participation standards into criteria for new members: "If someone comes from out of nowhere and says 'My great-great-great-grandfather was an Indian,' forget it."[67] This illustrates a clear difference between a set of individuals sharing Native descent and a cultural community, and in these distinctions both blood and culture come into play.[68]

For southeastern New England tribes, ethnic discourse is often brought to bear in opposition to non-Native ideas about racial admixture, both Black and White. In the past, being considered Black or having African American ancestry was seen as limiting Native peoples' opportunities, especially in terms of education and employment. Native people know that many non-Natives continue to privilege skin color, facial features, and hair texture over culture in identifying individuals and groups. To some Whites, "not looking Indian" signifies mixed ancestry and cultural dilution. Rejection of the priority of appearance leads Native people to define themselves through "blood" – genealogies and genetic descent – or "culture" – adherence to group traditions.[69] As ethnic symbols, blood and culture are used to define individual and group identity but vary contextually. The explicit relative importance of blood versus culture is seldom discussed, but Indian people in southeastern New England differentially weight them in defining the continuity and traditional character of their group and evaluating individuals as members.

In southeastern New England, there are no contexts – except tribal communities – where Native people are immediately recognized. Local tribes often find their identity claims opposed by insinuations that they are largely of African American ancestry. As suggested previously, early-twentieth-century pan-Indianism and public cultural practice grew out of Native attempts to be recognized as Indians within a bipolar racial framework and demonstrate the continued existence of local Indians, despite continued evaluation of individuals and groups based on physical appearance and admixture with African Americans. From these roots, personal research about Indian culture and history and tribal reorganization expanded. While some research involved reconstructing tribal histories and culture, other Indian people focused on their personal history, examining their links to the past through genealogy and family traditions. Relative evaluation of other Native people with regard to phenotype and ancestry did not end in the 1930s but continues to pervade ethnic self-identity and cultural expressions because of the persistence of racial thinking and, in particular, the equivalence of race and culture. As Fogelson suggests, individuals and groups maintain a faceted identity comprised of multiple parts, including an "ideal identity, an image of oneself that one wishes to realize; a feared identity, which one values negatively and wishes to avoid; a 'real' identity, which an individual thinks closely approximates an accurate representation of the self or reference group; and a claimed identity that is presented to others for confirmation, challenge, or negotiation in an effort to prove the 'real' identity closer to the ideal and further from the feared identity."[70]

For many Indian people in southeastern New England, the feared identity is to be thought racially African American rather than culturally Indian. With classifications based on physical appearance and folk biology, Native people must move themselves into arenas where more flexible cultural and ethnic symbols – blood, culture, and history – are more important.[71] As ethnic groups, Native tribes can act on their shared interests and defend themselves as ethnic groups, resorting to history and the negotiation and use of ethnic symbols.

Both "blood" and "culture" are folk terms rather than anthropological concepts. As the folk category "race" draws on physical appearance as an indicator of ancestry and concomitant social position, blood also has variable meanings in different situations.[72] For southern Whites in the past, blood was either pure or polluted: "It may only take one drop of Black blood to make a person a Negro, but it takes a lot of Indian blood to make a person a 'real' Indian."[73] In southeastern New England, the situation is sometimes identical, but public practice of culture and genealogical links to those recognized as Indians help mitigate such accusations.

BLOOD AND CULTURE AND THE INDIVIDUAL

In the same way tribes rely on history and Indian ethnic symbols to prove distinctiveness as ethnic rather than racial groups, individuals use genealogy and recitations of cultural ancestry (sources of their cultural knowledge) to demonstrate personal identity, especially when faced with accusations that they are not Indian or to position themselves hierarchically within groups. Federal statutes require Native groups to define membership by absolute blood quantum and/or descent from members of historic tribal rolls, and considerable resentment exists over the necessity of defining one's identity: "If you say you're Italian, I don't ask you how much: I take your word for it. Why is percentage important?" (*Marianne Easton*, Narragansett, 8/1992). Genealogies are used to document relationships and define membership, so blood – established genetic ancestry – is the primary ethnic symbol for many groups in differentiating themselves from non-Natives: those who validate their blood are admitted to tribal membership.

While blood and genealogies are important for many groups, symbolic use of genealogies is individual.[74] Native people may register for only one tribal roll even if their ancestors represent different groups. When asked their affiliation, they mention their tribal membership and any other connections. Children simply know they are "Indian," although a parent may say the child is "Narragansett and Mashantucket Pequot." As adults, they can apply for membership in either group, and stating all affiliations is appropriate until that point. Individuals who lack sufficient proof to register for tribal membership also mention all their affiliations. At powwows where participants introduce themselves publicly, one can see "*Red Raincloud*, a woman of Many Nations," or "*Geronimo Sacred Pipe*, Lenni Lenapé–Chippewa–Chiricahua Apache."

Although individuals can manipulate their genealogies within the context of New England Native society and powwow culture, tribal genealogists – who determine fitness for tribal membership – may see blood differently. Individuals orally maintain genealogies and treat them as factual statements of blood, often transforming the earliest remembered generation – even those born during the 1900s – into full-bloods despite widespread intermarriage. Personal genealogies can be easily manipulated, so individuals can claim a quarter Indian-blood by identifying a dark-haired, dark-eyed grandmother as a full-blood. Because of centuries of intermarriage, being one-quarter Native is eminently respectable and implies a significant cultural heritage as well.[75] However, to gain tribal membership, it may not be sufficient simply to mention Native ancestry. For example, in the 1920s, Sarah Ciscoe – a Nipmuc woman whose father called himself "colored" while she called him a Narragansett chief – tried to denigrate a well-known Mohegan family by suggesting they were mostly "White trash."[76] Although the Mohegans ignored this, some racial strictures did apply: historically, Mohegans who married Blacks were expelled from the tribe and their children unrecognized. Not realizing this, some phenotypically Black individuals call themselves Mohegan today but are not recognized by the tribe.

Tribal genealogists perform research to validate or deny claims of applicants to membership, and each tribe has specific rules illustrating that absolute blood quantum is not the sole criterion for admission.[77] Despite tribal genealogists' recourse to records proving or disproving individuals' claims to membership, these records do not affect individuals' own genealogical positioning within tribal hierarchies of heritage and knowledge. Many use real or imagined knowledge about others' genealogies to evaluate individuals or families with claims to high status, attempting to reduce their influence by suggesting their Native ancestry is mixed – in other words, not all Narragansett – or that their African American ancestors are more numerous than their Native forebears.[78] The intent of such private statements is simultaneously to denigrate others and advance the speaker's claims to heritage by comparison. While such statements are common in intragroup situations where blood and culture together define heritage and individuals negotiate tribal hierarchies, they are sometimes used in intergroup contexts. For instance, in devaluing a popular Wampanoag lecturer, members of other tribes suggest that his ancestry is almost entirely Portuguese.

Individuals and tribal genealogists alike focus attention on Indian descent and seldom articulate non-Indian ancestry, except to state that it is White or specifically Portuguese.[79] In particular, Wampanoag individuals may mention Portuguese or Azorean ancestry because it is obvious from their surnames. Many individuals state that they have White parents or grandparents, but few claim Black ancestors, except those who consider themselves descendants of two traditionally subjugated groups. In addition, the literal statement that one's non-Native ancestry is White is an instrumental assertion that it includes no Blacks. Physical traits stereotyped as African American place some constraints on individuals' ability to claim their Indian identity, but Native people who are phenotypically White are less inclined to argue their genealogies: Whiteness generally needs no defense.[80] Other individuals whose appearance suggests some African American ancestry do not mention those ancestors in their genealogies and instead focus heavily on articulating their Native ancestry.

Where Native surnames survive, these are considered perfect genealogies and are considered part of "blood"; such individuals have little trouble setting themselves up as cultural authorities, even where they lack traditional knowledge.[81] Changing one's name legally or using a Native name informally also lends credibility with Whites: a respected Native educator goes by the name *Corbitant* (a seventeenth-century sachem) rather than *Bruce Richards*, while *Frances Yancey Charles* became *Frances Tatobaum* (an ancestral surname of Native derivation). Although these names may not be readily recognizable as Indian, they are useful symbols given non-Natives' tendency to identify ethnicity on the basis of surnames: a fair-haired woman named O'Malley is assumed to be Irish even if her maiden name is Giancarlo.

In addition to truly Native names that establish blood, there are also "Indian names" that are used to demonstrate culture. Bestowal of these names marks an individual's transition between life stages, and having an Indian name is additionally an expectation of non-Natives. Indian names are given at tribal powwows or "naming ceremonies" and supposedly represent individual qualities. Individuals choose their own names or their children's, relying on their sense of appropriateness, including a young man taking the name "Stomping Coyote" or new parents calling a small baby "White Fang." Many believe they are transformed by taking a name and alter their regalia – traditional dress worn at powwows and ceremonial occasions – accordingly. During tribal or powwow activities they refer to themselves by their Indian name and call others (now their peers) by Indian names, thus establishing themselves as cultured.

Where Native people claim bodies of traditional knowledge, establishing "cultural heritage" via symbolic descent is important; individuals claim their knowledge comes from respected individuals in the same way they mention genetic ancestors. These "cultural ancestors" are symbols, and their "meanings" and social positions are negotiated. Among the Mashpee, Eben Queppish – an elderly tribal member who died in 1933 – was transformed posthumously into a carrier of traditional knowledge: his nephew maintained that Queppish had secretly taught him ancient dances and ceremonies. Queppish was used as a symbol by his nephew's faction to support a "traditional" slate of officers for tribal government.[82] In another instance, Princess Red Wing, a Narragansett-Pokanoket active in the 1930s' Narragansett revival, was disavowed by the Narragansett tribal genealogist and labeled Portuguese after her death in 1986. Although many still speak proudly about Red Wing's important work as a culture carrier, Red Wing's rejection by powerful Narragansetts devalues her as a symbol: those who based claims to traditional knowledge on links to Red Wing can no longer maintain those claims, because cultural heritage is only as good as one's cultural ancestors. The individuals in question can ignore the tribal genealogist, gossip about her genealogy in retaliation, or refashion their "cultural heritage" to include past individuals who have maintained their cultural reputations.

BLOOD AND CULTURE AND THE TRIBE

For some Native groups in southeastern New England, blood is preeminent in constructing self-identity. For instance, the Gay Head Wampanoags are accepted as Indians by non-Native neighbors and many Indians although their lives may seem nearly identical to those of non-Native Vineyarders. Their genealogies, the fact that they "look Indian," and that they have a set of recognizable surnames convince their neighbors and themselves that they are Gay Head Wampanoags (*Bruce Richards*, Wampanoag, 11/1991). However, at the 1992 Gay Head Wampanoag History Conference, younger tribal members were defensive and spoke more about keeping traditions alive than what those traditions were. The traditions discussed included oral history (collected by a White anthropologist) and specific foodways, such as harvesting cranberries, scallops, and herring using techniques developed by Whites, including locating swordfish with a helicopter and using harpoons equipped with explosive charges.[83]

Younger tribal members' defensiveness may stem from confrontations with Native people who emphasize "culture" more than "blood" and doubt the integrity of Gay Head traditions. Once exposed to Native Americans "off island," many young Wampanoags have recognized their ignorance of wider Native symbols and have attempted to remedy this by adopting pan-Indian traditions.[84] Some have begun a western-style drum and dance group (the tribe's first), while others support national Indian causes such as the movement to free Leonard Peltier (*Stephanie Waters* and *Darcy Edwards*, Gay Head Wampanoags, 11/1992). Exposure to national Indian rhetoric has also prompted sudden reminiscences of overt "racial" discrimination in the schools. White Vineyarders of the same generation remember the young Wampanoags as pleasant and popular and recall none of the racial tensions described by the Gay Headers.

Among the Wampanoags, nonfederally recognized groups who attempt to claim Indian identity are also challenged by Native people themselves. In a discussion of the Native American Graves Protection and Repatriation Act – which guarantees federally recognized tribes mechanisms to reclaim human remains and artifacts from museums and federal agencies – a Pokanoket man noted that unrecognized groups deserve the same rights. A Gay Head woman countered that there are many amalgamated groups – the Assonet Band of Wampanoag in particular – who claim Wampanoag ancestry without proof: "They just know somewhere back in history there was an Indian somewhere, and they assume that person was Wampanoag because of where they lived." To the Pokanoket's statement that proof of Indianness is "in their hearts," she coldly replied, "But that doesn't make them an Indian" (*Donald Hanson*, Pokanoket, and *Andrea Bache*, Gay Head Wampanoag, 9/1993). Although the Gay Heads, Pokanokets, and Assonets all consider themselves Wampanoags, the Gay Head Wampanoags' position as the only federally recognized

Wampanoag tribe and the only recognized tribe in Massachusetts, as well as the infrequency of African American intermarriages, gives them a feeling of superiority over other Wampanoag groups.

At the same time, Pokanoket individuals whose White ancestry may be apparent use derogatory terms for members of other tribes, for instance, calling the Narragansetts and sometimes the Pequots "muskies," which may be drawn from the historical term "mustee." Pokanokets who use such racial terminology for members of other tribes do not use it in talking about their own kin who, by appearance, exhibit some degree of African American ancestry and who aspire to admission to the Narragansett or Mashantucket Pequot tribal rolls. The selectivity of this usage is tied up with the Pokanokets' need to show themselves as "real Indians," especially in contrast to the Narragansetts, who they suggest lack sufficient ancestry to be Indian. However, Pokanoket enmity toward the Narragansetts is not solely about who is Indian and who is not. Pokanokets who use racial epithets in describing the Narragansetts specifically suggest that the recent ancestry of the prominent Narragansett "medicine family" includes a Cape Verdean (that is, Black) woman.

Emphasizing blood over culture does not mean Native people lack culture, only that it is secondary in those situations. Those lacking the security of recognizable phenotypes (and unquestioned acceptance by non-Natives) or unimpeachable genealogies resort to culture and tradition as ethnic symbols, shifting the focus from personal ancestry and history to that of their group. Unlike the Gay Head Wampanoags, who rely on genealogies to illustrate continuity, the Mashpee Wampanoags must try to downplay the "facts" of their genealogies – filled with Europeans and African Americans – to show their Native cultural heritage. As James Clifford suggests, the Mashpees are not generally recognized as Indians by their neighbors or by the courts, but they try to make cultural continuity visible through links with the land, traditional foods, their church, pow-wows, oral traditions, and the like, symbols subsumed under the ethnic symbol "culture."[85] In addition, throughout the 1980s, the Mashpees used the Supreme Sachem and Supreme Medicine Man of the Wampanoag Nation, both members of the Mashpee community, as examples of their superior position as keepers of traditional Wampanoag knowledge.

Race and racial labeling also pose problems within groups. The Narragansetts and Pequots have historically intermarried with African Americans and Whites, and for more than a hundred years the Narragansetts and the Pequots have been identified as heavily mixed with Blacks. Rejecting Narragansett identity on the basis of phenotype and presumed racial admixture remains common: in 1983, when the announcement of the Narragansetts' federal acknowledgment was published in *The National Register*, the Bureau of Acknowledgment and Recognition received objections that "expressed the opinion that the Narragansetts could not meet a blood degree requirement," apparently based on perception of a heavy degree of Black admixture.[86] Many active Narragansett tribal members are those who would likely be judged by non-Natives as having some African American ancestry, and this is recognized by many Narragansetts: "We are not to be judged by you, by the color of our skin, the length of our hair, where we live, what you have seen on television, or written in the newspapers, but by our blood. For you can destroy or take away all material things, but we still live, the Narragansett Indians."[87] Individuals who call themselves "Narragansett" but are phenotypically White are less often involved in tribal activities and may not be on the tribal rolls. These individuals are more often involved in regional nontribal pan-Indian events and associate with members of western tribes and others who claim Indian identity but are not enrolled members of any local tribe.

Among the Pequots, divisions based on phenotype are also significant at some levels. Historically, many Pequots intermarried with both Whites and African Americans, with some marriages to African Americans occurring in the most recent generations. With the rise of gaming profits in the 1990s, a number of Mashantucket Pequots who are descended from the Sebastian family – whose genealogies are in part Portuguese and African American – noted discrimination within the tribe based on skin color, suggesting that they were not recognized as tribal members in their own casino and that darker skinned individuals were seldom chosen for high-paying tribal jobs.[88] With the rise of the Sebastian family in Mashantucket politics, tensions appear to have dissipated to some extent, but the issue of phenotypic variability and how it came about is seldom addressed publicly and is virtually ignored in the exhibits of the tribe's own Mashantucket Pequot Museum and Research Center. Despite the lack of explicit discussion of racial intermarriage and admixture in the museum's exhibits, the issue was of such great importance to the tribe that the skin tone of each exhibit mannequin was said to have been reviewed and approved by tribal members during the museum's construction.

Other groups are also divided over matters of blood. The Paucatuck Eastern Pequot Indian Tribal Nation and the Eastern Pequot tribe – both of which are applying for federal recognition and control over a single reservation – are at odds over the identification of a single woman and how this affects genealogy, membership, and leadership (*Eagle* 9[6], 6).

Tamar Brushell Sebastian (ca. 1822–1915) is considered by the Eastern Pequot tribe as a full-blood Pequot, which affects her descendants' genealogies to a large extent since Connecticut recognizes those Indian people who can prove a ⅛ Indian blood quantum. On the other hand, the Paucatuck Eastern Pequot Indian Tribal Nation has identified Tamar Sebastian as a person of mixed, unknowable ancestry who lived on the Eastern Pequot reservation but was not a tribal member because she did not maintain relations with the tribe; thus those who claim Pequot ancestry only from her would not be eligible for tribal membership. Differential intermarriage factors for the two groups complicate this issue: while both groups historically intermarried with Whites and Blacks, the Paucatuck Eastern Pequot Indian Tribal Nation has more recently had more unions with Whites, while the Eastern Pequot tribe (almost all descended from Tamar Sebastian and related to the Mashantucket Pequot Sebastians) are generally darker skinned. As a result, the Sebastians claim that the members of the Paucatuck Eastern Pequot Indian Tribal Nation are racists who discriminate against the Sebastians on the basis of skin color, even though the issue – from the Paucatuck Eastern Pequot Indian Tribal Nation's perspective – is really about degree of Pequot blood and maintaining tribal relations. Tamar Sebastian's degree of Pequot blood has also been revised in more obvious ways: in documents at the Indian and Colonial Research Center in Mystic, Connecticut, a visitor changed Tamar's identity by scratching out "colored" and replacing it with "full-blooded Pequot."[89]

CONCLUSION

From the examples provided, readers may correctly assume that race and racial attitudes are a matter of discussion as well as a source of discomfort and reticence in Native communities. Race is seldom discussed in public since few want to draw attention to it as a facet of identity, either in terms of self-perception or external identification. Nor do Indian people who feel strongly about the effects of race on Native ancestry and heritage want to be thought of as open racists. As a result, in working on similar problems and sharing draft publications with Native consultants, I have received varied reactions to some of my interpretations.[90] These ranged from being lauded for openly discussing past and present racial discrimination based on physical appearance to being accused of being racist for suggesting that racial judgments existed within Indian communities and that they continue to affect how Indian people present themselves. What I continue to maintain is that cognizance of the effects of race on Indian identity – both internally perpetuated and externally perceived – does not mean that Indian people are racists: their actions in positioning themselves with regard to the racial attitudes of others are pragmatic responses, and they cannot be faulted for "working" the system.

Examining race as a factor is crucial in understanding Native identity over time and extends into other arenas. Indian people in southeastern New England appear to have been the first Native Americans to work toward recognition as an ethnic group – based on historical and cultural factors – as opposed to a racial group or an ambivalent category of mixed-race individuals. Native people continue to be aware of the problematic nature of their appearance to non-Indians, especially in the modern context of racialized ethnicities. Against these perceptions, Native people have negotiated the Indian "self" – one's response to others and internalized outside attitudes – and social action as tribal members to effect recognition as Indian. Native people have acted and reacted in response to regional non-Native racial ideologies to position themselves in society and demonstrate Indian identity, recognizing all the while that race – as a social construct – could and should be managed in ways beneficial to them.

Like all others, Native people today are concerned with improving their position in American society and must constantly react to wider social environments to ensure the effectiveness of symbols and ethnic expression. Increasingly, Native groups are trying to rewrite their identities by rewriting their histories. One power of history involves illustrating how the past gave way to the present and justifies present conditions and action. Besides reinterpreting histories of specific events, Native people rely on history to help prove their distinctiveness as ethnic rather than racial groups. Since racial classifications are based on largely immutable physical appearance and folk biology, Native Americans must move into an arena where symbols they can manipulate – blood, culture, and history – are more important to establishing identity.

In recognizing that Native people are attempting to position themselves as part of American society and contradict widespread notions that they are either White or African American rather than Indian, we must also recognize that blood and culture are brought to bear in different contexts for individual and group identity and that concepts of "ideal identity," "feared identity," and physical appearance are all variables that affect the presentation of self and group identity. As with other Americans who simultaneously negotiate the need for community versus individuality, Native people balance blood and culture in defining themselves, using cultural heritage where blood evidence is irrelevant or unworkable and vice versa.[91] This is especially apparent when individuals compare themselves with others: they may share the same blood quantum but can position themselves within a hierarchy via recourse to culture, which is representative of their effort to maintain identity and their own linkages with other "cultural ancestors" or those who are recognized as traditional. In sharing culture with others – even in varying degrees – individuals also align themselves with the tribe as a whole, including persons who share different degrees of blood validated by tribal authorities. Within the context of tribal culture, individuals are judged mainly by their claimed experience and are evaluated on whether their cultural holdings resonate well with other community members. Overall, those who value blood over culture as a marker of identity are less likely to be active members of tribal communities. For instance, urban Indians and those heavily involved in intertribal pan-Indian activities are less specific in their cultural actions than those who are members of active communities where hierarchy is established through tribally specific cultural knowledge and practice.

However, in all situations where recognition as Indian is complicated by phenotype – whether White or African American – Native people are more likely to use cultural demonstration and knowledge to be recognized by Natives and non-Natives alike. In these settings, Native people fight against folk ideas about the causal relationship between "loss of blood" and loss of culture: for them, the amount of blood is less important than articulating the specific individuals they descend from and how they gained knowledge of their cultures. While non-Indians may see intermarriage as leading to a "depreciation" of heritage, individuals can actually "amortize" cultural heritage by identifying themselves through those they are descended from and unrelated individuals from whom they learned cultural practices.[92]

As Joane Nagel suggests, problems of individual and group identity cannot easily be separated.[93] What began in southeastern New England as the rise of individual efforts to be recognized as Indian in the 1920s led to "collective ethnic renewal" and the rebuilding of tribal communities in the 1930s. Recent growth of stronger tribal communities and tribal economic development have also bred a rise in individual ethnic renewal among those whose ancestors passed into Black and White society and have themselves returned to burgeoning Native communities.

Despite this renewal and the decrease in stigmatization felt by Indian people, the racial history of the United States and non-Indians' belief that they can identify Indians and others on the basis of phenotype make necessary the continued use of ethnic symbols such as blood and culture in marking and proving identity. As long as race is salient in America – and physical appearance is part of the way individuals are judged and identified by others – it will remain salient in Indian country and in the way that Indian people present themselves and evaluate one another. Today, the legacy of race and caste in southeastern New England and other parts of the country remains, creating ongoing struggles and negotiations on the matter of who is or is not Indian, both in Indian communities and in the wider world.

NOTES

Data and conclusions presented here are dealt with in much greater depth in my dissertation, "Culture by Design: Native Identity, Historiography, and the Reclamation of Tradition in Twentieth-Century Southeastern New England" (Brown University, 1996), based on ethnographic and ethnohistorical fieldwork from June 1990 through May 1994 as well as continuing research. Fieldwork and research were funded by the Haffenreffer Museum of Anthropology, Brown University; the Wenner-Gren Foundation for Anthropological Research; and the Center for the Study of Race and Ethnicity in America, Brown University. I gratefully acknowledge this assistance here. I would also like to thank Dan Odess for comments and discussion on an earlier version of this essay.

1. Formerly known as the "Mohegan Tribe and Nation," this group is now "Native American Mohegans," although another unrecognized group operates under the name "Mohegan Tribe and Nation, Inc." as opposed to the "Mohegan Tribe," which is the federally recognized entity. At issue is whether these individuals – who are active in pan-Indian cultural activities – are truly descended from the historic Mohegan tribe.

2. This figure (compiled from U.S. census data available at http://www.census .gov) is a total of the self-identified Native Americans living in Connecticut, Rhode Island, and Massachusetts. However, this total includes members of non–New England tribes and tribes indigenous to western Massachusetts and Connecticut.

3. At this writing, the Paucatuck Eastern Pequot Indian Tribal Nation, the Eastern Pequot tribe, and two Nipmuc groups await final determinations on their petitions for federal recognition.

4. T. J. Brasser, "The Coastal Algonkians: People of the First Frontiers," in *North American Indians in Historical Perspective*, ed. E. B. Leacock and N. O. Lurie (Prospect Heights IL: Waveland Press, 1971), 64–91; Ann McMullen, "Native Basketry, Basket Styles, and Changing Group Identity in Southern New England,"

in *Proceedings of the Dublin Seminar for New England Folklife*, ed. P. Benes (Boston: Boston University, 1993), 76–88; McMullen, "Under the Bridge: Woodsplint Basketry and the Identification of Hidden Native Communities in Historic New England" (paper presented at the annual meeting of the American Society for Ethnohistory, Kalamazoo MI, 2–5 November 1995).

5. See Jack D. Forbes, *Africans and Native Americans: Language and Race and the Evolution of Red-Black Peoples* (Urbana: University of Illinois Press, 1993).

6. Gillian Cowlishaw, "Colour, Culture, and the Aboriginalists," *Man* 22 (1987): 229.

7. Ronald Takaki, *A Different Mirror: A History of Multicultural America* (Boston: Little, Brown, 1993), 55–67.

8. Raymond D. Fogelson, "Interpretations of the American Indian Psyche: Some Historical Notes," in *Social Contexts of American Ethnology, 1840–1984*, ed. J. Helm (Washington DC: American Anthropological Association, 1984), 9, 46.

9. Hazel W. Hertzberg, *The Search for an American Indian Identity: Modern Pan-Indian Movements* (Syracuse NY: Syracuse University Press, 1971), 306.

10. Fogelson, "Interpretations," 14–15; see also Robert E. Bieder, *Science Encounters the Indian, 1820–1880: The Early Years of American Ethnology* (Norman: University of Oklahoma Press, 1986).

11. Takaki, *Different Mirror*, 80.

12. Margaret Mead, "Ethnicity and Anthropology in America," in *Ethnic Identity: Creation, Conflict, and Accommodation*, ed. Lola Romanucci-Ross and George A. De Vos (Walnut Creek CA: Altamira Press, 1995), 301.

13. Ethel Boissevain, *The Narragansett People* (Phoenix: Indian Tribal Series, 1975); Paul R. Campbell and Glenn W. LaFantasie, "Scattered to the Winds of Heaven: Narragansett Indians, 1648–1880," *Rhode Island History* 37, no. 3 (1978): 67–83; Daniel R. Mandell, "Shifting Boundaries of Race and Ethnicity: Indian-Black Intermarriage in Southern New England, 1760–1880," *Journal of American History* 85, no. 2 1998: 466–501.

14. Barry O'Connell, introduction to *On Our Own Ground: The Complete Writings of William Apess, a Pequot*, ed. Barry O'Connell (Amherst: University of Massachusetts Press, 1992), xlix.

15. Joanne Pope Melish, "'Real Indians': The Racial Reconfiguration of the Narragansett in the Nineteenth Century" (paper presented at the annual meeting of the American Society for Ethnohistory, Mashantucket CT, 1999); Boissevain, *Narragansett People*. Rhode Island passed a gradual emancipation law that made all those born of slaves after 1784 free by birth. In 1842, those still living in slavery were freed by state law; see Ruth Wallis Herndon and Ella Wilcox Sekatau, "The Right to a Name: The Narragansett People and Rhode Island Officials in the Revolutionary Era," *Ethnohistory* 44, no. 1 (1997): 462 n.88. In some Massa-

chusetts Indian communities, Black men were said to take Indian wives because their children would be free by birth (Mandell, "Shifting Boundaries," 469).

16. Thomas Doughton, "Unseen Neighbors: Native Americans of Central Massachusetts, a People Who Had 'Vanished,'" in *After King Philip's War: Presence and Persistence in Indian New England*, ed. Colin G. Calloway (Hanover NH: University Press of New England, 1997); Melish, "Real Indians." Herndon and Sekatau ("Right to a Name," 445, 437) illustrate how "mustee" – a term commonly used in Rhode Island for the offspring of any mixed union, came to be replaced by "Black" or "Negro" after the Revolutionary War. The terms "Narragansett" and "Indian" were seldom used, resulting in a "documentary genocide."

17. *Annual Reports of the Commission on the Affairs of the Narragansett Indians for the Years 1880–1883*. 4 vols. (Providence RI: E. L. Freeman, 1881–84).

18. Forbes, *Africans and Native Americans*, 262; Herndon and Sekatau, "Right to a Name," 453.

19. Ann Marie Plane and Gregory Button, "The Massachusetts Indian Enfranchisement Act: Ethnic Contest in Historical Context, 1849–1869," *Ethnohistory* 40, no. 4 (1993): 587–618.

20. *Report of the Commissioner on the Narragansett Tribe of Indians, Made to the General Assembly, at its January Session, 1858* (Providence RI: Knowles, Anthony, 1858); *Narragansett Tribes of Indians: Report of the Committee of Investigation; A Historical Sketch, and Evidence Taken. Made to the House of Representatives at its January Session, A.D. 1880* (Providence RI: E. L. Freeman, 1880).

21. Larence R. Baca, "The Legal Status of American Indians," in *Handbook of North American Indians*, vol. 4. *History of Indian-White Relations*, ed. W. E. Washburn (Washington DC: Smithsonian Institution, 1988), 230.

22. Vine Deloria Jr. and Clifford M. Lytle, *The Nations Within: The Past and Future of American Indian Sovereignty* (New York: Pantheon Books, 1984); Oliver LaFarge, "Termination of Federal Supervision: Disintegration and the American Indian," in "American Indians and American Life," ed. G. E. Simpson and J. M. Yinger, *Annals of the American Academy of Political and Social Science* 3 (1957): 2; William T. Hagan, "Reformers' Images of the Native Americans: The Late Nineteenth Century," in *The American Indian Experience*, ed. P. Weeks (Arlington Heights IL: Forum Press, 1988), 207–17; Hertzberg, *Search for an American Indian Identity*; Frederick E, Hoxie, *A Final Promise: The Campaign to Assimilate the Indians, 1880–1920* (Lincoln: University of Nebraska Press, 1984).

23. Duane Champagne, *American Indian Societies: Strategies and Conditions of Political and Cultural Survival*. Colonial Survival Report 22 (Cambridge MA: Cultural Survival), 34; Mandell, "Shifting Boundaries," 471.

24. Walter Prichard Eaton, "In Old South County," *Outing Magazine* 60, no. 3 (1912): 265–66.

25. Mandell, "Shifting Boundaries," 472, 487.

26. Frank Speck, "Notes on the Mohegan and Niantic Indians," in "The Indians of the Greater New York and the Lower Hudson," ed. C. Wissler, *Anthropological Papers of the American Museum of Natural History* 3 (1909): 184 n.3.

27. Racial attitudes of early-twentieth-century anthropologists who worked in southern New England – especially Frank Speck – are examined in greater detail in Ann McMullen, "What's Wrong with This Picture? Context, Coversion, Survival, and the Development of Regional Native Cultures and Pan-Indianism in Southeastern New England," in *Enduring Traditions: The Native Peoples of New England*, ed. L. Weinstein (Westport CT: Bergin & Garvey, 1994), 123–50; McMullen, "'The Heart Interest': Native Americans at Mount Hope and the King Philip Museum," in *Passionate Hobby: Rudolf Frederick Haffenreffer and the King Philip Museum*, ed. Shepard Krech III (Bristol RI: Haffenreffer Museum of Anthropology, Brown University, 1994), 167–85; McMullen, "Culture by Design." For racial divisions among the Mohegan, see Mandell, "Shifting Boundaries."

28. Stephen Steinberg, *The Ethnic Myth: Race, Ethnicity, and Class in America* (Boston: Beacon Press, 1989), 174, 181, 201–3, 206.

29. Melish, "Real Indians."

30. Indian Council of New England, Scrapbook of Thomas Bicknell's correspondence, newspaper clippings, photographs, etc. Museum of Anthropology, Brown University, Bristol RI.

31. Herndon and Sekatau, "Right to a Name," 447. Mandell ("Shifting Boundaries," 474–76) has also suggested that competition for Indian women as mates, as well as the competition over influence and resources such intermarriages engendered, could have made Indian men hate Blacks.

32. McMullen, "What's Wrong with This Picture?"

33. The Native trend toward differentiating themselves from Blacks may have begun earlier, for instance, as a result of abolitionist plans to "expatriate" Blacks and resettle them in the Caribbean, as was supported by Thomas Jefferson (Takaki, *Different Mirror*). Abolitionist rhetoric may also have prompted New England Native people to reconsider their position within society. However, I have not yet ascertained the extent of Native knowledge of these ideas and whether it affected self-perception and concerted action in reclaiming overt Indian identity.

34. George A. De Vos, "Ethnic Pluralism: Conflict and Accommodation," in Romanucci-Ross and De Vos, *Ethnic Identity*, 28.

35. Nathan Glazer and Daniel Patrick Moynihan, *Beyond the Melting Pot: The Negroes, Puerto Ricans, Jews, Italians, and Irish of New York City*. 2nd ed. (Cambridge: MIT Press, 1970), xxiii.

36. James Axtell, "The White Indians of Colonial America," in *The European and the Indian: Essays in the Ethnohistory of North America* (Cambridge: Cambridge

University Press, 1981); John Demos, *The Unredeemed Captive: A Family Story from Early America* (New York: Alfred A. Knopf, 1994).

37. Mandell, "Shifting Boundaries," 470. Minority strategies in unequal plural situations include accepting minority status and stigma; working to change the system; passing in the dominant society but maintaining covert identity in the subordinate community; and abandoning community ties and passing completely (George A. De Vos and Hiroshi Wagatsuma, "Cultural Identity and Status in Japan," in Romanucci-Ross and De Vos, *Ethnic Identity*, 275).

38. Mandell, "Shifting Boundaries," 474–83; see also Plane and Button, "Massachusetts Indian Enfranchisement Act."

39. De Vos, "Ethnic Pluralism," 18.

40. Glazer and Moynihan, *Beyond the Melting Pot*, xiii; Steinberg, *Ethnic Myth*, 3; Takaki, *Different Mirror*, 3.

41. Richard D. Alba, *Ethnic Identity: The Transformation of White America* (New Haven CT: Yale University Press, 1990), 2–3, 9; De Vos, "Ethnic Pluralism," 30; Steinberg, *Ethnic Myth*.

42. De Vos, "Ethnic Pluralism," 31; Russell Thornton, "The Demography of Colonialism and 'Old' and 'New' Native Americans," in *Studying Native America: Problems and Prospects*, ed. Russell Thornton (Madison: University of Wisconsin Press, 1998), 17–39.

43. Thornton, *Studying Native America*; C. Matthew Snipp, *American Indians: The First of this Land* (New York: Russell Sage, 1989), 308. Snipp's analysis (47–49) of American Indian figures from the 1980 U.S. census suggests that there is little stigma to admitting Native ancestry. Approximately 1.5 million people identified themselves as members of an American Indian race, while 6.8 million reported American Indian ancestry, with a vast majority identifying themselves as White.

44. Pierre L. van den Berghe, *Race and Racism: A Comparative Perspective* (New York: John Wiley & Sons, 1967), 9.

45. Joane Nagel, *American Indian Ethnic Renewal: Red Power and the Resurgence of Identity and Culture* (New York: Oxford University Press, 1996); Snipp, *American Indians*, 27. Some sociological studies include American Indians under the category "U.S. born Whites," for example, Alba, *Ethnic Identity*. It is also possible to consider individual tribes as ethnic groups as well as to see "Indian" as a generalized ethnic group analogous to African American; see Nagel, *American Indian Ethnic Renewal*, 9.

46. Steinberg, *Ethnic Myth*, 265; Glazer and Moynihan, *Beyond the Melting Pot*, xxxvii.

47. Snipp, *American Indians*, 37; Mary C. Waters, *Ethnic Options: Choosing Identities in America* (Berkeley: University of California Press, 1990).

48. Waters, *Ethnic Options*, 158; Cowlishaw, "Colour, Culture and the Aboriginalists."

49. Alba, *Ethnic Identity*, 12; Waters, *Ethnic Options*, 102; Snipp, *American Indians*, 157.Census figures show that 2.1 percent of Indian men marry Black women, and 1.1 percent of Indian women have Black husbands. The relative percentages for Black-White intermarriage range from 0.1 to 2.6 (Snipp, *American Indians*, 157).

50. Raymond D. Fogelson, "Perspectives on Native American Identity," in *Studying Native America: Problems and Prospects*, ed. Russell Thornton (Madison: University of Wisconsin Press, 1998), 45; Waters, *Ethnic Options*, 18, 75–80.

51. Waters, *Ethnic Options*, 18, 75–78.

52. Within the text and notes, I have used italicized pseudonyms to disguise informants' identity, but individuals deceased during the period of my research or cited in published works retain their true names.

53. Snipp, *American Indians*, 28.

54. Fogelson, "Perspectives," 43–47.

55. Snipp, *American Indians*, 29.

56. Herbert Gans, "Symbolic Ethnicity: The Future of Ethnic Groups and Cultures in America," *Ethnic and Racial Studies* 2 (1979):, 1–20; Alba, *Ethnic Identity*, 61; Waters, *Ethnic Options*, 36. Selection depends on preconceptions of ethnic character: "Thus what people believe a certain ethnic identity to be is important for the identity they consciously choose to become or choose to maintain" (Waters, *Ethnic Options*, 130).

57. Fogelson, "Perspectives," 40, 41, 43.

58. Fogelson, "Perspectives," 52; Alba, *Ethnic Identity*, 17, 19, 139; Glazer and Moynihan, *Beyond the Melting Pot*, xxxiii.

59. Alba, *Ethnic Identity*, 37, 149; De Vos, "Ethnic Pluralism," 18; Waters, *Ethnic Options*, 161.

60. De Vos, "Ethnic Pluralism," 24.

61. Fogelson, "Perspectives," 53; George L. Hicks and David I. Kertzer, "Making a Middle Way: Problems of Monhegan Identity," *Southwest Journal of Anthropology* 28, no. 1 (1972): 1–24; George A. De Vos and Lola Romanucci-Ross, "Ethnic Identity: A Psychocultural Perspective," in Romanucci-Ross and De Vos, *Ethnic Identity*, 361.

62. George L. Hicks, personal communication, 1991.

63. Max Gluckman, "Gossip and Scandal," *Current Anthropology* 4 (1963): 309; see also Nagel, *American Indian Ethnic Renewal*, 62; De Vos and Romanucci-Ross, "Ethnic Identity," 367, 371.

64. Franz L. Wojciechowski, "Big Business and Modern Eastern Algonquian Identity: The Casino Connection," *European Review of Native American Studies* 11,

no. 2 (1997): 39–42. The New England Indian population – based on self-claimed identity – doubled from 1970 to 1980 (Snipp, *American Indians*, 75).

65. Nagel, *American Indian Ethnic Renewal*, 119.

66. James A. Clifton, "Alternate Identities and Cultural Frontiers," in *Being and Becoming Indian: Biographical Sketches of North American Indians*, ed. J. A. Clifton (Chicago: Dorsey Press, 1989), 1–37.

67. Ella Sekatau, Narragansett tribal genealogist, quoted in John Hill, "Membership Claims Divide Tribe," *Providence Journal* 14 May 1993. The Narragansett, who trace all members from their 1880 roll, also explored the genealogies of current tribal members in an effort to weed out those who were assumed – because of their surnames – to be tribal members but who lacked the actual genealogical links those names imply. Those whose membership was repudiated understood the attempt as an effort to increase remaining members' individual gains from the profits of proposed gaming operations (*Irving Davidson*, Narragansett, 8/1995).

68. Wojciechowski, "Big Business."

69. Although blood and culture are the ethnic symbols most commonly manipulated by southeastern New England Native people, a number of the "components" of ethnic identity mentioned by Harold R. Isaacs in *Idols of the Tribe: Group Identity and Political Change* (Cambridge: Harvard University Press, 1975) are bound up in "culture" or "blood." Names and land, along with religion, language, and other fragmented aspects of local Native tradition, are all included as part of "culture" as an ethnic symbol. See Ann McMullen, "Soapbox Discourse: Tribal History, Indian-White Relations, and Southeastern New England Powwows," *Public Historian* 18, no. 4 (1996).

70. Fogelson, "'Perspectives," 41.

71. Karen Blu, *The Lumbee Problem: The Making of an American Indian People* (Cambridge: Cambridge University Press, 1980).

72. Blu, *Lumbee Problem*, 6.

73. Blu, *Lumbee Problem*, 25.

74. Although Native people in southeastern New England were probably originally matrilineal, there were some shifts toward patrilineality during the contact period, especially in reckoning the lines of chiefs (Kathleen Bragdon, *Native People of Southern New England, 1500–1650* [Norman: University of Oklahoma Press, 1996]). Today, more flexible bilateral descent prevails.

75. High rates of intermarriage are also typical of the present: due to the small size of many tribes, at 9.4 percent, New England has the lowest rate of Indian-Indian marriages nationwide (Snipp, *American Indians*, 158).

76. Indian Council of New England, Scrapbook. Ciscoe sought to elevate her own position and gain authority within the Indian Council of New England (McMullen, "Culture by Design").

77. Not all tribes define their membership explicitly by blood quantum: for the Mashantucket Pequots, membership must be traced from the 1900 or 1910 tribal rolls, with a minimum blood quantum of ¹⁄₁₆ (*David Tremblay*, Mashantucket Pequot, 11/1991; Christopher Rowland, "The Big Gamble: The Pequots Bet on a Casino," *Providence Journal Sunday Magazine*, 11 August 1991, 6–14). Membership in the Mohegan tribe requires documentation of descent from one of the families listed on the 1861 roll (*Nancy Grant*, Mohegan, 2/1992). The Gay Head Wampanoags require that members have an ancestor on the 1870 census (*Bruce Richards*, Wampanoag 11/1991).

78. High status is ordinarily based on descent from historic leaders or high blood quantum.

79. See also Waters, *Ethnic Options*, 22.

80. Waters, *Ethnic Options*, 19; George L. Hicks, "Separate But Similar: Adaptation by Two American Indian Groups," in *Ethnic Encounters*, ed. G. L. Hicks and P. E. Leis (North Scituate MA: Duxbury Press, 1977).

81. Among the Mohegan, Niantic, Nipmuc, and Wampanoag groups, anthropologist Frank G. Speck focused on families with Indian surnames, although survival of these names was solely the result of tracing patrilineal descent. Indian women who took non-Native names at marriage had less bearing on Speck's work. See the following works by Speck: "Notes on the Mohegan and Niantic Indians"; *Decorative Art of the Indian Tribes of Connecticut*, Canada Department of Mines, Geological Survey, Memoir 75, Anthropological Series 10, 1915; "Native Tribes and Dialects of Connecticut: A Mohegan-Pequot Diary," in *Forty-Third Annual Report of the Bureau of American Ethnology 1925–1926* (Washington DC: Government Printing Office, 1928), 199-287; "Territorial Subdivisions and Boundaries of the Wampanoag, Massachusett, and Nauset Indians," *Indian Notes and Monographs* 44 (1928); "A Note on the Hassanamisco Band of Nipmuc," *Bulletin of the Massachusetts Archaeological Society* 4, no. 4 (1943): 49–56.

82. Jack Campisi, *The Mashpee Indians: Tribe on Trial* (Syracuse NY: Syracuse University Press, 1991), 134–35.

83. See William S. Simmons, "Gay Head Oral Traditions" (paper presented at Gay Head Wampanoag History Conference, Edgartown MA, 11–12 November 1972).

84. See Blu, *Lumbee Problem*.

85. James Clifford, *The Predicament of Culture: Twentieth-Century Ethnography, Literature, and Art* (Cambridge: Cambridge University Press, 1988), 278.

86. John W. Fritz, "Announcement of Narragansett Recognition," *Federal Register* 48, no. 29 (1983): 6178.

87. Lucille Dawson, *We Still Live: The American Indians*. Part 1 (n.p., ca. 1975), 3.

88. Wil Haygood, "Did the Pequots Hit the Jackpot? Foxwoods' Riches Have Fulfilled the Tiny Tribe's Dreams, But Not All Are Happy about the Price," *Boston Globe*, 17 August 1995.

89. Beth Dufresne, "Written in Bloodlines: One Woman's Genealogy Could Be Key to Two Tribes' Recognition," *New London Day*, 14 December 1997.

90. The paper in question became Ann McMullen, "The Heart Interest: Native Americans at Mount Hope and the King Philip Museum," in *Passionate Hobby: Rudolf Frederick Haffenreffer and the King Philip Museum*, ed. Shepard Krech III (Bristol RI: Haffenreffer Museum of Anthropology, 1994), 167–85.

91. Waters, *Ethnic Options*, 147.

92. See Alba, *Ethnic Identity*.

93. Nagel, *American Indian Ethnic Renewal*, 10.

10. A Most Secret Identity
Native American Assimilation and Identity Resistance in African America

RON WELBURN

Twentieth-century Native American Indians in African American communities know a tenuous identity, one furtive and usually silent as apart from and within them.[1] Often, Native Americans abided in rural and newly suburbanized communities where their ancestry was ambiguous but they were considered Colored people or Negroes, and they saw their communities absorbed into an expanding African American community of which unwittingly they became part. East of the Mississippi, White perceptions and opinions and legal dispositions and documents collapsed these two peoples into one identity, benefiting an intractable and uneasy White-Black biracialism. That Indians of the eastern seaboard had either vanished, departed for the West, or had lost their identities through intermarriage with the White or especially the Black race remains a widely held assumption and was the bland response given me during my childhood through college years in southeastern Pennsylvania in the 1950s and 1960s.

Most of us living on the Indian-Negro color line grew up with mixed signals and coded information. Our elders had learned to protect us from the ridicule and abuse they had experienced as Indians or from which their parents had sheltered them. They instilled in us the sense that we were "different" from our peers; but that we were Indian or of Native descent, when it was raised, was a covert issue. Why we should live such a covert identity was seldom explained. At best, in some families, we were to view ourselves as "Americans" or as "Colored people," which actually provided an inclusive ring for non-Indians and a social safety valve. Perhaps I was minimally fortunate in being told that since my parents bore a strong Native heritage, so did I. Many offspring do not take the assumption for granted or may not have had it explained to them as it was vigorously impressed upon me. Many children of the 1940s and 1950s did not or could not conceptualize or imagine themselves as Indians since the idea of being part-Indian seemed to stop with a parent or grandparent. A humorous aside for this conundrum is in the following exchange:

Non-Indian: "My grandmother was an Indian."
   Indian: "So was mine."

Amid the usual activities and perceptions of being socialized, I endeavored to know all I could about Indians, especially the Cherokees claimed by my mother's side. Though I knew I was also part Black, as a youngster I assimilated a kind of sovereignty of the spirit that paid allegiance to my indigenous ancestry as eons older than the construct called "the United States." I also was intrigued that members of my family possessing strongly obvious "Indian qualities" were identifying themselves (ourselves) as Negroes. In the 1970s, as I encountered more Indians in New York State, I wondered how an Indian who was three-quarters or more White could be Indian while Indians who were a quarter Negro had to be Negro. I can only explain my sustained desire to know and live by my heritage as what I was supposed to do; perhaps the loosening of my once firm grip on a mostly Indian identity during the Black consciousness period of 1964 to 1976 was also inevitable and necessary. The young Seneca man visiting the University of Arizona in 1969 who told me that many Indians back East were like me instigated a protracted turnaround marked by soul searching and self-doubt.

You know, when Mother died, the doctor present asked us what race we wanted him to fill in on her death certificate. I said, "Why do you ask that? She's a Colored woman, a Negro."

"If you say so; but she wasn't."

"What do you mean? What are you talking about?"

"I mean that your mother's bone structure and body build are definitely like Indians in the Southwest, and the Maori. I've served as a physician in Arizona and New Zealand, and I'm familiar with these qualities."

Then, Ron, I remembered that she had spoken a few times about her relatives when my brother and I were kids, that she had family both in the South Seas and out West; but she never said anything more about it. We just assumed she was Negro. Even Daddy's part Indian, but we never saw ourselves as anything more than Colored people.

Indian identity consciousness may survive through an aloofness that African Americans often resent. In the racial identity politics of the past three centuries, many eastern Indians lost their identities, in the slave community, due to pressures from Blacks and through their children for whom friendships and the attractions of African American life were compelling. The key question is: At what point and under what circumstances does a Native American Indian become an African American? Does this come about simply through intermarriage? And why are Indians so vulnerable?

The color line that constructs the phenomenon of Indians in African America differs markedly from its Black-White counterpart. Indians become Blacks easily through sociological, psychological, and documentational processes. Their efforts to protect their loved ones by remaining silent about Indianness resulted in their becoming Black by default.

This essay will draw upon personal and family experiences, observations shared with other part-Black Indians, and insights derived from scholarly discourse in order to illuminate some of the dynamics of Indians who have interacted or who continue to interact in or at the edges of African America. Examples from what little literature pertains to this topic will serve both experience and memory as a way to analyze and deconstruct some of the standardized assumptions about East Coast Indians and how part-Black Natives have perceived ourselves. A summary of my family lineages may serve what I understand as typicalities that configure the dynamics of Indian-to-Black identity.

As a topic of discussion in Native American Indian studies, Indian and Black relations is at this writing emerging from neglect and an almost orchestrated obscurity. Discourse on Indians' relationships with the non-Indian world has almost exclusively concerned White America. Declassified and presumed extinct, eastern tribes have been reasserting their identities since the 1960s, and the dynamics of their survival and social interaction have attracted the attention of journalists and the curiosity of the scholarly community and western Indians. The standard rhetoric involving Indians having to deal solely with Whites is slowly being dismantled by the need to formulate at least a tripart equation. The explosion of both multiculturalist theory and new immigrants midwifes this intense new interest. Indians themselves must configure the terms of their historicism and socialization from the centers of this discourse rather than from its margins, and this pertains emphatically to eastern Natives confronting the biracial equation.

In early 1999 a symposium at the Mashantucket Pequot Tribal Museum and Research Center discussed Black Indians, and several papers delivered at the American Society for Ethnohistorians' annual meeting that October either directly or inadvertently addressed this relationship. The Native American Studies Institute and the Program in African and African American Studies at Dartmouth College hosted a conference, "Eating Out of the Same Pot," in April 2000. That such discussions elsewhere have or will occur should be no surprise. *American Indian Quarterly* devoted a section to the topic in its winter/spring 1998 issue.[2] Concerted efforts began in the 1970s that included William Loren Katz's popular *Black Indians* and Daniel F. Littlefield's four volumes: *Africans and Seminoles*, *Africans and Creeks*, *The Chickasaw Freedmen*, and *The Cherokee Freedmen*. Theda Perdue and R. Halliburton produced valuable studies linked with Littlefield's focus on Blacks as free persons, slaves, and eventually freedmen among the Five Civilized Tribes.[3] Laurence Foster's dissertation from the University of Pennsylvania, published privately in 1935 as *Indian-Negro Relationships in the South-East*, is the forerunner among book-length studies.[4] Blacks among the Seminoles, Cherokees, and other major southern Indians removed from their homelands in the 1830s remain the dominant focus. Scholars like Frank Speck and A. Irving Hallowell surveyed the topic, and Helen Rountree in a series of books, essays, and lectures has scrutinized Virginia's efforts to transform Indians into Negroes. Paul T. Murray examined the issue in "Who Is an Indian? Who Is a Negro?" to demonstrate how the older tensions affected Virginia Indians who resisted being inducted into the military as Negroes.[5] *Africans and Native Americans*, by its subtitle a study of "Red-Black" peoples, is Jack Forbes's major contribution to the general discourse, taking a singularly historical approach. His short story "Only Approved Indians Can Play," while not about Blacks and Indians, adroitly illuminates the issue of color among Indians.[6] Still, there remains little discussion of the dynamics of Indian and Black relations in northeastern tribes.

Also motivating my approach to this topic is not having encountered in discourses of the past twenty-five years voices willing to articulate the warp and woof of Native and Black relations from inside its sometimes turbulent and resentful understandings, voices whose combined identity confusions, knowledge of Indian life east of the Mississippi, and struggles with family members, neighbors, and friends have been painful and frustrating yet at the same time instructive and fulfilling. I write this essay without asking the reader's indulgence when scholarly discourse slips into autobiography, when example and anecdote merge, and for the intangible meanings and memories for which there simply is no documentation.

My mother's lineage is Assateague Cherokee and African American.

Today's Assateague Peoples on the Delmarva Peninsula are remnants of various Algonquin groups such as the Assateagues proper, Choptanks, possibly Conoys (Joshua London Gray, an ancestor, living in Baltimore Hundred in Sussex County, Delaware, in 1810, was of one of these groups), Occohannocks, and, for us, the Gingaskins (née Accomacs) dating to a James West in Northampton County, Virginia, born in 1802, and possibly through him to a Ned West (possibly Occohannock), indentured at age sixteen in 1667. The Cherokee memory among the Wests resulted from one or two generational intermarriages between some Gingaskins and Cherokees that Assateague legacy holds sought refuge on the eastern shore prior to the Trail of Tears. This undocumented Delmarva Cherokee legacy, learned in 1981 from extended family elders, is affirmed in Assateague oral history. That my great-great-grandfather's name was Wat(t) West suspends any doubt: Wat, a form of Watie, resonates in Cherokee as "the Ancient One."

Chenie Greenhill, whom Wat and Martha's eldest son, Edward, married, was perhaps Nottoway; that Viola West Welburn visited "her mother's reservation in Virginia, south of Richmond going toward Petersburg" was one of my late oldest uncle's memories. The Nottoway reservation was terminated over a protracted period during the nineteenth century, but as a homeland it may still have been called a "reservation" in 1918 when my uncle was a boy.[7]

Cousin Clarence Greenhill, Viola's favorite cousin, was a tireless genealogist who visited us annually when I was growing up to tell of new relatives and ancestors he had found. His rolled-up window shade contained hundreds of names and dates. As a child I was expected to greet him, then was sent off to play because children didn't sit with adults speaking of their affairs. When at fourteen I was allowed to see the family tree on the shade, I asked Cousin Clarence about our Indian heritage. "Now, now," he uttered in his soft-spoken voice. And that was all.

Of my own father I know little except that he was born in Darlington County, South Carolina, and that his mother, Annie Eliza Elliott, the daughter of Daniel and Fannie Fields Elliott, was reputedly Cherokee. Annie Elliott married Henry Webster Leaver, an African American. Both my blood grandmothers died leaving young children, and much was lost with them.

My maternal grandfather's mother, an ex-slave from Frankford, Delaware, assumed the duty of raising Viola's children in 1924 when she was about seventy-eight – she died in 1942, and to her, Lucy Townsend Welburn, do I owe thanks for preventing her oldest daughter from putting the six children into an orphanage.

I was raised in my stepfather's household with his mother and sister – they are my "Dad" and "Nana" – and my grandmother's Indian ancestry was substantial and typically secret. Laura Lavinia Gover Watson's father, Charles Henry Gover, was described as a man of copper complexion and straight, white hair. It is no mystery in my aunt's recall that, despite his features and that he "had Indian in him," "he was not an Indian!" He was from a line of Govers from Penns Grove, Pennsylvania, in the nineteenth century a district of the town of West Chester, the county seat of Chester County. His mother, whose name is unknown, is also reputedly Cherokee; his grandfather, also named William, is listed in the 1840 Pennsylvania census as a Free Negro. Prior to that, Govers lived in northeastern Maryland in the lower Susquehanna River watershed. Whether they were Nanticoke, Piscataway, Lenape, or Susquehannock or of some other tribe is unknown. The Govers married other Indians, notably Cooks of Chester County. Except for what I can only acknowledge as the allegation of Cherokee – the ubiquitous Cherokee! – for Nana's grandmother, we regrettably have no other specific tribal identities for her ancestral lines. When she could twist Dad's arm to visit relatives in Cumberland County, New Jersey, no one ever said we were visiting the Lenni Lenape-Nanticoke community there or that our Gover Pierce relations had a Seneca ancestor. On the matter of race and Negroes, she was emphatic: she was "Colored," not a Negro, and "my ancestors were not slaves!" as she admonished my father once in the mid-1960s, "they were Americans!" She adopted "Negro" only in the 1970s when "Black," a term she despised, became popular. Perhaps more valuably ironical here is that Laura Gover Watson never admitted she was Indian either, except during an admonishment to me when I was about sixteen: "We can't be Indians any more, so forget about it."

I did not let this all go so easily, though from about age twenty to thirty-three I de-emphasized the Indian in favor of the Black, largely due to the lack of reinforcement for my considerable knowledge of Indian history, culture, and belief. As is common in what are shared circumstances with my peers, my family showed me things without describing them as "the Indian way," such as caring for all living things and becoming adept at certain skills. My grandmother, who owned a tailor and laundry establishment in West Philadelphia, valued a particular sweetgrass-filled pincushion and bade me show deference to Indian elders in the neighborhood I told her I had met in my travels. I treasure two memories of dancing by her and Dad. Many Sundays she dragged my siblings and me to her Holiness church. When the spirit overcame the women, they danced; but her movements, like those of one or two others, I recognized in adulthood as the Iroquois women's shuffle dance. My father, a skilled welder, also worked in leather. He loved loafers, and after having worn out the soles of his favorite pair for the last time, he ripped the complete bottom off, essentially creating a moccasin, and danced in them like I had never seen him do before. Inexplicably, when I congratulated him for his work and the dancing, he stopped as if caught unexpectedly. His and his brother's hunting buddies, fellow Philadelphians, included a Miles (Powhatan) and a Beverley (Monacan or Buffalo Ridge Cherokee).

In 1999, over twenty years after his death, I learned from my aunt and my mother that a painting in our cellar of an Indian astride a horse with his arms wide apart in a praying mood was painted by him in high school. The painting sat for many years above his workbench, and I admired it the innumerable times I had to go there. It seems that he painted it while a student at Mastbaum High School, one of Philadelphia's three high schools for technical training, and that the teachers entered it in a contest which he won, resulting in a scholarship to an art school. But Nana for some reason wouldn't let him go. That part of the story I already knew, not that he himself painted that portrait which I looked at almost every day for thirteen years.

No, I could never fully forget about it, and it obviously never left. In appearance I often was considered "from the islands" or Hispanic; admitting to Indian heritage brought mixed responses. In my college dorm room a Georgia boy and I nearly came to blows when I countered a notion about the Republic of New Africa's scheme for Black repatriation to five Southern states with the idea that Georgia and the others were already stolen land for which the original people should be consulted despite their having been removed. In the mid 1970s, as genealogical inquiry in my family, long prior to Alex Haley's inspiration, sparked my generation, I also answered the inner voices that for several years something had not been right. I had been going along without having properly decoded the subtle language and circumstances of Indian identity. In the New York metropolitan area and at affairs in Pennsylvania and southern New England, I encountered people like myself who had been confused by the Native and Black color line and had misread its signals, experiencing its ridicule and its embarrassing ignorance, and who had been advised by their families to "forget about it." Their families' refusal to engage Indian identity except through coded language, and their silence, translated to a "Colored" identity, which in the argot of race relations meant African ancestry. Fortunately, I never forgot what I knew as a lad of eight, twelve, and eighteen, but I gained keener insight that the withholding of information was a practiced carry-over from a time when Native families took seriously sheltering their children from verbal and physical abuse. One couldn't pressure or interrogate one's elders, annoying them with our desire to know.

"Nana, why haven't you considered yourself an Indian?"
"Never mind!"

INDIAN LANDS AND BLACK CLASSIFICATION

At the heart of this Indian-Black issue is the possession, dispossession, and sovereignty of Indian Country. We must contextualize the de-Indianization of Indians into becoming Blacks by default as part of the grand design by the English and Americans and their political and colonialist objectives to divest Native peoples of their homelands and later their reservations. Swallowing the land is a principle of Manifest Destiny. All European groups took captives to Europe; however, each came with different objectives for their place in North America. English avarice established settlements that required Indian removal or reservation confinement.

Native Americans know and innumerable studies describe how Indians were separated from their lands through land sales, often without tribal consensus and involving individuals unauthorized to act in any capacity to approve such a sale; as a result of pathogens that wiped out whole villages; and numerous infamous massacres of, for example, the Pequots and Narragansetts in the Northeast, and Powhatans, Tuscaroras, and Yemasis in the Southeast, all resulting in the enslavement of many survivors that often meant warriors being shipped to Bermuda, the Caribbean, and sometimes Spain or North Africa. African Americans and many eastern Indians agree that the early unions between Indians and Blacks occurred under these constraints. Indian communities not in the direct path of White racialist influences sheltered fugitive Blacks as the act so celebrated in African American lore; but plausibly, some of these fugitives could also have been Indians. Every Indian knows that over the past five hundred years Whites religiously break one of the Ten Commandments – the one involving the coveting of a neighbor's possessions – when Indian land is involved. An automobile bumper sticker in the late 1960s read: "We gave an inch; they took 3000 miles!" In our collective DNA perhaps is the only promise Whites ever kept to Indians – "They promised to take away our land, and that's what they did." Deploying every concoctable scheme to enforce taxation on Indian lands, what better method for obtaining Indian lands than removing Indians, perceiving and identifying them as de-Indianized and subsequently de-classifying them, and if necessary enforcing the removal of recalcitrants and resisters or otherwise making their continued presence unsafe. Whites adjudged Indians as disappearing when Blacks and poor Whites married into reservations and cohesive communities. Prior to Columbus, any infusion of non-Indian blood by any explorer from any part of Europe, the Mediterranean, Africa, or the Pacific, as surely there must have been some infrequent visitors, never prevented the offspring from being, for example, Micmac or Tuscarora. The English enforced the change, forcing Indians and Blacks to step to the piper's tune accordingly. In the wake of Indian Removal legislation, Indians in antebellum Southern states could not legally own land. However, free Blacks/mulattoes/Colored people could. Native groups in the Tidewater and the Piedmont thus sustained some form of land sovereignty in the midst of their tribal "disappearance."

Mrs. M., a "Black" schoolteacher living in metropolitan New Jersey, once remarked, during a visit to her neighbor, that "many years ago, our tribe's council met to discuss how to avoid giving up our lands, because in the state of North Carolina, Indians couldn't own land. The tribal council decided that in order for our people to keep their lands, they would register themselves as Negroes. That was the only way they could keep their lands" (1988).

Helen Rountree compared how disenfranchisement affected three Indian communities in Virginia. Termination of the Nottoway reservation began in the late eighteenth century; the Gingaskin reservation family allotments were sold by 1832; yet the Pamunkey reservation managed to elude termination. Confronting each was the imposed African American common denominator.[8] Frances Bibbins Latimer, a genealogist in Eastville, Virginia, and a Gingaskin descendent, holds the opinion that people are what they identify themselves to be; but I would agree with Charlotte Collins, another Gingaskin descendent active in Assateague Peoples affairs, that such individuals may have complex motivations about identities they chose in order to ensure their safety. Daniel R. Mandell offers an example involving the Wampanoag town of Mashpee and the attempt to convert its Indians into Negroes.

When the question of detribalization was brought by state officials to a hearing [there] in 1869, the testimony of African American men who had married into the community highlighted how changes in New England over the previous century had made intermarriage a liability for Indian villages. Three of the five men who openly supported the change in the strongest terms were African Americans. . . . [U]nder Mashpee's current rule, [George Sewell, "a free black man from the South"] observed, "My wife possesses land that *she* holds; if she dies to-morrow I can have no benefit from it, and all my labor and improvements go to somebody else. You can see that is not right." Sewell asked the legislature "to make us men, and give us all the dignity of manhood. I can't conceive, if our people are rightly informed, how they can remonstrate against so just a thing, and if they do, I want you to consider your duty to make us men."[9]

For Blacks, owning land confirms masculinity; for Indians, land is inseparable from spiritual identity and national and tribal sovereignty. This lack of a land-owning prerogative did not emasculate eastern Indian warriors, for example, who understood their responsibilities within a strongly matrilineal and matrilocal culture. I understand Black masculinity in this context of land as signifying Black patriarchy and the ever-present Indian grandmother motif celebrated by Blacks. Meanwhile, African Americans remain oblivious to the subtle hostility eastern and southern Indians may have about them over the dynamics of this land issue. They see "uppity" Negro snobs or people who "may be your color but not your kind," failing to take into account the spiritual issue of Indian land as a defining principle of Indian identity and that Indians' relationship to their lands differs from anyone else's.

MYTHS AND REALITIES OF THE SHARED EXPERIENCE

From John Blassingame, *Slave Testimony: Two Centuries of Letters, Speeches, Interviews, and Autobiographies*. Baton Rouge: Louisiana State University Press, 1977

Edinbur Randall, "a mulatto man," was born in Alabama and enslaved in Florida. "My mother was of Indian, and my father was of negro descent"; neither were slaves. He stowed aboard a merchant ship to Martha's Vineyard where he was rescued by a Vanderhoof/Vanderhoff woman of Gay Head (321–22). From *The Liberty Bell*, Boston 1858, 29–43.

From the "Narrative of James Fisher," born October 1817, recorded by Valentine Nicholson in Ohio in 1843

"My mother's name was Mary Davis. Though an unmixed Cherokee Indian, she was kept in slavery all her life." Father, Thomas Fisher, "fled from bondage when I was a small child" and remained uncaught (230). His mother did, however, buy the freedom of herself and his two sisters, saving "by washing and ironing" and paying $1,900 to do so. She died before reaching the goal of freeing her son (231).

From a narrative written as a letter to the editor of the *Liberator*, 1 November and 7 November 1862 by Rosa Barnwell, born in South Carolina and endured slavery for twenty years

"My mother was of Indian descent, and a free woman, but was kidnapped by a man named Leo Edwards, and doomed to a life of servitude." One of her twelve children was "sold to Texas"; five died; she knew not the fate of her mother or the others (698).

In a "P/S. Judge Lane holds an Indian woman, with her six children, as slaves. She is of the Creek nation, and her name is Susan . . ." (237). She was a full-blood, and tried to stab her master, Mr. Lane, as he whipped her daughter. He fled, never retaliating. The Creeks passed the house where she and other servants lived on their relocation to Arkansas. "Susan went out, with some of the other servants, to look at them. The moment they looked at her, they knew she belonged to their tribe. They stopped and gathered around her, and made signs for her to go with them. She could not understand their language; but they pointed to her and her children, and then at their women and children, and then along the road they were traveling. They took one of her children and carried it some distance, and we had trouble to get it away from them. Susan would have gone . . . , but Judge Lane . . . pleaded hard, [telling her] the Indians ate raw meat, and were often nearly starved, and many frightful stories: until she gave up to stay" (238).

Mother, who grew up between the two world wars, recalled that no one wanted to say much about their Indian heritage because Indians were considered mean.

The common reference by African Americans discussing Blacks and Indians not only invokes Indians sheltering Blacks but both peoples experiencing slavery. Colonialism and racism have injured both. Europeans coming to the Western Hemisphere made its indigenous peoples their first slaves, and Anglo-Americans in the southern United States held Indians in bondage with Africans until slavery's end. Indians not taken to

Bermuda or the Caribbean to be enslaved might be kept in their regions but more likely were sold in other colonies: Narragansetts from Rhode Island Colony to the South, Powhatans to Connecticut.[10]

Proclaiming a shared suffering functions to reduce ethnic distinctions and anxieties between African Americans and Indians and makes social disengagement by individualistic Indians the brunt of ridicule. Like Blacks, Eastern Native slaves fought their masters and tried to escape. A newspaper advertisement for an escaped slave might identify the person as "a negro of the Indian type." Almon Wheeler Lauber asserts that it is impossible to know the percentages of Native slaves in each colony or state because slave owners kept no distinctions between Indian and Black slaves (105).

From Freddie L. Parker, ed., *Stealing a Little Freedom: Advertisements for Slave Runaways in North Carolina, 1791–1840*. New York: Garland, 1994.

Fayetteville Observer. 25 April 1838. "Ranaway . . . a mulatto Girl Slave named HANNAH, alias Tillah. She is thought to be lurking in the neighborhood of Laurel Hill at present. She has on a former occasion made her way to Robeson County, and lived there among the free coloured people a considerable time . . ." (599–600).[11]

Newbern Spectator and Literary Journal. 8 August 1840. "$25 Reward. RAN AWAY, . . . my negro fellow named SHADRACH, . . . about 21 years of age, . . . well made and proportioned, a dark copper colour. . . . I understand he went immediately on Neuse, Craven County, among the free negroes and called himself Jim Sampson and took passage in some boat for Newbern, no doubt to but he will try to get north in some vessel" (796).[12]

Just as new historicist interpretations of terms like "Free Colored People" force reconsiderations of assumptions, the focus on Indian slaves in the nineteenth century should likewise force everyone to rethink some of the dynamics of "Black" slavery. In his compilation published in 1926, *Free Negro Heads of Families in the United States in 1830*, Carter G. Woodson, the father of Negro history, listed surnames of the kind implicit to this essay's objectives.[13] I challenge Woodson's criteria; he pursued his objective according to the "vanished Indian" thesis of his day. Today's ethnohistorians and social historians must better understand who lived in these communities and what other documents besides the federal census both reveal about them and obfuscate.

In the oversimplifying rhetoric of "eating out of the same pot" and sharing the same or similar experiences, African Americans unwittingly incorporate Indians into their world as a Black caste group. Indians thus absorbed either have no voice at qualifying this relationship and perception, or their efforts to do so are stifled and ridiculed. African Americans firmly chastise others of color whom they feel should be satisfied with being "like the rest of us"; the Black parent and family of the children of intermarriage reinforce Black cultural identity as the path of least resistance; in other words, be what the society assumes you are. There are no stronger believers that African Americans have absorbed Indians than African Americans themselves.

Privileging Indian heritage creates a breach in Black community stability, cohesion, pride, and unity. Many African Americans feel betrayed by, and sometimes react belligerently toward, anyone they perceive as Black professing to be Indian. In vigorously upholding the one-drop-of-African-blood rule, they maintain such persons should be "Black first." Blacks deploy a unique cultural mechanism in verbal criticism; the barbed words accompanying the chides, ridicule, and haughty ironical put-downs can be emotionally devastating when aimed at those among them who they want to "put back in line." They tell Indians they, too, had a Indian ancestor; "so quit trying to be something you're not." Quipping that "the white man isn't interested anyhow" betrays a colonized reaction. Blacks espousing Afrocentricity, meanwhile, proclaim "everybody is Black since humanity began in Africa." Several years ago I winced when a Black matron related that she did not want to tell two children she was raising of their Indian ancestry "because I didn't want them to grow up thinking they were better than we are." An Indian is essentially not allowed to be Indian or to assert a mixed-blood Indian pride. I have experienced this as born of the anxiety over skin color, social advantages, and being chided as one who fits the image of the half-White "house nigger." This anxiety threatens the closure of the perceived phenotypic difference and the significations that determine one as a member of the Black community. Around 1980, Clyde Pulley in Chicago privately published a book I have never been able to obtain, *Blacks Who Pass for Indians and White*. Contrary to its title, the overwhelming examples I know represent the deconstruction of Black-community Indians as persons whose survival is determined by *passing as Blacks*, submerging an identity known to few if any of their neighbors and peers. Anyone not White becomes part of African American society with ease. African Americans are an inclusive people. Native Americans today may not be so inclusive, having lost so much, and can be exclusive when they perceive that an Indian has been socialized Black. Mixed-blood Indian elders today still hesitate to acknowledge other eastern Natives they do not know, betraying their own anxieties about that stranger's identity. In Indian Country even "lost birds" still must prove themselves, at large and to their people.

Whites respond to the Indian corollary in the Black-White equation with related objectives betraying their avoidance of Blacks. The land-grab thesis is part of the web of attitudes and schemes involving the two peoples. Indian slavery, removals, annihilations, and religious conversions occurred in direct proportion to the introduction of African chattel slavery and the formation of the plantation system. White individuals from the postslavery era down to the present feel more at ease among non-White people they believe (and hope) "are not really Black." Those qualifying as "different" include persons of mixed heritage from the Caribbean, North American Black-White mixtures and triracials, and (mixed-blood) Indians, people representing a gradient of features away from the African. Characteristics mollifying White anxieties include hair texture and length, facial features, complexion, and speech mannerisms.

INDIANS IN BLACK MUSIC AND LITERATURE

Indians have ever been active in jazz, blues, and popular music, where they highlight the Red-Black-White color lines. Jazz trumpeter Adolphus "Doc" Cheatham, who played with Sam Wooding and Cab Calloway, was Creek and Choctaw, and was gracious about the honors Black cultural organizations bestowed on him. One-time Lionel Hampton drummer and journalist Lewis McMillan was vocal about his quarter-Cherokee heritage. Lester Young's original tenor saxophone sparring partner with the Bennie Moten and Count Basie orchestras, Hershel Evans, who invented the "whoop" for the style called the "Texas tenor," was strongly of Indian descent. Other performers include several Cherokees: blues guitarists Scrapper Blackwell (Eastern Cherokee) and Lowell Fulsom (Oklahoma Cherokee), innovative Duke Ellington bassist Jimmy Blanton, and soul singer Percy Sledge. Singer Tina Turner revealed her Navajo and Cherokee ancestry in her autobiography, *I, Tina*.[14] Motown saxophonist Junior Walker's 1960s' hit "Shotgun" directly resembles the call-and-response melody pattern of some Cherokee and Creek stomp dance songs. Some members of the International Sweethearts of Rhythm, a "Black" all-female orchestra, were, judging by their photographs, Native. A few lengthy interviews in the Jazz Oral History Project of the National Endowment for the Arts offer minor but revealing information about Indians. Basie alumnus trumpeter Buck Clayton recalled the great ex-Ellington band tenor saxophonist Ben Webster as "more Indian than anything else," and Charlie Green, a trombonist with Fletcher Henderson in the late 1920s, as a "big three-quarter Indian."[15] When I asked veteran bassist, photographer, and oral historian Milt Hinton (affectionately known as "The Judge") about how the famous and innovative Creek-Cherokee bassist Oscar Pettiford was perceived in the South Side Chicago community where they lived, he responded with, "Oh, he was just part of the community." As a rule Blacks perceive Indians among "their own."[16]

In literature, Montauk-Shinnecock writer Olivia Bush-Banks participated in tribal affairs and celebrated Indianness in a poem, "Mornings on Shinnecock," and a drama, *Indian Trails; or Trail of the Montauk*; she also participated in the Harlem Renaissance. The Hartford author Ann Plato, a member of Rev. James Pennington's Colored Congregational Church in the 1840s who taught in one of its African schools before disappearing, was possibly of Montauk and Narragansett descent.[17]

BLACK INDIANS

"Black Indian" is an ambiguous term. I reluctantly used it a few times, though I believe, as do most Indians, that one is either an Indian or not an Indian. To be "part-Indian" may be important for non-Indians, but it is superfluous for Indians. I see no Indians with European ancestry rushing to call themselves "White Indians," leaving that for writers of sentimental romances. Therefore, I see no reason why Indians with African ancestry should use this superfluous qualifier, which supports a peculiar caste, for their Indian identities. Indian ancestry in Whites and Blacks does not make them in their self-images any less White or Black. Why should Black ancestry in Indians do otherwise?

Some eastern tribal communities possess some African ancestry. It may be recent in their bloodlines, stem from several generations in the past, or be due to a consistent pattern of intermarriage (for example, an African infusion, however slight, every third generation). Overlapping Indian slavery and Indians sheltering Blacks, starting in the middle eighteenth century, some Indian communities began to shun Blacks and Indian-and-Black mixed-bloods. During the nineteenth century more Indians avoided Blacks, and some in the South became slave bounty hunters. Enslaved Indians in the South had few choices socially; yet many Indians who became Blacks by default continued to preserve their cultural ways.

Although the term is not new, "Black Indians" drew attention when

William Loren Katz used it in *The Black West* in 1969 before employing it as his book title in 1986.[18] Katz concentrates on Blacks among the Seminoles and other former southern tribes, but he seems to have misidentified as Black or part-Black some Plains and southwestern Indians in photographs who to me and other Indians appear to be full-bloods. "Black Indians" provokes the adjective-noun debate and seems more appropriate for the freedmen of the Five Civilized Tribes, some of whom are of Indian descent and who are either bicultural or culturally Native. "Indian Blacks" may better describe what Black Indian attempts to mean – in my definition, African Americans who cite Indian ancestry without desiring entry into Native life. Black ancestry among the Mashantucket Pequots, a federally recognized tribe in southeastern Connecticut, occasionally enters journalism describing them as "Black Pequots" and "Black Indians."[19] I suspect those involved vary in their self-identifying language, for other Pequots possess no discernible Black ancestry. Black Indian and Indian Black should be voluntarily self-ascribed and respected. Indians professing one or more African ancestors deserve respect as Indians, not Black Indians.

EASTERN RURAL AND URBANIZED INDIANS

Some Indian groups in rural eastern communities are likely to be remnants from tribes the majority of whose members relocated, or they constitute remnant families who remained after intending to settle temporarily in a region. The population distribution is dynamically mobile, the result of Indians being constantly uprooted and displaced, seeking some measure of a tranquil existence on land poor for farming in remote areas. Those moving into cities usually did so for employment opportunities. Rumors circulated during the last century of southern tribal councils, elders, or chiefs de-enrolling Indians who preferred to live away from home indefinitely and who married Blacks. It is plausible that some "Blacks" documented as having lived within a city and what evolved to become a city's exurbia were indeed Indians. The Matinecocks along the border of New York City's Queens County and Long Island's Nassau County struggle to survive culturally, and Orange, New Jersey, has a long-standing community of Lenape and Ramapo Indians from the New Jersey–New York border.

The farmsteads of old-family Indians became less remote with the influx and settlement of more Whites and free or ex-slave Blacks. This certainly characterized my West, Gover, and Cook ancestors near Richmond and West Chester. With increased population density and the gradual wearing down of their uniqueness, some families intermarried without fully acknowledging Indian identity; and remarkably, Indians not identifying as Indians found each other, too. Full-bloods and three-quarter-bloods acknowledged "part-Indian" identity, a survival strategy equating themselves both with those having less Indian ancestry and with African Americans. For the generation coming of age during 1890–1910, Indian identity in these then presuburban communities was ignored, denied, downplayed, or shunned as Indians internalized their self-image as defeated, persecuted, mean, and ridiculed heathens. Displays of intense anger were usually attributed to Indian heritage. The "bad nigger" syndrome of the slave era thus had its variation reflecting an African American who was "probably more Indian than anything else."

From Parker, *Stealing a Little Freedom*

The Star (Raleigh): 30 September 1814. "RANAWAY from Raleigh, a month or two ago, a mulatto man named ANTHONY, well known . . . as . . . the body servant of Gen. Jones, and more lately as a pressman and news carrier in the Star Office. Anthony is about 25 or 26 years of age, 5 feet 8 or 10 inches high, is a mongreal [*sic*] white, tuscarora, and negro, has a tolerably large aquiline nose, bushy hair, though sometimes he cuts it short, . . . when in a good humour has a pleasing countenance, but if intoxicated the Tuscarora shows itself. – . . . His master vice . . . is a fondness for strong drink, though sometimes he will abstain for months" (422–23).

Eventually, these Colored Americans with copper complexions and straight or wavy hair bettered their fortunes among African Americans when they balanced their individualistic ways with upward social mobility into "the good life" offered by Black society. Their descendants were among the Indians-as-Blacks most likely to belong to light-complexioned Black groups like the Jack & Jills (youth whose parents were of some relative means), be introduced to society at debutante cotillions, or own property in Sag Harbor on northeastern Long Island or in Oak Bluffs on Martha's Vineyard. Many could not take advantage of Indian programs at Hampton Institute (1878–1924) and the Carlisle Indian School (1879–1912); instead, they were educated at Black colleges such as Lincoln University in Pennsylvania and Atlanta, Howard, and Fisk Universities. According to my great-aunt, Charles Henry Gover was sent to Edgewater College in New Jersey by his mother.

"Sixty years or so before the founding of the school, the Cherokee Indians who lived in Georgia were forced to leave their homes and walk, through the snow, to resettlement camps in Oklahoma. A third of them died on the way. But many of them refused to leave Georgia. They hid out as Colored people and eventually blended with us. Many of these mixed-race people were at Spelman. Some remembered who they actually were, but most did not. If they thought about it at all (and it became harder to think about Indians because there were none around) they thought they were yellow or reddish brown and wavy haired because of white ancestors, not Indian" (Alice Walker, *The Color Purple*: as the narrator recalls Samuel's observation about Corinne, 241).

Whether or not they received higher education as formal preparation for business, the trades, or the professions, these Indians were among the emerging Black middle class of schoolteachers, entrepreneurs, professionals, and entertainers and were often among the "first Negro" businesspeople in a town or city neighborhood. They excelled at public service. T. Thomas Fortune, a close associate of Booker T. Washington, was one of these. I offer two others, one an individual my wife and I knew well.

Legions of Native schoolteachers have taught Native, Black, and mixed-ancestry children. Madge Barnes Allen (1906–89), a remarkable individual, was among them, and during her last decade she related the following details to us. Her mother, Nancy Enos, was Shinnecock and Poosepatuck from eastern Long Island and part-Narragansett. Nancy's grandfather was not allowed to enlist in the Union navy as an Indian, only as a Negro. In later years Nancy Enos Barnes worked for Hull House in St. Louis. Madge's father, George Barnes, was a "going-back" Cherokee, meaning a person or descendent who returned to the old Cherokee homeland in the Southeast after he, she, or ancestors had walked the Trail of Tears during 1838–39. Born in Tahlequah into the Cherokee Nation in Indian Territory in 1867, George traveled back over a four-year period to his family's homestead in Rome, Georgia, most of the way carrying his brother Russell who was born lame, working where possible for food, shelter, and money and hiding from Ku Klux Klan–like vigilantes who had not given up on enslaving, persecuting, or even murdering Blacks or Indians. George Barnes proceeded to graduate from Atlanta University and became a contracting associate to Booker T. Washington. He and his fellow Indian workers, two being his Trice cousins, installed the steam-heating systems at Bryn Mawr College hospital and the Rockefeller estate. Mornings after Halloween, he and his two sons knew they had to whitewash the outer walls of their Atlanta home on which "Squaw Man" had been painted. When he died in 1930, the Black mortician steadfastly refused to identify him as an Indian on the necessary documents, insisting to his widow and children that he was a Negro (they appealed successfully to the state of Georgia for the correction). One of Madge's brothers, by the way, joined the Omega Psi Phi fraternity, the second-oldest Black Greek organization, and graduated from Howard University Medical School.

While teaching art in Greenville, North Carolina, Madge Barnes married Travis Allen, an African American housing contractor who, when they moved to Montclair, New Jersey, supported her desire to make and sell silverwork jewelry on the northeastern powwow circuit. When they lived in North Carolina, the railway authority issued her a pass allowing her as an Indian to avoid segregated seating, but she never used it as she traveled during summers to Columbia University to earn her master's degrees in art history and art education – North Carolina gave her the travel pass while it paid her tuition and expenses in New York because she was not allowed to attend one of its own universities! She was proud to have been among the schoolchildren who sang "Lift Every Voice" (the Black national anthem), newly composed by the brothers J. Rosamand and James Weldon Johnson, for its first public performance. Raised by parents who instilled Indian identity in their children while demanding they respect others, she identified as Indian and was a member of the Cherokee Nation of Oklahoma and the Shinnecock Nation; yet she often referred to her innumerable Black pupils in North Carolina and Newark and Montclair, New Jersey, as "our own."

I encountered an obituary in the 3 June 1983 *New York Times*. Entitled "Laura McCoy, Started Black Girl Scout Troop," it proceeded to describe Laura Belle McCoy as a former resident of New Haven who died at age ninety-three. "She founded Girl Scout Troop 24" in that city in 1928. What captured my interest, however, was the sentence: "Mrs. McCoy, a nurse, was a Mohawk Indian, born in Carlisle, N.Y."[20] Clearly it seems that members of the Barnes family and Laura McCoy, *knowing who they were* as well as where they were living, did not hesitate to serve young African Americans.

Some mixed-blood Indians and triracial people sought mates from among Whites and other groups of color such as Filipinos, Japanese and Japanese Americans, Latinos, Cape Verdeans and Portuguese, and British Caribbean individuals of multiracial heritage (African, indigenous, Asian

Indian, British Isles, and occasionally Syrian). Wampanoag and Cape Verdean mixed-bloods like to call themselves "Wamp-Verdeans."

THE INDIAN GRANDMOTHER SYNDROME

A high percentage of African Americans proudly acknowledge a grand-mother or great-grandmother who was Blackfoot, Seminole, or Chero-kee – sometimes a full-blood, sometimes part-Indian, sometimes a "Prin-cess," whatever that means. Indian women who marry Black husbands become Indian matriarchs while tending to lose their matriarchal cultural advantages and sometimes their tribal enrollment status. They go home with their husbands, for Black marriages, like White marriages, are gener-ally patrilocal. Marrying out intensifies when Indians believe they will find no suitable mates like themselves or when motivated by social advantage and attaining prestige. Marrying an Indian is believed by a few to be too close to home. Black men choose Indian/light-skinned Black women for similar reasons, the social value signified by their complexions and the texture and length of their hair. Blacks and default Blacks close to an Indian elder figure in their families may seek replicating that person by marrying an Indian or mixed-blood Indian. Indian grandmothers and great-grandmothers impress one as lonely figures who are proud of their children's and grandchildren's achievements while suffering in silence at the invocation of "Mother Africa."

CRUCIAL YEARS OF 1820 TO 1950

The memory of annihilations, conversions to Christianity virtually under the threat of force, and being removed from or otherwise losing their homelands and places of refuge have traumatized eastern Native Ameri-cans since the sixteenth century in ways Plains and other western Indians, Blacks and Whites, cannot imagine. The Indian Removal Act of 1830 forced southern tribes to leave their homelands or adopt other survival strategies. The Fugitive Slave Law of 1850 compelled many Piedmont Siouan families to flee north of the Ohio River, part of their ancient homeland; their flight is embedded in the free Black migration into Ohio, Indiana, and southwestern Michigan of Free Negroes.[21] News of western tribes' victories and defeats also must have affected eastern peoples. As these Indian wars in the West peaked between 1860 and 1890, Indians in eastern communities experienced anxieties about their own survival, anxieties directly proportionate to their hoping to escape detection *as Indians* in off-reservation communities. They would have internalized the Indian-hating remarks they heard around them. Consider how they were likely affected by White responses to the major Indian events of that period: the Sand Creek Massacre (1864); the death of Cochise (1870); the annihilation of Custer and his portion of the Seventh Cavalry (1876); Chief Joseph's trek (1876–77); Geronimo's resistance and eventual surrender (1870s-1886); the Ghost Dance movement (1880s-1890); and the Wounded Knee Massacre (December 1890). East Coast Indians must have viewed these events as the bumpy and treacherous ride undulating downhill to oblivion. This is likely the era in which the deepest shame back East about being Indian or having Indian ancestors was instilled, a time for the greatest apprehension about vigilantes seeking Indians to intimidate or kill. Learning of the bad news, their survival strategies entertained ways to reconcile their ambiguous community status and the assimilation of their futures into their subconscious. They knew an irony of choice in Indian socialization in contrast to western Indians. In the West, Whites predominated as the non-Indians Native people were going to encounter on a regular or irregular basis. The farther east of the Mississippi Indians lived, they often encountered as many Blacks as Whites, and sometimes, because of de facto segregation, they lived in Colored neighborhoods. Antimiscegenation laws in some states forbade them from legally marrying a White person. They socialized and married either within their own enclaves or with African Americans.

Where Indians constituted a widely situated off-reservation community such as throughout Chester County, Pennsylvania, that community consisted of differing tribal and cultural heritages: coastal Algonquians, southern Iroquoians as well as Six Nations Iroquois who voluntarily relocated, and eastern Siouans like the Saponi and the Monacans. In present-day Philadelphia and Baltimore there are many second- and third-generation Lumbees, Saponis, and Cherokees. In older times as today, many of these families knew one another, but preparing their offspring for mate selection was a family, not necessarily a communally driven matter. The sense of extended community caveats, admonitions, and encouragements about who was acceptable for marriage, taken for granted in the reservation and cohesive Native communities like Nanticoke in Millsboro, Delaware, lacked the same stringencies in off-reservation and urban Native communities where neighbors and friends were more likely to mind their own business and where Indians still felt the pressure to conform to the standards abided by and dictated by the African Americans around them. Indian identity in southern Delaware has its peculiarities similar to other Native communities. Millsboro and Frankford are roughly about six miles apart. The former is Indian; the latter, Black. Despite little difference in casual appearance, of whatever complexion, those living in Millsboro are considered Indians; Indians in Frankford are considered Negroes. The Burtons and Tyres whose ancestors married the half-Indian–half-Black daughters of George and Mary Gray Welburn in the nineteenth century are essentially Indians living around Frankford. Meeting my relations at family reunions in Devon, Pennsylvania, and in Frankford compounded the mixed signals I grew up with, for here were people as Indian as any depicted in classic western photographs but who identified themselves variously as Negro, Black, or simply Colored; some belonged to the African Methodist Episcopal denomination.

THE POST–WORLD WAR II ERA

In the post–World War II decades, eastern Indians in and connected to tribal communities and reservations sustained as much of their cultural integrity as changes in their circumstances allowed. There were meetings like the American Indian Chicago Conference in 1961.[22] In 1946, Chief Thunderbird (Henry Bess, the man for which the Ford Thunderbird was named) started the Shinnecock Pow Wow, a Labor Day celebration that evolved with the three-day weekend and is capable of drawing crowds in excess of thirty thousand people. Urban and suburban/rural Indians sustained their contacts with tribal communities and with Native culture in subtle and clandestine ways. While living side-by-side with African Americans, they literally slipped off to "family reunions" that were actually tribal gatherings and powwows, or a family might host a "Sing" with dancing and potluck foods in their basement. Indians whose loyalties were uncertain were not informed about these clandestine occasions.

A dramatic action by an eastern Native group occurred in 1958 when the Lumbees in Robeson County, North Carolina, routed a Ku Klux Klan meeting in one of their cornfields. During the Civil Rights protests, marches, and sit-ins, some eastern Indians were involved, and Indians from northern and trans-Appalachian and western tribes participated in the Poor Peoples March and the tent cities in Washington DC. Allegedly, Cinque, leader of the Symbionese Liberation Army that captured heiress

Patti Hearst, was of a northeastern Indian community. In the 1970s and 1980s, Black artists like Quincy Troupe invoked his Cherokee grandmother in several poems, and novelist Alice Walker and composer-pianist Cecil Taylor, who had previously spoken of a Native ancestor, occasionally referred to themselves as African American Indians. Black super model Beverly Johnson and singer Chaka Khan professed to Blackfoot descent.[23]

Eastern Native Americans, however, did lose cultural ground amid the Black identity preoccupations during and since the 1960s. For many, a complete loss of Indian identity occurred; for a few, it was but a temporary exploration that over time manifested its revelation that "something wasn't right," a phrase that arose in several conversations. Many young East Coast Native people were easily lured by Black culture's dynamism, their resorting to it facilitated by their not having been told much about their Indian heritage, or their not believing it, or their having simply ignored it, all such responses being by-products of their parents and grandparents trying to hide their identities or forget them. Lighter complexion and wavy or straight hair were mantralike attributed to slave masters. Young Indians adopting Afro or "freedom" hairstyles sought to fit in with their Black peers. After all, having friends is important to all adolescents. As Black identity accelerated, youth of color assumed its rhetoric and style. Hairstyle is, of course, fluid, as some non-Black women – Indians included – still adopt the Afro style merely as an alternative. Urbanized Indians responded to Motown and Stax; in rural Indian enclaves one heard more country-and-western and rock. Into midcentury, speech enunciation in northern urban and rural communities tended to be distinct. I am a product of a belt of speech patterns ranging from York County, Pennsylvania, through the Philadelphia area to the New Jersey and Delaware shores. Incoming Blacks and Whites rehomogenized this dialect, and the urbanized teenagers of mixed-blood Indians adopted "ebonics" to reinforce their Blackness, criticizing their parents for "trying to sound White." These parents had in their youths been admonished from speaking both the urban hip jive and the southern dialect. The voice sounds in my household and among mixed-Indian friends and their parents were distinct and not terribly unlike the voice sounds one hears from Indians elsewhere. Food offered another distinction, at least in my family, where, not adhering to southern roots, my mother and her siblings ate hominy, not hominy grits. Only occasionally did we eat "soul food."

Black unity adversely affected Indians who could not or refused to try to fit in. It brought forth self-appointed sentinels and "identity police." In 1969, my sister, then finishing high school in Philadelphia, related to me how a marauding pack of Black girls in isolated incidents attacked two or three girls of color whose long hair they proceeded to cut off – one wore a waist-length braid. Indians who voluntarily cut their hair short may not have responded consciously to such violent acts, but the atmosphere unnerved them. People of color who were no longer consciously Indian became Blacks, virtually completing the process of de-Indianization. The route for survival taken by those mixed-blood Indians who felt assimilation difficult took alternative paths. Some gravitated toward White society; some buried their confusions in substance and alcohol abuse; and some aspired to a cosmopolitan Blackness. To start with, many of these young people were the same youths who had not listened about their Indian ancestry or believed they could not respond to it because part of their ancestry was African American.

THE CHILD REMEMBERS WHAT THE PARENT TRIED TO FORGET

While it was not solely responsible for the turnaround in consciousness of "lost birds" and de-tribalized Indians, Alex Haley's celebrated quest, which produced *Roots* in 1976, inspired Americans of all backgrounds to engage in genealogical research. People seeking documented Indian ancestors, of course, seldom found them until they learned to decode the documentation language. Some began returning to Indian Country, sometimes along a protracted journey. Getting family elders to talk about a subject in their lives that they had buried for decades has never been easy, for the apprehensions and fear of detection and ridicule hold tenaciously, stifling their psychological freedom. Meanwhile, some elders are relieved at their grandchildren's and children's new-found interest, though they may be skeptical about its longevity. "Learning to be Indians all over again" characterizes some eastern Native groups, as cultural centers and stalwarts in a community assist the young in learning what can be retrieved of the tribal language and the old ways.

Indian identity invokes some contradictory and ironic conditions. For example, there are both "lost bird" Indians and non-Indians desperate to imagine an Indian ancestor. They apply for tribal enrollment motivated only by the fallacious assumption that Indian status will end their tax responsibility and provide free educational benefits for their children. Then there are individuals who have never lived as Indians but can be tribally enrolled based upon an ancestor's enrollment; and there are individuals at the opposite end of the spectrum, having lived the life faithfully since childhood but whose parents cannot determine their own tribal identity, are thwarted by destroyed or missing data, or were themselves abused as children by some relations into forgetting it.

The takeover of Alcatraz Island in 1969 and the second Wounded Knee of 1972–73 kindled pride in default-Blacks who had believed, as their elders advised them, that Indian identity should be abandoned. Their children were now asking more pointed questions. Whether as adults or adolescents, many began to recognize and acknowledge their having lived a compromised existence, living in African American communities and having Black schoolmates and friends, and talking the talk but harboring feelings of being unsettled about *belonging* to an identity of the New World African. Not surprisingly, many cannot articulate what being an Indian means, even if their lineage is overwhelmingly Indian. But they possess an intangible sense that in the biracial scheme of Native American and African American, they could only proceed along the African path on a limited basis, and some probably abandoned it. Their consciences prevail upon them to gravitate toward people who they feel are more like themselves, even if on a superficial level for the time being and despite whether their families agree with them or find them renegades from Blackness. Whole families often experience this Native American disruption by one person or one family branch.

The rationale for such behavior may never impress many western Indians that there are still Indians east of the Mississippi. I suspect that the criteria eastern Native peoples set for themselves about Indianness and who is an Indian – whether they are reservation, off-reservation, community enclave, or urban-exurban-rural "lost birds" – will need to respond to and be measured by the unique destructive legacies eastern Native peoples have experienced. For so many Indian-and-Black mixed-bloods, Indian Country eastern style is the only place they can go to experience wholeness of being and a sense of personal integrity. Each person must arrive at these terms with personal honesty, that having African ancestry need not nullify them, as it did for over two hundred years, from being Native American or American Indian connected with a tribal community. There simply is nowhere else for them to go.

NOTES

1. Throughout this essay I will use Native American, American Indian, Natives, and Indians interchangeably, just as I will use African American and Black. I

will use "Negro" in its historical conversational context through the 1950s. Considering that, with few examples, virtually all Native Americans east of the Mississippi who are indigenous to that region are of mixed ancestry, I will occasionally employ "mixed-blood" to indicate such individuals in the context of describing their identity dynamics in association with African Americans; that is, to be a mixed-blood Indian does not nullify one's being an Indian. I am, for this essay, determining that persons are "Indian" because they have Indian ancestry whose cultural tenets they strive to maintain. Another term I will use is "lost birds," which typifies Indians who for various reasons have been disconnected from their tribal/nation communities since their early childhoods or from one or more generations.

2. See the "Special Issue" section of *American Indian Quarterly* 22 (winter/spring 1998): 123–258.

3. William Loren Katz, *Black Indians: A Hidden Heritage* (New York: Atheneum, 1986); Daniel F. Littlefield, *Africans and Creeks: From the Colonial Period to the Civil War* (Westport CT: Greenwood, 1979); Littlefield, *Africans and Seminoles: From Removal to Emancipation* (Westport CT: Greenwood, 1977); Littlefield, *The Cherokee Freedmen: From Emancipation to American Citizenship* (Westport CT: Greenwood, 1978); and Littlefield, *The Chickasaw Freedmen: A People Without a Country* (Westport CT: Greenwood, 1980). See R. Halliburton Jr., *Red Over Black: Black Slavery among the Cherokee Indians* (Westport CT: Greenwood, 1977); and Theda Perdue, *Slavery and the Evolution of Cherokee Society, 1540–1866* (Knoxville: University of Tennessee Press, 1979).

4. *Indian-Negro Relationships in the South-East* (1935; reprint, New York: AMS Press, 1978) was the first study of its kind. Foster chaired the sociology department at my alma mater, Lincoln University, and I am honored to have taken one course from him. At our last brief meeting in June 1969, a year after I graduated, we discussed this topic, about which he remained interested. He died several weeks later, however. While I harbored no desire to be his "successor," I dedicate this essay to his initiative and his memory. See Yolanda Moses, "Laurence Foster: Anthropologist, Scholar, and Social Advocate," in *African-American Pioneers in Anthropology*, ed. Ira E. Harrison and Faye V. Harrison (Urbana: University of Illinois Press, 1999), 85–100.

5. Frank Speck, "The Negroes and the Creek Nation," *Southern Workman* 37 (1908): 106–10; A. Irving Hallowell, "American Indians: White and Black: The Phenomenon of Transculturalization," *Current Anthropology* 4, no. 5 (December 1963): 519–31; Helen Rountree, *Pocahontas's People: The Powhatan Indians of Virginia Through Four Centuries* (Norman: University of Oklahoma Press, 1992); Rountree and Thomas Davidson, *Eastern Shore Indians of Maryland and Virginia* (Charlottesville: University Press of Virginia, 1998); Paul T. Murray, "'Who Is an Indian? Who Is a Negro?': Virginia Indians in the World War II Draft," *Virginia*

Magazine of History and Biography 95, no. 2 (April 1987): 215–31. Brewton Berry's *Almost White* (New York: Macmillan, 1963) argues that triracial groups were racial islands not accepted by Whites while avoiding Blacks. Berry's study has ignited vigorous debates about the cultural integrity of mixed-blood Indians in the Southeast, including Melungeons, who may have admixtures from throughout the Mediterranean; see N. Brent Kennedy, *The Melungeons: The Resurrection of a Proud People*, rev. ed. (Macon GA: Mercer University Press, 1997).

6. Jack D. Forbes, *Africans and Native Americans: The Language of Race and the Evolution of Red-Black Peoples* (Urbana: University of Illinois Press, 1993); and Forbes, "Only Approved Indians Can Play," in *Earth Power Coming: Short Fiction in Native American Literature*, ed. Simon J. Ortiz (Tsaile AZ: Navajo Community College Press, 1984), 262–63.

7. See Helen C. Rountree, "The Termination and Dispersal of the Nottoway Indians of Virginia," *Virginia Magazine of Life and History* 95, no. 2 (April 1987): 193–214.

8. Helen C. Rountree, "Pressured into Being 'Vanished Indians': The Gingaskin, Nottoway, and Pamunkey Reservation Cases, 1750–1850" (paper read at the meetings of the American Historical Association, Washington DC, 28 December 1992).

9. Daniel R. Mandell, "Shifting Boundaries of Race and Ethnicity: Indian-Black Intermarriage in Southern New England, 1760–1880," *Journal of American History* 85 (September 1998): 498. Also worth reading is Thomas L. Doughton's "Unseen Neighbors: Native Americans of Central Massachusetts, a People Who Had 'Vanished,'" in *After King Philip's War: Presence and Persistence in Indian New England*, ed. Colin G. Calloway (Hanover NH: Dartmouth College/University Press of New England, 1997), 207–30.

10. Remarkable for its thoroughness and resilience is Almon Wheeler Lauber, *Indian Slavery in Colonial Times within the Present Limits of the United States* (1913; reprint, New York: AMS Press, 1969).

11. That is, she lived among the Lumbees. She, too, may have been a Lumbee or of some other tribe.

12. These "free negroes" on the Neuse may have been Tuscaroras whose ancestors did not join the Five Nations in 1722.

13. Carter G. Woodson, *Free Negro Heads of Families in the United States in 1830* (Washington DC: Association for the Study of Negro Life and History, 1925). Listed are names of Indians among, for instance, the Nanticokes (Delaware) and the Shinnecocks (Suffolk County, Long Island).

14. Tina Turner, with Kurt Loder, *I, Tina* (New York: William Morrow, 1986).

15. Buck Clayton, interview by Stanley Dance, 1979, Jazz Oral History Project of the National Endowment for the Arts, Institute of Jazz Studies, Rutgers University, Newark NJ.

16. This list is not meant to overlook other Native jazz and pop artists or those acknowledging Indian ancestry: a sample includes saxophonist Jim Pepper (Creek and Kaw); trombonist and Louis Armstrong–Lester Lanin alumnus Russell "Big Chief" Moore (Pima); vocalists Kay Starr (Cherokee and Iroquois), Keely Smith (Sioux), Mildred Bailey (Coeur d'Alene), and Lee Wiley (Cherokee); saxophonist Frankie Trumbauer (Cherokee); clarinetist Pee Wee Russell (Cherokee); pianist Dave Brubeck (tribe unidentified); rock and roll guitar innovator Link Ray (Shawnee); and vocalist Clea Bradford, who proclaimed her Choctaw Indian and Ethiopian parentage.

17. Olivia Bush-Banks (1869–1944) was born in Sag Harbor on eastern Long Island. She claimed both parents to be of Montauk descent and attended the Indian school at Poosepatuck at Mastic on the South Shore where her paternal relatives lived. She described herself as a "Colored person" and, according to Bernice F. Guillaume, "concurrently retained a Montauk Indian and Afro-American ethos"; see the Schomburg Library of Nineteenth-Century Black Women Writers series, *The Collected Works of Olivia Bush-Banks* (New York: Oxford University Press, 1991).

Very little is known about the enigmatic Ann Plato, who presents a much more difficult study. Risky inferences about her can be drawn when one attempts to decode her writings and idiosyncrasies. Her book, *Essays, Including Biographies and Miscellaneous Pieces in Prose and Poetry*, was published in 1841 in Hartford, Connecticut, while she was a member of the Colored Congregational Church, whose pastor, Rev. James C. Pennington, wrote the book's "To the Reader." From 1844 into 1847 she taught at the Elm Street School, which was supported by the church. While Plato's place in African American literary history is taken for granted, her parentage and lineage remain far from certain, and her dates and places of birth and death are unknown. It is possible, based upon allusions in her poetry, that she was born between 1823 and 1825, thus being an adolescent prodigy. Her poem "To the First of August" rather blandly acknowledges the abolition of slavery in the British Caribbean; her longest poem, "The Natives of America," narrates in the impassioned voice supposedly of her father telling her of his people's legacy. A tribe is never mentioned; however, she may have been the daughter of one of a series of Platos who relocated to Connecticut between 1815 and 1824 or later from eastern Long Island. I suspect that she was of Montauk or Narragansett descent or both, which does not negate her having either some African or European ancestry or both.

18. William Loren Katz, *The Black West* (New York: Arno Press/New York Times, 1969).

19. African American popular magazines have featured articles on the casino-gambling rich Mashantucket Pequots, focusing on their high percentage of members mixed with African American. See Kevin Chappell, "Black Indians Hit Jack-

pot in Casino Bonanza," *Ebony*, June 1995: 46, 48, 50 and Leslie Goffe, "Hitting the Genetic Jackpot," *Emerge*, February 1999: 78, 80, 82–84.

20. *New York Times*, 3 June 1983.

21. Richard L. Haithcock and Vicki L. Haithcock, "Occaneechie Saponi and Tutelo of the Saponi Nation: aka Monacan and Piedmont Catawba, Includes Eastern Cherokee." TS, 1996.

22. Laurence M. Hauptman and Jack Campisi, "The Voice of Eastern Indians: The American Indian Chicago Conference of 1961 and the Movement for Federal Recognition," *Proceedings of the American Philosophical Society* 132, no. 4 (1988): 316–29.

23. African Americans predominate in asserting an ancestor who was a Blackfoot or part-Blackfoot Indian from the southern United States; I have encountered a small number of Whites who make this assertion. These Blackfoot have nothing to do with the Plains Black*feet*. The term "Blackfoot" seems to have come into use toward the end of the nineteenth century, and one likely possibility lies in its being a pejorative term given by Whites or other Indians for Blacks who proclaimed an Indian ancestor such as a Cherokee but were mistaken. Some Blackfoot today who identify as Indians also proclaim a Cherokee lineage. Independently, Richard Haithcock and Vicki Haithcock (see "Blackfoot and Blackfeet," 20 May 1997, online posting, Mississippi State University) and myself concur that some southeastern Blackfoot are Saponi descendants. The Haithcocks, members of the Saponi Nation of Ohio, have found their surnames in nineteenth-century documents in Virginia and the Carolinas as Free Colored Persons; they were among the Blacks migrating across the Ohio River in the wake of the Indian Removal Act and with Blacks before and especially after the passage of the Fugitive Slave Law of 1850. The Saponis, with the Occaneechis, Enos, Tutelos, and others, are an eastern Siouan People who constituted an extensive colonial and slavery-era diaspora throughout the eastern United States and Canada. The name "Saponi" appears to be a Siouan language derivation from a term that can be signified as "black foot." This is a remarkably extensive subject; see the essay "Who Are the Southeastern Blackfoot?" in my *Roanoke and Wampum: Topics in Native American Heritage and Literatures* (New York: Peter Lang Publishing, 2001), 9–23. See also George K. Hesslink's social history of Cass County, Michigan, *Black Neighbors: Negroes in a Northern Rural Community* (Indianapolis IN: Bobbs-Merrill, 1968).

11. Making Christianity Sing

The Origins and Experience of Lumbee Indian and African American Church Music

MALINDA MAYNOR

Sing because the holy ghost is saying sing.
Sing because the spirit said sing.
Amen.
But don't sing because you want to sing.
Just sing because thus said the spirit –
Sing.

Rev. Herbert Chavis (Lumbee)

Some months ago I screened one of my short films, *Sounds of Faith*, for a symposium on Black and Indian cultural connections. The film documents my Lumbee Indian family's transference of Christian faith through music and follows my uncle Michael Cummings, a preacher, and his son as they sing in church services, family gatherings, and the annual Lumbee powwow in Robeson County, North Carolina. During the question-and-answer period, an African American gentleman told me that he did not see much "Indianness" in the film, that my family's singing must be a reflection of our "Black" and "White" blood. He went on to say that our spiritual experience of the music was "Black" but the rhythm was "White." I explained that Lumbee music is neither White nor Black but something else. Yet his challenge to our "Indianness" persisted. Fortunately, my uncle (the preacher) was also in the audience; he stood up and said, "Well, you know, *Indians* have rhythm too."

His quiet reminder pointed to the cultural amnesia that surrounds southeastern Indians.[1] In Indians' quest to revitalize "contact-traditional" cultures, or in non-Indians' attempts to identify themselves with us, the basic elements of all cultures – spirit, song, relationships – disappear as we struggle to connect with elements of culture that are considered obviously "Indian."[2] Furthermore, the authenticity of these "Indian" elements is determined by how Euro-American culture and politics delineate "Indian" culture, not by how Indians understand culture. For both Indians and non-Indians, perpetuation of "traditional" culture becomes a convenient gauge of authenticity, defined by otherness. The need to be as exotic as possible, while "leapfrogging" over the political, ethnic, and religious contexts that have influenced our development, solidifies the very color lines that our ancestors, through their persistence and intelligence, struggled to undermine. Black Americans succumb to the same amnesia, not only concerning Indians but in the tendency for Black leaders to deny their own subjectivity, describing themselves primarily in terms of White society as victims of White oppression.[3] Consequently, we *all* forget that people are more than just their skin color, their economic status, or their political affiliation.

We all share religious music. The subtleties of performance and practice may differ across Black and Indian communities, but in both groups, music transmits our oral traditions and keeps our communities together. I have chosen to focus on worship music that is not performance-oriented to illuminate the ways in which music reflects and informs everyday experience. In both Indian and Black communities, music is sustained by oral, rather than written, tradition; the oral tradition can be viewed as the glue between our indigenous traditions and the supposedly "detribalizing" force of Christianity.[4] The history of religious music shows us that the dichotomies of "indigenous" and "Christian," "Black," and "White" do not accurately reflect the development of Indian cultures and the very real examples of cultural persistence that Christian Indian communities demonstrate. Beverly Diamond-Cavanagh's work among Eastern Woodland communities in New England and eastern Canada illustrates the role of oral tradition in cultural persistence. She explains the difference between the oral and the literate: "In the [oral], words do not merely connote meaning; they are an enactment of it. Their utterance has power and dramatic intensity."[5] Such "enactment" of meaning in the spoken (and sung) word provided continuity throughout the transition from indigenous to Christian worship in both Indian and Black communities. Valuing the everyday enactment of meaning allows us to understand what has and what has not changed.

Historian James Merrell describes continuity when he discusses the shocking population reduction that tribes in the Upper Pee Dee region of South Carolina endured. He writes, "Though diseases decimated them, the compass points – kin, village, hunting, planting, celebrating, mourning – around which people oriented their existence remained."[6] Today, Lumbees maintain that it was Christianity itself that enabled us to maintain these "compass points," and our religious music is a vibrant, constantly evolving example of that spiritual and cultural orientation. Christianity is critical to our persistence as a people.

Four factors influenced the postcolonial evolution of Lumbee religious music: indigenous traditions, the long-meter hymn (brought by eighteenth-century Baptist and Methodist missionaries), the call-and-response spiritual (popularized by the Second Great Awakening in 1800), and shape-note tune books (introduced by circuit-riding preachers in the late nineteenth century). African Americans' experience with these forces helps us understand the continuities and changes in Lumbee music. While Lumbees and Blacks had different responses to these influences, both relied on oral tradition and the "rhythms of faith" to shape spiritual beliefs and cultural structures.[7]

INDIGENOUS SOUTHEASTERN TRADITIONS

Lumbees are descendants of the Cheraws, Tuscaroras, Hatteras, and other tribes, some of the more than fifty groups that inhabited what is now Virginia, North Carolina, and South Carolina.[8] Even before these peoples encountered the Spanish in the 1560s, this area was extremely complex; hundreds of villages dotted the landscape, each belonging to one of three different linguistic families – Siouan, Algonquian, or Iroquoian. Seasonal migration was quite common, so intercultural contact and change were commonplace. The precolonial Southeast was already a kind of frontier, even before Europeans and Africans arrived.[9] The variety of religious practice prior to European invasion and the information that has been lost since then make any discussion of our ancestors' pre-Columbian music necessarily speculative. I rely on early European observers' accounts and the information gained by anthropologists to make some tentative connections between Christian and indigenous musical styles.

John Lawson published an account of his travels through North Carolina in 1714 and probably provided the most thorough and accurate description of our musical traditions prior to conversion. Lawson seems to call all the Indians he describes "Tuskeruros" but separates them into five "nations" – "Totero's, Sapona's, Keiauwee's, Aconechos, and Schoccories" – and then fifteen separate towns.[10] His apparent confusion over village organization hints at the difficulty Europeans had with describing Indian groups. In the early 1930s John Swanton's research indicated that, for example, the Keyauwee and Shakori were Siouan groups and not related to the Iroquoian Tuscaroras. He identified Lumbee ancestors as mainly Siouan language speakers and descendants of the Keyauwee, Cheraw, Shakori, and other groups, with possible (but unlikely, according to Swinton) "contributions" from Algonquian or Iroquoian groups.[11] Given that Lawson's account seems to describe (although mislabel) many of our ancestors, his descriptions of our musical practices are applicable:

They have . . . Feasts and Dances, which are always when the Harvest of Corn is ended and in the Spring. The one to return Thanks to the good Spirit for the Fruits of the Earth; the other, to beg the same Blessings for the succeeding Year. . . . At these Feasts which are set out with the Magnificence their Fare allows of . . . There is commonly a Fire made in the middle of the House . . . where sit two Men on the Ground upon a Mat; one with a Rattle, made of a Gourd, with some Beans in it; the other with a Drum made of an earthen Pot, covered with a dressed-Deer-Skin, and one Stick in his Hand to beat thereon; and so they both begin the Song appointed. At the same time one drums and the other rattles, which is all the artificial Musick of their own making I ever saw amongst them. To these two Instruments they sing, which carries no Air with it, but is a sort of unsavory Jargon; yet their Cadences and Raising of their Voices are formed with that Equality and Exactness that, (to us Europeans) it seems admirable how they should continue these Songs without once missing to agree, each with the others Note and Tune.[12]

Lawson described the ceremonial context of Indian music as a thanksgiving for the harvest, a holiday that Lumbees today see in explicitly religious terms. Drums and rattles as the only instruments is consistent with many (though not all) churches' musical preferences, but foot stomping has replaced the drum in church. Finally, Lawson depicted religious music as being without a melody (an "Air") but perfect in the singers' agreement with one another. The spirit behind this way of singing survives in the practice of lining-out hymns (see below). Characterizing these Indians' spiritual worldview, Lawson wrote,

They all believe that this World is round, and that there are two Spirits; The one good, the other bad. The good one they reckon to be the Author and Maker of every thing, and say, that it is he, that gives them the Fruits of the Earth, and has taught them to hunt, fish, and be wise enough to overpower the Beasts of the Wilderness. . . . They say, it is a bad Spirit, (who lives separate from the good one) that torments us with Sicknesses, Disappointments, Losses, Hunger, Travel, and all the Misfortunes, that Human Life is incident to.[13]

It is possible, of course, that Lawson is reading his own Christian philosophy into that of the Indians he observed, but the passage makes for a powerful comparison between indigenous religion and the Christianity that Lumbees now embrace. In his seminal work *The Southeastern Indians*, Charles Hudson writes:

The basic unit of Southeastern music was the song. . . . The length of the songs is variable. Some are only ten seconds long, and even the longer ones last only a few minutes. A great many consist of short sections which are repeated and combined in various ways. Characteristically, the Cherokees combine these phrases in fours and sevens, the typical song consisting of seven phrases repeated four times. . . . Many of the Southeastern Indian melodies have a throbbing or undulatory movement which gradually descends. They are sung with a moderate amount of vocal tension. . . . [The songs] often begin and end with shouts or yells, and some of the songs employ antiphonal and responsorial techniques, in which a group of singers repeats phrases sung by a group leader.[14]

Many of these elements of southeastern Indian music and ceremony are present in contemporary Lumbee music, which also reflects the various European influences that will be discussed below.

CONTEMPORARY LUMBEE MUSIC AND CEREMONY

There are four main musical settings in the Lumbee community: the home, church services (including revivals), gospel sings, and the pow-wow. This last has been introduced only in the last thirty years; the singing style is either northern or southern Plains and not indigenous to the Lumbees or the southeastern United States. Powwows are primarily social rather than religious events, and the singing style has not so far pervaded religious music.

Religious music dominates the other three settings, revealing multiple levels of cultural communion with this world and the world to come. These three spaces knit together secular and sacred lives and are permeated by the security of kinship. One approaches each space with respect for appropriate gender and generational roles, as well as for the history that inhabits each space (other cultures may say "spirits" instead of "history"). Everyday rituals of birth, death, and teaching take place in the home and church settings, while the gospel sing and the revival host more elaborate rituals of performance, cleansing, and rebirth. One's outward behavior and inner attitude, as well as the music that is sung in each place, are critical to maintaining the effectiveness of this year-round cycle.

While many features of Lumbee religion and music may seem easily transferable from indigenous to Christian practice, as John Lawson's description attests, Christianity is by no means incidental to our modern spiritual practice. Biblical scripture has a profound impact on our experience of the sacred and secular, as this conversion story reveals:

When I had accepted the Lord I was sitting at a piano seat,
And at that time I was fighting that battle of getting off drugs, you know,
And I found out that working with the youth choir was helping me.
One Sunday morning, Brother Jerry Lowry preached on Doubting Thomas.
He had to stick his fingers in his holes to believe that it was Jesus when He arose.
Well I was a Doubting Thomas, I had been struggling from drugs for five years.
And, it's like me and the Lord got into a little conversation –
"You can't save me – I mean you *can't get me off drugs*, I have *tried*."
"Try me," He said.
I said "Okay." That's just the way our conversation went.[15]

Singing, getting straight, and salvation meld together, bound by stories heard from the Bible.

Family bonding and intimacy take place in the home, spontaneously singing with whatever instruments might be at hand – a piano, guitar, or simply a cappella if that suits the singers. Church services are more formal places of worship, where extended families come together, a message is preached, and prayers are explicitly offered with songs. The spontaneous singing style, however, is maintained. Both the home and church settings include repertoire from hymn books, some accompanied by instruments and some lined out by a song leader. Rev. Michael Cummings provides the best description of the experience of Lumbee religious music, in which he touches on both the home and church settings, and reveals the important connections between family and community, music, memory, and spirituality.

My dad was a piano player, my daddy was a singer,
he was the musician of the church, and understand his father was too
but my dad was the music leader, very much involved in the church's singing,
And at home, we had the piano at home. . . .
I never got tired
of listening to dad play and us sing with him.
It was as if there was some kind of attraction,
some kind of power

that you felt, that just kind of bound you

to be there in that particular place in that room, don't leave you don't *want* to leave,

you just want to sit here and sing and let daddy play the piano. . . .

I felt like there was something growing between us something drawing us together

And that sitting together singing together, singing about God and

singing about things about Heaven or singing about dying,

brought to our minds, you know

ultimate kinds of concerns, life and death kinds of things. . . .

So our singing as a boy was In the Sweet By and By

When the Roll is Called Up Yonder I'll Be There

Which causes you to think about

you know, not just life now but life later on in the presence of God. . . .

In the Sweet By and By

I liked the way daddy played that song

He Whispers Sweet Peace To Me

If I Could Hear My Mother Pray Again

When the Roll is Called Up Yonder I'll Be There, When We All Get to Heaven, The Old Rugged Cross

Now those are hymns.

When I hear them being sung you know it's kind of like I get this

Almost like a homesick feeling

And I might cry, I'm just a big

mush when it comes to that kind of singing you know in the church

And my daddy's brother

both of them

were some of the best we had

among our people to sing those old hymns they had these real powerful

voices that would fill up a church

And singing with the audience was –

you could feel it swelling in the church,

and it's almost as if it would just pick you up, just move you

to the presence of God at the feet of Jesus or something

And that kind of singing

is my favorite kind.[16]

Although I am mainly concerned here with music sung in homes and churches, the gospel sing is an important bridge between contemporary and traditional expressions and deserves a mention. This is both a social and religious event and possibly the most obvious evidence of the persistence of "traditional" indigenous worship among the Lumbee. Several times a week during the summer and fall, during the traditional time of the Southeast's Green Corn ceremonies and stomp dances, Lumbees from all over the county gather at different churches to hear Lumbee gospel singers (often quartets from that particular community, a youth choir, or a multigenerational family group).

Gospel sings bring together the larger community outside the nuclear family and Sunday worship settings, and the song repertoire is quite different. A prayer or homily starts the event, and sometimes shouting and testifying take place, as in a church service. The choirs and groups perform original material that they have written, as well as arrangements of classic country/gospel hit songs (some of which go back to the 1930s and 1940s, while others are quite recent). Electronic instruments dominate these events. This shift in repertoire represents the performance-oriented function of these events and their role as a meeting place for Lumbees from different parts of the county, all of whom have slightly different religious and singing traditions. While some churches may still line out hymns and others have moved to a karaoke-style of singing, nearly everyone enjoys the fine performance of gospel standards and the freshness of original songs.

Non-Lumbee observers have struggled to describe what our music sounds like; invariably, they shrug their shoulders and say, "it's indescribable." They often begin by describing what it does not sound like: you cannot dance to it, but it can be fast; there is not much ornamentation, but a Lumbee group's sound has depth; it is not syncopated, but it has a swing to it. Most often, they say that it sounds like a mixture between Black and White music, but when pressed, they cannot give an example of *how*. Certain characteristics of our music can be traced to southeastern Indian styles. For example, traditional church singing can be accompanied by rattles, tambourines, or foot stomping, Lumbee voices have an open-throated, nasal quality, and we generally carry a different sense of pitch from standard Western music when singing informally or as a congregation. In traditional Lumbee congregational singing, there is more emphasis on heterophony (where a congregation sings in "unison," but the melody is sung by individuals at different tempos, with different ornaments, creating an impression of harmony) than part-harmony. Long-meter hymns are a cappella, led by one song leader, with a smooth, elevating, and haunting quality, as if the church is being visited by the past.

Lumbee descriptions of music, on the other hand, often reference an emotional or life experience. Mike Cummings says that when he hears it he gets "a homesick feeling, and I might cry." To me, hearing it feels like home. Singing it feels like searching. Its indescribability perhaps comes from the unfamiliarity that non-Lumbee observers have with those feelings in the Lumbee context – "home," "homesick," and "searching" mean that when my family harmonizes together on the last note of a song, our voices waver as we find the right pitches. We are searching together for our home in Heaven, with loved ones who have gone on. But our definition of the "right" pitch signifies that we are present together as well, with a constant awareness of our relationship to one another in *this* world. The standard of good Lumbee singing is rarely whether the singers correspond to a Western key or pitch – rather, the standard is set by how well the singers function *together* and how well our pitches fit each other. The sound is also determined by context – one does not sing the same way at home as one would at a gospel sing. In music, our emphasis is on the community rather than on the individual.

On the whole, Lumbee church music is less influenced by current trends than that of either Blacks or Whites. Whether in the home, in the church, or at a gospel sing, the style of singing is determined foremost by the spirit in the room, the context of the event, and the relationship of the singers. Lumbee musical change reflects changes in our spiritual experiences, not trends in the Top 40.

LUMBEE CONVERSION TO CHRISTIANITY

How did our religious music develop such variations? Our musical and spiritual response to Christianity accounts for much of our development, but the changes happened gradually, over as many as three hundred years. While missionary activity accounts for much of the conversion of Indians to Christianity in the United States, our Lumbee ancestors may have had at least some knowledge of Christianity before any significant missionary activity took place. Such knowledge was probably gained during migrations undertaken by Indians, Africans, and Europeans in the sixteenth, seventeenth, and eighteenth centuries.[17]

After initial contact with Europeans, however, disease, the deerskin trade, and war created such instability in daily life that a number of these groups were probably searching for a sanctuary. They found the Lumbee River and its swamps in Bladen County (now Robeson County), a watershed whose swamps and streams provided sustenance. By the 1730s, the

Indians that were once distinct tribal communities found themselves on the Lumbee River, near the border that now divides North and South Carolina.[18]

African slavery brought on a political and economic upheaval in the Southeast that drove other settlers into the Bladen County area. In 1701, an English visitor complained that North Carolina "only tis a place which receives Pirates, Runaways, and Illegal Traders." A Virginia governor added, "Carolina (I meane the North part of it) always was and is the sinke of America, the Refuge of our Renegadoes."[19] The colony did not have its own government until 1712, and Europeans and Africans who could not or did not want to participate in South Carolina's and Virginia's booming plantation economies found a place to escape.[20] Many of the colony's White inhabitants were debtors trying to elude authorities in Virginia and South Carolina, indentured servants who had been released from bondage and granted a piece of land, or pirates who marauded between the West Indies and North Carolina's coast. Slaves escaping from the port towns of Wilmington or New Bern and even from the Cooper River and low country plantations of South Carolina may have also found a home along the Lumbee River.[21] "Tribes" of Indians, escaped African and Indian slaves, Highland Scots, and other "renegade" elements of colonial society converged on southeastern North Carolina.[22]

Migration probably played a significant role in Indians' conversion to Christianity. We would have encountered Protestant and Catholic Europeans; African Americans who practiced Christianity, Islam, indigenous African religions, and West Indian traditions; and other Indians who had been converted to Christianity from contact with Spanish Catholics.[23] Members of other ethnicities and religious creeds were also assimilated into migrating indigenous groups, creating a mélange of religious practices that must have functioned quite well in this multicultural frontier environment.[24] As a group, my Lumbee ancestors settled on a Protestant Christianity that allowed for a direct relationship to God and the earth. Because of Baptists' and Methodists' general lack of emphasis on hierarchical authority, Indians could set up churches that reflected complex and extensive kinship networks and established leadership patterns without needing to establish a rigid church hierarchy.[25] Today, the majority of Lumbees are Baptists, followed by Methodist, Pentecostal Holiness, and other unaffiliated churches. However, religious belief and its musical expression can be traced back to several core influences, regardless of denomination. Many of these influences have parallels in the African American experience – long-meter singing, call-and-response singing, and shape-note singing.

Until fairly recently, Lumbees regularly sang long-metered hymns, an old form of congregational singing that does not use instruments or song-books. George Pullen Jackson, one of the leading authorities on religious folk music in America, credits the evolution of long-meter singing to the early Puritan church in America.[26] Since the Puritan style and the style adapted by Lumbees are similar, we might make some suppositions about how this style came to us and why it gained so much influence.

In the seventeenth and eighteenth centuries, Puritan congregations sang psalms from the Bible using various hymn tunes. Because the psalm verses were translated with four lines and eight syllables per line, con-gregations could sing any psalm that had four phrases and eight beats per phrase.[27] Unlike much music in the contemporary Protestant church, however, these churchgoers did not see music as entertainment. John Cal-vin instructed that music should be unaccompanied and unharmonized, which focused one's mind on heavenly rather than earthly things. These hymns and the spiritual lessons they reinforced could be transferred from church to town meeting to school to home, without the encumbrances of instruments or songbooks. Nor did the congregation need to memorize a large repertoire to make singing both instructional and emotionally fulfill-ing. "Such songs would be a means to spiritual joy and would distinguish the truly sacred from mere entertainment."[28] In describing the features of Lumbee long-meter singing in the early 1940s, one observer said, "one will easily recognize sincerity and genuine pleasure in participation – not for the benefit of the listener, but for the benefit of the singers."[29]

Baptist, Methodist, and Presbyterian missionaries traveled south from New England in the mid–eighteenth century, bearing many Puritan sing-ing traditions. By 1800, Baptist and Methodist doctrine and worship per-haps had been incorporated into Indian oral and musical traditions. The lack of authoritarian control in Baptist and Methodist churches lent an improvisational, spontaneous style to their worship and their singing.[30] These denominations were perhaps attractive to our Lumbee ancestors because of their emphasis on community worship and because they did not require literacy for spiritual understanding. The style of singing that missionaries promoted coincided with a fairly unstable community that was recovering from several generations of movement and turmoil.

Some Indians of Robeson County were familiar with the long-meter style and the tenets of Christianity, as seen in this hymn allegedly written by a missionary who visited Robeson County's Indian settlement before 1776. According to a Lumbee family historian, the missionary wrote in an

Indian dialect that he heard while staying with James and Priscilla Lowry. James Lowry was one of the first Indians to receive a land grant from King George in Bladen County (now Robeson). He migrated to the area with his wife's family from the Pamlico Sound, near North Carolina's outer banks. According to family tradition, they were already practicing Christianity before arriving at the Lumbee River. This hymn roughly follows the long-meter form:

> De joy I felt I cannot tell
> To tink dat I was saved from Hell
> Through Jesus streaming blood
> Dat I am saved by grace divine
> Who am de wurst of all mankind
> O glory be to God.
> So me lub God wid inside heart
> He fight for me, he take um part.
> He save um life before
> God hear poor Indian in de wood.
> So me lub him and dat be good.
> Me prize him evermore.[31]

In the long-meter style, the role of the song leader was particularly vital. Because few church members had songbooks and many were illiterate, the leader would stand in front of the congregation and "line-out" the hymn, chanting the first phrase. Someone in the congregation then gave a starting pitch. This method led to a very slow pace and numerous variations on the melody by individual singers, producing the heterophony that John Lawson may have heard on his travels.

Gradually, long-meter singing disappeared in most New England churches, as preaching and prayer became more important and access to songbooks and instruments increased.[32] It persisted in many southern churches, particularly Black churches, through the nineteenth century, but has been particularly stubborn in the Lumbee church. Only in the last twenty to thirty years has unaccompanied hymn-singing in Lumbee churches declined.

Examining the long-meter style's history in the Black church illustrates the role of oral tradition in perpetuating the style among Lumbees. George Pullen Jackson argues that African American long-meter singing, similar to Lumbee long-meter singing, originated in the Calvinist Puritan church and the Wesleyan Methodist church. Jackson arrives at his conclusion through a comparison of hymn texts and tunes in Black and White churches and through analyzing the history of Black conversion. Eighteenth- and nineteenth-century missionaries transmitted the style of singing lined-out hymns in unison. Missionaries feared for slaves' souls in a plantation environment that was hostile to slaves' conversion. Laws did not allow masters to build places of worship for slaves, and they also restricted Black preaching and integrated church worship. Consequently, according to historian C. Eric Lincoln, Black Christians "met and worshipped with the preachers of their choice in the swamps and forests as far from the Big House as possible in what came to be called the 'Invisible Church.' "[33] Jackson attributes the development of heterophony in Blacks' long-meter singing to those churches' relative cultural isolation and their lack of supervision by church authorities; thus "Invisible Churches" were left to form and control their own worship.[34]

Other historians see Africa as more important in the origin of Black lined-out hymn singing. Rather than emphasizing text, these scholars name musical and oral conventions such as call-and-response singing and the use of pentatonic, hexatonic, and heptatonic scales as elements of African music that survived the Middle Passage to be re-created in long-meter hymns.[35] Religious historian John Boles writes: "One thing is clear: more than perhaps any other aspect of African culture, music survived the ordeal of the Middle Passage to play a significant role in the lives of American slaves and contribute greatly to indigenous forms of American music."[36] Boles goes on to describe slaves' music as "communal and improvised . . . [with] little solo singing. Rather, the group sang together, sometimes in response to a leader who lined out the verse (particularly when the song was a white-influenced religious one – frontier whites lined out their hymns too) and other times singing the chorus after verses sung out by the leader. . . . Special situations, individuals, and events thus entered the realm of song."[37]

There is perhaps a parallel between the role of these "special situations" in forming Black music and the importance of religious context in Lumbee music. Rather than allowing denominational doctrine or written hymns to influence the function of music, we always maintained local control over our spiritual life. Christianity did not change Indian and African music and religion beyond recognition in these early years. The changes brought by hymn books were significant, but in each case oral tradition guided the Indian and Black community's response.

The enactment of meaning through oral tradition paved the way for the necessary emotional and immediate spiritual experience of Puritan, African American, and Lumbee churches and permitted the continued influence of those religious forms through the present day. Even though literacy is nearly universal and all except the most orthodox Primitive Baptist churches have instruments, there is a recognized and sustained value in a layperson feeling a hymn spontaneously and leading the congregation. In the case of Lumbees, the persistence of oral tradition into the late twentieth century, in spite of the omnipresent written word, is a tribute to the significance of the "power and dramatic intensity" of singing and hearing the gospel according to long-developed structures and forms of worship.[38]

CALL-AND-RESPONSE SINGING AND THE CAMP MEETING

Beginning on the Southern frontier (mainly western Tennessee and Kentucky) in 1800, the social and political circumstances around the Second Great Awakening hastened a divergence in Black and Indian worship and singing.[39] Corresponding to the entrenchment of slavery and their greater contact with Whites, Blacks largely abandoned the long-meter form and adopted call-and-response spirituals, while sociopolitical circumstances isolated Lumbees, who maintained the long-meter style and diversified our worship.

During the Second Great Awakening, large gatherings of churchgoers converged at a central area for a few days or a week, socialized with people from other communities, and attended worship services. Spread-out populations with few church facilities necessitated these meetings. It was a form uniquely suited to the lifestyle of the American frontier, where isolated populations meant scarce resources for church facilities, an environment similar to Robeson County in 1800. These camp meetings emphasized a transformational experience as a prerequisite for salvation. Hence, the focus of the music similarly became emotional and, indeed, "spiritual," designed to carry the gospel to the listener's heart rather than head. Perhaps not coincidentally, the Presbyterians, General Baptists, and Methodists who organized the camp meetings were also among the first antislavery agitators. In their early years in the mission field, missionaries taught Blacks to read and write, and camp meetings were racially integrated events where Blacks often outnumbered Whites (although seating may have been segregated).[40]

Eileen Southern speculates that Black activities at camp meetings may have been quite controversial for the "church fathers," based on "complaints" that were made to White organizers.

First, the Blacks were holding songfests away from proper supervision, and this was undesirable in the eyes of the church fathers. They were singing songs of their own composing, which was even worse in the eyes of the officials. The texts of the composed songs were not lyric poems in the hallowed tradition of Watts, but a stringing together of isolated lines from prayers, the Scriptures, and orthodox hymns. . . . Finally, for their composed religious songs the Blacks used tunes that were dangerously near to being dance tunes in the style of slave jubilee melodies. None of this was acceptable to the orthodox. Nevertheless, from such practices emerged a new kind of religious song that became the distinctive badge of the camp-meeting movement.[41]

From this description, one sees the powerful role of oral tradition in creating the camp-meeting spiritual – prayers, Scriptures, and hymns that originated in different written contexts took on a new meaning when transmitted into an oral, spontaneous setting.

Southern goes on to say that rather than Blacks adopting a White singing style at the camp meetings, Whites adopted a Black style. Responsorial singing began to spread to communities all over America, replacing the more subdued Puritan-influenced psalmody. The turn of the nineteenth century was a chaotic time in American life, especially in the South. The doctrine of states' rights was gaining popularity, slavery was expanding into "frontiers" like Kentucky and Mississippi, slave insurrections became more prevalent, and the cotton gin had created an even wider gulf between rich and poor Whites. These factors may have contributed to an upheaval in religious doctrine and practice as well. During this time, Baptists and Methodists changed their stance on slavery, deciding to conflate the absolute authority of God and the White master.[42] The spiritual song was perhaps a key to the emotionalism that swept the South; it shifted Black worship toward a greater interaction with White forms. Partly because of White population expansion in southeastern North Carolina, enslaved Blacks (whose population was also growing in Robeson County) began to live in closer proximity to Whites than they did to Indians. The widely shared experience of the camp meeting drew White and Black Baptists and Methodists closer together, even as the denominations endeavored to suppress Black freedom.[43]

Meanwhile, camp meetings certainly influenced Indians, who regularly attend them still today. Judging by our contemporary worship style and doctrine, the theology that camp meetings articulated held a particular power for Lumbees. Unlike their Black and White neighbors, however,

Lumbees did not move wholeheartedly toward spiritual songs as a means of religious expression. Rather, we continued the long-meter form and began officially to establish our own churches. Circumstances seemed to necessitate this shift in survival strategy. Unlike the colonial period, when we were ready to embrace change as a means of survival, shifting racial attitudes and growing local hostilities toward Indians caused us to retreat further into our swamplands.[44] Neither Black nor White, Lumbees occupied a precarious racial, economic, and political position. Obscurity offered protection, as it had during the migration period, and social interaction became more limited. Lumbee churches also offered a spiritual refuge.

At the same time that Lumbees perpetuated a more conservative singing style, we moved aggressively to establish a diverse worship practice and institutional role for religious life apart from both Blacks and Whites. The earliest documentation for a separate Lumbee church actually dates from 1792 – Saddletree Meeting House.[45] The second known instance was in 1854, when William Jacobs and Stephen Locklear deeded land to trustees Allen Lowrie, William Jacobs, and Jesse Oxendine for the founding of Locklears Church Congregation. The church was established on the "[e]ast side of Lumber River" and later became New Hope Church.[46] By the 1870s, Indians had established at least four other Methodist churches, and in the 1880s they formed their own Indian Methodist Conference. The Burnt Swamp Baptist Association formed in 1881 and at first included three Indian Baptist churches, which numbered fifteen by 1898. Ownership and the desire for local decision-making and control motivated Indians to formalize their own churches. Many more churches of various denominations have followed these initial efforts.[47]

We can shed light on this unique historical trajectory from less insular worship to more insular worship by using models presented by the study of Lumbee English. In analyzing Lumbee linguistic features, Natalie Schilling-Estes writes, "Contrary to popular belief about rural and otherwise marginalized communities, the Lumbee have not traveled a straightforward path from greater to lesser insularity with the progress of time." The development of Lumbee dialects causes her to believe that "insularity promotes rather than hinders innovation." She explains,

When speakers in non-insular communities come into contact with language features from varieties other than their own, linguistic confusion among forms often results, leading speakers to level out distinctions among varieties, as well as any internal heterogeneity in their own variety. . . . In isolated communities, however, there is little interference from outside dialectical systems or from unfamiliar speakers, and so it is possible to maintain and transmit quite subtle linguistic distinctions and for language changes to proceed unchecked.[48]

The isolation of the Lumbee community led to subtle distinctions in worship, akin to the development of dialect in insular communities. Similarly, the popularity of the spiritual songs that emerged from the camp meeting is like the contact between speakers in noninsular communities (in the case of spirituals, between the Black and White communities). The subtle varieties between musical forms are leveled out, and call-and-response patterns dominate religious music among both Blacks and Whites. In contrast, Indians' perpetuation of the long-meter form may have indirectly sparked a movement toward greater variation in religious worship, as represented by formal organization of various Indian churches of different denominations.

THE INFLUENCE OF SHAPE-NOTE TUNE BOOKS

Lumbees' visibility as a third race in the explicitly biracial Jim Crow era that emerged after the Civil War brought us again into greater contact with the outside world. In 1885, North Carolina officially recognized Lumbees as Indian people and established a separate school system for us.[49] The introduction of shape-note tune books was the musical manifestation of this contact. In contrast to the oral forms of long-meter and call-and-response styles, tune books were perhaps the first exclusively written form to influence Lumbee singing.

Shape-note tune books, and the singing schools that accompanied them, appeared around 1770 in New England, prior to the Second Great Awakening. George Pullen Jackson writes that they spread from New England to the South via Protestant missionaries.[50] Singing schools offered roughly organized musical instruction that often accompanied missionary efforts in frontier America. The increasing democratization of religion after the early Puritan period in New England gave rise to interdenominational forums where groups of children and adults learned to celebrate their faith through song, apart from the strict regulations of who could participate in Puritan worship. Using tune books, the Sacred Harp, Southern Harmony, and other shape-note systems were taught in these singing schools. Paradoxically, the text of some of these early shape-note hymns often celebrated the defeat or Christianizing of Indians, reflecting many of the religious and social concerns of frontier Whites.[51]

Lumbees took up shape-note singing and part-harmony enthusiastically in the late nineteenth and early twentieth centuries, probably following greater exposure to their White neighbors or to circuit-riding preachers who had been taught in the singing schools. The appeal of the shape-note system was that "a population with strong roots in traditional singing [could acquire] the simplified shape-note system of musical notation that enabled them to transform familiar tunes into three- and four-part spirituals."[52] Thus shape-note singing became a way for Lumbees to incorporate the popular spiritual style with the tunes, texts, and institutional contexts with which we were familiar.

The first documented music instruction in Robeson County's Indian community was in 1885, at Old Magnolia Church, by S. A. Lockee, an Indian man who had learned the shape-note system from a prominent White family in the county, the Prevattes.[53] The Burnt Swamp Baptist Association held the first "singing convention" in 1891, and Indian choruses from all over Robeson County participated.[54] Since that time, Indian choruses have proliferated, largely due to the ease of the shape-note system and the energy that Indians applied to forming their own singing schools and gathering regularly to sing. Instrumental accompaniment was fairly rare until the mid–twentieth century, when some Indian churches acquired pianos.

Shape-note singing did not replace the "traditional" long-meter singing, which persisted throughout this period, perhaps as an alternate form to tune-book singing. The cross-pollination of these forms, existing side-by-side in the Lumbee community, led to a distinctive experience of both "traditional" long-meter singing and the more "nontraditional" influence of tune books.

But how did "traditional" long-meter singing in Lumbee culture fare against these forces of change? Ethnomusicologist Brett Sutton's study of tune books among Black and White Primitive Baptist churches provides an appropriate model to explore how these schools influenced Lumbee long-meter singing. Primitive Baptists' insistence on orthodoxy and their relative isolation from popular trends make them somewhat analogous to Lumbee churches around 1900. Long-meter hymn singing seemed to suit Primitive Baptists, as it did the Puritans, particularly well because of their doctrine of predestination and reliance on strict interpretation of Scripture. While most Protestant churches sing part-harmony in hymns, Primitive Baptist churches sing unharmonized, like the early Puritans. In the Appalachian churches that Sutton has visited, however, each singer sings a slightly different melody than the next, creating an overall impression of heterophony rather than either monophony or strict harmony, or part-singing.[55] In his study, Sutton asks if heterophony emerged from the influence of singing schools and tune books, and he notes several differences between the use of heterophony in Black and White churches. Sutton concludes that singing schools were particularly influential among the White churches, whereas Black churches were more comfortable working within an already established oral tradition to develop a singing style that suited their culture and their religious doctrine.

Furthermore, Sutton argues that the influence of the tune books was more widely felt by White churches because the books' compilers had closer proximity to White traditions: "The occasional and nonstandardized use of harmony . . . is doubtless due to the influence of tune books, singing schools, and secular harmonizing traditions such as bluegrass."[56] In contrast, Black Primitive Baptist churches "have always preferred to work within the oral tradition and were either never exposed in a comprehensive way to the singing schools or had less interest in the reading of music in tune books than their white neighbors. Thus it is the spirituals, not tune books, that now compete with the old hymns in the black church."[57]

In this analysis, Sutton demonstrates how a popularized form such as the spiritual is passed down through oral tradition *within* the Black community, whereas in the White community, exposure to different mediums and secular forms introduces innovation. While more specific research can be undertaken in this area, we can speculate that the Lumbee adaptation of tune-book hymns corresponds more closely to what Sutton found in the Black Primitive Baptist church. Sutton's analysis of the influence of tune books on "traditional" forms in the Black Primitive Baptist church results in a perceptive observation about music in the Lumbee church and indeed the entire influence of Christianity as a "nontraditional" form: "[W]hether a tune book functioned as a support for tradition or as a source for change [in the church] depended not on the book itself so much as on the particular combination of the book and the repertory already available in the . . . tradition of the community."[58]

These three musical forms – long-meter, call-and-response, and shape-note – all combined with an available religious structure and oral tradition to create a distinctive form and experience of music in the Lumbee church. Since contact with Europeans and Africans, Lumbees have perpetuated and enriched these traditions through the use and adaptation of other forms. Christian hymns represent neither strictly a support for tradition nor a source for change among the Lumbees. Instead, they are a mechanism by which we combine the versatility and spiritual strength of the hymns with our own history of long-developed religious structure and experience.

CONCLUSION

Music is a language that is both spoken and unspoken. It brings together facets of culture that are unarticulated in daily life – gestures, migrations, stories, food, prayers, dialects, yearnings. These unspoken qualities make music a reservoir of power, a place from which individuals and communities derive guidance for appropriate behavior. Religious music, in particular, taps into these personal and cultural spaces and value systems.

The subtle power of religious music reminds us that power itself is not held as much by dominant force as it is by controlling the language we use to describe our relationships. Using a fixed, dichotomous language to describe the ever-shifting pool of religious expression excludes groups such as the Lumbees, who value the process of exchange and relationships above maintaining a strict boundary of ethnic identity. From a Lumbee perspective, holding such a strict boundary maintains the dominant paradigm of racial markers and limits the possibility of new revelations, from whatever origin, that will help us perpetuate our families, homeplace, kinship networks, and religious experience.

The transformations brought about by social and political circumstances caused Indians and Blacks to rely even more on the traditional approaches that had worked to keep their communities intact. James Merrell's "compass points" of culture retained their integrity with the help of a variety of outside musical, political, and religious influences. These communities' traditions of musical and oral transmission have survived the influences of wider society's standards, absorbing new information and reinterpreting it for the benefit of the community's continued growth.

NOTES

I am indebted to Peter Nabokov, Theda Perdue, and Judy Kertész for their revisions, research assistance, and encouragement.

The epigraph is from a videotape I made of a sermon made October 1996 at God's Holy Assembly Church, Shannon, North Carolina. There are several quotes sprinkled throughout the essay that I gathered when I was videotaping with my family in Robeson County, North Carolina. My goal in using them is to expand the reader's sense of the experience of Lumbee church music, because at the foundation of Lumbee religion and culture, experience shapes belief. Therefore, the text is transcribed in such a way as to hint at the nature of this experience for the speaker and for the hearer. There are poetics to our preaching and rhythms to our faith that are difficult to understand in a literal transcription. See Glenn Hinson, *Fire in My Bones: Transcendence and the Holy Spirit in African American Gospel* (Philadelphia: University of Pennsylvania Press, 2000), 25–26, for further information on this transcription style.

1. See Charles Hudson, *The Southeastern Indians* (Knoxville TN: University of Tennessee Press, 1976), for an analysis of this cultural amnesia.

2. J. Anthony Paredes, "Paradoxes of Modernism and Indianness in the Southeast," *American Indian Quarterly* 19, no. 3 (1995): 344.

3. Cornel West, "The Pitfalls of Racial Reasoning," in *Race Matters* (Boston: Beacon Press, 1993), 33–49.

4. In his brief essay "Black Music in North Carolina," Wilson James Bastin asserts that Africans were "detribalized" upon their arrival in the Americas and consequently were more accepting of Christianity. According to this logic, one would infer that Indians who suffered similar dislocations due to migration, warfare, and disease were not "detribalized" and therefore "naturally" resistant to Christianity. In making this assertion, Bastin crystallizes the simplistic assumption that often underlies the scholarship of Black and Indian Christian history: indigenous Africans had no ability to maintain their tribal traditions and were blank slates for missionaries, while indigenous Americans stuck to increasingly "irrelevant" tribal traditions as their world changed beyond their control. Wilson James Bastin, "Black Music in North Carolina," in *The Heritage of Blacks in North Carolina*, vol. 1, ed. Philip N. Henry and Carol M. Speas (Charlotte: North Carolina African-American Heritage Foundation, 1990), 70. See also Jon Butler, *Awash in a Sea of Faith: Christianizing the American People* (Cambridge: Harvard University Press, 1990), for his interpretation of the African spiritual holocaust.

5. Carol E. Robertson, ed., *Musical Repercussions of 1492: Encounters in Text and Performance* (Washington DC: Smithsonian Institution, 1992), 389.

6. James Merrell, *The Indians' New World: The Catawbas and Their Neighbors* (Chapel Hill: University of North Carolina Press, 1989), 45.

7. Hinson, *Fire in My Bones*, 25.

8. Julian T. Pierce et al., "The Lumbee Petition for Federal Acknowledgment" (Mary H. Livermore Library, University of North Carolina-Pembroke, 1987, photocopy), 17–18.

9. Pierce et al., "Lumbee Petition," 11. There are several excellent historical studies that realistically cast the frontier: see James Merrell, and Richard White,

The Middle Ground: Indians, Empires and Republics in the Great Lakes Region, 1650–1815 (New York: Cambridge University Press, 1991).

10. John Lawson, *Lawson's History of North Carolina* (Richmond VA: Garrett and Massie, 1937), 255. Lawson may have been referring to peoples whom we now call Tuscaroras, Tutelos, Saponis, Keyauwees, Occaneechis, and Shakoris.

11. John Reed Swanton, "Probable Identity of the 'Croatan' Indians," in *Report on the Siouan Indians of Lumber River*, 73rd Cong., 2nd sess., S. Doc. 204 (Washington DC: Government Printing Office, 1934), quoted in Pierce et al., "Lumbee Petition," 17. Swanton's own understanding of Lumbee ancestry is limited, however – he seems to have ignored some of the cultural similarities between the Lumbee and Iroquoian (Tuscarora, especially) and Mississippian groups (Cherokee).

12. Lawson, *History of North Carolina*, 186–87.

13. Lawson, *History of North Carolina*, 223–24.

14. Hudson, *Southeastern Indians*, 402–3. Hudson goes on to note that Indians' call-and-response style is also "characteristic of Negro music," but he disagrees with some scholars' suggestions that the style "represents an African influence." He cites Frances Densmore, "Choctaw Music," in Bureau of American Ethnology, *Anthropological Paper* 28, *Bulletin* 136 (1943), as advocating the African origin of call-and-response singing among southeastern Indians.

15. Eunice Cummings Chavis, interview by author, recorded, December 1996, Pembroke NC.

16. Rev. Michael Cummings, interview by author, recorded, October 1996, Pembroke NC.

17. Indians in North Carolina made their first contact with Europeans in 1524, and a steady stream of Spanish explorers came through our territory until the 1560s. The English attempted to establish a permanent colony on Roanoke Island in the 1580s. See Pierce et al., "Lumbee Petition," 3–5.

18. Swanton, "Probable Identity," 18–20.

19. William L. Saunders, ed., *The Colonial Records of North Carolina*, vol. 1 (Raleigh NC: P. M. Hale, 1886), 527; Edmund Morgan, *American Slavery, American Freedom: The Ordeal of Colonial Virginia* (New York: W. W. Norton, 1975), 239.

20. Harry Roy Merrens, *Colonial North Carolina in the Eighteenth Century: A Study in Historical Geography* (Chapel Hill: University of North Carolina Press, 1964), 18; Hugo Prosper Leaming, *Hidden Americans: Maroons of Virginia and the Carolinas* (New York: Garland, 1995), 20.

21. Freddie L. Parker, *Running for Freedom: Slave Runaways in North Carolina, 1775–1840* (New York: Garland, 1993), 33.

22. Leaming, *Hidden Americans*, 9–12; Pierce et al., "Lumbee Petition," 6–10. See also Duane Meyer, *The Highland Scots of North Carolina, 1732–1776* (Chapel

Hill: University of North Carolina Press, 1961); Malinda Maynor, "Violence and the Racial Boundary: Fact and Fiction in the Swamps of Robeson County, 1831–1871" (A.B. thesis, Harvard University, 1995).

23. Leaming, *Hidden Americans*, 9–10.

24. See Jack D. Forbes, *Africans and Native Americans: The Language of Race and the Evolution of Red-Black Peoples* (Urbana: University of Illinois Press, 1993).

25. Pierce et al., "Lumbee Petition," 159–65, 227–28.

26. George Pullen Jackson, *White and Negro Spirituals: Their Life Span and Kinship* (Locust Valley NY: J. J. Augustin, 1943), 279–82.

27. Brett Sutton, "Shape Note Tune Books and Primitive Hymns," *Ethnomusicology* 26, no. 1 (1982): 12.

28. Beverly Patterson, *The Sound of the Dove: Singing in Appalachian Primitive Baptist Churches, Music in American Life* (Urbana: University of Illinois Press, 1995), 16.

29. Elma Louise Ater, "A Historical Study of the Singing Conventions of the Indians of Robeson County, North Carolina" (master's thesis, Ohio State University, 1942), 26.

30. Jackson, *White and Negro Spirituals*, 10–11, 18–19, 279–82.

31. Joseph Michael Smith and Lula Jane Smith, *The Lumbee Methodists: Getting to Know Them* (Raleigh: Commission of Archives and History, North Carolina Methodist Conference, 1990), 61–62. More information about the Lowry family genealogy can be found in Pierce et al., "Lumbee Petition."

32. Jackson, *White and Negro Spirituals*, 17.

33. C. Eric Lincoln, "Black Religion in North Carolina: From Colonial Times to 1900," in *Black Americans in North Carolina and the South*, ed. Jeffrey J. Crow and Flora J. Hatley (Chapel Hill: University of North Carolina Press, 1984), 77.

34. Jackson, *White and Negro Spirituals*, 279–82; Dena J. Epstein, *Sinful Tunes and Spirituals: Black Folk Music to the Civil War* (Urbana: University of Illinois Press, 1977), 105–7; Alan Gallay, "Planters and Slaves in the Great Awakening," in *Masters and Slaves in the House of the Lord: Race and Religion in the American South, 1740–1870*, ed. John B. Boles (Lexington: University Press of Kentucky, 1988), 20–21.

35. Epstein, *Sinful Tunes*, 25–44; and John Lovell, *The Black Song: The Forge and the Flame* (New York: Macmillan, 1972), 63–70.

36. John Boles, *Black Southerners: 1619–1869* (Lexington: University Press of Kentucky, 1983), 147.

37. Boles, *Black Southerners*, 149.

38. Cavanagh, in Robertson, *Musical Repercussions*, 389. The power of religious experience that resists the written word is further demonstrated by the work of ethnomusicology student Elma Louise Ater. In the early 1940s, she noted the rich

and intricate harmony in Lumbee churches of long-meter hymns and commented that while Lumbees sing many of the same hymns that Appalachian mountain churches sing, "the mountaineers do not characteristically harmonize their hymn tunes." Although Appalachian churches are just as isolated as Lumbee churches, the distinct ways of worship and community influences have created different styles of singing the same texts. The equally isolated circumstances of both communities result in styles that are suited to the particular spiritual needs of each community rather than conforming to an outside standard. Ater, "Historical Study of the Singing Conventions," 24.

39. Sutton, "Shape Note Tune Books," 17–18.

40. Lincoln, "Black Religion," 76; Eileen Southern, "The Religious Occasion," in *The Black Experience in Religion*, ed. C. Eric Lincoln (Garden City NY: Anchor Press, 1974), 53.

41. Southern, "Religious Occasion," 55.

42. John B. Boles, "Evangelical Protestantism in the Old South: From Religious Dissent to Cultural Dominance," in *Religion in the Old South*, ed. Charles Reagan Wilson (Jackson: University Press of Mississippi, 1985), 29.

43. Blacks at this time were continuing to perpetuate and reinterpret African forms, such as the ring shout and Jonkonnu, "[sublimating] them into religious ritual" to coincide with the Protestant prohibitions on dancing. Southern, "Religious Occasion," 63.

44. See Maynor, "Violence and the Racial Boundary." Other communities that perpetuate long-meter hymn singing into the late nineteenth and twentieth centuries, such as the Primitive Baptists, have Calvinist religious philosophies that dictate unaccompanied hymn-singing. Lumbee ancestors' emphasis on Arminian doctrine would lead one to believe that our singing would drift more toward the spiritual songs, but on the whole we continued to develop psalmody until quite recently (and the form of long-meter music, with a song leader and familiar verse, continues today). This is a topic that bears further investigation.

45. Pierce et al., "Lumbee Petition," 41.

46. Robeson County Register of Deeds, Book CC, 120 (Robeson County Courthouse, Lumberton NC).

47. Pierce et al., "Lumbee Petition," 45; Adolph Dial and David K. Eliades, *The Only Land I Know: A History of the Lumbee Indians* (San Francisco: Indian Historian Press, 1975), 107; Smith and Smith, *Lumbee Methodists*, 11–22.

48. Natalie Schilling-Estes, "Investigating Intra-ethnic Differentiation: /ay/ in Lumbee Native American English" (forthcoming).

49. After the Civil War, the Lowry War (1864–72) also forced Lumbees to take a more active role in local and state politics. See Dial and Eliades, *Only Land I Know*; William McKee Evans, *To Die Game: The Story of the Lowry Band: Indian*

Guerillas of Reconstruction (Baton Rouge: Louisiana State University Press, 1971); and Gerald M. Sider, *Lumbee Indian Histories: Race, Ethnicity and Indian Identity in Southern United States* (New York: Cambridge University Press, 1993).

50. George Pullen Jackson, ed., *Spiritual Folk-Songs of Early America: Two Hundred and Fifty Tunes and Texts* (New York: J. J. Augustin, 1937), 23–24.

51. Jackson *Spiritual Folk-Songs*, 182–83.

52. Jackson *Spiritual Folk-Songs*, 12.

53. Ater, "Historical Study of the Singing Conventions," 19.

54. Ater, "Historical Study of the Singing Conventions," 16.

55. Sutton, "Shape Note Tune Books," 20–21.

56. Sutton, "Shape Note Tune Books," 21.

57. Sutton, "Shape Note Tune Books," 17.

58. Sutton, "Shape Note Tune Books," 18.

12. Estrangements

Native American Mascots and Indian-Black Relations

C. RICHARD KING

Near the conclusion of the 1999 college football season, ABC Sports began promoting the 2000 Nokia Sugar Bowl, pitting the Virginia Tech Hokies against the Florida State Seminoles. The main advertisement for the much anticipated national championship game to be played in New Orleans centered on the carnivalesque reputation of the host city: in the French Quarter, a multiethnic crowd of revelers parties into the night, perhaps celebrating an unnamed victory. Enlivening the carnival atmosphere of the spot, literally transforming the scene from another night of carousing in the French Quarter, are a series of Mardi Gras Indians bedecked in their finery performing amid the hoopla. To be sure, many in the audience missed the inclusion of the renowned folk artists or imagined them to be a vivid reiteration of the spectacular excesses of media, carnival, and/or sport. To viewers familiar with the Mardi Gras Indians, the advertisement may have evoked more jaded responses, confirming the insatiable appetite of the media for the new and different, underscoring the drive of popular culture to appropriate symbols and practice from marginalized peoples for mass consumption, and mapping the awkward spaces available to disenfranchised peoples in public culture.[1]

Easily overlooked in viewing the advertisement was not simply the possible significance of its content but also its connection with playing Indian at the 2000 Nokia Sugar Bowl.[2] Florida State University, which won the game, has a much celebrated, if openly contested, mascot, Osceola, a white student in racial drag and his thundering mount, who opens every home game by charging to midfield where he dramatically thrusts a flaming lance into the ground.[3] As at any home game, at the Sugar Bowl, the scattered fans donning face paint and feathers accentuated the atmosphere created as the band plays "Cherokee," a rendition of "Indian" music familiar from Hollywood soundtracks, accompanied by the mass chanting of the audience and the tomahawk chop, a repetitive arm motion in time to the music, which purportedly began at the southern school. Alumni and fans, Black and white, students and citizens, enthusiastically engaged in such practices, and the endorsement of the absent Seminole Tribe of Florida legitimated both the official and vernacular enactments at the game. At the 2000 Nokia Sugar Bowl, this tradition framed the play of two predominantly Black football teams.

Two forms of racial cross-dressing both revolving around Blacks and Blackness intersected in the staging of the 2000 Nokia Sugar Bowl: what does it mean for two football teams, largely composed of African American players, to meet in a context delimited by the intersection of a historic tradition of playing Indian at halftime and the commercialization of the Mardi Gras Indians? Both traditions share in common efforts to stage self, craft community, secure interpretations of the past, and project visions of the future through enactments of Indianness. They produce these cultural effects in decidedly different ways. Whereas, since the late nineteenth century, working-class African American men in New Orleans, organized in tribes or gangs, collectively have elaborated a folk idiom hinging on signs of Indianness (songs, language, and social organization) and individually have fashioned new sequined and feathered costumes annually for Mardi Gras parades, individuals and institutions (schools, colleges, clubs, and athletic teams), largely Euro-American, have spontaneously initiated and officially sanctioned logos, images, dances, songs, and cheers in the context of athletic contests increasingly centered on the exploits of African American bodies. Moreover, the Mardi Gras Indians, observers have argued, have assembled a counterhegemonic tradition; speaking truth to power, they stake claim to social space, recuperate collective memory, and oppose dominant cultural categories. In contrast, playing Indian at halftime has emerged over the course of the twentieth century as a privileged and powerful means of inscribing and effacing the colonization of North America, working through some of the crises of modernity, and reiterating racial hierarchies. Finally, whereas discussions of the Mardi Gras Indians have stressed the historical, genealogical, and symbolic ties between African Americans and Native Americans, accounts of mascots have largely neglected Blacks and Blackness and their relations with Indians and Indianness. Whiteness and Indianness and the relations between the two have dominated efforts to make sense of mascots. Blacks do not appear as players, fans, alumni, or activists.[4] This absence is noteworthy for two reasons. First, contemporary athletics pivots around images and exploits of African Americans. Second, Indians and Blacks as well as

Indianness and Blackness have been articulated in multiple, complex, and often contradictory ways around mascots.

Native American mascots offer important lessons about Indian-Black relations because they unsettle many taken-for-granted assumptions about these relations. They challenge us to think about the affinities and the animosities, to consider the historical circumstances and the human actions that both facilitate and discourage mutual recognition between African Americans and Native Americans. Indeed, whereas many public and scholarly discussions assume a natural affinity, if not solidarity, between marginalized peoples, the ongoing enactments of and oppositions to mascots remind us that these are social constructions emergent as people act in historically contingent social fields. Furthermore, because mascots direct our attention to the diverse, situated, and translocal relations binding Indians and Blacks, they push us beyond the rather limited perspective afforded by the Mardi Gras Indians, which paints African American Indian play as a fundamentally oppositional practice. Mascots promote the invention, refashioning, and even fracturing of identities, communities, and histories. Importantly, these processes are never monolithic and are always contradictory, for at any given moment, because all social groups are uniquely positioned in relation to domains of *difference*, racial identities necessarily are "the product of encounters between and among differently located groups."[5] Finally, mascots provide an occasion to theorize the more general structures of feeling, ideological networks, and material conditions (dis)connecting Indians and Blacks.

In focusing on Native American mascots, I want to reframe prevailing interpretations of Indian-Black relations through close readings of the images and practices that have knitted together and torn apart Blacks and Indians. I concern myself primarily with the ways in which Blacks have imagined, enacted, ignored, and opposed signs of Indianness in the domain of sports and the manner in which American Indians, in turn, have responded to such actions. Noting silences, tensions, and alliances, I not only endeavor to make sense of the uneasy locations and uneven possibilities open to Indians and Blacks but to ascertain the arrangement of social structures and signifying practices shaping them as well. Throughout, I attend to the racial identities, imaginaries, and alliances that have been elaborated and challenged, reproduced and resisted, in the context of athletic symbols and spectacles because they afford unique insights into contemporary Indian-Black relations. Indeed, examining Native American–African American relations in association with mascots permits a richer understanding of mascots and reveals a fundamental feature of current

Indian-Black relations: Native Americans and Africans Americans are linked, often only symbolically, yet, to their detriment, are also alienated and disconnected from one another. I discuss three moods or modes of interrelation: indifference and silence, playing Indian, and imperfect alliances.

TEAM SPIRITS

Native American mascots, despite recent efforts to retire them, remain a ubiquitous feature of American culture, fundamental to athletic events, individual identities, and imagined communities. Dozens of professional and semiprofessional sports teams have employed such symbols. A quarter of a century after Stanford University and Dartmouth College retired "their" Indians, the National Coalition on Racism in Sports and Media reports that more than eighty colleges and universities still use Native American mascots.[6] And countless high schools still retain such imagery, referring to themselves as the Indians, Redskins, Braves, Warriors, or Red Raiders.

Euro-Americans began to incorporate images of Indians in athletic contexts precisely because a set of social relations and cultural categories made it possible, pleasurable, and powerful. First, Euro-Americans have always fashioned individual and collective identities for themselves by playing Indian. Native American mascots were an extension of this long tradition. Second, the conquest of Native America simultaneously empowered Euro-Americans to appropriate, invent, and otherwise represent Native Americans and to long for aspects of indigenous cultures destroyed by conquest. Third, with the rise of public culture, the production of Indianness in spectacles, exhibitions, and entertainment proliferated, generating new symbolic configurations in sporting contexts.

Increasingly, mascots have been the subject of local struggles and national debate. Individuals and organizations, from high school students and teachers to the American Indian Movement (AIM) and the American Anthropological Association, have challenged the use of Native American mascots, forcing public debates and policy changes. During the past decade, school boards such as the Minnesota State Board of Education and the Los Angeles School District have mandated the alteration of offensive mascots; colleges and universities have revised (the University of Utah and Bradley University) or retired (St. John's University, the University of Miami [Ohio], and the University of Tennessee at Chattanooga) their mascots; and the Federal Trademark Commission revoked the trademark of the Washington Redskins.[7] Of course, many other schools have retained them, often generating intense protest and controversy, such as the highly visible struggle continuing to unfold at the University of Illinois at Urbana-Champaign.[8] For all the success and tumult of recent intervention, it is likely the controversy over mascots will persist given that the public still embraces them as unproblematic.[9]

INDIFFERENCE

Wichita North High School in Kansas, the alma mater of famed professional football player Barry Sanders, like many educational institutions, has retained its Native American mascot and team name, the Redskins, in the face of mounting pressure to retire it. Alumni, students, and staff at the racially diverse school maintain the symbol honors American Indians, reflecting their collective pride for the native nations of North America. Associate Principal Wardell Bell, himself of mixed African American and Cherokee ancestry, has defended the school's team name publicly against charges of racism: "I've see the real thing all my life, police stopping me, questioning me and no one else when there's lots of white people around, people staring hard at me. Trust me. . . . The Redskins name is not racism."[10] To be sure, Bell's comments express the popular sentiment that American Indian mascots generally and the Redskins team name particularly are not offensive or problematic, but more important, he articulates the most prominent response of African Americans to such symbols and spectacles.[11] Many, if not most, African Americans are indifferent to mascots; they do not give them a second thought when reading the sports page or watching an athletic event, or if they do have problems, they remain silent. As significant and common as these moments are, it is difficult to access or analyze them. Thus, while the support of countless Black fans is noteworthy, the positions and entanglements of African American athletes are more remarkable, if only for their visibility.

In the late 1960s, even as the Civil Rights movement reshaped race relations in American culture, at Florida State University (FSU) sports teams were ostensibly inspired by a tradition of playing Indian on the field and in the stands and by large numbers of spectators brandishing the Confederate flag, often while the band chimed "Dixie." Actually, Rebel banners had become ubiquitous at sporting contests and other public events in the

Deep South ever since the 1940s – with the start of the eventual collapse of a segregated Jim Crow society of southern states. These expressions of nostalgia for a bygone era of de jure white supremacy served to further complicate the racial spectacle at FSU athletic events, as members of a mostly white audience played at being Indian – with face paint and feathers – while also asserting a version of whiteness marked by Rebel paraphernalia. Meanwhile, the presence of African Americans was confined to the playing field, even if more frequently it was a presence more likely noted on the opposing team (given FSU's tardiness to integrate its sports teams).

In October 1968, in the wake of the recent formation of the Afro-American Student Union, an alleged racial incident occurred at a football game that sparked a number of protests by African American students.[12] Using his lit cigarette, a white student burned holes in the shirt of a Black student. This white student was a member of a fraternity that used the Confederate flag as a symbol, and members of this fraternity were responsible for a number of incidents in which Confederate flags were waved in the faces of Black students. The Black victim confronted his attacker, but security officers removed both students from the stadium before a fight could occur. However, the officers did not take the names of the students, and an officer discouraged the Black student from filing a complaint. A white student, in support of the Black student, attempted to identify the officer's badge number and was promptly arrested.

In response, the Afro-American Student Union issued a number of demands, including that the incident be investigated by the administration and that Black security officers and more Black faculty be hired. The demand that stirred the most controversy, however, was a request that the school band stop playing "Dixie" and that students stop displaying the Confederate flag. The administration did make some effort to appear to respond to the students' demands, first by investigating the incident at the football game and dropping charges against the arrested student, and then by actually meeting with and talking to representatives of the Afro-American Student Union. Regarding the matter of the Confederate symbols, university president John Champion was reluctant to order students to desist from carrying the flag because it might infringe upon their rights of expression. His suggestion that the "Battle Hymn of the Republic" be played immediately following "Dixie" was unacceptable to the group.

By the time the Afro-American Student Union had been renamed the Black Student Union (BSU) in the fall of 1969, the enrollment of African

Americans had increased to between three hundred and four hundred.[13] The new BSU president was John Burt, a junior; particularly noteworthy, he was also a scholarship member of the basketball team. Of the team's twelve players, eight were African American, including four of the five starters. Burt, however, was not merely a token leader chosen for his popularity as an athlete. On the contrary, during the tenure of his two-year leadership, the BSU greatly advanced its campus presence and political power. His identities as a student and as a person of color superseded his identity as an athlete. "If you have to give up your manhood to be a basketball player," Burt reasoned, "then basketball isn't worth anything. If you can't be a man, and if you can't have dignity, then you're nothing."[14]

Burt encouraged his teammates to strive to maintain politically relevant voices, reminding them that "whatever happen[ed] to those students in the Black Student Union [was] also going to happen to [Black athletes]."[15] One of the first concerns tackled by the BSU under Burt's leadership was the segregated cheerleading squad. Although many Black women had auditioned to be cheerleaders, none had ever been selected. At the urging of Black players, the FSU athletic department finally added a Black woman, Gail Andrews, to the squad. However, a number of games had passed and Andrews still had not been allowed to cheer on the court.[16] On 27 January 1970, the popular rivalry between FSU and Jacksonville University would resume in a statewide televised match. As the game approached, Burt consulted with the Black basketball players, and all eight agreed to confront the coach. They made it clear that they would refuse to play unless a Black woman appeared as an FSU cheerleader during the game. Andrews indeed made her first of many appearances during the Jacksonville game, and the cheerleading squad soon became more fully integrated. This incident reveals the power student athletes wield, often unwittingly, as a result of their importance to a lucrative system of spectacle and sport. This platform would seem to be especially important to African American students since their presence, on the field and on the court, has so often provided the key aspect of "Blackness" to these performances.

The events at FSU are noteworthy, if easily forgotten, moments in the broader Civil Rights movement. African American athletes animated the shifts within public culture at FSU. Importantly, even as they agitated against the racist symbols of the Old South and their effects, however, they ignored the equally repugnant uses and understandings of Indianness. Their understandings of race and racial politics remained myopic. They could not grasp the connection between their disenfranchisement, stereotypical uses and understandings of Indians, and white supremacy as both a set of structural relations and as a collection of symbols and sentiments.

Although the political role of African American athletes has softened with the de-emphasis of the Civil Rights movement and commercialization of the Black sporting body, African American athletes have had occasion to address racial asymmetry within and beyond the domain of sports. For instance, in April 1998, the Presidential Commission on Race examined the articulations of race and sports. Televised on ESPN, the event afforded a unique opportunity for African American athletes, including legendary running back and social activist Jim Brown and basketball great Patrick Ewing, to discuss the racial stratification of contemporary sports. Not surprisingly, they commented on the exploitation of the Black athlete, the broader milieu of marginalization, and the underrepresentation of Blacks in administrative roles. Significantly, all present remained silent about Native American mascots.

More recently, an interview in *Sports Illustrated* with John Rocker, then a relief pitcher with the Atlanta Braves, sparked a moral outrage about the lingering sediment of racial ideologies in sports. Rocker, in a voice inflected with rage and disgust, made disparaging comments about gays, crime, and women but saved his most acerbic rhetoric for racial and ethnic groups. He described his feelings for New York City, home to bitter rivals, the Yankees and the Mets, in xenophobic terms: "The biggest thing I don't like about New York are the foreigners. I'm not a very big fan of foreigners. You can walk an entire block in Times Square and not hear anybody speak English. Asians and Koreans and Vietnamese and Indians and Russians and Spanish people and everything up there. How the hell did they get in this country?" More familiar prejudice emerged in his conversation as well. He nonchalantly referred to one of his Black teammates as "a fat monkey." And he read the treatment received by professional basketball player Latrell Sprewell following his much publicized choking of his coach as evidence of a racial double standard and even reverse discrimination.[17]

A massive outcry followed Rocker's comments. Commentators, fans, and even politicians immediately criticized the young athlete for his views, dismissing his racism as individual prejudice. Among the most prominent critics of Rocker was Hank Aaron, a former baseball player famous for career home-run record and now an executive with the Braves. On a sports talk show on One-on-One Sports Radio, he commented: "I played for 23 years and had everything under the sun happen to me, like most Black players. But never has anything happened to me that made me feel like I did reading that in *Sports Illustrated*. When I first read that, I was sick, absolutely sick. I thought we had passed the stage where things like that were no longer tolerated."[18] Aaron, like many Americans, believed racism to be a thing of the past and was shocked by Rocker's sentiments. In fact, he had a very visceral reaction to the interview: it sickened him. At the same time, African American community members and political organizations denounced Rocker's comments, demanding his resignation, asking the Braves to fire him, and calling for official condemnation of his comments. Following much public debate and formal apologies from Rocker, the Braves, and others to offended parties; disciplinary action by both the Braves and Major League Baseball Incorporated; and a series of media panics, as when Rocker made his first appearance in New York City after the interview, the young reliever remained an integral part of Atlanta's baseball team until traded to the Cleveland Indians in the summer of 2001. Also still in place, although not the subject of public outcries, corporate contrition, or official sanctions, were the legitimate and popular versions of Indianness associated with the Atlanta baseball team – the franchise name incorporating a stone tomahawk; an image of a regal, defiant, and strong whooping warrior; and fans engaging in the infamous tomahawk chop and war chant, with many of them wielding oversized foam tomahawks. Indeed, apparently lost on Aaron and other critics was that Rocker played for the Atlanta Braves. Their actions and comments suggest that on the one hand many African Americans, in common with the majority of Euro-Americans, understand stereotypical representations of African Americans and immigrants to be false, denigrating, and damaging, while on the other hand they believe teams' Indian names and mascots to be harmless, ennobling, and fun.

RACIAL CROSS-DRESSING

If many African Americans take Native American mascots for granted, as natural symbols of fun and identification, others have embraced the pleasures and possibilities of playing Indian at halftime. Surely, African American fans and alumni identify with the traditional uses of Indianness employed by their favorite teams or alma mater, and some even passionately defend them as respectful and honorific. Jerry Strothers, an activist of mixed heritage in the Cleveland area, reports that in conversations with friends and debates with supporters of Chief Wahoo, the Cleveland Indians mascot, Blacks and whites contend, "There is nothing offensive about Wahoo," or worse, "It is an honor, you people should be proud of it."[19] In common with their Euro-American counterparts, moreover, some African American fans and athletes have seized upon popular uses and understandings of Indianness to fashion individual and collective identities. Black players frequently find themselves entangled in promotional stunts and media events employing symbols and motifs thought to embody Indianness. In the early 1990s, for instance, members of the National Football League's Kansas City Chiefs' defense posed for a charity poster. Each athlete donned regalia, including feathers and face paint, and was given an "Indian" name as well.

Black fans also often eagerly embrace Indian play. On any given Sunday that the Washington Redskins and the Kansas City Chiefs play a home game, one can find African Americans not only on the field but in the stands singing the team fight songs, participating in war chants and other antics such as the tomahawk chop, some dressed in feathers and others donning war paint, all cheering "their" Indians to victory. For some, the pleasures and possibilities of identification, of staging self through an imagined other, become so powerful as to be all encompassing. In January 2000, one such fan was inducted into the Visa Hall of Fans at the National Football League Hall of Fame in Canton, Ohio. Zema "Chief Zee" Williams, like all other inductees, was selected for his enthusiasm for and dedication to his local team, his integral role in boosting player morale, and his contribution to the sport. Chief Zee has worn a Plains headdress and red buckskin shirt to all Washington Redskins home games since 1978. He has become something of an unofficial mascot for the town and the team. He engages in colorful antics, particularly when the Redskins play the Dallas Cowboys, to excite the crowd. He has been more than a mere cheerleader. After the offensive line was playfully nicknamed "the Hogs," for example, he regularly brought a hog to home games. This Black man cross-dressing as an Indian came to symbolize Washington DC as well when 7 November 1985 was officially dubbed Chief Zee Day.[20]

Playing Indian has produced tense moments as well, which begin to reveal the complex meanings of racial cross-dressing. Jay Rosenstein's film *In Whose Honor?* captures one such incident.[21] Native American activist Charlene Teters, protesting the continued uses of Indian icons and imagery by the Washington Redskins franchise and its fans, encounters a Black vendor who is wearing a huge Plains-style feathered headdress and face paint and is peddling Redskins merchandise. She rather aggressively questions the man's motives, precipitating a shouting match between the two.

The vendor, yelling over Teters, exclaims, "I love your people. Your blood is the same as mine. I have nothing against you. I am not making fun of you . . . the dollars is what I am concerned with . . . it comes down to one simple thing, dollars, money." Following his departure, Teters, in tears, laments, "It is the same as if I were dressed in blackface . . . it symbolizes our chief and he is turning it into a mascot." As Teters's response makes plain, when Blacks play Indian, whether for fun or profit, it still hurts. In fact, for many Native Americans, it is more painful and problematic to witness African Americans and other marginalized groups familiar with the impact of racial stereotypes, if not the history of racial oppression secured through such representations, appropriating aspects of their heritage and imitating them through stereotypes.[22]

As common as such displays and discord have become, they are fleeting, spontaneous, and/or individual efforts. In at least one instance, however, African Americans have elaborated a tradition of playing Indian in an institutional context under their control. Students, alumni, and administrators at Alcorn State University (ASU), the first Black land-grant institution, established in 1871 in Lorman, Mississippi, have taken great pleasure in imaging themselves in racial drag within and beyond athletic spectacles. The historically Black college, built on the grounds of Oakland College, an antebellum school for planters' sons, was to be modeled after the University of Mississippi, but indifference, segregation, inadequate funding, and racist policies made such aspirations nearly impossible to attain. While the school fielded an independent baseball team four years after its founding, it did not begin competing in intercollegiate athletics until 1890. In about a quarter century, its teams were known as the Braves. The origins of the name remain unclear; it appears, however, to have coincided with the inauguration of football in the early 1920s. A robust tradition of incorporating Indianness had crystallized by the 1930s. A succession of Indian symbols have been created to represent the school and its athletic teams, and a student in Indian attire has long played Indian at halftime. In the past, fans have dressed in feathers; they still perform the tomahawk chop and do a war whoop at games when the band plays "Cherokee." The campus came to be popularly known as "the academic reservation" or just "the reservation"; students, alumni, and fans have resisted recent efforts to rename the campus "the academic resort." The administration recognizes the ongoing discussion of mascots but has yet to seriously consider changing the name or otherwise revising the uses and understandings of Indianness on campus, at least in part because there has been no real pressure to do so.[23]

Of course, the name "Braves," as several administrators noted, is not meant to offend or be derogatory; there is no racist intent. Whether intended or not, the symbols and practices observed during Homecoming festivities in October 1999 suggest a rather more complex situation

Homecoming at ASU, like many colleges and universities, is a week-long series of events, including the coronation of queen and court, step show (a series of synchronized dance routines), bonfire, and pep rally. Undoubtedly, the parade is among the most vibrant and popular activities. Several thousand African Americans and perhaps a dozen Euro-Americans (students, administrators, and alumni, along with local fans and supporters) attend the annual happening, which snakes through the campus grounds. The 1999 parade brought together a surprising array of groups, interests, and messages: a few floats, a pair of Cub Scout troops, several Reserve Office Training Corps (ROTC) groups from surrounding communities, a steady stream of young women representing various campus organizations (sororities, scholastic, residence halls, and extracurricular) in the Miss Alcorn Pageant, a handful of candidates for local offices, and countless marching bands. Indian motifs animated the parade. At the center of the parade route, a collection of mostly young sorority women encouraged others to "Become a Brave, get your face painted." An impressive truck was perhaps the most flamboyant expression of local attitudes toward Indians and Indianness. Painted in glittery purple and gold and adorned with arrowheads and several striking profiles of southeastern Indian heads, the vehicle featured an epic, polychromatic interpretation of *The End of the Trail*. Arguably the highlight of the parade was the ASU marching band, dubbed "The Sounds of Dynamite." A quartet of drum majors, "The Fantastic Four," led the procession, followed in turn by a drill team and the rather massive band. Images evoking Indianness emblazoned the front and back of their uniforms. A tomahawk imposed on the ASU logo appears on the front, while on the back a more intricate design situates an Indian head between the band's name. Sounds of dynamite and a pair of tomahawks cross at the bottom. Intermixed with the drill team was a student dressed as a brave.

The Homecoming game pitted the Prairie View A&M Panthers against the ASU Braves. Although not a sellout, perhaps as many as ten thousand fans were in attendance, most in the school colors of purple and gold. And while tailgating and the marching band appeared to attract as many adherents as the football team, Indianness clearly centered the spectacle. According to tradition, during warm-up drills, as the ASU players run and turn, they mark the transition with a tomahawk chop. After scoring a touchdown, the marching band plays "Cherokee" and fans do the toma-hawk chop while letting out a series of syncopated war whoops. To urge their team on or celebrate a good play and at the behest of the marching band, fans cheer, "Hooah! Hooah! Hooah! Let's Go!" Throughout, the mascot entertains the crowd and cheers the Braves. He dresses in a purple tunic and pants, fringed in yellow. Atop his shoulders he wears an en-larged fiberglass head with long, black hair and a menacing grin on his face. Standing along the sidelines with cheerleaders, he makes fun, does funny antics, dances, and entertains. There is nothing authentic about the outfit, appearance, or antics; nor is there any pretense of authenticity. Little effort is made to authenticate. The dance appears to be spontaneous or at least improvised, incorporating elements of hip-hop, break, and other modern dances. After each touchdown when the cheerleaders do push-ups, the mascot feigns inability and playfully fails.

Outside the stadium, overlapping renderings of Indianness continue to anchor the local formulations of identity and community. Multiple Indians populate the ASU campus. In addition to the T-shirts, hats, and other memorabilia, the mascot and marching band, and the parking decals, the Health, Physical Education, and Recreation Building contains two addi-tional Indians: a Southeast-style Indian head on the floor and a Plains-style Indian head logo on plaques noting inductees in the ASU Sports Hall of Fame. A display case in the library contains several items that reinforce these patterns: a football helmet with a Southeast-style Indian head on it, a miniature golden football with a Plains motif Indian head, a baseball cap again with an Indian head in Southeast style, and a "scalpin'" scarf – white towel with purple lettering. T-shirts, moreover, frequently contain images of Indians, invariably an Indian head, most often in profile. These are monochromatic and polychromatic images, usually more or less realistic, most frequently in southeastern style – braids, one or more feathers, face painted for war, occasionally a war whoop à la the fans of the Atlanta Braves. Hats, car flags, and parking decals follow a similar pattern. They also incorporate other markers of Indianness, tomahawks primarily. Other T-shirts bearing phrases like "Hooah Wartime" and "Always ready to rum-ble" restage self through romantic, bellicose, and ultimately hypermascu-line renderings of Indianness. Occasionally, the surrounding community draws upon this tradition. One such poster giving the "ASU Scalping Braves" schedule includes a line drawing of a feather-fringed tomahawk in the background. The geographic remoteness of ASU, perhaps combined with the fact that it is a historically Black institution, undermines deep imprecation between campus and community. Only one example is visible.

The eatery adjacent to the campus's north gate has Alcorn with a toma-hawk painted on its corrugated roof. Importantly, Indianness is not the exclusive means of imagining/imaging ASU; as with many schools, some version of the school's name is used frequently, as is a stylized rendering of the Oaklawn Chapel pillars. Indianness is, however, the preferred and the most pleasurable and powerful means for individuals at ASU to imagine themselves.

PROMISES, PROMISES

To this point, I have described two key relations between African Ameri-cans and Native Americans in association with American Indian mascots, playing Indian and indifference. Both of these sets of relations are largely symbolic; they do not involve physical relations between Indians and Blacks, but rather entail relations between African American actors and imagined Indians. A third set of relations exists that is fully embodied, hinging on the lived relations, encounters, efforts, and exchanges between African American and Native American agents. Although much less com-mon, Indians and Blacks have forged alliances against Native American mascots. Undoubtedly, some African American individuals (it is impossi-ble to count) have long sympathized with and actively participated in efforts to retire particular mascots. For instance, Black students, in collab-oration with their Indian, white, and Latino peers, have played an impor-tant role in efforts to retire Chief Illiniwek at the University of Illinois at Urbana-Champaign. Similar informal and individual commitments have marked protests in the Cleveland area against the local Major League baseball franchise, and throughout the 1990s, whenever the World Series or Super Bowl has featured teams with Native American mascots, protests have been integrated. More tangible have been the linkages among politi-cal organizations with diverse membership and agendas. More often than not, the construction of solidarity between Native Americans and African Americans occurs largely on the local level. In many cases these have been cooperative endeavors, as in August 1999 when the National Peoples Democratic Uhuru Movement and African Peoples Solidarity Committee joined with the Florida chapter of AIM to stage protests against the Cleve-land Indians when they played the Tampa Bay Devil Rays.[24]

On other occasions, African American political organizations have acted independently. At its 21 April 1998 monthly meeting, the Cham-paign County (Illinois) Branch of the National Association for the Advancement of Colored People (NAACP) passed a resolution opposing the use of Native American mascots at the University of Illinois at Urbana-Champaign. The resolution was impressive for its scope and vision, calling upon

- the University of Illinois Urbana-Champaign President and Chancellor to take a public stance against "Chief" Illiniwek;
- the University of Illinois Board of Trustees to retire "Chief" Illiniwek;
- the Governor of the State of Illinois to use his influence to retire "Chief" Illiniwek and other racist mascots and symbols throughout the state;
- the State Legislature to create and pass legislation that rejects the use of historically oppressed people and their cultural traditions as sports mascots and symbols, and affirms their commitment to respectful racial and cultural inclusion in all aspects of public life;
- other predominately African American community institutions and organizations to join the NAACP in public opposition to "Chief" Illiniwek and other racist mascots and symbols;
- African American community members to refrain from purchasing items with the "Chief" logo and to cross out the logo on apparel already in their possession

In a press conference, members of the Champaign County branch argued that they were affirming the core values of the NAACP and taking a stand against racist attitudes that had residual effects upon African Americans in the broader community. The branch member Abdul El Jamal, moreover, "reminded members of the historic political and familial relationships between African Americans and Native Americans, as well as their parallel struggles to define and name themselves in the face of pervasive, unrelenting racial stereotypes."[25]

For their part, Native Americans have long sought to alert African Americans of the racial politics of mascots. For nearly thirty years, activists have used analogy and juxtaposition to foster recognition among Black (and white) individuals of the dehumanizing symbols and illegitimate power central to the tradition of playing Indian at halftime. In his biting essay "Tribal Names and Mascots in Sports," Dennis Banks, a founding member of AIM, poses the uncomfortable query: "The Cleveland Indians or the Atlanta Braves – why not change their names to the Niggers? I wonder how many blacks would play for them (or whites for that matter)."[26] A leading opponent of Native American mascots, Charlene Teters compares mascots to "'Black Sambo' or the 'Frito Bandito.'"[27] Jeffrey

Newman, assistant director of the Association for American Indian Affairs, who drew on racial analogy nearly thirty years ago to critique Chief Noc-a-Homa, then the mascot of the Atlanta Braves, offers a final example of this political strategy: "It is outrageous, I feel, to have a man dressed as an Indian, sitting in an alleged tepee outside the outfield fence, doing a silly dance every time some player hits a home run . . . would they hire a black man to sit in a tar paper shack out there and come out picking cotton every time a player hit a home run? No, they wouldn't dare." Newman lamented the ease with which young and old rooted for the Washington Redskins, when they "wouldn't think of calling a team the 'Blackskins' or the 'Yellowskins.'"[28] Activists have not only sought to hail individual African Americans through juxtaposition, but they have on occasion employed this strategy to address political organizations as well. Dissatisfied with the unwillingness of either the local or national offices of the NAACP to support their efforts to change the Wichita North High School Redskins name and mascot, Matthew Richter and Clem Iron Wing created an elaborate and nuanced Web page asserting that the NAACP was a racist organization.[29] The multimedia site incorporates familiar analogies and introduces a series of novel linkages: mock helmets for the Washington Blackskins, Sambo beside Chief Wahoo, a photograph of a lynching paired with a photograph of Chief Bigfoot following the massacre at Wounded Knee. The accompanying text unpacks and extends these themes. Undoubtedly, the site is, by turns, inflammatory, sincere, and effective (see below). Taken together, juxtaposition makes race tangible, marks oppression, and ultimately calls upon African Americans (and others) to challenge mascots.[30]

To be sure, the recognition of mutual oppression embedded in Native American mascots and the sorts of alliances built in opposition to them offer a promising, hopeful opening for counterhegemonic politics; they often also are promissory, unfulfilled, rhetorical commitments expressing the difficulties of racial solidarity in post–civil rights America. In Cleveland, according to local activists, the local branch of the NAACP publicly condemned the continued use of Chief Wahoo by the Cleveland Indians on a radio talk show, only to disavow the condemnation the following day. Jerry Strothers even suggested that "the lame NAACP in Cleveland is fully against our efforts."[31] More broadly, the NAACP, on the national level, has been both reserved and evasive in struggles against Native American mascots. At least rhetorically, the organization has taken a strong stance against mascots. It has passed two resolutions against mascots, the most recent at its annual meeting in 1999. In the words of Kwesi Mfume, president of the NAACP, the organization "strongly opposes the use of Native American people, images, symbols, and cultural and religious traditions as sports names, logos, and mascots."[32] Despite this position, it has refused to support local movements against mascots. Indeed, although purportedly opposed to such signs and stagings of Indianness, it has not advocated or assisted in concrete efforts to retire specific mascots. The organization's very public role in other struggles over racial signs, most notably its ongoing crusade against the Confederate flag, heightens the tensions between its words and its deeds. While Native American activists I spoke with supported the antiracist interventions of the NAACP, they were deeply troubled by the organization's silence and inaction. In fact, it was the NAACP's failure to respond to efforts to remove the Redskins as the team name of Wichita North High School that prompted Matthew Richter and Clem Iron Wing to charge that the NAACP was a racist organization. And it may have been the negative publicity generated by the Web page that facilitated the recent decision of the NAACP and its Wichita branch to enter the controversy. Clearly, alliances between Native Americans and African Americans have great promise in struggles against mascots; however, too often this promise remains unrealized, dashed by narrow agendas and competing interests.

CONCLUSION

Indian-Black relations around Native American mascots display multiple, conflicted interpretations of race, culture, and history. African Americans have embraced and ignored mascots, remained silent about them and romanticized them, created and contested them, taken pleasure in them and taken to the streets against them. These (dis)engagements with Indianness in locales as diverse as Wichita, Washington DC, Atlanta, Cleveland, Kansas City, New Orleans, Tallahassee, and Lorman, Mississippi, outline three prevailing ways of relating to and through Indianness: indifference, mimicry, and affiliation.

Although indifference, the refusal to question the signs and spectacles of Indianness central to Native American mascots, and mimicry, the celebration of Indian play, are distinct modes of Indian-Black relations, the two intersect in important ways around questions of irreflexivity, identity, and imagination. Thus I will consider the two together. Whereas indifference accepts existing means and meanings of playing Indian at halftime, mimicry enacts and even invents novel signs and performances. Mimicry and indifference clear a space in which African Americans not only accept imagined Indians as natural facts – playful, idealized, renderings devoid of cultural significance or empirical grounding – but also often know themselves and their social worlds through them. They adopt these images as unproblematic, incorporating them as meaningful markers not of embodied Indians and their histories but as symbols of power and powerful symbols through which to name themselves and their experiences, to cultivate pleasures and fulfill desires, and to participate in public culture as equals.

In contrast, efforts to forge alliances between African Americans and Native Americans turn on embodied relationships. They emphasize the shared circumstances uniting Indians and Blacks, particularly a history of oppression, ongoing racism, and persistent co-optation. The interpersonal relations and mutual vision grounding movements against mascots call into question the social structures and cultural categories legitimating these signs and spectacles as well as the racial imaginaries and injuries central to them. Animating opposition to mascots have been efforts to alert African Americans (and others) to their significance, particularly through racial analogies that recall the oppression of African Americans. And while indifference and mimicry appear to be more or less secure as ways of relating to and through (imagined) Indians, alliances remain especially emergent, fragile, and imperfect.

At the heart of Indian-Black relations around Native American mascots are the problems and possibilities of recognition. Often, in fact, mascots facilitate, even demand, misrecognition. Many African Americans remain unable or unwilling to see, touch, feel, and know racial politics of mascots or imagine social justice outside the bounds of Black and white. Neither Chief Zee nor students, fans, and administrators at Alcorn State University seem aware of the effects of their enactments or the marginal positions they share with the Native Americans they misrepresent in their performances. More pronounced perhaps is the mass reservation of Blacks, exemplified by the pregnant silence of fans and the refusals of African American athletes and activists to speak out against dehumanizing images of American Indians, even as they challenge racist sentiments. African Americans and Native Americans do not see one another; they likely do not know the shared histories joining them and cannot identify the conditions presently uniting and dividing them. Against this background, activism and organizing have sought to make race tangible, power legible, and history meaningful. Above all else, Native American and African American activists not only struggle against mascots but struggle to make them recognizable as cultural constructs, charged with privilege, pleasure, and pain. The overwhelming estrangement and emergent rapprochement characterizing the relations between Native Americans and African Americans is both imposed and embraced, part forgetfulness, part erasure. Consequently, I propose a dialectical understanding attuned to both the import of sociocultural formations and to the creativity of human subjects, arguing that a historically situated constellation of "signs and practices, relations and distinctions, images and epistemologies" shapes the contours and possibilities of human action – here, the ways in which individuals insert themselves within spectacular stagings of Indianness.[33]

bell hooks has suggested that the contemporary disconnections between Indians and Blacks derive from historic processes of dislocation, primarily the forced relocation and confinement of Native Americans in the nineteenth and the later mass migration of African Americans to northern cities and the alienation fostered by mass mediated stereotypes.[34] Although somewhat simplistic and overly romantic, hooks helpfully reminds us that the present estrangement is the product of human work in particular sociohistorical fields. Five structural factors begin to account for the prevailing misrecognition in the context of Native American mascots. First, African Americans and Native Americans occupy very different positions in the contemporary United States; thus Black players, fans, and administrators often do not share the same interests or objectives and when they do cannot articulate this mutual condition. Second, many younger African Americans do not remember overt stereotypes of Blacks or popular misappropriations of Blackness and thus lack an appreciation for what it means to be mocked.[35] Third, inundated with mass culture, many African Americans, like others in American society, accept stereotypical images as authentic, faithful, and true. In fact, Blacks may have a more romantic understanding of Indianness than do their white counterparts: a recent survey found that a plurality of Blacks would prefer to be American Indians, 35 percent of African Americans compared with 20 percent of Euro-Americans.[36] Fourth, it is not simply that African Americans reiterate dominant interpretations of Native Americans. Rather, they have revised and reinterpreted them in light of their sociohistorical positions. Discussing the attractiveness of Indianness to Blacks in New Orleans and particularly the emergence of the Mardi Gras Indians, Joseph Roach has succinctly observed, "Those a generation away from slavery, exiled from a home they would never know, could identify with Native Americans, bitter exiles in their own land. The slave-holding propensities of the Five Civilized Tribes (so-called by whites in part *because* they held slaves) emphasize the double, inverted nature of the Indian as a symbol for African Americans: the nonwhite sign of both power and disinheritance."[37] Finally, African Americans in general seem to subscribe to the predominant understanding of culture and semiosis that suggests that Native American mascots are insignificant, trivial, and natural. The irreflexivity facilitated by this perspective obfuscates mascots and the work of other racially charged representations as well. For instance, it shapes the debate over Confederate symbols. Although individuals and organizations in some communities with high schools named to honor heroes of the Confederacy and former slave owners or that have team names such as the Rebels have endeavored to change them, for many African American students, staff, and athletes at such institutions, these signs are "unimportant," unproblematic.[38] Together, these structural factors not only promote a misrecognition of Native Americans and the linkages binding African Americans to them, but also transfigure and shroud power.

Of course, neither African Americans nor Native Americans are cultural dupes, manipulated by dominant discourses. Instead, in association with mascots, they actively relate to and through (images of) one another to produce identity and dignity, to claim and counter authority and privilege. At root, under circumstances not of their own making, they creatively engage prevailing signs and structures. The efforts of Blacks and Indians to forge multiethnic coalitions for social justice clearly exemplify this creative agency. Protests and proclamations seek to speak truth to power, while racial juxtaposition draws upon the experience and understanding of the African American experience to challenge mascots and hail Blacks. Less comfortable may be assertions that the mimicry and indifference associated with playing Indian also actively engage power. In this light, mimicry cannot be read as mockery, particularly when African Americans mimic Native Americans. It is, in fact, an active borrowing. Chief Zee appropriates a popular idiom of Indianness to fashion himself, command prestige, and shape social relations. Similarly, at Alcorn State University, the tradition of playing Indian borrows power to proclaim the validity of Blackness in a remote context, foster community, and enliven the remote campus's public culture. More significantly, these appropriations are borrowings of whiteness and white power: white versions of Indianness, the noble warrior, for instance; the very symbols invented in white contexts, such as the use of the song "Cherokee," the tomahawk chop, and images that appear to be nearly exact copies from regional teams with Indian mascots, particularly the Atlanta Braves; and the power and privileges of Indian play. Finally, the most circumscribed response to power would be indifference. Many Blacks exhibit indifference not simply because they have been absorbed into the mass and thus accepted aspects of the dominant ideology but rather because they have adapted to the unevenness of the social field.[39] Remaining indifferent to mascots, they may assert their whiteness, reassure themselves that race and racism are historical artifacts, declare their Americanness, and/or ensure the success of specific political projects.[40] Indifference allows them to reclaim themselves in the rather limited terms of dominant culture and cope with these limitations.

If estrangement hinges on the misrecognition of interconnectedness and on the transparency of power, recognition of the arbitrariness of power and the symbols that legitimate it is central to its undoing. Indeed, as Pierre Bourdieu has argued, "what creates the power of words and slogans [and by extension representations more generally], a power capable of maintaining or subverting social order, is the belief in the legitimacy of words and those who utter them."[41]

NOTES

Research for this essay was made possible by a generous grant from the Drake University Humanities Center. Matthew Richter, David Sansing, Jerry Strothers, Rudolph Waters Jr., and Roy Wenzl were kind enough to share with me their understandings of Indian-Black relations in specific contexts and at times valuable primary documents. I doubt whether the essay would have been conceivable without their assistance. Charles F. Springwood and Marcie Gilliland provided intellectual support and critical suggestions. Finally, Gary Dunham and James Brooks are to be applauded for their encouragement and patience.

1. A massive literature has examined the history and significance of the Mardi Gras Indians. See Samuel Kinser, *Carnival, American Style: Mardi Gras at New Orleans and Mobile* (Chicago: University of Chicago Press, 1990), 151-94; Kinser, "Violence Ritually Enjoined: The Mardi Gras Indians of New Orleans," *Cahiers de Littérature Orale* 37: 115–50; George Lipsitz, "Mardi Gras Indians: Carnival and Counter-Narratives in Black New Orleans," in *Time Passages: Collective Memory and Popular Culture* (Minneapolis: University of Minnesota Press, 1993), 233–91; Laura L. Lovett, "'African and Cherokee by Choice': Race and Resistance under Legalized Segregation," *American Indian Quarterly* 22, nos. 1–2 (1999): 203–29; Reid Mitchell, "Mardi Gras Indians," in *All on Mardi Gras Day: Episodes in the History of New Orleans Carnival* (Cambridge: Harvard University Press, 1995), 113–30; Joseph Roach, "Mardi Gras Indians and Others: Genealogies of Ameri-

can Performance," *Theatre Journal* 44 (1992): 461–83; Michael P. Smith, *Mardi Gras Indians* (Grenta LA: Pelican Publishing, 1994); and Smith, *Spirit World: Pattern in the Express Folk Culture of AfroAmerican New Orleans* (New Orleans: New Orleans Urban Folklife Society, 1984), 81–105.

2. Dennis Banks, "Tribal Names and Mascots in Sports," *Journal of Sport and Social Issues* 17, no. 1 (1993): 5–8; Ward Churchill, "Let's Spread the Fun Around," in *Indians Are Us? Culture and Genocide in Native North America* (Monroe, ME: Common Courage Press, 1994), 65–72; Rosemary J. Coombe, "Sports Trademarks and Somatic Politics: Locating the Law in a Critical Cultural Studies," in *SportCult*, ed. Randy Martin and Toby Miller (Minneapolis: University of Minnesota Press, 1999), 262–88; Laurel Davis, "Protest Against the Use of Native American Mascots: A Challenge to Traditional, American Identity," *Journal of Sport and Social Issues* 17, no.1 (1993): 9–22; C. Richard King and Charles Fruehling Springwood, eds., *Team Spirits: Essays on the History and Significance of Native American Mascots* (Lincoln: University of Nebraska Press, 2001); Cornell D. Pewewardy, "Native American Mascots and Imagery: The Struggle of Unlearning Indian Stereotypes," *Journal of Navaho Education* 9, no. 1 (1991): 19–23; L. Sigelman, "Hail to the Redskins? Public Reactions to a Racially Insensitive Team Name," *Sociology of Sport Journal* 15, no. 4 (1998): 317–25; Synthia S. Slowikowski, "Cultural Performances and Sports Mascots," *Journal of Sport and Social Issues* 17, no. 1 (1993): 23–33; Charles Fruehling Springwood and C. Richard King, "Race, Ritual, and Remembrance Embodied: Manifest Destiny and the Ritual Sacrifice of 'Chief Illiniwek,'" in *Exercising Power: The Making and Re-making of the Body*, ed. Cheryl Cole and Michael Messner (Albany NY: SUNY Press, forthcoming); Charles Fruehling Springwood and C. Richard King, "Race, Power, and Representation in Contemporary American Sport," in *The Color Line at the Dawn of the 21st Century*, ed. Peter Kivisto and Georganne Rundblad (Thousand Oaks CA: Pine Valley Press, 2000); and Ellen Staurowsky, "An Act of Honor or Exploitation? The Cleveland Indians' Use of the Louis Francis Sockalexis Story," *Sociology of Sport Journal* 15, no. 4 (1998): 299–316.

3. C. Richard King and Charles Fruehling Springwood, "The Best Offense . . . : Dissociation, Desire, and the Defense of the Florida State University Seminoles," in King and Springwood, *Team Spirits*, 129–56.

4. For noteworthy exceptions to this pattern, see King and Springwood, "The Best Offense"; and Springwood and King, "Race, Power, and Representation." For a broader discussion of the interplay of redness, Blackness, and whiteness in contemporary sports, see C. Richard King and Charles Fruehling Springwood, *Racial Spectacle in College Athletics* (Albany NY: SUNY Press, forthcoming).

5. Cameron McCarthy and C. Crichlow, eds., *Race, Identity, and Representation in Education* (New York: Routledge, 1994), xv.

6. Roberto Rodriguez, "Plotting the Assassination of Little Red Sambo," *Black Issues in Higher Education* (11 June 1998): 20–24.

7. See King and Springwood, *Team Spirits*; Davis, "Protest"; Springwood and King, "Race, Ritual, and Remembrance."

8. On the ongoing struggles at the University of Illinois, see C. Richard King, "Spectacles, Sports, and Stereotypes: Dis/Playing Chief Illiniwek," in *Colonial Discourse, Collective Memories, and the Exhibition of Native American Cultures and Histories in the Contemporary United States* (New York: Garland, 1998), 41–58; C. Richard King and Charles Fruehling Springwood, "Choreographing Colonialism: Athletic Mascots, (Dis)Embodied Indians, and EuroAmerican Subjectivities," *Cultural Studies: A Research Annual* 5 (2000): 191–221; David Prochaska, "At Home in Illinois: Presence of Chief Illiniwek, Absence of Native Americans," in King and Springwood, *Team Spirits*, 157–85; Carol Spindel, "We Honor Your Memory: Chief Illiniwek of the Halftime Illini," *Crab Orchard Review* 3, no. 1 (1998): 217–38; Springwood and King, "Race, Ritual, and Remembrance."

9. See Sigelman, "Hail to the Redskins?"

10. Roy Wenzl, "'Redskin' Mascot Foe Wins NAACP as Ally," *Wichita Eagle*, 20 September 1999.

11. Sigelman, "Hail to the Redskins?"

12. James Louis Palcic, "The History of the Black Student Union at Florida State University, 1968–1978" (Ph.D. diss., Florida State University, 1979), 84.

13. Palcic, "History," 103.

14. Palcic, "History," 104.

15. Quoted in Palcic, "History," 105.

16. Palcic, "History," 105.

17. Jeff Pearlman, "At Full Blast," *Sports Illustrated*, 27 December 1999.

18. Quoted in "Rocky Reaction: Minority, Gay Groups call for Rocker's Retirement," *Des Moines Register*, 23 December 2000.

19. Jerry Strothers, personal communication, December 1999.

20. "Visa and the Hall of Fame Welcome Newest Fan Honorees to the Visa Hall of Fans," press release, author's files; also available online: *http://www.pro footballhof.com/new/visa.html* (last accessed 27 July 2000). See also Courtland Milloy, "Redskins Rally Sounds Different to Indians," *Washington Post*, 8 January 2000.

21. Jay Rosenstein, *In Whose Honor? American Indian Mascots in Sports* (Hohokus NJ: New Day Films, 1996).

22. Rosemary J. Coombe, *The Cultural Life of Intellectual Properties: Authorship, Appropriation, and the Law* (Durham NC: Duke University Press, 1998), 196.

23. Rudolph Waters Jr., executive vice president, Alcorn State University, per-

sonal communication, 7 October 1999. See also W. Milan Davis, *Pushing Forward: A History of Alcorn A.& M. College and Portraits of Some of Its Successful Graduates* (Okolona MS: Okolona Industrial School, 1938); Melderson Guy Dunham, *The Centennial History of Alcorn Agricultural and Mechanical College* (Hattiesburg: University and College Press of Mississippi, 1971); Neil R. McMillen, *Dark Journey: Black Mississippians in the Age of Jim Crow* (Urbana: University of Illinois Press, 1989), 103–8; Josephine McCann Posey, *Against Great Odds: The History of Alcorn State University* (Jackson: University Press of Mississippi, 1994).

24. "Florida Aim to Protest Washington Redskins at Raymond James," press release, author's files.

25. "Local NAACP Chapter Speaks out in Public," press release, author's files.

26. Banks, "Tribal Names," 5.

27. Quoted in Rodriguez, "Plotting the Assassination," 22.

28. Marty Ralbovsky, "An Indian Affair: American Indian Students Concerned about Nicknames, Mascots in Sports," *New York Times*, 14 November 1971.

29. Available online: *http://www.iwchildren.org/naacp* (last accessed 27 July 2000).

30. See King, "Borrowing Power," for a fuller account of racial juxtaposition.

31. Jerry Strothers, personal communication, December 1999.

32. Letter from Kweisi Mfume to Clem Iron Wing and Matthew Ritcher, 3 September 1999. In contrast with Mfume's outspokenness, efforts to locate the resolutions at the NAACP's headquarters were met with reticence. In fact, repeated calls to the national office failed to produce the resolution.

33. John Comaroff and Jean Comaroff, *Of Revelation and Revolution: Christianity, Colonialism, and Consciousness in South Africa* (Chicago: University of Chicago Press, 1991), 21. See also Jon Fiske, *Power Plays, Power Works* (London: Verso, 1993); Stuart Hall, "Gramsci's Relevance for the Study of Race and Ethnicity," *Journal of Communication Inquiry* 10, no. 2 (1985): 5–27; and D. V. Kurtz, "Hegemony and Anthropology: Gramsci, Exegeses, Reinterpretations," *Critique of Anthropology* 16, no. 2 (1996): 103-35. Joane Nagel offers an instructive application of this framework to Native American identity in *American Indian Ethnic Renewal: Red Power and the Resurgence of Identity and Culture* (Oxford: Oxford University Press, 1996).

34. bell hooks, "Revolutionary 'Renegades': Native Americans, African Americans, and Black Indians," in *Black Looks* (Boston: South End Press, 1992), 185.

35. Jerry Strothers, personal communication, December 1999.

36. Peter Noel, "Cutting on the Bias: Readers Sound Off on the Racism Quotient Test," *Village Voice* 38, 9 March 1993, 24, 26.

37. Joseph Roach, *Cities of the Dead: Circum-Atlantic Performance* (New York: Columbia University Press, 1996), 205.

38. Dennis Cauchon, "Many Indifferent to Racist School Names," *USA Today*, 9 February 1998.

39. See Robin E. Sherriff, "Exposing Silence as Cultural Censorship: A Brazilian Case," *American Anthropologist* 102, no. 1: 114–32.

40. Coombe, *Cultural Life*, 196.

41. Pierre Bourdieu, *Language and Symbolic Power*, ed. John B. Thompson (Cambridge: Harvard University Press, 1991), 170.

Epilogue
Seeing Each Other through the White Man's Eyes
Reflections and Commentary on the "Eating Out of the Same Pot" Black Indian Conference at Dartmouth College

VALERIE J. PHILLIPS

I read with great interest and anticipation the 1998 special issue of the *American Indian Quarterly* that was devoted to the subject of Indian-Black relations. My copy arrived in the mail the day before I was to attend the Black-Native conference at Dartmouth College 20–22 April 2000. I devoured the journal on the airplane, completely unaware of how much the social-political dynamics of growing up Black and Indian in the city of Chicago would be replayed at the impending conference.

Growing up in Chicago, I learned to live in fear. Black youth seldom saw me for who or what I was. Instead, they saw me through the white man's eyes, deciding during the height of the Black is Beautiful era that all that mattered was my relatively light skin and "good" hair, both of which made me a target, a substitute for the white man they never dared to touch.[1] My initial insistence that I was Indian as well as Black lapsed into silence for many years in the face of that hostility. Looks matter, especially in the war zones of Chicago.

One young Black boy derisively called my mother and me "White-faced Indians" loudly enough for everyone in a South Side grocery store to hear. Everybody within earshot, except us, laughed. Little did they, the young boy, and even I at that time know how succinctly he had expressed the flawed perspective that continues to manifest itself today among Blacks, American Indians, and the people at the conference in Dartmouth.[2]

There is a big difference between pragmatic adaptation to the dominant culture and an assimilative embrace, a distinction that Jo Carrillo makes clear in her commentary on the land struggles of the Mashpee Wampanoags.[3] The social-political dynamics of Black-Indian relations, so prominent in my childhood, were replayed throughout the Dartmouth conference. The dynamics at Dartmouth underscored how politics, oppression, academics, too much selective silence, and personal pain mesh in the real world.

The Dartmouth conference was a stimulating mix of academia and lay-people. Academia dominated, perhaps adding to the confusion occasionally felt by some participants about what to expect. In spite of the proliferation of various ethnic studies departments and general lip service that universities give to notions of diversity, academia is still very dominated by the white man's approach and viewpoint. However, at the conference, people seemed on the verge of seeing each other through our own eyes, rather than filtered through the white man's. Speakers came from across the country and represented thought from disciplines as varied as Native American studies, ethnic studies, African/African American studies, Latin American/Caribbean studies, history, religious studies, English, film, government, psychology, genealogy, and sociology.

During the opening session, Donna Roberts, repatriation and site protection coordinator of the Abenaki Nation, talked about how much more difficult repatriation was for her tribe since it is not federally recognized. She told of her shame that some of her ancestors had enslaved others of her ancestors. She theorized that decolonization would come to the United States as well as to the rest of the Western Hemisphere. However, the whole idea of decolonization of the Americas, including decolonizing our minds, seemed rather lost during later portions of the conference.

Miss Navajo Nation, 1997–98, Radmilla Cody, gave an emotional account of growing up on the Navajo reservation and the reactions of her tribe to the fact that she is half-Black. She introduced herself in the traditional way as being of the Red Bottom People clan, born for the African Americans. She had seemingly translated being "born for the African Americans" into a personal mission of acting as an ambassador between the Red and Black races even though her reign as Miss Navajo Nation had ended.

She introduced her Navajo grandmother and explained how important she was in teaching Cody traditional Navajo ways. Her grandmother kept Cody grounded in her culture and who she was. Cody displayed a strong sense of herself as a Navajo as well as a healthy respect for her Black heritage.

During her talk, Cody referred to a letter written to *Indian Country Today*. It was from a Navajo who complained that Cody looked too Black to be Miss Navajo Nation. Another letter to the editor appeared later. The second letter defended Cody and her right to the title as well as roundly denounced the racism expressed in the first letter. One wonders how many previous Miss Navajo Nations had been mixed-white and whether such a mixture had ever inspired similar commentary.

Jewelle Gomez spoke last. She related that her ancestry was Cape Verdean on her paternal side and Ioway/Wapanoag through her maternal great-grandparents. She observed that there was little room for such complexity during the heyday of the Black Power movement so she remained silent. The conventional wisdom of Black Power said that if one identified as part-Indian then one was necessarily also claiming to not be "that lesser thing," Black. She also feared being labeled a wannabe.

Gomez believed that it was her marginalization as a lesbian within the Black community that nevertheless kept her great-grandparent's Indian heritage alive. Marginalization as a phenotypically and culturally more Indian than Black person within an awakening Black community can produce the same result. It was because the symbiotic relationship between Blacks and Indians continued in some measure into the twentieth century that my family was able to find refuge within the Black community after the Cherokees had become too acculturated.

During the remainder of the conference, speakers assumed a dizzying array of approaches to their respective topics. Some took a very exploratory and open-minded approach. Such an approach has the most potential for moving past the limitations of "uncritical multiculturalism" into the diverse realm of indigenous and community thought. These speakers included Russel Barsh, Patrick Minges, Claudio Saunt, Sharon Holland, Donald Pease, Ron Welburn, and others.[4]

WHITE-FACED INDIANS?

If the white man cannot dominate other cultures and races, as he has throughout the history of the United States, then his "answer" to the "problem" of diversity is the "uncritical multiculturalism" and "uncritical diversity" that Joseph Jordan referred to in his presentation. According to Jordan, uncritical multiculturalism is the acknowledgment of the different kinds of diversity without an analysis of their accompanying intellectual and political meanings. This has led to confusion in the otherwise more progressive units of academia.

Jordan noted that, at their inception, African and cross-cultural studies were developing a theoretical approach that looked past uncritical multiculturalism to theory building and problem solving that was firmly grounded in the community itself. However, this new theoretical approach in African and cross-cultural studies later degenerated into simply putting old wine into new bottles.[5] Jordan stated that Native American studies currently faces the same dilemma that African and cross-cultural studies did years ago. It therefore is currently at a crossroads.

In my view, the old wine is the white man's conception of the world, in which his vision still dominates everything: economics, social relations, academia, and so forth. The new bottles are the lip service paid to diversity and multiculturalism. Jordan maintained that academia must confront this problem within its ranks because it is only creative disobedience that promises actual change.

The white man favors the kind of empty diversity and multiculturalism that Jordan described at the conference for a very practical reason. In today's supposedly postcolonial world, uncritical multiculturalism is the only way that whites can still keep their dominant position vis-à-vis non-white peoples without resorting to the more obvious modes of oppression prevalent during the earlier stages of colonialism. Whites have devised an empty definition of diversity and effectively superimposed that definition on the rest of the world before all the vestiges of colonialism have been eradicated. Whites in the twenty-first century thus continue to avoid the painful efforts that decolonization within countries such as the United States would necessarily require while maintaining an outward, conscience-soothing pretense of equality and tolerance. Any attempts at even approaching decolonization of the Americas are then shouted down with self-righteous charges of reverse discrimination, separatism, and antidemocratic activity by indigenous peoples.

Indigenous peoples within the United States and African Americans have exacerbated the entrenchment of neocolonialism by continuing to internalize and blindly mimic the white man's way of seeing things in so many aspects of their lives. This blindness is at the heart of the gulf that still exists between Blacks and Indians today. Uncritical multiculturalism was also implicit within a discouraging number of the comments made at the conference.

The presentation by Angelia Means, "Multicultural Citizenship and the Delgamuukw Case," was infuriating. Means, a Harvard Law School graduate and a Black woman, teaches government at Dartmouth College. Her basic premise was a confused amalgam of assertions that: (1) Native American interests are not really any different than those of immigrants and the gay community; (2) Native Americans have sovereignty because they reject democratic principles and the U.S. Constitution; (3) Native morals may be destructive to democracy; and (4) traditional forms of oral history may not be amenable to the rules of evidence used in the Western legal system. She used the Canadian Delgamuukw case to illustrate this last, rather obvious point. However, this was the most intelligible thing that she said during her entire presentation.

Means's first assertion completely ignored the fact that this country resulted from colonialism. The resulting waves of immigration were and continue to be voluntary, as well as heavily influenced by the prospect of economic gain. Her assertions with respect to gays ignored the difference between culture and sexual orientation that even gay and lesbian studies is coming to acknowledge in some ways. Her second assertion completely ignored the nature of sovereignty as well as the long line of court cases that do address the concept, although from a colonialist and imperialist perspective. Her third assertion assumed that the white man (the implicit model for all of her assertions) is qualified to judge native morality and the nature of democracy. This country was founded on the backs of Black slaves and Indian lands. Democratic principles were intended to apply only to white males and have only been extended in recent years to others after much civil unrest, lawsuits, and even death.

Indigenous peoples would be much better off looking to and strengthening their own native legal, social, academic, conceptional, and economic frameworks rather than focusing on trying to fit the round hole of indigenous ways into the square peg of the white man's laws and ways. Means was also apparently unaware that the American common law system, like that of England, is ultimately based on the white man's oral tradition.[6] Overall, Means's thinking seemed garbled and perhaps even intellectually dishonest. Nevertheless, Means will no doubt be joining Clarence Thomas on the U.S. Supreme Court someday if she continues along the same lines of thinking during the rest of her career.

Angelia Means and other speakers intentionally or unintentionally illustrated the problems inherent in the African American tendency to see American Indians almost exclusively through the white man's eyes. Yet part of what was so provocative about this conference was the potential for openly exposing the limitations of this kind of thinking. Exposure teased around the edges but was never fully explored.

Like Means, others illustrated the problems inherent in the American Indian tendency to see African Americans almost exclusively through the white man's eyes. In one of its more "benign" forms, American Indians today display an alarming tendency to sacrifice mixed-Black members for what they think is politically expedient. For example, Melinda Micco presented on contemporary tribal politics among the Seminoles of Oklahoma. On 1 July 2000 the tribe voted on whether to amend its 1969 constitution to institute a blood quantum requirement for membership that, according to Micco, would probably have the effect of disproportionately disenfranchising its Black Seminoles. Before the vote, the Seminoles had no blood quantum requirement to be tribal members, although tribal officeholders must demonstrate one-quarter Seminole blood. After the vote, the tribe instituted a one-eighth blood quantum requirement for tribal membership, thus excluding those Black Seminoles who cannot prove they have Indian blood from sharing in monies awarded to the tribe for land ceded in Florida more than 160 years ago.

Perhaps like the Black Seminoles to whom Micco referred, mixed-Black Indians within the United States are generally at a disadvantage in documenting their Indian blood vis-à-vis mixed-white Indians due to the federal government's deliberate attempts to "erase" them from tribes regardless of how much Indian blood they actually possessed. It is no accident that the federal government is the producer and custodian of the records that are currently used by tribes to determine who is or is not an Indian.

Although tribes now have the power to correct the inequities in the enrollment process that result from historical subjugation by the United States and its history of eugenics and racism, the overwhelming majority seem to have chosen not to take much advantage of this opportunity. Instead, they seem to devote an inordinate amount of attention on what they think is politically and economically expedient. Increasingly, tribal governments and tribal members are exhibiting more fundamental similarities to state governments and state citizens than they would like to admit.

Often overlooked are the power and strength to face modern problems that a tribe could gain from consolidating with the most indigenous of its people, regardless of their racial mixture. This would certainly be a complex task that would require a more fundamental reemphasis on the indigenous in every sphere of Indian life, including the social, political, cultural, educational, and academic. The survival of tribes "as tribes" depends on such a refocus at the collective and individual tribal levels to see clearly other alternatives.[7]

Melinda Micco openly disagreed with the institution of a blood quantum requirement among the Seminoles of Oklahoma. However, she also stated that she would defer to whatever the outcome of the tribe's vote is, in the interests of sovereignty, since the tribe's cultural connections with the Black Seminoles will remain unbroken regardless of the vote's outcome. Her position with respect to sovereignty was understandable, especially in light of the realities of the legalized neocolonialism that this country has never addressed on any level.

Yet Micco also pointed out that her tribe's Black Seminoles have threatened to try to seek federal recognition on their own if the blood quantum requirement is approved. Threats about seeking federal recognition raises suspicions about just how strong the cultural and social connections between the Blacks and Indians within the tribe really are. Perhaps the white society's cultural values were swaying both groups much more than Seminole values.

In her commentary, Theda Perdue began by advocating that we wage war against the residuals of colonialism, including: Western ideas that one can tell who people are simply by looking at them; the artificial distinctions of race; blood quantum requirements; and Aristotelian logic's demand that contradictions must be reconciled.

To illustrate the basic thrust of her comments, Perdue related how the Cherokees dealt with an African American slave woman who was first brought into the Cherokee Nation as a result of the Cherokee law of "blood atonement."[8] She was purchased by a white man who had beaten his Cherokee wife to death as the wife's replacement within the tribe. She was accepted and adopted into the Deer clan and eventually raised a Cherokee family of her own. Later, a white woman claimed ownership of this woman and her two sons but the Cherokee council refused to countenance the claim, upholding the citizenship of the woman and her sons in 1833. Their refusal of the white woman's claim was particularly significant because it occurred after the Cherokees themselves had outlawed miscegenation with Blacks in their Constitution of 1827, mimicking in a somewhat milder form the U.S. Constitution.[9]

PASSING AND STRADDLING

The session titled "Reading Sources, Writing Lives: Themes and Methodologies in Black-Indian Studies" plunged headlong into an eclectic focus on Black-Indian relations. The morning and afternoon speakers took a variety of approaches. Some speakers examined the evidence of such relations in ostensibly African American literary sources that nevertheless crossed over into native themes. Others spoke of more obvious Afro-Native nuances in works that had not previously been examined in this light.

Russel Barsh spoke on the Afro-Indians in New England and the abolitionist movement. In his research, Barsh found extensive kinship and economic ties between Blacks and Indians, particularly in the New England fishing communities such as Gay Head, Pequot, and Mashpee. Barsh also noted that the early-nineteenth-century literature revealed that Blacks and Indians at that time were very strongly connected, displaying a very healthy identification of themselves as Black without disconnecting from the Indian. As the abolitionist movement grew stronger, many stories on Indians even appeared in the abolitionist press. Approximately a third of the stories appearing in the *Liberator* were on Indians, including the Creek and Seminole Wars and the Cherokee Removal. Barsh noted further that Black regiments from New England during the Civil War were either heavily Black-Indians or Indian by choice. According to Barsh, an internal tension seemed to arise among Afro-Indians in New England with the rise of the abolitionist movement. He recounted how one Black-Indian struggled with the contradiction between the pro-integration abolitionist view and the Black-Indian view that avoiding whites was best.

One of the more poignant moments of the conference occurred during two films in the oral history portion. Both films underscored how the white man's worldview has negatively impacted Blacks and Indians. Malinda Maynor's *Real Indian* and Saundra Sharp's *Picking Tribes* also highlighted the bind in which Indians who have mixed heavily with whites and Blacks are likely to find themselves as a direct result of U.S. Indian policy. Both films showed the fundamental difference between how heavily mixed-white Indians and heavily mixed-Black Indians reacted to this policy, even within the same tribe.

While Maynor's *Real Indian* was her own view of her tribe, the Lumbees, it served as a perfect introduction to David Wilkins's presentation the following day, "Racial Identity and the Federal Recognition Process: A Case Study of the Lumbee Indians." Wilkins elaborated on Maynor's oral history of the Lumbees. He stated that one of the main reasons why the Lumbees have not gained federal recognition is that they have too much mixture with non-Indians, specifically with Blacks. That is, the Black mixture is seen as an impermissible "dilution" of the tribe while their extensive mixture with whites is essentially ignored. Yet Wilkins also admitted that tribal members always seemed more willing to beat up Blacks than whites.

Mixed-Black Indians have historically been less amenable to federal policy objectives precisely because of their racial mixture and the heritage that goes with it. Mixed-Black Indians, because of the nature of the Black community and how the white man has historically chosen to define Blacks, historically had the "option" of preserving some semblance of their Indianness by retreating into the relative refuge of the Black community.[10] Mixed-white Indians have historically not had this option vis-à-vis the white community, unless they were willing to give up their Indianness completely. Of course, now it can be rather chic to be an Indian in a white community, as long as one does not bring up too many discomfiting substantive issues at the same time, but this is a more recent phenomenon.[11] Whites today love flirting with the idea that they may have an Indian somewhere among their ancestors, although they recoil from the more likely possibility that they have a Black ancestor.

Blacks also have lingering ties to their own indigenous roots as descendants of Africans, although the exact African tribe is usually unknown. Sharp's short film *Picking Tribes* underscored the satisfaction and frustration that Blacks can derive from this knowledge. In that film, the young protagonist is eventually laughed into silence about her Indian heritage by her Black peers who refuse to believe that she is part-Indian because she is phenotypically Black. However, she later arbitrarily picks an existing African tribe, the Fulani, as her own as part of her awakening Black consciousness. Her friends accept her choice. Although the protagonist's claim to being part-Indian but unaware of the tribe is much more recent genetic history than her claim to being Fulani, for which she has no evidence at all, her friends accept her adaptation of Fulani tribal characteristics.

James Brooks's presentation on "Indian-Black Mixed-Race Identity" covered the question of passing and straddling from a different angle. Brooks examined the "Black Ute clan" of the Southern Ute tribe. According to Brooks, one family in particular, the Taylors, were by the 1990s only ¹⁄₃₂ African American. Yet their matriarch, Euterpe Cloud Taylor, made continual references to the strength of her family's African heritage and its positive influence on the family. Brooks stressed Taylor's tendency to "erase" other bloodlines in the family (specifically, the Hispano and non-Ute Indian lines) in spite of contemporary social ties with both of the latter outside the family. At the same time, Taylor never seemed to erase the Black or the Ute Indian strains in her family. Instead, she engaged in a continual and rather seamless "switching" between Black and Ute identifications. Brooks referred to this switching as a bifurcated identification of herself.

. . . loving a white man, loving an Indian . . .

Robert Warrior read Joy Harjo's poem to the audience at Dartmouth. He explained that Harjo's poem was intended to present a list of things more culturally relevant to Indians than a list that had appeared in *Cosmopolitan* magazine. When did "loving a white man" become culturally relevant for Indians?[12]

Historians today continue to extol and otherwise emphasize Indian women like Nancy Ward, Pocahontas, and *La Malinche*.[13] They tend to judge the intrinsic worth of Indian women by the degree of their cooperation or collusion with whites in some aspect of their lives. There is even a Nancy Ward Chapter of the Daughters of the American Revolution (DAR), a largely white supremacist organization. The DAR and the white man's vision of Indian women represent one point of view. Such views are an outgrowth of the white man's die-hard vision of the Indian woman as squaw, whose worth is measured primarily from her status as an exotic and reputedly very available bedmate for the white man. Nancy Ward was a Beloved Woman among the Cherokees for tribal cultural reasons. However, she is beloved by most historians and the DAR precisely because she betrayed Dragging Canoe to white Americans, not because she was a Ghigau (Beloved Woman) among the Cherokees.

American Indian Radio recently asked what was the meaning behind the current popularity of romance novels that feature muscular Indian bucks and fluttering white women coupling (without any troublesome substantive issues between the races getting in the way of all that sex, naturally). The answer is that sex does not necessarily equal love or even respect. However, superficial interracial sex, like uncritical multiculturalism, can fool the participants into believing that progress between the races has somehow automatically occurred as well.

The Indian woman and the Black woman historically were and continue to be portrayed as existing solely for the sexual titillation of the white man. The popular portrayal of each female has historically had somewhat different connotations. Details on all the different connotations are beyond the scope of this commentary. Suffice it to say that it was assumed that the Indian female (Miss Exotica) was flattered to be the subject of the white man's sexual fantasies as well as his bedmate. Nobody cared whether the Black female was flattered by the same thing. Seldom do we talk about the destructive impact of the white man's past and present attitudes toward Indian and Black females on all male-female relationships, regardless of race. Yet that impact continues to be evident into the twenty-first century and threatened to erupt between two mixed-Indian participants at the Dartmouth conference.

Silence remains the norm in the realm of sexual colonialism today. Open acknowledgment of these issues would be the first step in a long-overdue and inevitably painful healing process. Instead, popular conceptions of the Indian male have joined those of the Black male as the new Mr. Exotica, sex studs who are allowed to service the white woman in relatively innocuous circumstances. Significantly, such liaisons do nothing to threaten the white man's domination of the world as a whole. The white man's view of Indian and Black females remains essentially intact. By not openly confronting these issues, at least within and between the respective communities, Indians and Blacks collude in their own oppression.

This complex sexual/political dynamic was played out in just a few minutes by two conference participants during the plenary session on the last day. This incident was an explosive encounter between a woman and a man, both of whom identified themselves as Indian. The woman was phenotypically Black. She had spoken extensively the previous day during audience participation about medicine, her five husbands, and other matters. On both days, she wore regalia. Finally, the moderator cut her off.

The man was clearly mixed-white but still had discernable Indian features. He identified himself as enrolled. He spoke in reaction to the woman's erroneous claim that Theda Perdue had asserted that the Cherokees did not have slaves. Initially, it seemed that his comments might clarify what Perdue said before the woman went into another long monologue. Then it seemed that he was trying to convey some of the dissatisfaction that the Indian students had privately expressed. This dissatisfaction apparently stemmed from the tendency of some of the Black participants to disrespect native creation stories by, among other things, claiming that Africa was the true origin of the indigenous peoples of this hemisphere.

However, the man moved from an attitude of understandable impatience with the woman's budding monologue to becoming extremely angry. The woman kept asking him why it was always the nappy-headed Black-Indians who were treated in this way, why did he talk in that manner to *her*. Even if she was annoying, one wonders why the man was so angry with her. Why did he emphasize that because she was not a Cherokee she could not address whether there was slavery within that tribe? Perdue, a white woman, was not Cherokee either. Nevertheless, the man chose to defend what she said. One wonders if he would have publicly spoken in such a hostile manner to a white wannabe or any other white person who was annoying or rambling. Was prefacing his comments by referring to his enrollment supposed to be his defense against uncomfortable questions about his attitude?

When the woman made a reference to "nappy-headed," it was clear that the encounter was going to become even more heated. In using the word "nappy-headed," she was referring to the rejection of their humanity that Black women have had to endure in this country for centuries. A colleague of mine, a social psychologist, frequently refers to the resentment that Black women today feel at having been forced to bear the white man's children, raise his and the white woman's children, and work themselves to death in this country both before and after slavery just to survive. To add insult to injury, they are expected to sit quietly in today's world while the white woman takes their Black men. Black women are not inclined to listen sympathetically when white feminists complain about how hard it has been for them to live with all the benefits arising out of the enslavement of Blacks.[14] White feminists, like white men and the academic environment they dominate, remain largely oblivious to the enormity of these problems.

The exchange between the man and the woman threatened to spin out of control. Not even the moderator seemed to know what to do at this point. It seemed the two might come to blows. The man shouted that the Cherokees never enslaved Cherokees. The woman left the room and the man stormed out saying, "They're taking over Native American studies." We could hear them shouting at each other in the hallway. Ward Churchill and perhaps a few others rushed out into the hallway. More shouting, then silence. The woman returned to the room, crying, and apologized to everyone. The plenary session ended with singing and prayers. The man did not return.

CONCLUSION

Obviously, my commentary barely touches upon the wealth of issues raised by the conference at Dartmouth. It was a simultaneously encouraging and discouraging event. Some readers might erroneously conclude from my comments that I advocate separatism and/or the deliberate destruction of the white man's world.

Today's mixed-white Indians too frequently overlook opportunities to come to terms with themselves and who they really are as indigenous people by not actively confronting the racism within themselves and their own tribes. Hiding behind the "shield" of enrollment, acculturation, and/or earlier federal recognition of their tribes is counterproductive and shortsighted on many levels. Mixed-Black Indians, in turn, would benefit greatly from looking to and through their own very strong indigenous roots rather than seeing their mixed-white brothers and sisters, as well as tribes as a whole, through the white man's eyes. Both groups have their own respective issues as indigenous people that cry out for redress. The only redress they will find in this world will result from turning to each other as indigenous people. Neither the white man nor his worldview will accomplish this for them.

Racial mixture in one form or another has always been a part of the world's history, as has intertribal mixing. Indian tribes traditionally had mechanisms for dealing with the differences between people with respect before the white man's oppression. Now, those mechanisms flounder in a sea of uncritical multiculturalism.

Africans and Indians are fundamentally tribal people, indigenous to the earth. Their blending only strengthens what they already are, if they remain true to their essence. Blacks and Indians who uncritically persist in looking at each other through the white man's eyes only undermine themselves. We strengthen ourselves by seeing the past clearly, changing our present, and consciously building our future on a solid, indigenous foundation.

Pushing past the white man, I can see it through my own eyes.

NOTES

1. I use the term "white man" rather than non-Indians because I think the use of the latter term in the context of this commentary would be so nondescriptive as to be meaningless. Non-Indians could conceivably include Japanese, Blacks, Tongans, Samoans, Ethiopians, Arabs, Jews – almost anyone under the sun. The term "white man" better embodies Euro-America's own conception of itself within this country.

2. Even today, I have noticed how quickly some Blacks retreat behind their own defense mechanisms upon realizing the depth of the Indianness within my family rather than confront the uncomfortable questions that our existence alone seems to raise about their own assimilation within American society.

3. "The Mashpee Wampanoag Tribe turned to federal law to validate what it regarded as its superior rights to its ancestral land. What the Mashpee Tribe

discovered was that federal law served as both resource and constraint; that is, the law that was applied to resolve the dispute ended up escalating it instead. . . . The law presumed Indian ways to be primitive, chaotic, timeless, simple. More troubling, it assumed that any tribal adaptation to colonial society was in fact an assimilative embrace of the mainstream." Jo Carrillo, ed., "Identity as Idiom: Mashpee Reconsidered," in *Readings in American Indian Law: Recalling the Rhythm of Survival* (Philadelphia: Temple University Press, 1998).

4. Available online, http://www.dartmouth.edu/student/sorg/aam/2000 conference/htmls/schedule.html

5. Joseph Jordan, "Formalizing Black and Native Studies: Challenges to African American and Native American Studies Programs" (paper presented at the conference, "Eating Out of the Same Pot: Relating Black and Native Histories," 20–22 April 2000, at Dartmouth College, Hanover NH).

6. For a fascinating analysis of nature of the customary law, tradition, and common law, see Leon Sheleff, *The Future of Tradition: Customary Law, Common Law and Legal Pluralism* (London: Frank Cass Publishers, 2000).

7. There seems to be some evidence that Indians may be re-evaluating whether more traditional governmental structures, such as substantive consultation by governments elected under the Indian Reorganization Act (IRA) with traditional clans and elders, should be tried. "Opinion Leaders Cast Doubt on Tribal Governments," *Indian Country Today (Rapid City)*, 24 May 2000.

8. A more detailed account of this incident may be found in Theda Perdue, *Cherokee Women: Gender and Culture Change, 1700–1835* (Lincoln: University of Nebraska Press, 1999), 150–51.

9. Article III, Section 4, stated: "No person shall be eligible to a seat in the General Council but a free Cherokee male citizen, who shall have attained to the age of twenty-five years. The descendants of Cherokee men by all free women, except the African race, whose parents may have been living together as man and wife, according to the customs and laws of this Nation, shall be entitled to all the rights and privileges of the Nation, as well as the posterity of Cherokee women by all free men. No person who is of Negro or Mulatto parentage, either by the father or mother's side, shall be eligible to hold any office of profit, honor or trust under this Government."

10. That is, if one admits to even a drop of Black blood then one is Black, a very convenient definition if one has no qualms about enslaving one's own children, which the white man has historically had no problem doing.

11. Today, of course, it is rather fashionable, not to mention exciting, for whites to have an Indian or two in one's midst or even in one's bed. Witness the white "medicine groupie," whom one can readily find on the Red Road.

12. The phrase "sexual colonialism" was coined by Arthur Einhorn after reading the unedited draft of this essay.

13. Nancy Ward betrayed Dragging Canoe to the whites and was half-white herself. Pocahontas saved John Smith's life and later married a white man. *La Malinche* betrayed her people, the Aztecs, to Cortez, to whom she was a mistress.

14. Kelly Ervin, Department of Comparative American Cultures, Washington State University, personal communication.

Contributors

Russel Lawrence Barsh has divided his time between teaching and advocacy for indigenous peoples' rights. Currently at New York University's School of Law, he has also taught at the University of Washington, Harvard Law School, and Dartmouth College and served as a lawyer, negotiator, and United Nations spokesperson for the Mi'kmaq Grand Council and other North American Native nations. His sixteen-year involvement in the Samish Indian tribe's successful struggle to regain federal recognition focused on the abuses of racial typologies and stereotypes by federal bureaucrats, including a presumption against the legitimacy of Afro-Indian communities.

James F. Brooks is assistant professor of history at the University of California, Santa Barbara. He has held NEH Fellowships at the Institute for Advanced Study in Princeton and the School of American Research in Santa Fe. His essays have received the Joan Jensen–Darlis Miller Prize for western women's history (1997) and the Arrell Morgan Gibson Award for Native American History (2000). Most recently, he authored *Captives and Cousins: Slavery, Kinship, and Community in the Southwest Borderlands* (Omohundro Institute of Early American History and Culture, University of North Carolina Press, forthcoming).

Daniel H. Calhoun is professor emeritus at the University of California, Davis.

C. Richard King is assistant professor of anthropology at Drake University. His work has focused on the representations of Native American cultures and histories in museums and tourist sites and the cultural, political, and racial significance of Native American mascots. He is the coeditor of two books on race and sports: *Team Spirits: The Native American Mascot Controversy* (University of Nebraska Press, 2001) and *Beyond the Cheers: Race as Spectacle in College Sport* (SUNY Press, 2001). He currently is conducting research on indigenous athletes and athletics in North America.

Laura L. Lovett is a visiting assistant professor of history at Dartmouth College. Her current research concerns how nostalgic and often idealized images of the family were used in the United States to justify various social and political agendas during the Populist and Progressive eras.

Malinda Maynor is a Lumbee Indian from North Carolina and is currently pursuing a Ph.D. in history at the University of North Carolina–Chapel Hill. She also holds an M.A. in documentary film from Stanford University and a B.A. in history and literature from Harvard University. Her films *Real Indian* and *Sounds of Faith* concern Lumbee identity and religion and have been screened at film festivals and in classrooms and conferences all over the country. She is the coproducer of *In the Light of Reverence*, a feature-length documentary for PBS on Native American sacred sites and religious freedom. Maynor has also completed a Web site and CD-ROM on Lumbee religious history and was an adjunct professor in American Indian studies at San Francisco State University.

Dedra S. McDonald is a lecturer in history at Hillsdale College in southern Michigan. She completed her doctorate in history at the University of New Mexico in 2000. Her dissertation examines domestic servants and gender in the Spanish colonial and Mexican northern borderlands. Her research interests include persons of African descent in the Spanish and Mexican northern borderlands; labor in the same region; and intermarriage in the borderlands. She has published articles in the *Colonial Latin American Review*, *American Indian Quarterly*, and in forthcoming anthologies on black women in the American West and on labor in the American West.

Ann McMullen holds a Ph.D. in anthropology from Brown University and is a curator at the Smithsonian Institution's National Museum of the American Indian. With Russell G. Handsman, she edited *A Key into the Language of Woodsplint Baskets* (Washington CT: American Indian Archaeological Institute, 1987). She has also authored "What's Wrong with This Picture? Context, Conversion, Survival and the Development of Regional Native Cultures and Pan-Indianism in Southeastern New England," in *Enduring Traditions: The Native Peoples of New England*, ed. Laurie Weinstein (Westport CT: Bergin and Garvey, 1994); "Soapbox Discourse: Tribal History, Indian-White Relations, and Southeastern New England Powwows," *Public Historian* 18, no. 4 (1996): 53–74; and numerous other articles.

Tiya Miles teaches in the departments of ethnic studies and African American studies at the University of California, Berkeley. Her research interests include African American and Native American related histories;

the histories, feminist theories, and life experiences of women of color in the United States; and gender and sexuality in African American history. She received her doctorate in American studies from the University of Minnesota and extends her gratitude to Jean O'Brien and David Roediger for encouraging her pursuit of historical research. Her monograph, *"Bone of My Bone": Stories of a Black Cherokee Family, 1790–1866*, is forthcoming from the University of California Press.

Celia E. Naylor-Ojurongbe is a doctoral candidate in the history department at Duke University in Durham, North Carolina. She is currently working on her dissertation on Cherokee slaves and freedpeople in Indian Territory (1838–1907). Last year she taught in the Women Studies Program at the University of New Mexico. Her interests include African American/Caribbean and Native American history, as well as women's history and literature in the African diaspora.

Valerie J. Phillips received a B.A. in political science from Wellesley College and a J.D. from the University of California School of Law in Berkeley. She is currently an assistant professor of business law at the University of Tulsa. Recent presentations include "The Research Exemption in Patent Law: Encouraging the Development of Collaborative Efforts with Indigenous Peoples" before the Seventh International Congress of Ethnobiology in Athens, Georgia, and "Sacred Justice and Indigenous Peoples" before the Third Community Congress on Race Relations at Gonzaga University, Spokane, Washington. She is of Eastern Cherokee and Black descent.

Claudio Saunt teaches American Indian history and early American history at the University of Georgia. His first book, *A New Order of Things: Property, Power, and the Transformation of the Creek Indians, 1733–1816* (Cambridge University Press, 1999), was awarded the Wheeler-Voeglin Prize for the best book in ethnohistory and the Charles S. Syndor Prize for the best book in southern history. His current research, which extends into the twentieth century, focuses on race and class in Indian Territory and Oklahoma.

Circe Sturm is an assistant professor of anthropology and Native American studies at the University of Oklahoma, Norman. Her research interests focus on the intersections of race, culture, and nationalism, particularly as these are expressed through the idiom of "blood." Her forthcoming book, *Blood Politics: Racial Hybridity and Identity in the Cherokee Nation of Oklahoma* (University of California Press), is an ethnographic and ethnohistorical study of multiracial and multicultural identities among Cherokee people.

Ron Welburn, from Berwyn, Pennsylvania, and Philadelphia, teaches in the English department and directs the Native studies program at the University of Massachusetts Amherst. He is Assateague Gingaskin and Cherokee Indian and of African American descent. He has published six books of poetry and a collection of essays, *Roanoke and Wampum: Topics in Native American Heritage and Literatures.* In 1992, he attended the historic Returning the Gift Festival of Native Writers. His ongoing interests include Indians and jazz and a developing a profile of Ann Plato, a nineteenth-century Connecticut writer of Indian descent.

Index

Chakwaina kachina, 22
Chavez, Angelico, 28–29
Cherokee Freedmen's Association, 231–32
Cherokee Indians: and division over slave-
    holding, 162–63; and fear of British
    enslavement, 54; and treaty granting
    freedmen citizenship, 225–26; tribal status
    of those of mixed descent, 12
Cherokee Nation: and Cherokee Supreme
    Court definition of Cherokee citizenship,
    148–49, 377; citizenship in, based on
    racial identity, 233–40, 247–53; and
    decline in membership of ex-slave descen-
    dants, 244–47; and resistance to enroll-
    ment of ex-slaves as members, 176–79,
    226–32, 246; status of ex-slaves in, 173–80
Chiaja (Creek-Seminole town): as site of
    Black community, 58–59
Choctaw Indians, 169–71
Clay, Henry (ex-slave), 166, 169
Cleveland Indians, 354–55, 359
Cody, Radmilla, 15–16, 372–73
Colbert, Polly, 170
Cole, Jefferson L., 170–71
Concho Indians, 28
Cornsilk, David, 247–49, 251–52
Creek Indians: and adoption of Blacks, 60–
    61; as allies with French and Spanish
    against British, 50–54; and attitudes
    toward slavery, 8–9, 47, 52–55; dissidents'
    alliance with Seminoles, 57–58; geo-
    graphic extent of settlements of, 48–49;
    and Redsticks faction, 48, 61–63; as
    slaveholders, 55–61; social structure of,
    49–51, 61
Cuffee, Paul, 97–98
culture: as element of Indian identity, 270–
    76, 278, 281–82; Indian cultural survival
    linked to racial purity of, 265; mixed
    descent Indians' desire to sustain customs
    of, 313; role of music in, for Lumbee
    Indians, 14, 322–23. See also acculturation
Cummings, Michael, 326–27

Davis, Lucinda, 168
Dickson, James, 117
discrimination, racial: against Blacks and

Indians in New England, 84, 95–96, 99–
    100; by Cherokee Indians against ex-slaves
    and descendants, 12, 173–80, 233–40,
    247–55; as protested by Blacks at Florida
    State University, 350–53
Dorantes, Esteban de (the Black Moor),
    21–22
DuBois, W. E. B., 208

Eastern Pequot Tribe, 279–80
"'Eating Out of the Same Pot': Relating
    Indian and Black (Hi)stories" (con-
    ference), 16, 371–83
employment: of minorities, 90–97, 109–10
eugenics, 206–7

Fitch, Tobias, 52–53
Florida: slavery in, 47, 55
Florida State University, 346–47, 350–53
Forbes, Jack D., 28–29, 112, 144–45
Freedonia Rebellion, 117

Gay Head Wampanoag Indians, 276–78
Georgia: slavery in, 55
Gillam, Cora, 137–38, 143–44, 154–55
Glaize, the (Indian settlement in OH), 111
Gomez, Jewelle, 373
Grayson, Mary, 168–69

haciendas, 109–10
Hallowell, A. Irving, 165
Hampton Normal and Agricultural Insti-
    tute, 203–6; racial typologies taught at,
    204–6
Hanke, Lewis, 111–12
Hawikuh (Zuni Indian settlement), 21–22
Henderson, Henry, 167–68
Herskovits, Melville: and studies of Indian
    ancestry among Blacks, 144–45, 192–93
Hooks, Rebecca, 196
Hopson, Moble, 210
Houston, Sam, 116
Hu-Dehart, Evelyn, 113–14
Hurston, Zora Neale, 192, 207

Indian Claims Commission, 231–32
Indians: and acceptance of White racial

Nantucket MA, 83, 90, 92

Naranjo (African man): as leader in Pueblo Revolt, 28–29

Narragansett Indians, 278–79; mixed descent presence threatens racial legitimacy of, 279

Narragansett Tribe: membership of, based on lineage and cultural participation, 271

National Association for the Advancement of Colored People (NAACP), 359–62

Navajo Indians, 15–16, 372–73

Nave, Cornelius Neely, 148, 162–63, 174, 241

Naylor-Ojurongbe, Celia, 147

Nero, Roger H., 232–33, 236–40

New Bedford MA: mixed descent population, 90–91

New London CT, 92–93

New Orleans LA, 199–203

Omi, Michael: argument that Europeans construct concept of race, 140–41

Otermín, Antonio de, 29–30

Pamunkey Indians, 213

Parras, Mexico: status of minorities in, 108–11

Parsons, Lucy, 120

Paucatuck Eastern Pequot Indian Tribal Nation, 279–80

Pequot Indians, 86–87; population decline of, 93

Perdue, Theda, 377

Perryman, Patsy Taylor, 167

Peter (free Black man): and escape of slaves to Creeks, 59

Phillips, Valerie, 16

Pino, Pedro Baptista, 39

Plecker, Walter Ashby, 207–8

Pokanoket Wampanoag Indians, 277–78

Portuguese: as replacements for minorities in New England seafaring, 94–95

Presidential Commission on Race, 353

Pueblo Revolt: participation of those of mixed descent in, 28–31

Quintana, Frances Leon, 1–2

race codes: in New Spain, 25–26

racial attributes: Blacks' view of Indians as savage, 203–4; and image of Indian resistance invoked by Blacks, 195–199; mixed descent individuals' attribution of virtues to Indian heritage, 154–55; scientific theories of, as biological, 192–93; Euterpe Cloud Taylor on mixed heritage and, 3–6. *See also* mixed descent peoples; racial identity

racial hierarchies, 13, 193–95; of Blacks, 197–98, 203; of Indians, 240–44, 275, 277–80; in New England, 93–97, 264–67; as portrayed in Mardi Gras, 199–203; in Spanish New Mexico, 7–8, 24–25, 30–31, 37–39. *See also* blood quantum; mixed descent peoples; racial identity; racial typologies; segregation

racial identity, 11, 13; contestation of, 10–11, 176–77, 240–47; as culturally constructed, 140–41, 145, 208–11, 268–69; definitions of, 148–49, 207–8, 233; as factor upon which identity is based, 162–65, 233–40, 267–83; imposition of, on Indians, 142, 145–46, 263–66, 292–93, 297–301, 304, 311–15, 378–79; of Lumbee Indians, 211–13; in Spanish New Mexico, 7–8, 30–31, 38–40. *See also* blood quantum; racial attributes; racial hierarchies; racial typologies; segregation

racial stereotypes: of Indians as sports team mascots, 14, 346–47, 349, 350, 354

racial typologies, 11; as applied to Mexican insurgents, 114–15; in colonial New England, 263–64; historiography of, 5–6, 111–12; influence of, on identity of minorities, 204–6, 374–76, 382–83; mixed descent individuals do not fit categories of, 146–47, 240–44; New England Indians respond to, 281–83; present binary categories of, 210–11, 266; as reflection of White conceptions, 141–42, 194–99, 204–7, 365, 374–76. *See also* blood quantum; racial attributes; racial hierarchies; racial identity; segregation

Redstick War, 8, 61–63

Richardson, Chaney, 180